THE ROMAN INSCRIPTIONS OF BRITAIN II, Fasc. 3

R.G. Collingwood and R.P. Wright

THE ROMAN INSCRIPTIONS OF BRITAIN

Volume II
Instrumentum Domesticum

(Personal Belongings and the like)

Fascicule 3

Brooches, Rings, Gems, Bracelets, Helmets, Shields, Weapons, Iron Tools, Baldric Fittings, Votives in Gold, Silver and Bronze, Lead Pipes, Roundels, Sheets and Other Lead Objects, Stone Roundels, Pottery and Bone Roundels, Other Objects of Bone.

(*RIB* 2421–2441)

Edited by S.S. FRERE and R.S.O. TOMLIN

Published for the Administrators of the Haverfield Bequest by
Alan Sutton Publishing
1991

First published in the United Kingdom in 1991 by
Alan Sutton Publishing Ltd · Phoenix Mill · Far Thrupp · Stroud · Glos.

First published in the United States of America in 1991 by
Alan Sutton Publishing Inc · Wolfeboro Falls · NH 03896–0848

Copyright © The Administrators of the Haverfield Bequest, University of Oxford, 1991

All rights reserved. No part of this publication may be reproduced, stored in a retrieval system, or transmitted, in any form, or by any means, electronic, mechanical, photocopying, recording or otherwise, without the prior permission of the publishers and copyright holders.

British Library Cataloguing in Publication Data

The Roman inscriptions of Britain.
  Vol. 2. Fascicule 3.
  1. Great Britain. Inscriptions in Latin
  I. Frere, Sheppard, *1916*–
  477

ISBN 0 86299 935 9

Library of Congress Cataloging in Publication Data applied for

Typesetting and origination by
Alan Sutton Publishing Limited.
Printed in Great Britain by
The Bath Press, Avon.

CONTENTS

		Page
Preface By R.M. Harrison, Chairman of the Administrators		vii
List of Plates		ix
Abbreviations		xi
Bibliography		xiii
2421.1–59	Brooches	1
2422.1–82	Finger-rings	15
2423.1–34	Gemstones, Amulets and Cameos	34
2424.1–2	Bracelets	43
2425.1–9	Helmets	44
2426.1–4	Shields and Armour	48
2427.1–28	Weapons and other Military Equipment	51
2428.1–20	Iron Tools	58
2429.1–18	Bronze Baldric- and Belt-fittings	63
2430.1–3	Votive objects and an Amulet in Gold	69
2431.1–11	Votive objects in Silver	70
2432.1–10	Votive objects in Bronze	74
2433.1–23	Miscellaneous objects in Bronze	78
2434.1–6	Lead Water-pipes	84
2435.1–14	Lead Roundels	86
2436.1–13	Lead Sheets (except *Defixiones*)	90
2437.1–6	Miscellaneous Lead objects	94
2438.1–7	Stone Roundels	96
2439.1–31	Pottery Roundels	98
2440.1–381	Bone Roundels	105
2441.1–19	Miscellaneous Objects in Bone, Horn or Ivory	170
Index of Sites		175

PREFACE

The third fascicule of *RIB* ii contains the following categories:

2421. Brooches
2422. Finger-rings
2423. Gemstones, Amulets and Cameos
2424. Bracelets
2425. Helmets
2426. Shields and Armour
2427. Weapons and Military Equipment
2428. Iron Tools
2429. Bronze Baldric- and Belt-fittings
2430. Votive objects and an Amulet in Gold
2431. Votive objects in Silver
2432. Votive objects in Bronze
2433. Miscellaneous objects in Bronze
2434. Lead water-pipes
2435. Lead Roundels
2436. Lead sheets (except *Defixiones*)
2437. Miscellaneous lead objects
2438. Stone Roundels
2439. Pottery Roundels
2440. Bone Roundels
2441. Miscellaneous Objects in Bone, Horn or Ivory

This fascicule, like its predecessors, has been compiled by S.S. Frere from the archive collected by R.P. Wright and from later records down to the end of 1986 in *JRS, Britannia* and elsewhere. Critical assistance, especially on readings, has been given by Dr. R.S.O. Tomlin. The Administrators are grateful to Mr. M.W.C. Hassall and to Dr. Tomlin for providing drawings or rubbings of objects published by them in the annual reports of discoveries in successive volumes of *Britannia*. They also wish to acknowledge the help of Mr. D.F. Mackreth in checking and amplifying the entries for *RIB* 2421 (the Brooches) and of Dr. Martin Henig for doing the same with 2422 and 2423 (the Finger-rings and Gems). The Editors wish to thank the Trustees of the British Museum and the Society of Antiquaries of London for permission to reproduce illustrations, and the following individuals or institutions for similar permission and for providing information, photographs or drawings:

Miss Lindsay Allason-Jones (Museum of Antiquities, Newcastle upon Tyne); Paul Bennett (Canterbury Archaeological Trust); R.E. Birley (Vindolanda Trust); Dr. M.C. Bishop; K. Blockley; G.C. Boon; S. Cracknell (Warwickshire Museum); K.L. Crowe (Southend Museum); Nina and Philip Crummy (Colchester Archaeological Trust); The Cumberland and Westmorland Antiquarian and Archaeological Society; Dr. A.P. Detsicas (Kent Archaeological Society); A. Down (Chichester District Archaeological Unit); English Heritage; R. Friendship-Taylor; Miss B.M. Gobel; J. Gould; Miss Barbara Green (Norwich Museum); Dr. S. Greep; Nicholas Griffiths; D. Gurney (Norfolk Archaeological Unit); R. Hattatt; Dr. M. Henig; J. Hinchliffe; Mrs. V. Holgate (Verulamium Museum); Mrs. P. Irving (English Heritage); D.

Jennings; Miss C.M. Johns (British Museum); Miss Christine Jones (Museum of London); Dr. L.J.F. Keppie (Hunterian Museum, Glasgow); Dr. R.H. Leech; Dr. I. Longworth (British Museum); A. Macgregor (Ashmolean Museum, Oxford); D.F. Mackreth; Professor W.H. Manning; D.P.S. Mason (Grosvenor Museum, Chester); J. May; Mme. Morrison (Cabinet des Medailles, Paris); D.S. Neal; Mrs. Rosalind Niblett; A.B. Page (City and County Museum, Lincoln); K.S. Painter; K. Parfitt (Dover Archaeological Group); Miss Georgina Plowright (Corbridge Museum); Dr. T.W. Potter; Dr. Warwick Rodwell; P.R. Sealey (Colchester Museum); Harvey Sheldon; Miss Alison Sheridan (National Museums of Scotland); Dr. Ian Stead; D. Viner; Professor J.S. Wacher; Dr. Susan Walker (British Museum); Dr. G.A. Webster; S.E. West (Suffolk County Council); Dr. J.P. Wild; Professor J.J. Wilkes; J. Wilson (Kent Archaeological Rescue Unit); Miss Carolyn Wingfield (Bedford Museum); York Archaeological Trust; J.D. Zienkiewicz.

Throughout *RIB* ii the term 'bronze' is used in its traditional sense of an uncertain copper alloy. Very few objects have been subjected to analysis.

R.M. Harrison

LIST OF PLATES
(at end)

I A–C	2421.43.	Gold crossbow brooch from Erickstanebrae, Strathclyde.
II A	2421.53.	Inscribed brooch from Wickford, Essex.
B	2421.49.	Inscribed brooch from Piddington, Northamptonshire.
C	2421.59.	Inscribed brooch from Kempston, Bedfordshire.
III A	2422.16.	Gold ring from Brentwood, Essex.
B	2422.30.	Silver ring from Billingford, Norfolk.
C	2422.42.	Silver disc or seal from Silchester, Hampshire.
D	2422.32.	*Impression* from a silver ring from Caistor St Edmund, Norfolk.
E	2422.38.	Silver ring from an unknown provenance.
F	2422.65.	*Impression* from a bronze ring from Caistor St Edmund, Norfolk.
G	2422.75.	Iron ring with bronze inlay from London.
IV A–E	2422.80.	Jet ring from (?) Chesters, Northumberland.
V A, B	2423.1.	Haematite amulet from Lockleys, Hertfordshire.
VI	2423.2.	Onyx gem from London.
VII A	2423.6.	Cornelian intaglio from Braintree, Essex, showing Asclepius and Hygieia.
B		*Impression* of 2423.6.
C	2423.8.	Jasper intaglio in an iron ring from Caistor St Edmund, Norfolk.
D	2423.11.	Onyx cameo from North Wraxall, Wiltshire.
E	2423.16.	Cast of the obverse of a bloodstone amulet from Silchester.
VIII A	2423.17.	Lapis lazuli amulet from Colchester: obverse, showing Harpocrates.
B		Reverse of A.
C	2423.19.	Onyx cameo from Bradwell, Essex, set in a gold ring.
D, E	2423.20.	Nicolo intaglio from Oxfordshire, obverse and reverse.
IX A	2423.21.	Cornelian intaglio from Kingsholm, Gloucestershire, showing wheat-stalks and a cow.
B	2423.23.	Cornelian intaglio from Akenham, Suffolk, showing Victory.
C	2423.25.	Cornelian intaglio from Caerleon, Gwent, showing Diana.
D	2423.30.	Intaglio of green prase from Caerleon showing clasped hands, a hippocamp, raven and other symbols.
E		*Impression* from D.
X A	2423.33.*	*Impression* of a plasma intaglio from Canterbury Cathedral, showing a lion-headed serpent.
B	2427.26.*	Bronze roundel showing legionary vexillations and a *venatio*.
XI	2426.1.	Bronze shield-plate from the river Tyne.

ix

LIST OF PLATES

XII	A, B	2425.2.	Neck-guard of a bronze helmet from London with punched graffiti.
XIII	A, B	2425.2.	Neck-guard of a bronze helmet from London with punched graffiti.
XIV		2427.21–24.	Four bronze pommel-stiffeners from Newstead.
XV	A	2429.6.	Bronze baldric-fitting from York.
	B	2429.7. and part of 8.	Bronze baldric-fittings from Aldborough.
	C	2429.16. and 17.	Belt-plates from Chesters, Northumberland.
XVI	A, B	2427.27.*	Obverse and reverse of a jasper pommel from Colchester, Essex.
	C	2427.2.	Iron spearhead from London with punched graffito.
	D	2440.15.	Bone roundel from Chichester.
	E	2440.51.	Bone roundel from Chichester.
	F, G	2440.68.	Obverse and reverse of a bone roundel from Chichester.

ABBREVIATIONS

This list contains only items not already listed in *RIB* i, pp. xix–xxii and in the Lists of Abbreviations in *RIB* ii, fascicules 1 and 2, which should be consulted for the remainder.

AJA	*American Journal of Archaeology.*
Bull. Soc. des Antiq. de France	*Bulletin de la Société Nationale des Antiquaires de France.*
Fasti Arch.	*Fasti Archeologici.*
HA	*Historia Augusta.*
Henig, *Corpus*	M. Henig, *A Corpus of Roman Engraved Gemstones from British Sites* (B.A.R. 8), 1974; ed. 2, 1978.
Mém. Soc. Ant. France	*Mémoires de la Société Nationale des Antiquaries de France.*
P. Dorset NHAS	*Proceedings of the Dorset Natural History and Archaeological Society.*
T. Lichfield and South Staffordshire A & HS	*Transactions of the Lichfield and South Staffordshire Archaeological and Historical Society.*
T. Radnorshire Soc.	*Transactions of the Radnorshire Society.*
Trierer Zeitschr.	*Trierer Zeitschrift.*
Vet. Mon.	*Vetusta Monumenta.*

BIBLIOGRAPHY

This list contains only items not already listed in the Bibliographies of *RIB* i (pp. xxiii–xxxi) and *RIB* ii fascicules 1 and 2, which should be consulted for the remainder.

Manning, *Cat.*   W.H. Manning, *Catalogue of the Romano-British Iron Tools, Fittings and Weapons in the British Museum* (1985).

Marshall, *Cat. of Finger-rings*   F.H. Marshall, *Catalogue of the Finger-rings, Greek, Etruscan and Roman, in the Departments of Antiquities, British Museum* (1907).

May, *Cat.*   T. May, *Catalogue of the Roman Pottery in the Colchester and Essex Museum* (1930).

Roach Smith, *Cat.*   C. Roach Smith, *Catalogue of the Museum of London Antiquities* (1854) (a collection acquired by the British Museum in 1856).

RIB 2421. BROOCHES

The vast majority of brooches carry no inscription. Of inscribed types the most frequent (41 examples here) is the Aucissa brooch, a type which was being manufactured on the Continent, probably in Gaul, during the first half of the first century and which was imported into Britain in some numbers during the period A.D. 43–60. For Continental examples see G. Behrens and J. Werner, *Reinecke Festschrift* (1950), 6–8; E. Ettlinger, *Die römischen Fibeln in der Schweiz* (1973), 114 Type 5.2; E. Riha, *Die römischen Fibeln aus Augst und Kaiseraugst* (1979), Type 29.

Many brooches of the Aucissa type have no inscription: see C.F.C. Hawkes and M.R. Hull, *Camulodunum* (1947), 321–3. The majority of the inscribed examples carry a version of the type name AVCISSA moulded across the head of the bow; but some examples of this type of brooch carry other names (for instance, ATCIVIOS, TARRA or QCOM). The inscriptions are thought to have been formed by hammering this part of the brooch into a metal former, in which the letters had been moulded; the variety of detail seen in the inscriptions testifies to the use of a number of moulds, and thus to the large numbers of these brooches which were manufactured.

Attention is also drawn to the important gold *Kaiserfibel* from a site near Moffat (*RIB* 2421.43).

2421.1. Norfolk, unknown provenance. Bronze plate brooch (1/1) with perforations, the area between them being decorated with blue and green enamel. Across the centre is a rectangular panel with moulded letters surrounded by green enamel. Found in or before 1984 when it was purchased from a dealer. In private possession. Reproduced from Hattatt.

Britannia xvi (1985), 329 No. 36. R. Hattatt, *Iron Age and Roman Brooches* (1985), 170 No. 604 with fig. 69.604.

moulded in the panel: [.]MAME
  Perhaps *[a]ma me*
  'Love me'

2421.2. Colchester (*Camulodunum*), Sheepen Farm, Essex. Distorted bronze brooch of Aucissa type (3/2), found in 1970 unstratified in ploughsoil during excavations. Colchester Museum. Reproduced from Niblett.

R. Niblett, *Sheepen: an early Roman industrial site at Camulodunum* (1985), 116 No. 25 with fig. 75.25 and Microfiche 3, C6.

moulded: ATCIVIO[.]
  Atcivio[s]

Compare *RIB* 2421.3–4. For another brooch by this maker see *CIL* xiii 10027.105.

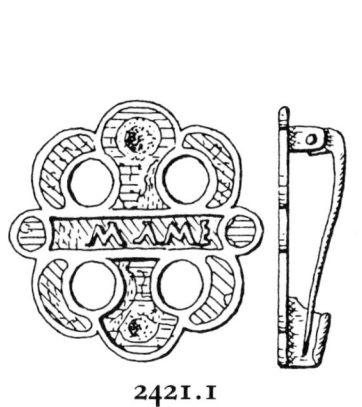

2421.1

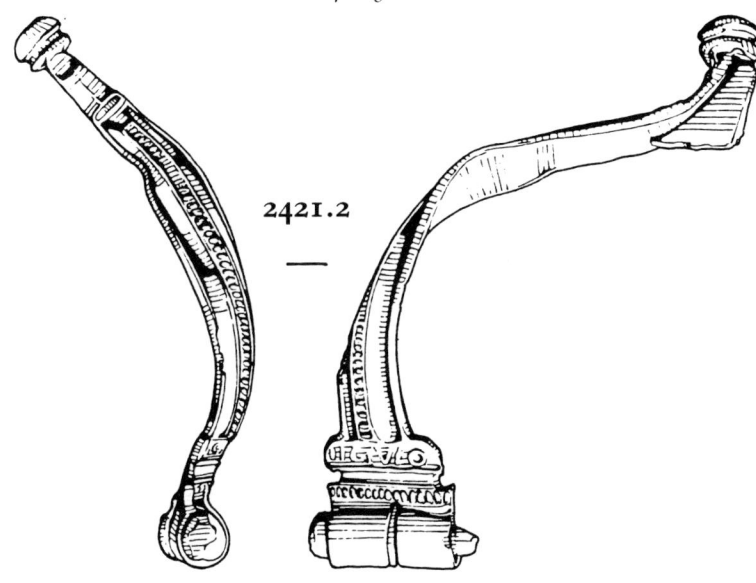

2421.2

2421.3. Wroxeter (*Viroconium*), Shropshire. Bronze brooch ($\frac{2}{1}$) of Aucissa type, found in 1923–27 during excavation below East Room 4 at the south-eastern corner of the forum. Rowley's House Museum, Shrewsbury. Drawn by S.S.F. from a photograph in Atkinson.

JRS xxxiii (1943), 81 No. 15. D. Atkinson, *Wroxeter* (1942), 199 No. 1 with pl. XLVII, H22.

moulded: ATGIVIOS

See note to *RIB* 2421.2.

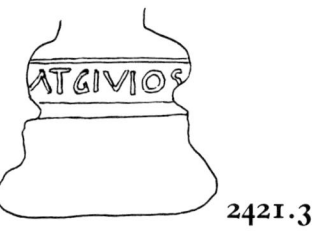
2421.3

2421.4. Ibid. Bronze brooch ($\frac{2}{1}$) of Aucissa type, found in 1973 during excavations in the basilica of the Baths. Wroxeter Museum. Drawn by D.F. Mackreth.

moulded: ATG·VIOS
   Atg(i)vios

See note to *RIB* 2421.2.

2421.4

2421.5. Alcester, Warwickshire. Bronze brooch ($\frac{1}{1}$), found in 1964–66 during excavations by C.M. Mahany. Warwick Museum. Drawn by D.F. Mackreth.

moulded: AVCIS[..]
   Aucis[sa]

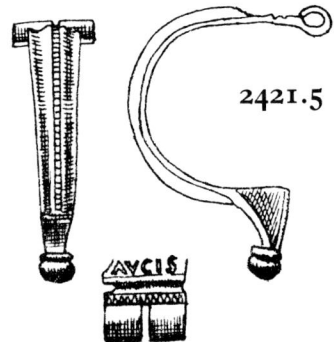
2421.5

2421.6. Ibid. Bronze brooch found in 1975 during excavations in the garden of Lloyds Bank. Warwick Museum. Not illustrated.

Britannia vii (1976), 331.

moulded: AVCISSA

2421.7. Alchester, Oxfordshire. Bronze brooch ($\frac{1}{1}$), found in 1928 during excavations in the Roman town. Ashmolean Museum, Oxford. Reproduced from Iliffe.

Iliffe, *Antiq. J.* xii (1932) 64 with pl. XVII d.

moulded: AVCISSA

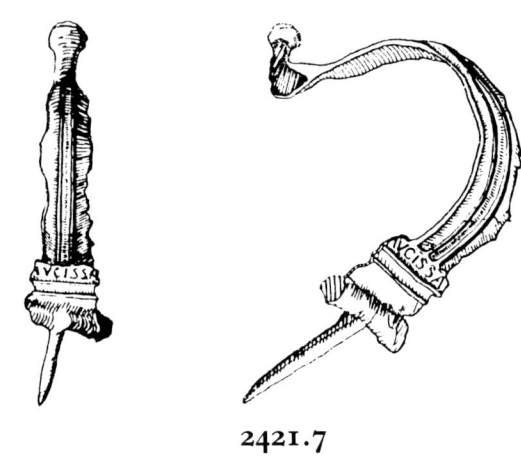
2421.7

2421.8. Avebury, Wiltshire. Bronze brooch ($\frac{1}{1}$), found in 1911 during excavation of an upper layer in the filling of the ditch of the Neolithic Circle, in Cutting VIII. Devizes Museum. Reproduced from Gray.

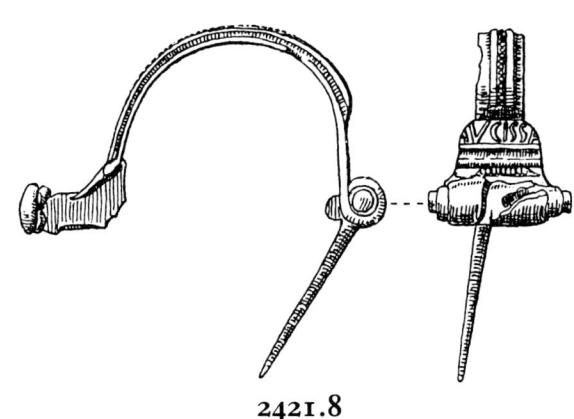
2421.8

EE ix 1313 g. Anon., *WAM* xxxvii (1911–12), 477. Devizes Museum Cat. ii (1934), 81. Gray, *Arch.* lxxxiv (1934), 155–6 with fig. 8.

moulded: ΛVCISSΛ

2421.9. Canterbury (*Durovernum*), Kent. Bronze brooch ($\frac{1}{1}$ and $\frac{2}{1}$), found in 1976–77 during excavations at the Rosemary Lane Car Park. Canterbury Museum. Drawing: Canterbury Archaeological Trust.

P. Bennett *et al., Excavations at Canterbury Castle* (The Archaeology of Canterbury, i (1982)), 172 No. 5 with fig. 88.

moulded: AVCISSA

R.H. Leech, *Excavations at Catsgore 1970–73* (1982), 105 with fig. 76.1

moulded: ΛVCISSΛ

2421.11. Charlton, Somerset. Bronze brooch ($\frac{1}{1}$), found in 1917 at a Roman site at Charlton, near Shepton Mallet. Shepton Mallet Museum. Reproduced from Gray, *Connoisseur*.

Gray, *The Connoisseur* 11 (1918), 221 with fig.; *Arch.* lxxxiv (1934), 156.

moulded: ΛVCISSΛ

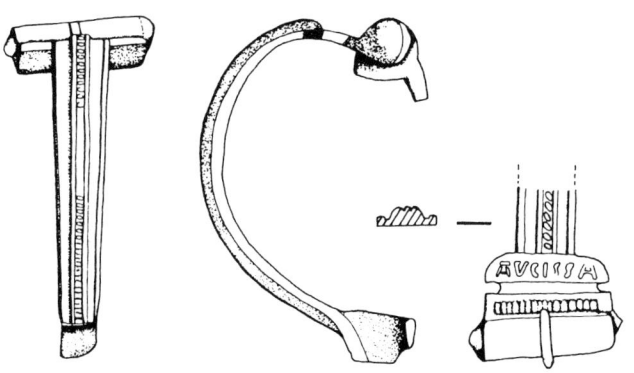

ΛVCISSΛ

2421.9

2421.10. Catsgore, Somerset. Bronze brooch ($\frac{1}{1}$), found in 1970–73 during excavations. Taunton Museum. Reproduced from Leech.

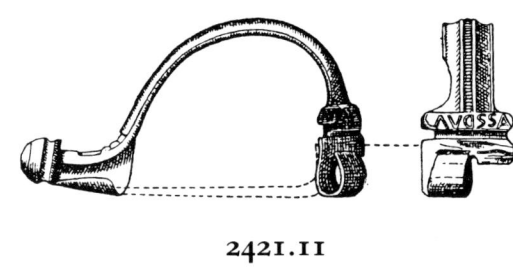

2421.11

2421.12. Charterhouse on Mendip, Somerset. Bronze brooch ($\frac{1}{1}$), found about 1875 with *RIB* 2421.38. Bristol Museum (A.C. Pass collection). Reproduced from Haverfield, *Arch. J.*

EE ix 1313 a. Haverfield, *Arch. J.* lx (1903), 240 No. 16 with fig. 5; *VCH* Somerset i (1906), 343 with fig. 98. Gray, *Arch.* lxxxiv (1934), 156.

moulded: ΛVCISS[.]
   Auciss[a]

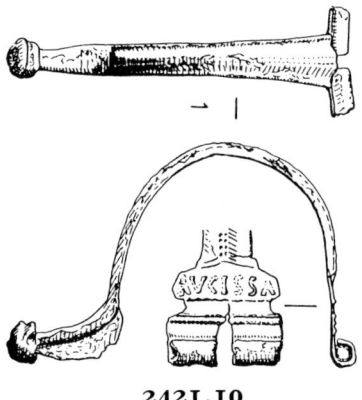

2421.10

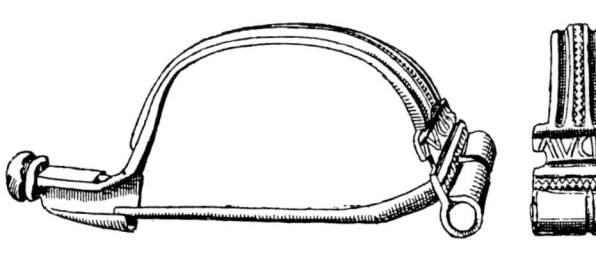

2421.12

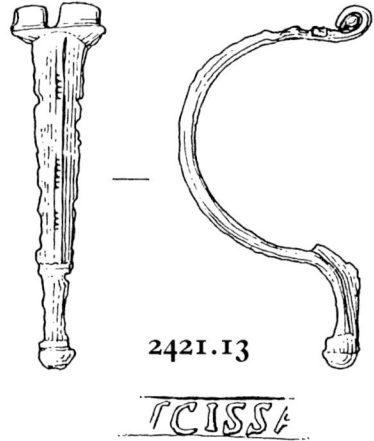

2421.13

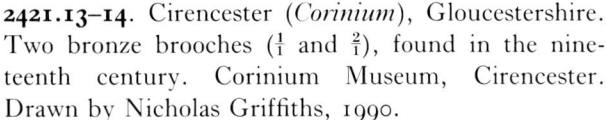

2421.13–14. Cirencester (*Corinium*), Gloucestershire. Two bronze brooches ($\frac{1}{1}$ and $\frac{2}{1}$), found in the nineteenth century. Corinium Museum, Cirencester. Drawn by Nicholas Griffiths, 1990.

EE ix 1313 d, e. Haverfield, *Arch. J.* lii (1905) 265 Nos. 22, 23. Gray, *Arch.* lxxxiv (1934), 156.

13. moulded: [.]VCISSA
    [A]ucissa
14. moulded: AVCISSA

2421.15. Ham Hill, Somerset. The bow of a bronze brooch, somewhat smaller than *RIB* 2421.16. Found in 1923. Taunton Museum. Not illustrated.

Walter, *Antiq. J.* iii (1923), 150. Gray, *Arch.* lxxxiv (1934), 156.

moulded: AVCISSA

2421.16. Ibid. Bronze brooch ($\frac{1}{1}$ and $\frac{2}{1}$), found in 1905 at Tor Point Quarry, Ham Hill. Taunton Museum. Reproduced from Gray, *P. Som. AS*.

EE ix 1313 c. Haverfield, *VCH* Somerset i (1906), 296. Gray, *PSA*[2] xxi (1906), 13; *Arch.* lxxxiv (1934), 156; *P. Som. AS* lvi.2 (1911), 56 with fig.; *The Connoisseur* 11 (1918), 221 with fig.

moulded: AVCISSA

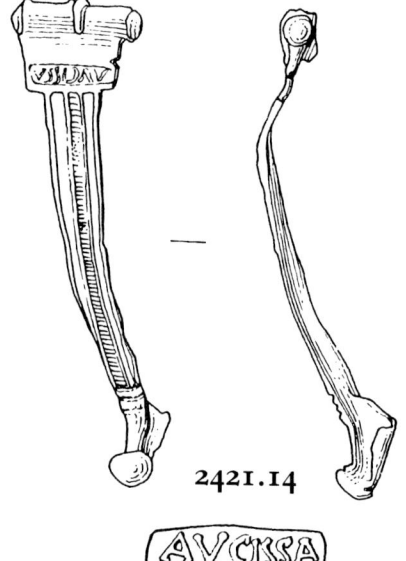

2421.14

2421.17. Harlow, Essex. Bronze brooch ($\frac{1}{1}$ and $\frac{2}{1}$), found in 1963 during excavations at the Romano-Celtic temple. Harlow Museum. Reproduced from France and Gobel; inscription drawn by S.S.F. from a rubbing by R.P.W.

JRS lvi (1966), 221 No. 19. N.E. France and B.M. Gobel, *The Romano-British Temple at Harlow, Essex* (1985), 76 No. 20 with fig. 39.20.

moulded: AVCISSA

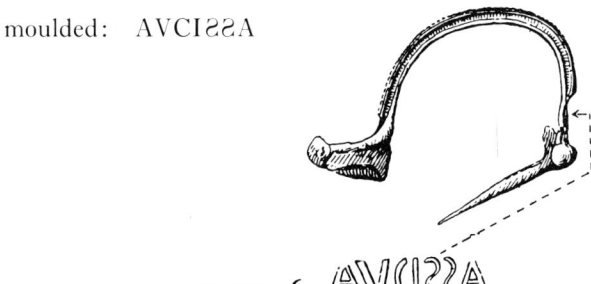

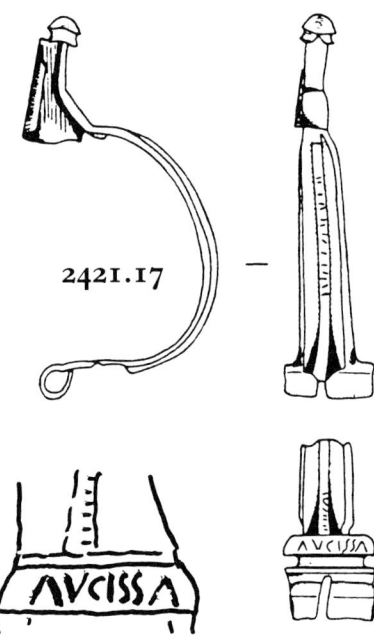

2421.18. London (*Londinium*). Bronze brooch ($\frac{1}{1}$), found before 1930 at Poultry in the City. Museum of London. Reproduced from Wheeler.

R.E.M. Wheeler, *London in Roman Times* (1930), 90 with fig. 25.

moulded: AVCISSA

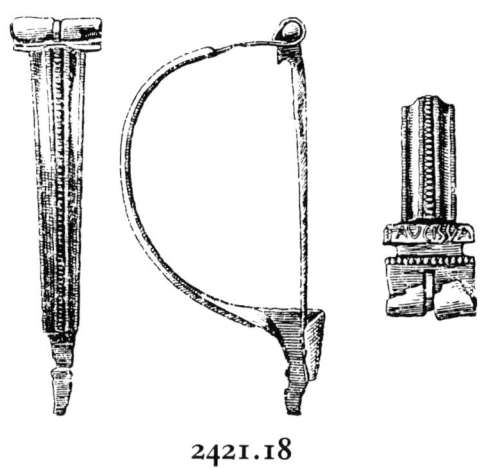

2421.18

2421.19. Mildenhall (*Cunetio*), Wiltshire. Bronze brooch ($\frac{1}{1}$), found in 1910. Devizes Museum. Drawn by D.F. Mackreth.

EE ix 1313 f. Devizes Museum *Cat.* ii (1934), 222 No. 8 with pl. LXXII.8. Gray, *Arch.* lxxxiv (1934), 156. Anon., *WAM* xxxvii (1911–12), 477. *VCH* Wiltshire i.1 (1957), 88.

moulded: AVCISSA

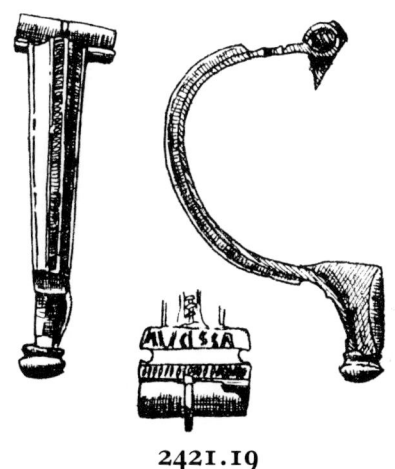

2421.19

2421.20. Nettleton, West Kington, Wiltshire. Bronze brooch ($\frac{2}{1}$) broken in three pieces, found in 1956–71 during excavations at the Shrine of Apollo at Nettleton Scrubb. Bristol Museum. Reproduced from Wedlake.

W.J. Wedlake, *The Excavation of the Shrine of Apollo at Nettleton, Wiltshire, 1956–71* (1982), 120 No. 6 with fig. 50.6.

moulded: AVC[. . .]
Auc[issa]

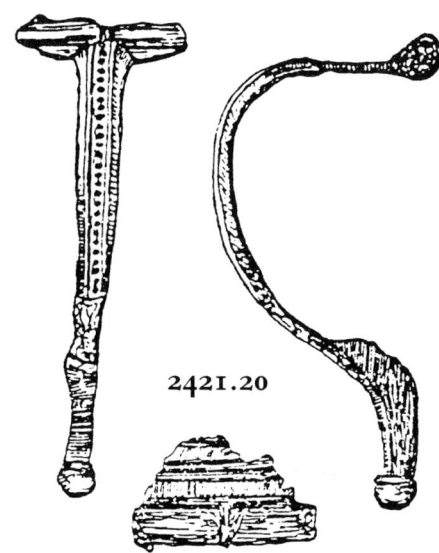

2421.20

2421.21. Richborough (*Rutupiae*), Kent. Bronze brooch ($\frac{1}{1}$), found in 1933–8 during excavation of the lower occupation-level of Area XX and thus earlier than A.D. 85. In store at Dover Castle. Reproduced from Cunliffe.

B.W. Cunliffe (ed), *Fifth Report on the Excavations of the Roman Fort at Richborough, Kent* (1968), 84 No. 42 with pl. XXX.42.

moulded: AVCISSA

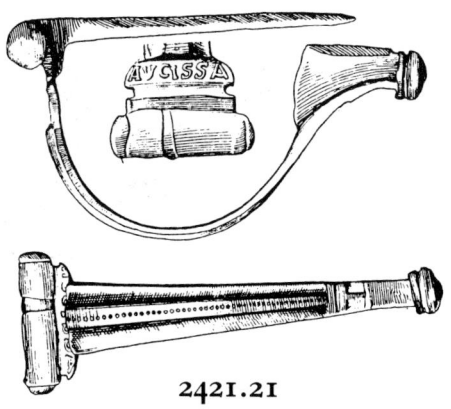

2421.21

2421.22. South Ferriby, Humberside [Lincolnshire]. Bronze brooch ($\frac{1}{1}$), found before 1905 with *RIB* 2421.40 'presumably in the Roman cemetery' (F.H.). Hull Museum. Reproduced from Haverfield, *Arch. J.*

EE ix 1313 i. Haverfield, *Arch. J.* lxii (1905), 266 No. 25 with fig. Sheppard, *Hull Museum Publication* No. 28 (1905), 3 with fig.; No. 39 (1907), 3 with pl. XXIX.7.

moulded: AVCISSA

2421.23. Usk (*Burrium*), Gwent [Monmouthshire]. Bronze brooch ($\frac{2}{1}$), found in 1971 during excavations at the fortress. National Museum, Cardiff. Drawing supplied by D.F. Mackreth.

moulded: [.]VCISSA

[A]ucissa

2421.24. Ibid. Bronze brooch ($\frac{2}{1}$), found in 1971 during excavations at the fortress. National Museum, Cardiff. Drawing supplied by D.F. Mackreth.

moulded: [.]VCIS[. .]

[A]ucis[sa]

2421.25. Wall (*Letocetum*), Staffordshire. Bronze brooch ($\frac{1}{1}$ and $\frac{2}{1}$) broken in two and heavily corroded, found in 1964–6 during excavation of the second-century filling of a military ditch of Punic type. Wall Museum. Reproduced from Gould, with enlargement of the stamp drawn by S.S.F.

Gould, T. *Lichfield and South Staffordshire A & H S* viii (1966–7), 17 No. 9 with fig. 7.9.

moulded: AVCISSA

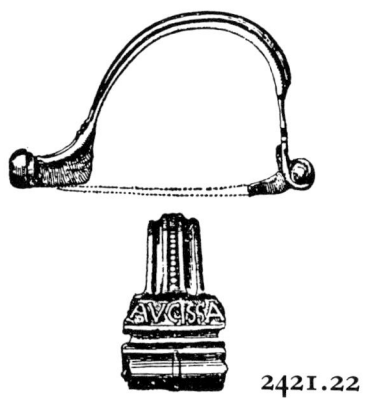

2421.22

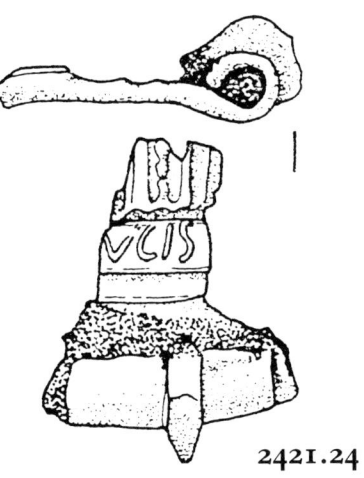

2421.24

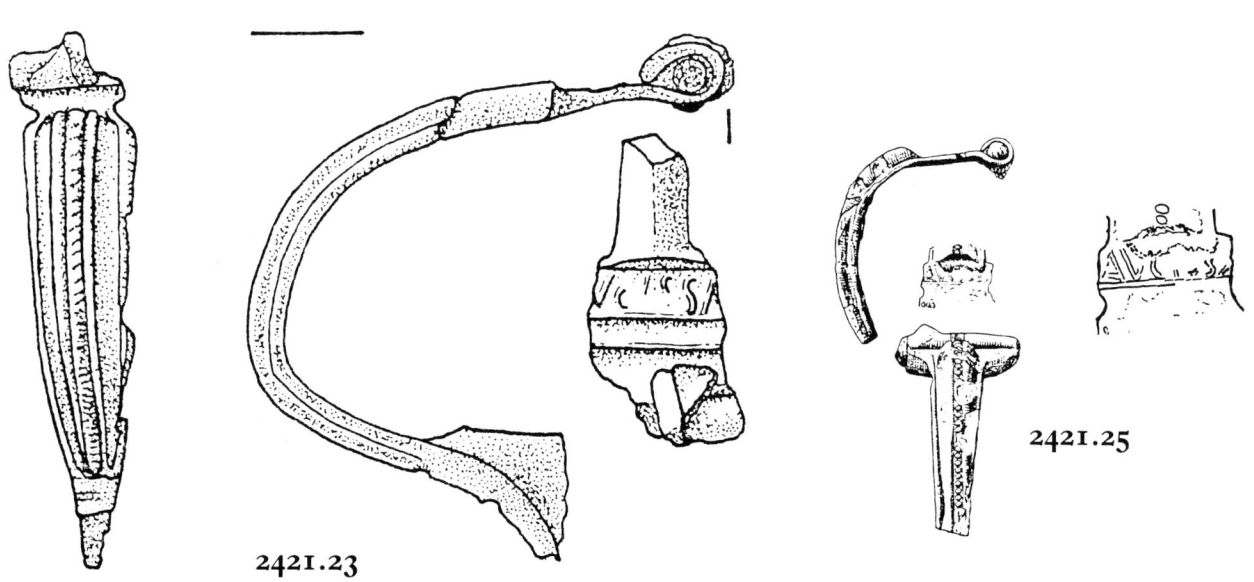

2421.23

2421.25

2421.26. Wanborough, Wiltshire. Bronze brooch ($\frac{1}{1}$ and $\frac{2}{1}$), found in 1921 during excavations at the *mansio*. Ashmolean Museum, Oxford. Reproduced from Passmore, with enlargement of the stamp drawn by S.S.F.

JRS xxxiv (1944), 90 No. 14; xlvi (1956), 152. Passmore, *WAM* xli (1921) 279 with pl. No. 3.

moulded: ΛVC.SSΛ
Auc[i]ssa

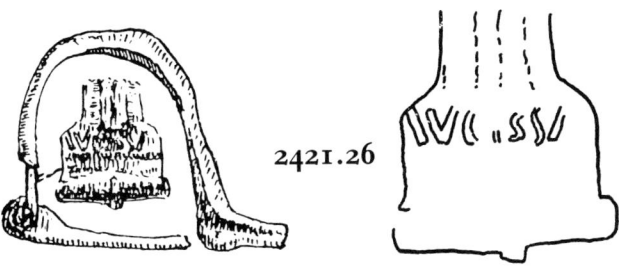

2421.27. Wroxeter (*Viroconium*), Shropshire. Bronze brooch ($\frac{1}{1}$), found in 1912 during excavation of a low level on Site I, associated with pottery dated c. A.D. 80–120. Rowley's House Museum, Shrewsbury. Reproduced from Bushe-Fox.

Haverfield, *Roman Britain in 1913*, 32 No. 9. J.P. Bushe-Fox, *Wroxeter* i (1913), 24 No. 5 with fig. 9.5. Gray, *Arch.* lxxxiv (1934), 157.

moulded: [.]VCISSΛ
[A]ucissa

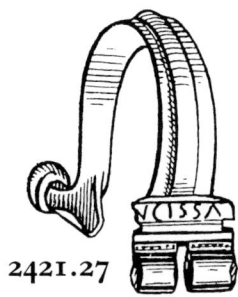

2421.28. Ibid. Bronze brooch ($\frac{1}{1}$), found in 1975–7 during excavations by P. Brown. Wroxeter Museum. Drawn by D.F. Mackreth.

moulded: ΛVCISSΛ

2421.29. Ibid. Bronze brooch ($\frac{1}{1}$), found during excavations by Dr. G.A. Webster. Wroxeter Museum. Drawn by D.F. Mackreth.

moulded: AVCISSA

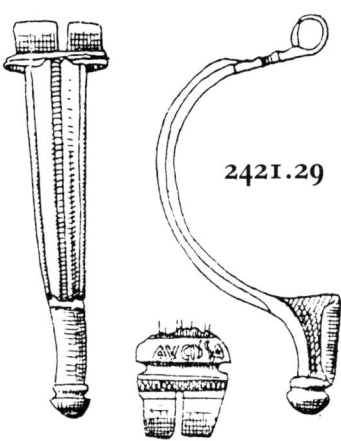

2421.30. York (*Eboracum*). Bronze brooch ($\frac{2}{1}$), now in the Hull Museum. Drawn by S.S.F. from a rubbing by R.P.W., 1951.

moulded: AVCISSA

2421.31. Unprovenanced. Bronze brooch, formerly in the E.J.W. Hildyard collection, where it was recorded by D.F. Mackreth. Not illustrated.

moulded: AVCISSA

2421.32. Unprovenanced, probably from Yorkshire or Humberside. Bronze brooch ($\frac{2}{1}$). Hull Museum. Drawn by S.S.F. from a rubbing by R.P.W., 1951.

moulded: AVCISSA

Another Aucissa brooch, but with the inscribed portion broken away and lost, is recorded from Chichester: Mackreth in A. Down, *Chichester Excavations* v (1981), 257 No. 14.

2421.33. Maiden Castle, Dorset. Bronze brooch (¹⁄₁ and ²⁄₁), found in 1934–37 unstratified in the filling of a trench dug in 1882 on the site of the temple. Dorchester Museum. Reproduced from Wheeler.

R.E.M. Wheeler, *Maiden Castle, Dorset* (1943), 262 No. 31 with fig. 85.31.

moulded: AVCISSAF
  Aucissa f(ecit)
  'Aucissa made (this)'

AVCISSAE, Wheeler.

D.F. Mackreth (to S.S.F., 30 April 1990) notes that this is the sole example of the *small* size of Aucissa brooch known to him to carry an inscription: but see also *RIB* 2421.15.

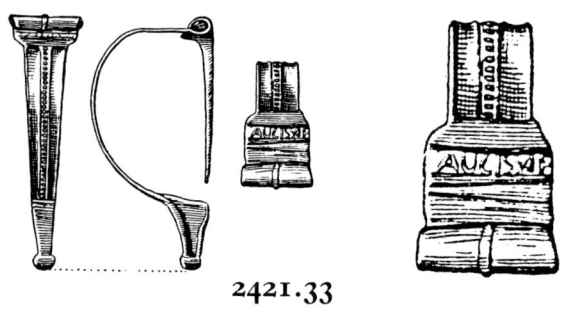

2421.33

2421.34. Kingsholm, Gloucestershire. Bronze brooch (¹⁄₁), found in 1983 during excavations. Gloucester Museum. Drawn by D.F. Mackreth.

moulded: IAVCISSA

The initial I is perhaps a space-filler or decorative edging rather than a letter. Compare *RIB* 2421.35, 36–40 and 2422.53, 54.

2421.34

2421.35. Rudston, Humberside [Yorkshire]. Bronze brooch, tinned (¹⁄₁), found in 1962–3 in excavations at the villa outside Building 4. Hull Museum. Reproduced from Stead.

I.M. Stead, *Rudston Roman Villa* (1980), 95 No. 2 with fig. 59.2 and p. 174.

moulded: IAVCIS.A
  Perhaps ⟨i⟩*Aucis*[*s*]*a*

See note to *RIB* 2421.34.

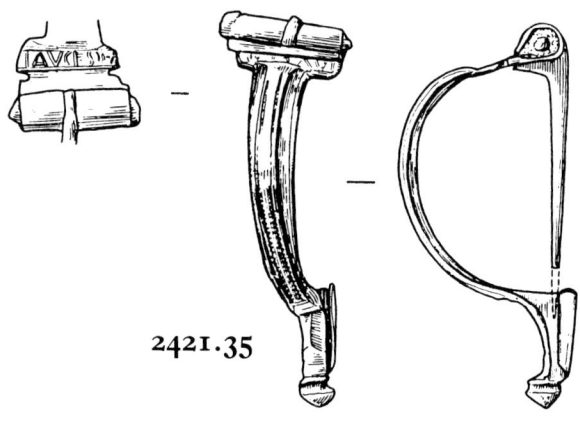

2421.35

2421.36. Baldock, Hertfordshire. Bronze brooch (¹⁄₁ and ²⁄₁), found in 1968–72 during excavations in Wall Field. Letchworth Museum. Reproduced from Stead and Rigby.

I.M. Stead and V. Rigby, *Baldock, The excavation of a Roman . . . Settlement 1968–72* (1986), 113 No. 104 with fig. 46.

moulded: IIAVCISSA

The initial double I is perhaps a space-filler or decorative edging rather than epigraphic. Compare *RIB* 2421.37, 34–35, 38–40. See also *RIB* 2422.53, 54.

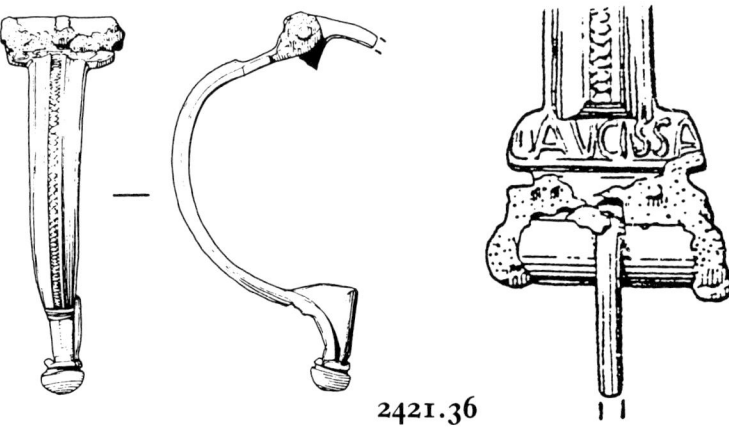

2421.36

2421.37. Wroxeter (*Viroconium*), Shropshire. Bronze brooch (¹⁄₁), found during excavations by Dr. G.A. Webster. Wroxeter Museum. Drawn by D.F. Mackreth.

moulded: IIIAVCISSA

See note to *RIB* 2421.36.

2421.38. Charterhouse on Mendip, Somerset. Bronze brooch (¹⁄₁), found *c.* 1875 with *RIB* 2421.12. Bristol Museum (A.C. Pass collection). Reproduced from Haverfield, *Arch. J.*

EE ix 1313 b. Haverfield, *Arch. J.* lx (1903), 240 No. 17 with fig. 5; *VCH* Somerset i (1906) 343 with fig. 98. Gray, *Arch.* lxxxiv (1934), 156.

moulded: IIIAVCISS

'No space for the A at the end', F.H.

The initial triple I is perhaps a space-filler or decorative edging rather than epigraphic. Compare *RIB* 2421.39–40, and 34–37. See also *RIB* 2422.53, 54.

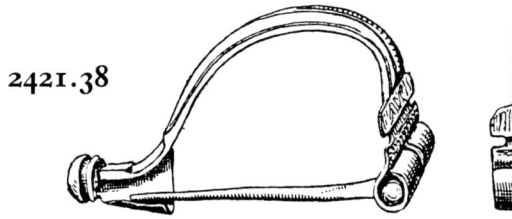

2421.39. Silchester (*Calleva*), Hampshire. Bronze brooch (¹⁄₁). Reading Museum. Reproduced from Boon.

G.C. Boon, *Roman Silchester* (1957), 113 fig. 17.5; *Silchester: the Roman Town of Calleva* (1974), 134 fig. 19.7.

moulded: IIIAVCISSA

See note to *RIB* 2421.38.

Boon states that the object is of brass, but quotes no analysis.

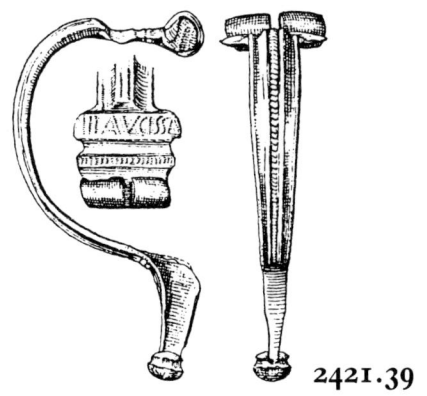

2421.40. South Ferriby, Humberside [Lincolnshire]. Bronze brooch (¹⁄₁), found before 1905 with *RIB* 2421.22 'presumably in the Roman cemetery' (F.H.). Hull Museum. Reproduced from Haverfield, *Arch. J.*

EE ix 1313 h. Haverfield, *Arch. J.* lxii (1905), 265 No. 24 with fig. Sheppard, *Hull Museum Publication* No. 28 (1905), 6 with fig.; No. 39 (1907) pl. XXIX.8.

moulded: IIIAVCISSA

See note to *RIB* 2421.38.

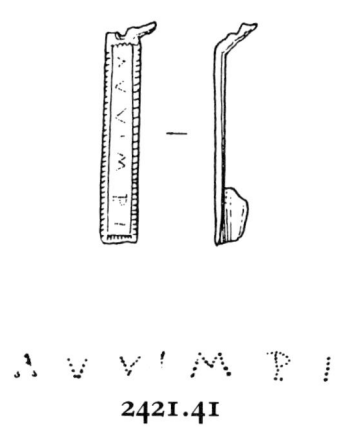

2421.41. Cirencester (*Corinium*), Gloucestershire. Bronze brooch (¹⁄₁ and ²⁄₁), found in 1885. Corinium Museum, Cirencester. Drawn by Nicholas Griffiths, 1990.

EE vii 1170 b. Watkin, *Arch. J.* xliii (1886), 286.

moulded: AVVIMPI

Auvimpus is otherwise unattested, whereas *Vimpus* was certainly a Celtic personal name (*CIL* xiii 4707; Oswald, *Index* s.v.; P. Wuilleumier, *Inscriptions Latines des Trois Gaules* (1963), 529 and 530). Perhaps therefore *Av(. . .) Vimpi* or *Au(reli) Vimpi*.

2421.42. Wroxeter (*Viroconium*), Shropshire. Bronze zoomorphic brooch (¼), length 57 mm, in the form of a dog, probably once enamelled. Found in 1860–61 during excavation at the Baths. Rowley's House Museum, Shrewsbury. Reproduced from Wright.

EE ix 1314. T. Wright, *Uriconium* (1872), 280 with fig. Scarth, *Arch. J.* xxi (1864), 131. Watkin, *Arch. J.* xxxviii (1881), 295. Haverfield, *VCH Shropshire* i (1908), 250 No. 20 with fig. 24.

moulded on the tail of the dog (forming the sheath of the pin): EECIT
   for *fecit*
   'made (this)'

The initial E, unless the draughtsman has misunderstood a serifed F (e.g. *RIB* 2423.28), was moulded in mistake for F. The maker's name may have been moulded on the dog and since lost; or possibly the dog itself was a rebus for the maker's 'dog' name (*Canio, Caninius, Cuno-*, etc.).

2421.42

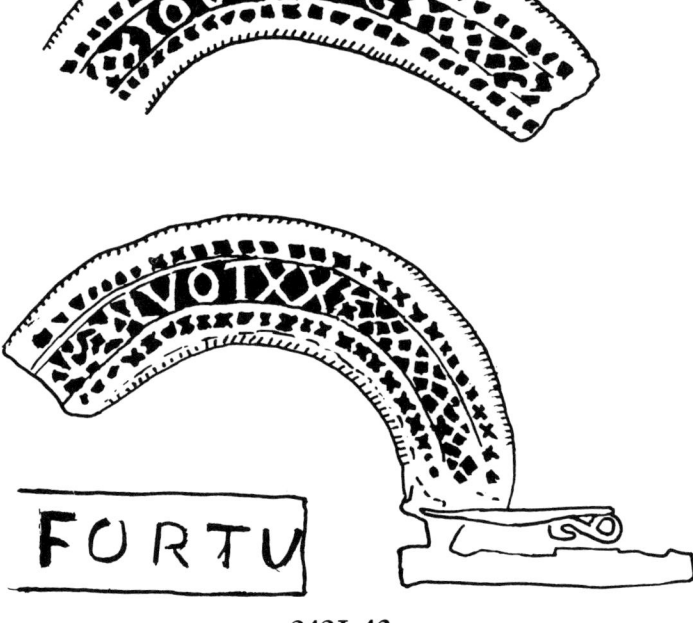

2421.43

2421.43. Erickstanebrae, Dumfries and Galloway [Dumfriesshire]. Foot and part of the semicircular bow of a gold brooch of elaborate cross-bow type (¼). The bow in cross-section forms a hollow triangle, the upper sides of which are decorated in openwork which includes inscriptions (a) and (b). Found in, or shortly before, 1787 during peat-cutting near the Roman road at Erickstanebrae, about four miles north of Moffat (*Gent. Mag.*). The Rev. G. Scott, in Sinclair (1792), places the discovery in his parish of Kirkpatrick Juxta about 2 miles south of Moffat; this is near the military sites at Milton. The *Gent. Mag.* account is to be preferred. Los Angeles County Museum; replica in the National Museums of Scotland, Queen Street, Edinburgh. Drawn by S.S.F. from a rubbing by R.P.W., 1954; see also PL. I.

CIL vii 1283. Anon., *Gent. Mag.* lvii (1787), 540, cf. 579. Sinclair, *Statistical Account of Scotland* iii (1792), 522. R. Stuart, *Caledonia Romana* (ed. 2, 1852), 235. Wilson, *Prehist. Ann.* (1863), 355. Haverfield, *Arch. J.* l (1893), 305. Curle, *PSAS* lxvi (1931–32), 335, 370–1 with fig. 54. *Fasti Arch.* vi (1951), No. 4199. Robertson, *Britannia* i (1970), 223. Noll, *BJ* 174 (1974), 227–30 with Bild 6 and 7.

(a) IOVIAVG
   Iovi(i) Aug(usti)
   '(Gift) of the Jovian Augustus'
(b) VOTXX
   Vot(is) XX
   '(On payment of) vows for twenty (years)'
(c) graffito on the plain underside of the bow: FORTV[...]
   Fortu[nati ?]
   '(Property) of Fortunatus (?)'

(c) PORTO, Curle, Noll.

(a) and (b) refer to the celebration of the twentieth anniversary (*vicennalia*) of Diocletian's accession. This took place on 20 November 303.
   Cross-bow brooches were worn by late Roman soldiers and officials, and in gold would have been presented by the Emperor to a person of high rank. This example may have been lost during the northern campaign of Constantius I in 306. The breakage of the brooch may suggest the division of captured spoil.
   This example is the only one of the eight recorded by Noll to be in openwork; the rest have solid bows.

2421.44. Unknown provenance. Bronze brooch (⅟₁) with raised moulded inscription set in a red enamel background. In private possession. Drawing by courtesy of D.F. Mackreth.

Detector User i.9 (June 1984), 62 with fig.

moulded on the two faces of the bow:
  F̂IBVLAEXEVT.. | LACITIENSE
  fibula . . .
  'brooch . . .'

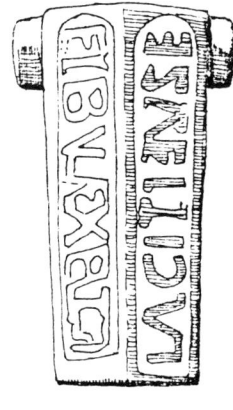

2421.44

2421.45. Exeter (*Isca*), Devon. Bronze brooch found before 1836. Now lost. Reprinted from Shortt.

Shortt, *Gent. Mag.* 1836 ii, 311.

'A bronze fibula, of elegant shape and workmanship, with the letter M on it.'

2421.46. Near Maidstone, Kent. Bronze brooch (⅟₁) of Colchester Type A, found some decades before 1971, presumably in the area round Maidstone. Maidstone Museum. Drawn by S.S.F. from a rubbing by R.P.W., 1971.

Britannia iii (1972), 357 No. 29.

moulded on the bow: NOИN·F
  Nonn(us) f(ecit)
  'Nonn(us) made (this)'

2421.46

2421.47. Ravensden, Bedfordshire. Bronze brooch (⅟₁ and ¼) of a variant of the Hod Hill type although lacking the normal tinned finish. Found in 1983–84 at the bottom of the bank of a stream south of Ravensden House. Bedford Museum. Drawing sent by M.W.C.H.

Britannia xvii (1986), 439 No. 22.

in punched letters on the bow: IS | IN | NO
or ON | NE | SI

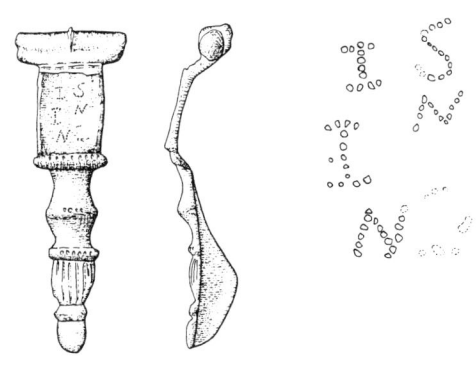

2421.47

2421.48. Unknown provenance, probably in Britain. Bronze brooch (²⁄₁) of Aucissa type, formerly in the E.J.W. Hildyard collection, acquired from a dealer. Drawn by S.S.F. from a rubbing by R.P.W., 1954.

moulded: QCOM

D.F. Mackreth (to S.S.F., 30 April 1990) notes that the brooch is of a type more usually found on the middle and lower Danube than in North Gaul or Germany.

2421.48

2421.49. Piddington, Northamptonshire. Bronze brooch of the Nertomarus variety of the Langton Down type ($\frac{1}{1}$ and $\frac{2}{1}$), found in 1985 in a first-century context during excavations at the Roman villa. In the possession of the Upper Nene Archaeological Society. Brooch drawn by D.F. Mackreth; stamp drawn by S.S.F. from a photograph. See PL. II B.

Britannia xvii (1986), 447 No. 69. R.M. and D.E. Friendship-Taylor, *Iron Age and Roman Piddington* (1989), 24 No. 7 with fig.

moulded retrograde on the spring-cover: ROMV

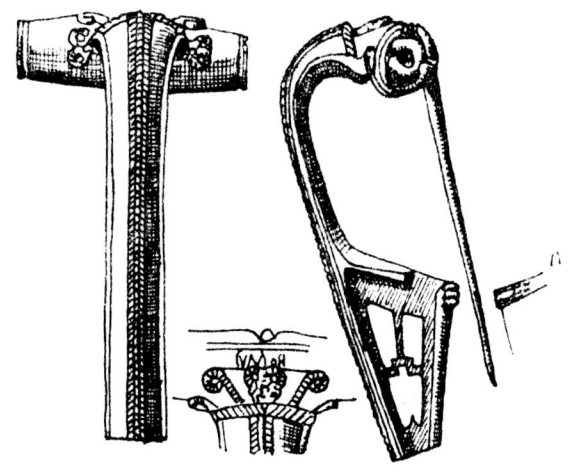

2421.49

2421.50. Richborough (*Rutupiae*), Kent. Bronze brooch ($\frac{1}{1}$ and $\frac{2}{1}$) of first-century Hod Hill type, found in 1931 during excavations within the Saxon Shore fort, in the drain of the north–south road. In store at Dover Castle. Brooch reproduced from Cunliffe; with inscription enlarged by S.S.F.

JRS xxii (1932), 228 No. 19. B.W. Cunliffe (ed.), *Fifth Report on the Excavations ... at Richborough* (1968), 87 No. 61 with pl. XXX.61.

in punched letters: SIΛ | MΛS | EGOP | LVS
Si amas ego plus
'If you love (me) I love (you) more'

Compare *CIL* xiii 10027.150 (two brooches from Étaples with the same words).

2421.51. St Albans (*Verulamium*), Hertfordshire. Bronze brooch ($\frac{2}{1}$). Found before 1954. Verulamium Museum. Drawn by S.S.F. from a rubbing by R.P.W., 1954.

moulded on the bow: SIBANI

2421.51

[. . .]BANI, R.P.W. The rubbing appears to give a reading SIBANI. The name *Sibanus* is not attested, but for *Sebanus* see *RIB* 2082.

2421.52. Lakenheath, Suffolk. Bronze brooch ($\frac{1}{1}$) of Langton Down type. The cylindrical head of the spring is decorated with curving lines and an inscription of punched dots. Found before 1985. In private possession. Reproduced from Hattatt.

R. Hattatt, *Iron Age and Roman Brooches* (1985), 36 No. 272 with fig. 15.272.

in letters punched with a point: TA

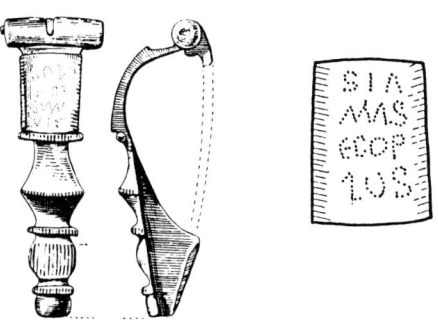

2421.50

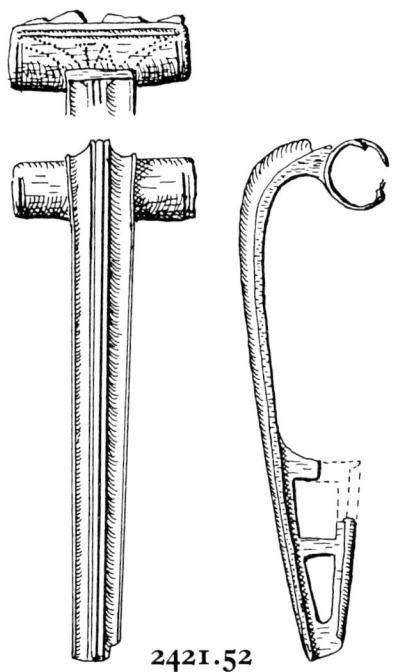

2421.52

2421.53. Wickford, Essex. Bronze brooch ($\frac{2}{1}$) of Aucissa type, found c.1977–78 during excavations by P. Neild. Southend Central Museum. Drawn by S.S.F. from a photograph. See PL. II A

moulded: TARRA

Compare *RIB* 2421.54. The name is also that of a samian potter (Oswald, *Index* s.v.).

2421.53

2421.54. Wroxeter (*Viroconium*), Shropshire. Bronze brooch ($\frac{1}{1}$) of Aucissa type, found during excavations by Dr. G.A. Webster. Wroxeter Museum. Drawn by D.F. Mackreth.

moulded: TARRA

Compare *RIB* 2421.53 (with note).

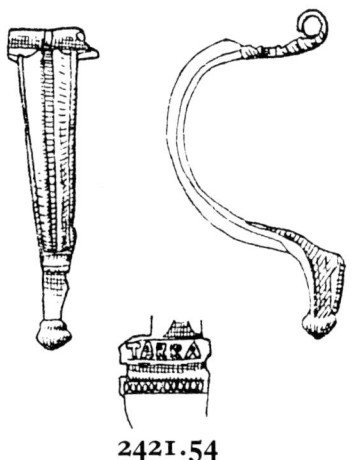

2421.54

2421.55. Walcot, Avon [Somerset]. Bronze brooch found in 1815 in the north-east part of Walcot near Bath, in association with coffins and much occupation-material. Sought in vain by F.H. Now lost. Reprinted from *EE*.

EE ix 1315. *Bath and Cheltenham Gazette*, 20 Nov. 1816. Haverfield, *VCH* Somerset i (1906) 283.

inscribed: TARRAS

ARRAS, F.H., *EE*; TARRAS, *VCH*.

F.H. compares *CIL* xi 6719, a brooch from Etruria inscribed .RRIC.

2421.56. Canterbury (*Durovernum*), Kent. Bronze brooch of 'Knee' type ($\frac{1}{1}$ and $\frac{2}{1}$), found in 1978 during excavations at No. 16 Watling Street. Canterbury Museum. Drawing: Canterbury Archaeological Trust.

Britannia xi (1980), 413 No. 45. *The Archaeology of Canterbury* v (1991), No. 111.

moulded along the bow in a recessed panel with a background of light blue enamel: VTĒREFĒLIX
  utere felix
  'Good luck to the user'

Compare *RIB* 2421.57, 58.

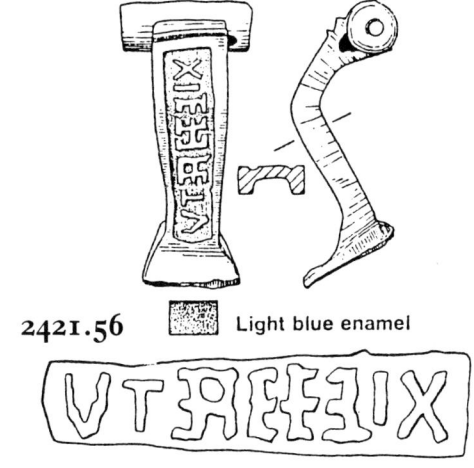

2421.56   Light blue enamel

2421.57. County Durham, no provenance. Bronze brooch ($\frac{1}{1}$) of 'Knee' type. Found in or before 1984 when it was purchased by a collector. In private possession. Reproduced from Hattatt.

Britannia xvi (1985), 327 No. 18. R. Hattatt, *Iron Age and Roman Brooches* (1985), 122 No. 483 with fig. 52.483.

moulded along the bow in a recessed panel with a background of green enamel: VTĒREFĒLIX
  utere felix
  'Good luck to the user'

Compare *RIB* 2421.56, 58.

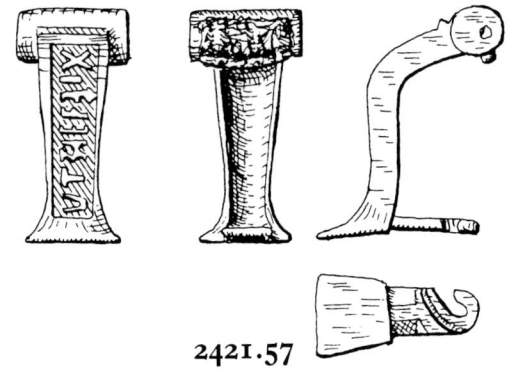

2421.57

2421.58. England, no provenance. Bronze brooch ($\frac{1}{1}$) of 'Knee' type, found in or before 1983, when it was purchased from a dealer. In private possession. Reproduced from Hattatt.

Britannia xvi (1985), 330 No. 40. R. Hattatt, *Iron Age and Roman Brooches* (1985), 122 No. 484 with fig. 52.484.

moulded along the bow in a recessed panel with a background of red enamel: VTEREFELIX

   utere felix

   'Good luck to the user'

Compare *RIB* 2421.56–7.

2421.60. Southwark, south London. Bronze brooch of Hod Hill type ($\frac{1}{1}$), found in 1970–72 during excavations at Toppings Wharf. Museum of London. Reproduced from Sheldon.

Sheldon, *T Lond. Middl. AS* xxv (1974), 90 No. 1 with fig. 41.1.

incised on the cross-arm: [. . .]X̣Ẋ[. . .]

The letters are almost certainly the remains of a line of decoration; compare examples illustrated in R. Hattatt, *Iron Age and Roman Brooches* (1985), 58, fig. 24. 318 and *Britannia* xvii (1986), 26 with fig. 18. 112.

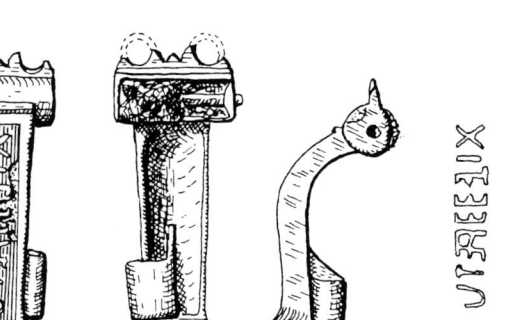

2421.58

2421.59. Kempston, Bedfordshire. Bronze brooch ($\frac{2}{1}$) of Colchester type, found before 1921 when it was acquired by Bedford Modern School Museum, probably from Mr. J.W. Lack; it is thought to have been discovered in the 19th century during gravel digging at the site of a wealthy Belgic and early Roman cemetery south-west of the village. Bedford Museum. Drawn by S.S.F. from a photograph. See PL. II C.

moulded in a recessed panel on the bow: V̇(*c.* 2)ĊIINV̇

   Perhaps a name in *-genus*

2421.59

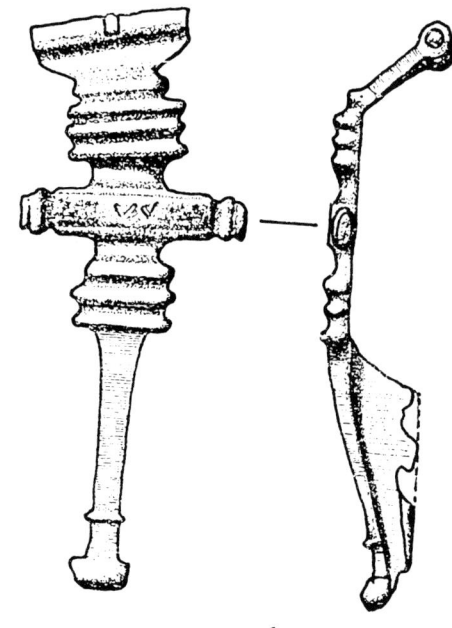

2421.60

RIB 2422. FINGER-RINGS

This chapter records rings whose inscriptions are cut in the bezel or hoop of the ring itself; inscribed gems which were formerly or are still displayed in the bezels of finger-rings are listed under *RIB* 2423. The rings in the present chapter have been arranged alphabetically under their respective materials: Gold (2422.1–17); Silver (2422.18–46); Bronze (2422.47–74); Iron (2422.75–77); Jet (2422.78–80); and unrecorded material (2422.81).

One bronze, one iron, two silver and three gold rings bear Greek inscriptions (2422.6, 10, 12, 35, 43, 57 and 76), in addition to those carrying a Chi-Rho monogram, of which there are two in gold, three in silver, two in bronze, one in jet and one in unrecorded material (2422.16, 17, 44–46, 69–70, 80, 81). Two other gold rings carry fuller Christian formulae (2422.14, 15), as does 2422.70, one of the bronze rings inscribed with the Chi-Rho.

Two gold and eleven silver rings (2422.9, 14, 20, 21, 23, 28–30, 36–40) carry invocations of, or dedication to, pagan deities. The names occur in the nominative or vocative (Nos. 14, 28), the genitive (No. 9) or the dative case (Nos. 20, 21); Nos. 29 and 30 are also conventionally restored in the dative. No. 52 refers to a *collegium* (guild) of Silvanus. Four bronze rings (Nos. 53–56), though from widely separated sites, are clearly the products of a single workshop: they carry permutations of what is possibly a magical formula of unknown significance (see note to *RIB* 2422.53). Two gold rings (Nos. 4, 7), carrying texts of loyalty to the emperor Constantine (?), are paralleled by numerous examples on the Continent (see note to *RIB* 2422.4). The majority of rings, however, carry either personal initials or simple secular wishes for good luck or for sexual partnership.

Unless stated, inscriptions are incised so as to be directly legible; such rings would be intended for ornament, gift or dedication. They are distinguished from rings bearing retrograde inscriptions, which would have been used as signets for sealing.

The term 'bronze' is used here in its traditional sense of an uncertain copper alloy; but one ring (2422.49) is known to be of brass.

(a) *RIB* 2422.1–17, Gold rings

Note: for other gold rings, carrying inscribed gems, see *RIB* 2423.4, 5, 7, 10, 15, 18 and 19.

2422.1. Corbridge (? *Coria*), Northumberland. Gold openwork ring ($\frac{2}{1}$), diameter 25.4 mm, weight 4.86 gm, consisting of fifteen facets, each bordered at top and bottom with two lunate cut-outs and each carrying an openwork letter or leaf-stop in the centre. Found in 1840 while pulling turnips in a field. Museum of Antiquities, Newcastle upon Tyne. Drawn by S.S.F. after *PSAN*.

CIL vii 1300. *EE* ix p. 668. Bruce, *LS* 655. *PSAN*[2] i (1884), 294 with fig. *Cat. of Edinburgh Museum* (1856), 59–60 with fig. Haverfield, *NCH* x (1914), 515. Charlesworth, *Arch. Ael.*[4] xxxix (1961) 24 No. 7 with pl. I.7. Wall, *Arch. Ael.*[4] xliii (1965), 216–17 with fig. 5 and pl. XII.2. Johns, *Antiq. J.* lxi (1981), 344. C. Thomas, *Christianity in Roman Britain to A.D. 500* (1981), 130. Sothebys' sale of antiquities, London, 13–14 December 1990, catalogue Lot 87, with colour plate.

moulded: ❦ AEMI ❦ LIA ❦ ZESES
Aemilia zeses
'Aemilia, long life to you'

For other rings in *opus interrasile* see *RIB* 2422.5 (with note) and 12.

2422.2. Carlisle (*Luguvalium*), Cumbria [Cumberland]. A diminutive gold ring ($\frac{1}{1}$), weight 1.88 gm, but with no dimensions recorded. Found in or shortly before 1860 during excavations in English Street. British Museum. Drawn by R.P.W., 1965.

JRS liii (1963), 163 No. 23. Braybrooke, *Arch. J.* xvii (1860), 182. O.M. Dalton, *Cat. of Finger-rings . . . bequeathed by Sir A.W. Franks* (1912), 4 No. 15 with fig. Henig, *Corpus* No. 772.

engraved on the oval bezel, with a palm branch:
ΛΜΛ ME
'Love me'

Compare *RIB* 2422.18 and 48.

2422.1

2422.3. London (*Londinium*). Heptagonal gold ring ($\frac{2}{1}$), found in 1974 during excavations on the New Fresh Wharf site, Lower Thames Street. Museum of London. Drawn by M.W.C.H.

Britannia vii (1976), 387 No. 43. T. Dyson (ed.), *The Roman Quay at St Magnus House, London* (Lond. Middl. AS Special Paper No. 8) (1986), 235 No. 14.1. T. Murdoch (ed.), *Treasures and Trinkets* (1991), 129 No. 297 with fig.

engraved retrograde on the bezel: Λ·P·D
    A(ulus) P(. . .) D(. . .)

2422.3

2422.4. Caistor St Edmund (*Venta Icenorum*), Norfolk. Gold ring ($\frac{1}{1}$) with eleven facets, diameter 25 mm, height 8 mm, found in 1823 about 2 miles south-east of the Roman city beside the Roman road and 'close to the windmill on Poringland Heath'. Norwich Castle Museum. Drawn by R.P.W., 1951.

CIL vii 1301. *EE* ix p. 668. Gurney, *Arch.* xxi (1827), 547 with fig. Woodward, *Arch.* xxxiii (1831), 366. Haverfield, *VCH* Norfolk i (1901), 311 with fig. 26. Noll, *BJ* clxxiv (1974), 243.

engraved: CONSTANṬFIDES
    Constant(ino) fides
    'Loyalty to Constantine'

CONSᴸVИTFIDES, F.H., *EE*.

Compare *RIB* 2422.7. The eighth letter could be an incomplete I or T, lacking either the second serif or the cross-stroke, but T is probable in view of the 16 rings found outside Britain with the legend FIDEM CONSTANTINO (see *Bonner Jahrb.* clxxiv (1974), 241–3). Hence also the expansion *Constant(ino)*, although *Constant(i)* or even *Constant(io)* are strictly possible.

2422.4

2422.5. Bedford. Gold openwork ring ($\frac{2}{1}$), diameter c. 20 mm, weight 5.93 gm, with a hoop, 8 mm wide and 1 mm thick, consisting of twelve facets; the edges of these are decorated with small peltas and each facet contains a letter, except one which has a leaf-stop. Found in 1980 by metal detector on a footpath leading from Honeyhill Farm, Queen's Park, to Biddenham. British Museum. Drawn by S.S.F. from a photograph.

Britannia xiii (1982), 411 No. 14 with pl. XL A. Johns, *Antiq. J.* lxi (1981), 343–5 with pl. LVIII a–c.

moulded: EVSEBIOVITA ✿
    Eusebio vita
    'Long life to Eusebius'

For other rings in *opus interrasile* see *RIB* 2422.1 and 12. Johns, op. cit., shows that this type of ring is not confined to the late Roman period but can occur as early as the second century. On the present example, however, the name *Eusebius* does suggest a fourth-century date.

2422.5

2422.6. Whittlesey, Cambridgeshire. Gold ring, weight 22.55 gm, found in or shortly before 1850 during ploughing on the Roman road near Whittlesey. Now lost. Reprinted from *Gent. Mag.*

EE iii p. 146. *IG* xiv 2573, 5. *Gent. Mag.* 1850 ii, 296.

engraved: ΕΥΤΟΛΜ
    Εὐτολμ(ίου)
    '(Property) of Eutolmius'

2422.7. Birchington, Kent. Gold ring with eleven facets, no dimensions recorded, found in, or perhaps before, 1860 (1850, F.H.) during ploughing. In 1889 it was in the possession of J.P. Powell, of Birchington. In 1892 Haverfield sought it in vain. Now lost. Reprinted from *Lit. Gazette*.

EE ix 1330. *Dover Chronicle* quoted by *Lit. Gazette*, 1 Sept. 1860, 166. Mowat, *Mém. Soc. Ant. France*[5] x (1889), 336. Haverfield, *Arch. J.* l (1893), 282; *VCH* Norfolk i (1901), 311. Noll, *BJ* clxxiv (1974), 243.

engraved: FIDES CONSTANI
    Probably *Constant(ino) fides*
    'Loyalty to Constantine'

Compare *RIB* 2422.4. Both rings had eleven facets and what could be read as CONSTANI, so it is probable that they bore identical inscriptions. See note to *RIB* 2422.4.

2422.8. Colchester (*Camulodunum*), Essex. Small gold ring ($\frac{1}{1}$) with oval bezel, 11 by 9 mm, bearing two opposed bearded busts within a border of dots. Found before 1860. British Museum. Drawn by R.P.W.

EE iii p. 146, b. Braybrooke, *Arch. J.* xvii (1860), 182; *T. Essex AS* ii (1863), 64. F.H. Marshall, *Cat. Finger-rings . . . in the British Museum* (1907), 17 No. 82. Henig, *Corpus* No. 785.

engraved retrograde on the bezel above the busts (drawn as *impression*): IMP

Imp(eratores)

'The emperor(s)'

2422.8

The busts may be those of Marcus Aurelius and Lucius Verus (Braybrooke, Henig).

2422.9. Backworth, Northumberland. Gold ring ($\frac{1}{1}$), diameter 25 mm, with oval bezel, found in 1812 with *RIB* 2414.36 (also dedicated to the *Matres*) in the Backworth Treasure. British Museum. Drawn by R.P.W.

CIL vii 1299. *EE* ix p. 668, *PSAN*² i (1853), 363 with fig. Hawkins, *Arch. J.* viii (1851), 37, 42 with fig. Hodgson, *Northd.* iii, facing p. 440. Ihm, *BJ* xciv (1893), 165. Haverfield, *NCH* ix (1909), 26–32. F.H. Marshall, *Cat. of Fingerrings . . . in the British Museum* (1907), 106 No. 636. Charlesworth, *Arch. Ael.*⁴ xxxix (1961), 24 No. A1 with pl. I.1.

engraved on the bezel: MATR|VM·C ❦ | C ❦ AE

Matrum C(. . .) C(. . .) Ae(. . .)

'(Property) of the Mother-Goddesses . . .'

MATR|VIA ❦ C ❦ | C ❦ AE, perhaps *Matr(ibus) via(libus)*, Huebner, *CIL*.

C·C·AE, perhaps *C(oloniae) C(laudiae) Ae(qui)*. No cult of the *Matres* is known at Aequum in Dalmatia, the origin of two second-century governors of Britain (Sex. Iulius Severus and Cn. Iulius Verus, cf. *RIB* 486, a legionary), but compare *ILS* 4794, *Matres Pannoniorum et Delmatarum*.

2422.9

2422.10. Stonham Aspal, Suffolk. Gold ring ($\frac{1}{1}$ and $\frac{2}{1}$), with carinated shoulders edged with chip-carved leaves and an uninscribed cabochon sapphire on the bezel; internal diameters 20 and 21.1 mm. Found in 1811. Ashmolean Museum, Oxford. Drawn by Keith Bennett, 1990.

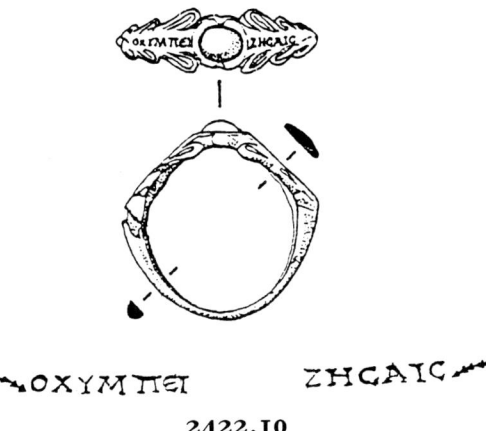

2422.10

CIL vii, p. 234. *IG* xiv 2573, 11. *Britannia* xix (1988), 507 item (f). Green, *Gent. Mag.* (1811) ii, 516 with pl. II.6. Mawer, *Britannia* xx (1989), 237–41 with fig. and pl. XVII B, C.

engraved on the shoulders, each side of the sapphire:
  palm branch ΟΛΥΜΠΕΙ | ΖΗCΑΙC palm branch
  Ὀλύμπει ζήσαις
  'Olympis, long life to you'

For this vocative form of Olympis (properly Ὄλυμπι) see Mawer, op. cit., 239 note 59.

2422.11. Essex, exact provenance unknown. Gold ring, found in 1873. Said to be in the British Museum (Huebner, *CIL*), but was sought in vain there by R.P.W. in 1961. Not illustrated.

CIL vii 1304 quoting Way.

engraved: OVIN | VSL

Ovin[i]us L(iberalis) or possibly *Quin[ti]us L(. . .)*, Huebner, doubting if a votive formula can be concealed in the letters VSL. O·V·N, Way.

2422.12. Corbridge (? *Coria*), Northumberland. Gold openwork ring ($\frac{2}{1}$), diameter 27 mm, weight 11.86 gm, consisting of sixteen facets; the edges of each are decorated with openwork peltas and each facet contains one letter or a leaf-stop. Found in 1935 during clearing of the top-soil inside the north-east corner of Site XI. British Museum. Drawn by S.S.F. after Ward.

Cowen, *Arch. Ael.*[4] xiii (1936), 310–19 with fig. by J.E. Ward and pl. XXV; xxvi (1948), 310. Charlesworth, *Arch. Ael.*[4] xxxix (1961), 24 No. A.6 with pl. 1.6. Wall, *Arch. Ael.*[4] xliii (1965), 217. Tait, *Jewelry through 7000 years* (1976), 251 No. 435. J.P.C. Kent and K.S. Painter, *Wealth of the Roman World* (1977), No. 128. Johns, *Antiq. J.* lxi (1981), 343–5 with pl. LVIII d, e.

moulded: ΠΟΛΕΜΙΟΥΦΙΛΤΡΟΝ leaf-stop
Πολεμίου φίλτρον
'Love-charm of Polemius'

For other rings in *opus interrasile* see *RIB* 2422.1 and 5 (with note).

2422.12

2422.13. London (*Londinium*). Gold ring ($\frac{1}{1}$), with a bezel carrying an intaglio gem representing a long-billed bird (perhaps an eagle) devouring a hare. Found in 1914 in a rubbish-pit during excavations at the General Post Office site. Museum of London. Drawn by R.P.W.

Haverfield, *Roman Britain in 1914*, 35 No. 12. RCHM, *Roman London* (1928), 175 No. 33. Henig, *Corpus* No. 700 (without mention of the inscription).

engraved on the narrowest part of the hoop: Q·D·D·
Q(uintus) D(...) D(...)

The tail of the Q is discernible, F.H.

2422.13

2422.14. Silchester (*Calleva*), Hampshire. Gold ring of ten facets ($\frac{1}{1}$), weight 12.02 gm, with a rectangular bezel depicting a bust of Venus, captioned retrograde, and a probably secondary inscription around the hoop. Found in or shortly before 1786 during ploughing. The Vyne, Basingstoke. Inscription drawn by R.P.W.; the ring reproduced from *VCH*.

CIL vii 1305. *EE* vii 1171. Arden, *Arch.* viii (1787), 449. Kempe, *Gent. Mag.* ciii (1833), (1), 124; *Arch.* xxvii (1838), 417. C.W. Chute, *A History of the Vyne in Hampshire* (1888), 7 with three figs. Haverfield, *TBGAS* xiii (1888–9), 203; *VCH Hampshire* i (1900), 283 with fig. Toynbee, *JBAA*[3] xvi (1953), 19–20 with fig. Goodchild, *Antiquity* xxvii (1953), 100–102. G.C. Boon, *Roman Silchester* (1957), 130–31; *Silchester: The Roman Town of Calleva* (1974), 133 with fig. 18.4. Henig, *Corpus* No. 789. C. Thomas, *Christianity in Roman Britain to A.D. 500* (1981), 131.

2422.14

engraved:
(a) retrograde on the bezel each side of the bust: VENVS
'Venus'
(b) around the hoop:
SE | NI | CI | A | NE | VI | VA | SII | NDE
Seniciane vivas i⟨i⟩n de(o)
'Senicianus, may you live in God'

NE VIVAS IN INDECENTIA Kempe, *Gent. Mag.*, corrected in *Arch.* VFNVS with the lowest bar of E worn away, F.H. *TBGAS*.

The original ring with its pagan inscription has, apparently later, been inscribed with a Christian formula. This is blundered, since the repetition of the I of *in* has left no room for the O of *deo*. The ring has often been identified with the ring mentioned in *RIB* 306, a *defixio* from Lydney, which records its loss by a certain Silvanus, who accuses Senicianus of the theft. F.H. (*TBGAS*, *VCH*) was cautious of the identity of the two Seniciani, for 'the name Senicianus is not uncommon', and he (wrongly) dated the Lydney *defixio* 'to the first or, at the latest, the second century: the Silchester ring is of the fourth century.' Toynbee thought that 'a connexion is by no means improbable', and Goodchild argued 'a strong probability'. Thomas calls it 'a strange coincidence; perhaps a genuine link'.

Senicianus and its variants are popular in Celtic-speaking provinces (there are three instances among the Bath tablets); the identity cannot be formally disproved, but seems unlikely, R.S.O.T.

2422.15. Brancaster (*Branodunum*), Norfolk. Gold ring ($\frac{1}{1}$ and $\frac{2}{1}$), diameter 23 mm, with a bezel (9 by 8 mm) bearing two confronting busts, one male, the other female, crudely engraved between the lines of the inscription, which is cut to give a retrograde impression. Found during ploughing in 1829. Norwich Castle Museum. Reproduced from Hinchliffe and Green.

CIL vii 1307. Woodward, *Arch.* xxiii (1831), 361. Fitch *JBAA* xxxvi (1880), 115. Haverfield, *VCH* Norfolk i (1901), 304 fig. 20. Toynbee, *JBAA*³ xvi (1953), 19 with pl. IV 6. R.R. Clarke, *East Anglia* (1960), 129, 230 with pl. XXXIX. Henig, *Corpus*, No. 790. J. Hinchliffe and C.S. Green, *Excavations at Brancaster 1974 and 1977* (East Anglian Archaeology No. 23, 1985), 195–7 No. 2 with fig. 85.2 and pl. XXII. C. Thomas, *Christianity in Roman Britain to A.D. 500* (1981), 131.

engraved on the bezel: VIVAS | INDEO
 Vivas in deo
 'May you live in God'

This is a betrothal ring. Toynbee suggests that the lettering may be a secondary addition.

2422.15

2422.16. Brentwood, Essex. Gold ring ($\frac{1}{1}$), diameter 19 mm, weight 8.29 gm, with a circular bezel. Found in 1948 in the garden of Wealdcote, Hillside Walk, at a distance of 61 m from the London to Colchester Roman road. British Museum. Reproduced from *JRS*. See also PL. III A.

JRS xxxix (1949), 115 No. 10 with fig. 25. *Britannia* xvii (1986), 453. *Illus. Lond. News*, 2 Oct., 1948. Toynbee, *JBAA*³ xvi (1953), 19 with pl. IV.5. Henig, *Corpus*, No. 793. C. Thomas, *Christianity in Roman Britain to A.D. 500* (1981), 124 fig. 13.5.

engraved retrograde on the bezel within a border of dots (illustrated as an *impression*):   X̂P
 'Chi-Rho'

2422.16

2422.17. Suffolk. Gold ring ($\frac{1}{1}$), internal diameter 21 mm, weight 27.55 gm (probably intended to weigh one *uncia* (27.288 gm), see Introduction to *RIB* 2412). It has a plain hoop with some longitudinal faceting and a raised bezel with bordering line. The inscription is placed beneath two trees, one supporting a bird which pecks fruit on the other. Found in or before 1980 and said to be from an unspecified site in Suffolk. British Museum. Drawn by P. Compton.

Johns and Rigby, *Antiq. J.* lxiv (1984), 393–4 with fig. 9 and pl. LI *a–b*.

deeply incised, retrograde, on the bezel: X̂P
 'Chi-Rho'

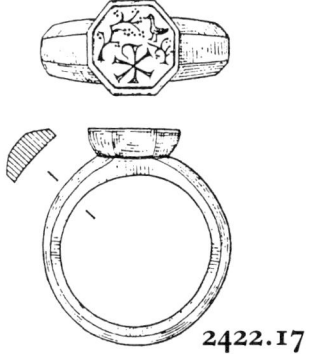

2422.17

(b) *RIB* 2422.18–46, silver rings

Note: for a silver ring carrying an inscribed gem, see *RIB* 2423.13.

2422.18. Portchester, Hampshire. Silver ring with overlapping terminals ($\frac{2}{3}$) and the bezel flanked by incised lines and ring-and-dot ornament. Found in 1961–72 during excavations within the Saxon Shore fort. Portsmouth Museum. Reproduced from Cunliffe.

B.W. Cunliffe, *Excavations at Portchester Castle* i (1975), 210 No. 49 with fig. 112.49

engraved: ΛM
 Perhaps *Am(a me)*
 'Love me'
Compare *RIB* 2422.2 and 48.
'Perhaps *A(nima) M(ea)*, 'My soul', R.P.W.

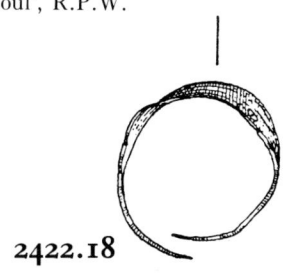

2422.18

2422.19. Castell Collen, Powys [Radnorshire]. Silver ring (¼), diameter 20 mm, height 18 mm, found in 1913 on a footing north of Room 17 in the *praetorium* of the fort. Llandrindod Wells Museum. Reproduced from Boon.

Haverfield, *Roman Britain in 1913*, 31 No. 6. White, *AC*⁶ xiv (1914), 34, 42 with pl. Boon, *T. Radnorshire Soc.* xliii (1973), 18 No. 3 with pl. I and fig. 1.3.

engraved on the bezel: AMOR | DVLCIS
amor dulcis
'Sweet love'

2422.19

2422.20. Corbridge (? *Coria*), Northumberland. Silver ring (¼), internal diameter 18 mm, width of bezel 12 mm. Found in 1947–80 during excavations at Corbridge, but the context has been lost. Corbridge Museum. Reproduced from Bishop and Dore.

M.C. Bishop and J.N. Dore, *Corbridge: Excavations of the Roman fort and town 1947–80* (1988), 159 No. 1 with fig.

engraved: DEO | MER̦
deo Mer(curio)
'To the god Mercury'

Compare *RIB* 2422.29–30.

Perhaps DEO MEI, 'to my god', L. Allason-Jones in Bishop and Dore. This interpretation is doubtful Latin and seems improbable, S.S.F.

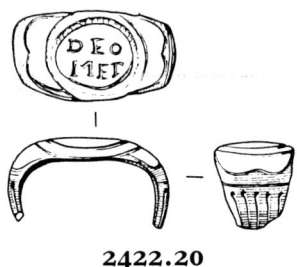

2422.20

2422.21. York (*Eboracum*). Octagonal silver ring (¼), maximum diameter 25 mm, height 13 mm, inscribed on one of the facets. Found in 1875 in the City moat in St Maurice's Road. Yorkshire Museum, York. Drawn by R.P.W.

EE iii 181 a. *ILS* 4689. Watkin, *Arch. J.* xxxv (1878), 68. RCHM, *York* i (1962), 133 No. 140 with pl. LXV.

engraved: DEO | SVCELO
deo Sucelo
'To the god Sucelus'

This is the only inscription from Britain of the god Sucellus (as the name is usually written), whose cult is well attested in Gaul.

2422.21

2422.22. Benwell (*Condercum*), Tyne and Wear [Northumberland]. Part of a silver ring (¼), diameter 25 mm, height of bezel 14.3 mm, found in 1938 during excavations at the Vallum crossing south of the fort. Museum of Antiquities, Newcastle upon Tyne. Drawn by S.S.F. after a sketch by R.P.W., 1947.

JRS xxxvii (1947), 181 No. 12.

engraved: DMT

DMI, R.P.W., *JRS*, treating the bar above I as a flaw. DMT, R.P.W.

Perhaps an abbreviated name *(D(ecimus) M(...) T(...))* but more likely a dedication to a deity (for instance Mars Toutatis or Matres Tra(ns)marinae).

2422.22

2422.23. Chesters (*Cilurnum*), Northumberland. Silver ring (¼), diameter 22 mm, with a hoop D-shaped in section and a flattened bezel. Found in 1885. Chesters Museum. Drawn by R.P.W.

EE vii 1173. Bruce, *Arch. Ael.*² xi (1886), 235 with fig. Watkin, *Arch. J.* xliii (1886), 289. Anon., *PSAN*² ii (1886), 164 with fig. Roach Smith, *Num. Chron.*³ v (1885) 253, in error assigning the ring to South Shields.

engraved on the bezel: DN | EP
d(eo) Nep(tuno)
'To the god Neptune'

2422.23

2422.24. London (*Londinium*). Broken silver ring ($\frac{1}{1}$ and $\frac{2}{1}$), diameter 16 mm, with an extended rectangular bezel, 12 by 20 mm, having filigree decoration and the figures of two standing Victories holding between them a wreath above an eagle. Found in 1985 in spoil from excavations at Billingsgate Lorry Park. Museum of London. Drawn by Nicholas Griffiths.

Britannia xvii (1986), 445 No. 63.

engraved below the figures: G·FL·G | FILIS◂
Presumably *G(aius) Fl(avius) G(ai) fili(u)s*
'Gaius Flavius, son of Gaius'

2422.26. Cirencester (*Corinium*), Gloucestershire. Silver ring ($\frac{1}{1}$), original diameter *c.* 19 mm, now distorted; the band is 1 mm wide thickening to 2 mm near the bezel, which measures 6.5 by 4 mm. Found in 1971–3 during excavation of Building XII.1 at Beeches Road. Corinium Museum, Cirencester. Reproduced from McWhirr.

Britannia xiv (1981), 343 No. 18; xv (1984), 349 corrigendum. A. McWhirr, *Houses in Roman Cirencester* (1986), 106 No. 9 with fig. 77.

incised on the bezel: IVṾ

IVLI, *Britannia* xiv.

Perhaps *Iuv(entii)* or similar; but MI or IVII are possibilities.

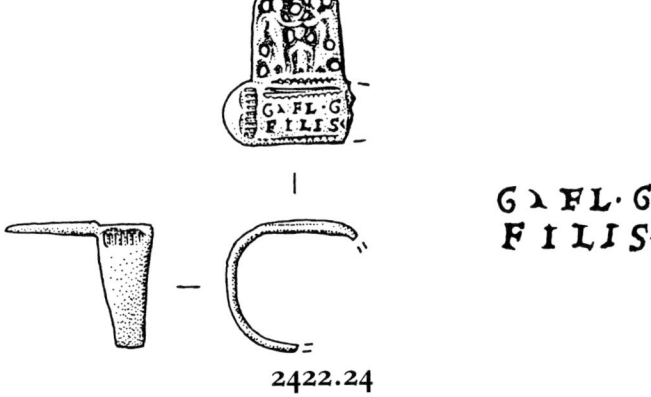

2422.24

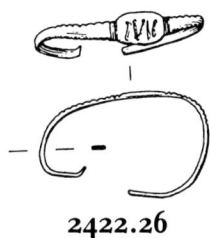

2422.26

2422.25. Silchester (*Calleva*), Hampshire. Silver ring with a circular bezel ($\frac{1}{1}$) engraved with a male bust, which is damaged from the base to the centre of the head. Reading Museum. Drawn by R.P.W., 1951.

EE ix 1331. Haverfield, *VCH* Hampshire i (1900), 254. Henig, *Corpus* No. 786.

engraved retrograde around the bust (shown in *impression*):
IVLBELLATORVIVAS
Iul(ius) Bellator vivas
'Julius Bellator, long life to you'

2422.27. Colchester (*Camulodunum*), Essex. Silver ring ($\frac{1}{1}$) with an octagonal bezel flanked by a leaf on either side. Found before 1768. Now lost. Drawing after Morant.

CIL vii 1302. P. Morant, *The History and Antiquities of the County of Essex*, i (1768), p. 195 No. 10 with pl. II facing p. 192.

engraved retrograde, on the bezel: LV|CIA|NI
'(Property) of Lucianus'

2422.25

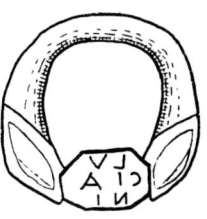

2422.27

2422.28. Carrawburgh (*Brocolitia*), Northumberland. Angular silver ring (¹⁄₁), diameter 22 mm, found before 1871 'at *Procalitia*' (Roach Smith). Blair (MS Sketchbook vi (1889), 66) labels the ring 'Chesters' but may merely be referring to the location of the object in the Clayton Collection there. Haverfield (1889) gives *Cilurnum* (Chesters) as the findspot, but in 1892 changed this to Carrawburgh. Stolen from Chesters Museum in 1967. Drawn by R.G.C., 1927.

EE iii p. 146. Roach Smith, *The Builder*, 2 Dec. 1871, 941. Watkin, *Arch. J.* xxxi (1874), 296. Blair, MS Sketchbook vi (1889), 66. Haverfield, *Arch. Ael.*² xiii (1889), 360; *Arch. J.* xlix (1892), 332 No. 30. Budge, *Cat.* (1907) 393 No. 66. Collingwood, *Guide to Chesters Museum* (1926), 42. Charlesworth, *Arch. Ael.*⁴ xxxix (1961), 24 No. A4 with pl I.4. L. Allason-Jones and B. McKay, *Coventina's Well* (1985), 20 No. 32 with pl. XII.32.

engraved on the bezel: MAT|RES
Matres
'The Mothers'

MAT(RIBVS) RES(TITVTVS), Roach Smith.

2422.28

2422.29. Chesterholm (*Vindolanda*), Northumberland. Silver ring (¹⁄₁) of flattened hexagonal profile, diameter 22 mm, height 18 mm, with a bezel 16 by 10 mm. Found in 1971. Vindolanda Museum. Drawn by S.S.F. from a rubbing by R.P.W., 1972.

Britannia iii (1972), 360 No. 47. R. Birley, *Vindolanda: A Roman Frontier-post on Hadrian's Wall* (1977), pl. VIII.

engraved within a rectangular border: MER
Mer(curio)
'To Mercury'

Compare *RIB* 2422.20 and 30.

2422.29

2422.30. Billingford, Norfolk. Silver ring (²⁄₁), internal diameter 17 by 15 mm, with a bezel 15 by 11 mm. Found in or before 1985 by metal detector. In private possession. Drawn by S.S.F. from a photograph. See PL. III B.

Britannia xvii (1986), 447 No. 66.

engraved on the bezel: MER
Mer(curio)
'To Mercury'

Compare *RIB* 2422.20 and 29.

2422.30

2422.31. Eastwood near Andover, Hampshire. Silver ring found in 1922 with a coin-hoard of A.D. 193–244. Whereabouts unknown. Not illustrated.

JRS xi (1921), 239 No. 17.

'inscribed with three letters, but only OQ is legible'

2422.32. Caistor St Edmund (*Venta Icenorum*), Norfolk. Part of a silver ring with an oblong bezel (²⁄₁), 10 by 8 mm, bearing the bust of a negro (?), cut in intaglio with letters of the inscription cut to give a positive reading on each side. Found in 1983 or 1984 by metal detector. In private possession. Drawn by S.S.F. from a photograph. See PL. III D.

Britannia xv (1984), 344 No. 40.

engraved: ⋀SR | DEDỊ

2422.32

2422.33. Kent, unprovenanced. D-shaped silver ring (¹⁄₁), diameter 14 mm. In private possession. Drawn by R.S.O.T.

Britannia xvii (1986), 444 No. 57 with fig.

engraved: S | DΛE | ENV

2422.33

2422.34. Corbridge (? *Coria*), Northumberland. Silver ring ($\frac{1}{1}$), diameter 22 mm, with an oval bezel. Found during excavations in 1907. Corbridge Museum. Drawn by R.P.W., 1946.

EE ix 1332. Forster, *Arch. Ael.*³ iv (1908), 268. Charlesworth, *Arch. Ael.*⁴ xxxix (1961), 24 No. A3 with pl. I.3.

engraved on the bezel: SVC|CES
  Presumably the common cognomen *Successus*

F.H., *EE* considered that it might be recent; but R.P.W. saw no reason to doubt its Roman origin.

2422.34

2422.35. Brandon area, Suffolk. Silver ring ($\frac{1}{1}$), diameter 15 mm, maximum height 14 mm, found in about 1974 'within thirty miles of Brandon on the surface'. In private possession. Drawn by R.S.O.T. from a photograph.

Britannia ix (1978), 481 No. 66, with pl. XXXII A.

engraved on the bezel: CYN|HΛΘH
  συν|ήλθη for σύνελθε
  'Marry (me)'

2422.35

See note *ad loc.* for the form and its translation.

2422.36. Lincoln (*Lindum*). Silver ring ($\frac{1}{1}$), internal diameter 17.5 mm, expanding at the front to form two triangular shoulders, both notched at top and bottom, on either side of a circular bezel, 8 mm in diameter. Found in 1984 during excavations at Michaelgate. Lincoln Museum. Reproduced from Henig and Ogden.

Britannia xviii (1987), 370 No. 18. Henig and Ogden, *Antiq. J.* lxvii (1987), 366–7 with fig.

engraved on the bezel: T[.]T
  Probably T[O]T

Perhaps *To(u)t(atis)*, Henig and Ogden. *Tot(atis Martis)*, Holder s.v. *Totatis*.

Compare *RIB* 2422.37–40.

2422.36

2422.37. York (*Eboracum*). Silver ring ($\frac{1}{1}$), diameter 23 mm, height 15 mm, found in 1875 during excavations at the Railway Station. Yorkshire Museum, York. Drawn by R.G.C.

EE iii 181 b. Watkin, *Arch. J.* xxxv (1878), 68. RCHM, *York* i (1962) 133 No. 141 with pl. LXV.141. Henig and Ogden, *Antiq. J.* lxvii (1987), 366–7.

engraved on the bezel: TOT

Perhaps *To(u)t(atis)*, Henig and Ogden. *Tot(atis Martis)*, Holder s.v. *Totatis*.

Compare *RIB* 2422.36, 38–40.

2422.37

2422.38. Unknown provenance, probably in Britain. Silver ring ($\frac{2}{1}$ and $\frac{1}{1}$), diameter 27 mm, weight 9.78 gm, with an oval bezel containing a sard intaglio depicting a hound catching a hare; the inscription is below this on the shoulder. The ring was originally in the Braybrooke Collection (and so probably found in East Anglia), and was received in 1887 by the British Museum in the Franks bequest. Drawn by S.S.F. from a photograph and the ring reproduced from Marshall. See PL. III E.

F.H. Marshall, *Cat. of Finger-rings . . . in the British Museum* (1907), 185 No. 1169 with fig. Henig and Ogden, *Antiq. J.* lxvii (1987), 367.

engraved on one shoulder: TOT

Perhaps *To(u)t(atis)*, Henig and Ogden. *Tot(atis Martis)*, Holder s.v. *Totatis*.

Compare *RIB* 2422.36–37, 39–40.

2422.38

2422.39. Tetford, Lincolnshire. Silver (?) ring, found two or three years before 1977. Lincoln Museum. Drawn by S.S.F. from a photograph.

Henig and Ogden, *Antiq. J.* lxvii (1987), 382 note 53.

engraved (?) on the bezel (?): TOT

Perhaps *To(u)t(atis)*, Henig and Ogden. *Tot(atis Martis)*, Holder s.v. *Totatis*.

Compare *RIB* 2422.36–38, 40.

2422.39

2422.40. Willoughby-on-the-Wolds (*Vernemetum*), Nottinghamshire. Silver (?) ring found shortly before 1987. In private possession. Not illustrated.

Britannia xx (1989), 340 No. 50. Henig and Ogden, *Antiq. J.* lxvii (1987), 382 note 53.

engraved (?) on the bezel: TOT

Perhaps *To(u)t(atis)*, Henig and Ogden. *Tot(atis Martis)*, Holder s.v. *Totatis*.

Compare *RIB* 2422.36–39.

For a gold ring in the Victoria and Albert Museum, unprovenanced, inscribed TOT on the shoulder, see S. Bury, *An Introduction to Rings* (1984), pl. 19.

2422.41. Brafield, Northamptonshire. Part of a silver ring ($\frac{2}{1}$), with a circular bezel, diameter 14.5 mm, found in or before 1977 during field-walking. In private possession. Drawn by S.S.F. from a photograph.

Britannia ix (1978), 480 No. 62 with pl. XXXII B.

engraved on the circular bezel above and below a line of triangular stops: VTER | FELIX
 uter(e) felix
 'Good luck to the user'

2422.42. Silchester (*Calleva*), Hampshire. Silver disc ($\frac{1}{1}$), diameter 11 mm, part of a seal or ring, with incised retrograde inscription above an engraved female head with two stars on each side. Found in 1908 during excavations. Reading Museum. Drawn by R.P.W., 1951. See also PL. III C.

EE ix 1335. Hope, *Arch.* lxi (1909), 485 (repr. p. 13). Henig, *Corpus* No. 787 with pls.

incised retrograde, above the head (shown in *impression*): VIVAS
 'Long life to you'

2422.42

2422.43. Corbridge (? *Coria*), Northumberland. About one third of the hoop of a gold-plated ring on a silver core ($\frac{2}{1}$), length 21.6 mm, width 20.6 mm, thickness 3 mm, weight 0.9 gm. Found in 1939 at the south edge of the main east-to-west street just north of Site IV. Corbridge Museum. Drawn by R.P.W., 1945.

JRS xxxvi (1946), 148 No. 4. Wright, *PSAN* x (1945), 269. Charlesworth, *Arch. Ael.*[4] xxxix (1961), 24 No. A5 with pl.I.5.

inscribed in niello: ΦΥΛΑ
 φύλα[ξαι]
 'Take care'

ΦΥΛΑ[ΞΑΙ], R.P.W. ΦΥΛΑ[ΞΟΜΑΙ], F.E. Adcock (quoted by R.P.W.): this would fill the space better but seems unmatched by other examples. See F.H. Marshall, *Cat. of Finger rings . . . in the British Museum* No. 585 for a silver ring from Rome, φΥΛΑΞΑΙ; compare also *IG* iv 7358 for a gem from Florence.

2422.41

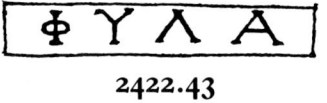

2422.43

2422.44. Fifehead Neville, Dorset. Silver ring (⅟₁), diameter 21 mm, with an oblong bezel 6 by 7 mm, found in 1881 during excavations at the Roman villa, together with *RIB* 2422.45 and 'a silver necklace or girdle-fastener, and nine bronze bracelets, with fragments of others', lying 'in a small hollow cut in the concrete floor of one of the rooms' (Middleton). Now lost. Reproduced from Middleton.

EE vii 1174 a. Middleton, *PSA*² ix (1881–3), 68 with fig. 1. Henig, *P. Dorset NHAS* xciii (1972), 191; *Corpus* No. 794.

engraved on the bezel: X͡P
  'Chi-Rho'

The X͡P is of the 'Constantinian' form current throughout the fourth century. See C. Thomas, *Christianity in Roman Britain to A.D. 500* (1981), 88.

2422.45. Ibid. Silver ring (⅟₁), diameter 20 mm, with oblong bezel 8 by 7 mm, found in 1881 with *RIB* 2422.44 (*q.v.* for details), during excavations at the Roman villa. Now lost. Reproduced from Middleton.

EE vii 1174 b. Middleton, *PSA*² ix (1881–3), 68 with fig. 2. Henig, *P. Dorset NHAS* xciii (1972), 191; *Corpus* No. 795.

engraved on the bezel: branch dove branch | X͡P
  'Chi-Rho'

This simplified form of X͡P seems to have become current during the second half of the fourth century. See C. Thomas, *Christianity in Roman Britain to A.D. 500* (1981), 88.

2422.46. Thruxton, Hampshire. Silver ring 'inscribed with the CHI-RHO', found in 1823 with another silver ring (uninscribed) at the site of the Roman villa. Now lost. Reprinted from Engleheart.

Engleheart, *P. Hants. FC* ix (1922) 215 (with no record of whereabouts).

inscribed: X͡P

The inscribed mosaic found in the villa will be found as *RIB* 2448.9 in Fascicule 4.

(c) *RIB* 2422.47–74, bronze rings

Note: for a bronze ring carrying an inscribed intaglio, see *RIB* 2423.28.

2422.47. Wroxeter (*Viroconium*), Shropshire. Bronze ring with oval hoop (²⁄₁), 19 by 15 mm, and an oval bezel, 15 by 7 mm, bisected by a groove. Found in 1973. Rowley's House Museum, Shrewsbury. Drawn by G. Webster.

Britannia v (1974) 468 No. 51.

engraved: ΛMΛ | MΛO
  For *ama amo*
  'Love (me), I love (you)'

2422.48. St Albans (*Verulamium*), Hertfordshire. Bronze ring (⅟₁) found in 1930–34 in a late third-century context in Building III.2. Verulamium Museum. Reproduced from Wheeler.

R.E.M. and T.V. Wheeler, *Verulamium: A Belgic and two Roman Cities* (1936), 216 No. 75 with fig. 47.75.

engraved on the bezel: ΛMΛ (?)
  'Love (me)'

If this interpretation is correct, an extra diagonal stroke was added to make the inscription identical either way up. For the legend compare *RIB* 2422.2 and 18.

2422.49. London (*Londinium*). Brass ring ($\frac{2}{1}$), diameter 17.5 mm, with a bearded male head on the bezel and the inscription moulded around the hoop. Found in 1954–55 during excavations at the Bucklersbury House site in the bed of the Walbrook. Museum of London. Drawn by Nicholas Griffiths, 1990, at $\frac{2}{1}$; and $\frac{1}{1}$ drawing by R.P.W. to show the bezel.

JRS l (1960), 240 No. 20. Guildhall Museum, *Small Finds from the Walbrook* (1954–55), 6 No. 9. T. Murdoch (ed.), *Treasures and Trinkets* (1991), 30 with fig. 4.3.

moulded around the hoop: AMICA
  'Friend' (female)

Compare *RIB* 2422.62, probably from the same workshop.

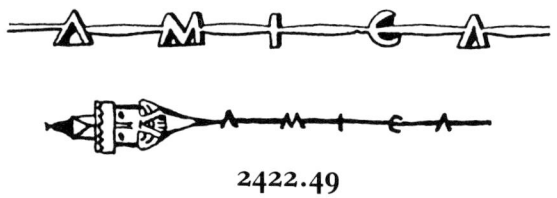

2422.49

2422.50. Colchester (*Camulodunum*), Essex. Bronze ring ($\frac{1}{1}$), diameter originally *c*. 18 mm, height at the bezel 5 mm, reducing to 2.5 mm in the hoop; the oblong bezel measures 10 by 5 mm. Found in 1977 during excavations at the Butt Road Roman cemetery. Colchester Museum. Reproduced from Crummy.

Britannia xii (1981), 384 No. 35. N. Crummy, *Small Finds* (1983), 49 No. 1787 with fig. 51.

punched within three scored guide-lines:
  SASV|AS V or A SV|ASVS

The letters were produced apparently with tiny punches; two would have been sufficient.

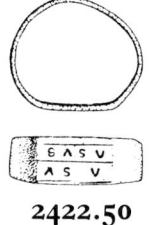

2422.50

2422.51. Croxton Kerrial, Leicestershire. Bronze ring ($\frac{1}{1}$), diameter 27 mm, formed of three cordons, together 20 mm wide at the front and tapering to 5 mm at the back. Found in 1983 by metal detector. In private possession. Drawn by S.S.F. from a photograph and a sketch by T. Ambrose.

Britannia xv (1984), 344 No. 34.

engraved within a rectangular panel on the central cordon: ƆMV or possibly ƆMAV

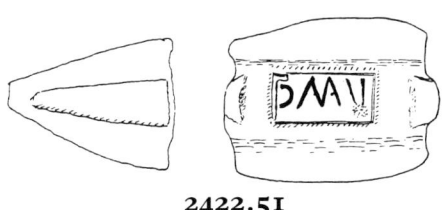

2422.51

2422.52. Wendens Ambo, Essex. Bronze ring ($\frac{1}{1}$), diameter originally *c*. 25 mm, cast in one piece with an enlarged rectangular bezel, 32 by 19 mm, from the sides of which project two (broken) ansa-like extensions. On the flat face of the bezel is a rectangular panel bordered by scored lines and surrounded by notches; it is divided by further scored lines into three zones which carry the inscription. Found in 1978. Saffron Walden Museum. Drawn by S.S.F. from a photograph.

Britannia xii (1981), 384 No. 36.

engraved: COL | DEI | SIL
  col(legium) dei Sil(vani)
  'The guild of the god Silvanus'

Perhaps for attachment to a votive offering.

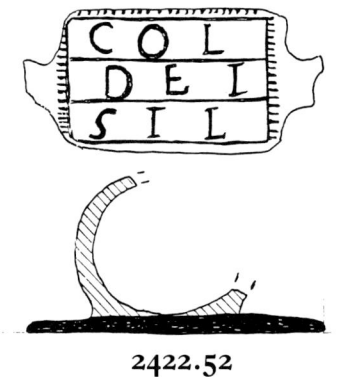

2422.52

2422.53. Caistor St Edmund (*Venta Icenorum*), Norfolk. Octagonal bronze ring ($\frac{1}{1}$), found in 1930 during excavations in the corridor of Building I in Insula VII. Norwich Castle Museum. Drawn by S.S.F. from an original by R.P.W.

Britannia ii (1971), 300 No. 64.

incised: IXSAONC three verticals

IXSAOSC, R.P.W.

Compare *RIB* 2422.54–6 and a ring of identical type found in 1990 near Devizes (*Britannia* xxii (1991), forthcoming), which reads: three verticals OΛSCNXI. The identical form of the five rings and the almost identical lettering mark them as the products of a single workshop. Each text is a different permutation of the same seven letters, with an eighth 'letter' as a spacer; in four of the texts it is three vertical lines (cf. *RIB* 2421.38–40 and *Britannia* xvii (1986), 350 fig. 8), in *RIB* 2422.56 a reversed C(?). The present text is the only one with a barred Λ; in view of the coincidence of the other letters, the V read by R.P.W. in the other three texts published by him is surely Λ. The retrograde S on its side as read by R.P.W. must be N, since each text already has an S of conventional form. The interpretation of these texts is unclear. Only one combination of letters is repeated even once, XΛN in 54 and 56, so the apparently random letter-sequence must be regarded as deliberate, not as confusions of an intended text. Since one ring (*RIB* 2422.54) was found at a temple-site, it is possible they had a religious or magical significance (as indeed is suggested by the permutation of the same *seven* letters), but this does not necessarily mean that the letters formed the name of a deity. R.S.O.T.

2422.53

2422.54. Yatton, Somerset. Octagonal bronze ring ($\frac{1}{1}$), found in 1969 in the upper filling of the temenos ditch of a Romano-Celtic temple at Henley Wood. In store with English Heritage. Drawn by R.P.W., 1970.

Britannia i (1970), 311–12. Wright, *Antiq. J.* l (1970), 257–8 with fig. 7. Wickenden, *Britannia* xvii (1986), 350 with pl. XXVII B.

inscribed: three verticals XΛNOCS I

ISCOSVX (stop), R.P.W. ISCONVX three parallel bars, Wickenden.

Compare *RIB* 2422.53, with note, and 55–56.

2422.54

2422.55. Owslebury, Hampshire. Octagonal bronze ring ($\frac{1}{1}$), found in 1968 in a late Roman context during excavations at Bottom Pond Farm. In private possession. Drawn by R.P.W., 1970.

JRS lix (1969), 240 No. 28. *Britannia* i (1970), 312. Wright, *Antiq. J.* l (1970), 257 No. (b) with fig. 7.

incised: three verticals INSXΛOC

ƆOVXSSI (stop), *Couxssi*, R.P.W.

Compare *RIB* 2422.53, with note, 54 and 56.

2422.55

2422.56. Ibid. Octagonal bronze ring ($\frac{1}{1}$), found in 1962 unstratified above a fourth-century corndrier during excavations at Bottom Pond Farm. In private possession. Drawn by R.P.W., 1970.

JRS liii (1963), 163 No. 24; lix (1969), 240 note 38. Wright, *Antiq. J.* l (1970), 257 No. (a) with fig. 7.

incised: SOICXΛNƆ

SVXƆIOSC, R.P.W.

Compare *RIB* 2422.53, with note, and 54–55. In this text the reversed C(?) corresponds to the three verticals in the other three texts, and since there is also a C of conventional form this was probably not a letter, but instead a spacer like the three verticals.

2422.56

2422.57. Rugby, Warwickshire. Bronze 'hoop-shaped' ring with a Greek inscription on the inner face. Found *c.* 1848 in an orchard close to St Matthew's Place, Rugby. Sought in vain by F.H. Now lost. Reprinted from *EE*.

EE iv 714. Bloxham, *Assoc. Archit. Soc. Rep.* i (1850–1), 229. Watkin, *Arch. J.* xxxiv (1877), 140; xxxv (1878), 67, 301. Haverfield, *VCH* Warwickshire i (1904), 248.

engraved: ESYNEPAEYNAICXE

'The sense is not at all clear, and I do not suppose [that the] reading is correct', F.H., *VCH*.

Greek letters were intended and S is probably a transcription error for C (repeated in *Arch. J.* xxxv (1878), 301).

2422.58. Unknown provenance, presumably somewhere in Britain. Bronze ring, diameter 21 mm, height 17 mm, with an oval bezel, found before 1864, when it was in the possession of G. Fortescue Wilbraham. Now lost. Reprinted from *EE*.

EE iv 715. Smith, *Arch. J.* xxi (1864), 186. Watkin, *Arch. J.* xxxiv (1877), 140.

engraved:
(a) on the bezel: FIDES | clasped hands within a wreath | CONCORDIA
(b) on the shoulders of the hoop: RVFVS·D·D VIATOR

Rufus d(ono) d(edit) Viator(i)
'Loyalty (and) Concord. Rufus gave (this) as a gift to Viator'

(b) RVFVS VIATOR, Watkin.

2422.59. Chichester (*Noviomagus*), West Sussex. Plain bronze ring, diameter 20 mm, height 4 mm. Found in 1968–75 during excavations at the Wool Store site. Chichester Museum. Reproduced from Down.

A. Down, *Chichester Excavations* iii (1978), 302 No. 106 with fig. 10.38.

engraved on the outer face: IIXVI or IAXII

2422.59

2422.60. Wroxeter (*Viroconium*), Shropshire. Bronze key-ring ($\frac{1}{1}$), found in or before 1872. Rowley's House Museum, Shrewsbury. Drawn by R.P.W., 1953.

T. Wright, *Uriconium* (1872), 283–4 with fig. Haverfield, *VCH* Shropshire i (1908), 250.

inscribed on the hoop: L[1–2]OR

[...]RIAI[...], F.H. As text, R.P.W.

2422.60

2422.61. Wanborough, Wiltshire. Bronze ring ($\frac{1}{1}$), diameter 18 mm, with an oblong bezel 9.5 by 2 mm, 1.5 mm thick, found in 1970 during road-construction. Swindon Museum. Drawn by S.S.F. from a rubbing by R.P.W., 1970.

Britannia ii (1971), 302 No. 82.   2422.61

incised on the face and the top and bottom of the bezel:
VENI | TERMO | (*inverted*) MANE
veni, Termo (?), *mane*
'Come, Termo (?), (and) stay (with me)'

MANE (inverted) | TERMO | VENI. '(T)hermo(don), come (and) stay (with me)', R.P.W.

Termo (Gk. Τέρμων) is used once by Ennius as a synonym for *Terminus*, but is not attested as a personal name. Nor is *Termomanus*. Perhaps therefore an abbreviated personal name of Greek etymology in *Thermo-*, e.g. *Thermodon* (thus R.P.W., citing *ILS* 4223).

2422.62. London (*Londinium*). Bronze ring ($\frac{2}{1}$), diameter 18 mm, with a circular bezel 7 mm in diameter. Found in 1984 at Billingsgate Lorry Park during commercial excavations. Museum of London. Drawn by Nicholas Griffiths, 1990.

Britannia xvi (1985), 328 No. 19. T. Murdoch (ed.) *Treasures and Trinkets* (1991), 30 with fig. 4.3.

engraved: MISCE MI
for *misce me*
'Stir me'

MISCE is often found on motto beakers (*CIL* xiii 10018.119) and MISCE ME and MISCE MI are also found (ibid., 123, 124). The verb is also used in a sexual sense (J.N. Adams, *The Latin Sexual Vocabulary* (1982), 180–1).

Compare *RIB* 2422.49, probably from the same workshop.

2422.62

2422.63. Old Winteringham, Humberside [Lincolnshire]. Part of a bronze ring ($\frac{1}{1}$), diameter 24 mm, height 6 mm. On the outside of the hoop at intervals are roughened areas formed by a small punch; on the inside of the hoop are three widely-spaced letters with space for two or three more. Found in 1979 during field-walking. In private possession. Drawn by S.S.F. from a photograph.

Britannia xv (1984), 345 No. 50.

punched inside the hoop: [...] O S T [...]
Perhaps *[n]ost[er]*
'our'(?)

O S T

2422.63

2422.64. Uncertain provenance. Bronze finger-ring (1/1) with bezel, 23 by 20 mm, worn down by wear; found some years before 1936 when the collection of C. Faulkner of Deddington was presented by his granddaughter, Mrs. Fuller, to the Ashmolean Museum. The object was not labelled, but the Accession Book gives the findspot as Kingsholm, Gloucestershire. Ashmolean Museum, Oxford. Drawn by S.S.F. from a cast by R.P.W.

engraved in capitals: PHIL | VIIC̣

The final letter could be C, G or possibly O, R.P.W.

2422.65. Caistor St Edmund (*Venta Icenorum*), Norfolk. Part of a bronze ring (2/1), 10 mm wide at the bezel, which is surrounded by an oval border of punched dots. Found in 1983 or 1984 by metal detector. In private possession. Drawn by S.S.F. from a photograph. See PL. III F.

Britannia xv (1984), 344 No. 39.

engraved on the bezel: PIA
  Pia
  Perhaps a personal name.

2422.66. London (*Londinium*). Octagonal bronze finger-ring (1/1), diameter 19 mm, with each letter of the inscription engraved on a separate facet. The ring is of third-century type. Found in 1982 during excavations at Rangoon Street. Museum of London. Drawn by A. Sutton.

T. Murdoch (ed.), *Treasures and Trinkets*, Museum of London 1991, 81 No. 55 with fig. 4.2 (p. 29).

engraved: VALIATIS
  for *valeatis*
  'May you have good health'

'Vulgar' confusion of unstressed ĕ and ĭ.

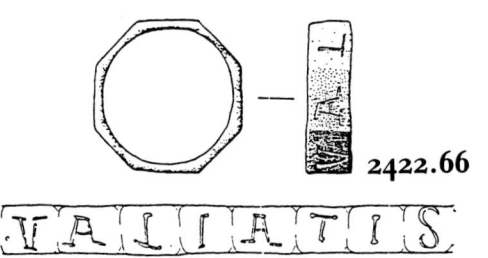

2422.67. Canterbury (*Durovernum*), Kent. Part of a bronze ring with inscribed oval bezel (1/1), found in 1946 in a late Roman level during excavations in the yard of the former Rose Hotel; Rose Lane. Canterbury Museum. Drawn by R.P.W., 1947.

JRS xxxvii (1947), 181 No. 13.

engraved: VITΛ
  vita
  'Long life'

Compare *RIB* 2422.77. For five examples of bronze rings inscribed VITA, of which two come from Mainz, see *CIL* xiii 10024.86 b–f.

2422.68. South Shields, Tyne and Wear [Durham]. Bronze finger-ring (1/1), diameter 24 mm, width 2 mm. Museum of Antiquities, Newcastle upon Tyne. Reproduced from Allason-Jones and Miket.

L. Allason-Jones and R. Miket, *Cat.* 122 No. 3.171 with fig.

incised on the raised oval bezel: VV *or* M

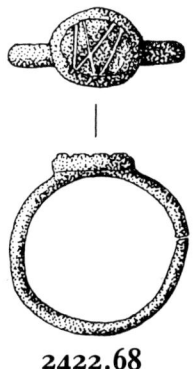

2422.69. Saham Toney, Norfolk. Bronze ring (2/1 and 4/1); on the bezel, cut in intaglio, is a bust with fourth-century hair-style, facing left between the letters of the inscription. In private possession. Drawn by Nicholas Griffiths, 1990 from an *impression*.

Britannia xi (1980), 415 No. 56.

engraved on either side of the bust, one of them retrograde: X͡P
  'Chi-Rho'

2422.70. Richborough (*Rutupiae*), Kent. Bronze ring with nine facets (⅟₁), found in 1931 during excavations within the Saxon Shore fort. Now lost. Reproduced from Cunliffe.

JRS xxii (1932), 228 No. 20. B.W. Cunliffe (ed.), *Fifth Report on the Excavations of the Roman Fort at Richborough, Kent* (1968), 98 No. 160 with pl. XLII.160. C. Thomas, *Christianity in Roman Britain to A.D. 500* (1981), 131 with fig. 7.3.

engraved:
(a) on the bezel: Λ (*inverted*) X͡P ω (*inverted*)
(b) around the ring with two letters on each facet:
IVSTINEVIV̇ASINDEO
Iustine, vivas in deo
'Justinus, live in God'

IVSTINI, *JRS*.

2422.70

2422.71. London (*Londinium*). Bronze ring (⅟₁) with oblong bezel, found before 1907 and said to have been discovered in Canon Street. Now lost. Drawn by R.S.O.T. after Montague.

Montague, *The Bazaar: Exchange and Mart* lxxvii (No. 5269: 14 Dec. 1907), 1707 with fig. 1.

engraved on the bezel: . . . | .Ṭ.

For Lt. Col. L.A.D. Montague see note to *RIB* 2422.74.

2422.71

2422.72. Chichester (*Noviomagus*), West Sussex. Plain bronze ring (⅟₁), diameter 20 mm, height 4.5 mm. Found in 1968–75 during excavations at Chapel Street. Chichester Museum. Reproduced from Down.

A. Down, *Chichester Excavations* iii (1978), 302 No. 101 with fig. 10.37.

incised on the face: I II III

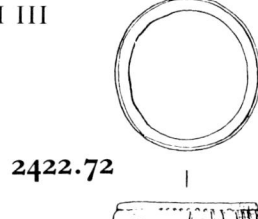

2422.72

2422.73. London (*Londinium*). Bronze ring, diameter 24 mm, with an oval bezel (⅟₁), date and exact location of discovery not recorded. London Museum. Inscription drawn by R.P.W., 1954, and ring reproduced from Wheeler.

R.E.M. Wheeler, *London in Roman Times* (1930), 99 No. 7 with fig. 30.7.

roughly incised retrograde on the bezel: VII
'Seven'

2422.73

2422.74. Dorchester (*Durnovaria*), Dorset. D-shaped bronze ring, diameter 17.5 mm, with bezel (⅟₁) measuring 16 by 6.4 mm, found in, or before, 1907. Exeter Museum (Montague Collection). Drawn by R.P.W., 1953.

Montague, *The Bazaar: Exchange and Mart* lxxvii (No. 5272: 21 Dec. 1907), 1778 with fig. 4.

engraved: XVII
'Seventeen'

2422.74

Lt. Col. L.A.D. Montague was a well-known collector and purchaser from dealers; the context of this ring as from Dorchester must be doubtful, especially as bronze rings with incised numerals are frequent outside Britain (F. Henkel, *Die römischen Fingerringe der Rheinlande* (1913), 316–8).

(d) *RIB* 2422.75–77, iron rings

Note: for other iron rings, carrying inscribed gems, see *RIB* 2423.3, 8, 27.

RIB 2422. FINGER-RINGS (IRON AND JET)

2422.75. London (*Londinium*). Iron ring ($\frac{2}{1}$), diameter 20 mm, with an oval bezel inlaid with three strips of bronze set crosswise, with six-pointed stars stamped within the angles of the arms of the cross. Found in 1974 during excavations at New Fresh Wharf, Lower Thames Street, in river-silt probably deposited in the first half of the second century. Museum of London. Drawn by S.S.F. from a photograph. See PL. III G.

Britannia xiii (1982), 416 No. 54. Henig, *T. Lond. Middl. AS* xxxv (1984), 17–18 with fig. T. Murdoch (ed.), *Treasures and Trinkets* (1991), 81 No. 54 with fig. 4.2 (p.29).

inscription filled with niello set within the cross to read:
- (a) horizontally, DA MI
- (b) vertically, VITA

da mi(hi) vita(m)
'Give me life'

Compare *RIB* 2422.77.

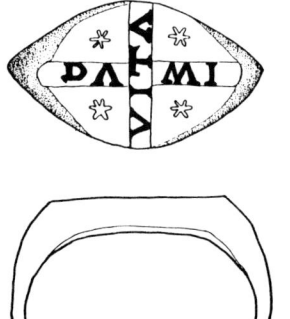

2422.75

2422.76. Unknown provenance, possibly in Britain. Iron ring ($\frac{1}{1}$) with circular silvered bezel, with inscription 'seemingly in Greek letters'. Formerly in Lt. Col. L.A.D. Montague's collection: since 1991 in the Museum of London. Drawn by R.S.O.T. from a photograph, 1991.

Montague, *The Bazaar: Exchange and Mart* lxxvii (No. 5272: 21 Dec. 1907), 1778–9 with fig. 4.

engraved on the silvered bezel:
MAYP|IANOY | YIѠI
Μαυριάνου | υἱῶ
'For the son of Maurianus'

VIIA or VIII, Montague. 'The last letter is not very clear because the silvering has scaled off'. As text, R.S.O.T. from a photograph.

MAYP suggests *M(arcus) Aur(elius)*, but the divine name *Ianus* is doubtful as a cognomen, and the text seems to require a patronymic of peregrine form. *Maurianus* is noted only once by Kajanto (*Cognomina*, 206), but would derive from the common *Maurus*.

For Montague see note to *RIB* 2422.74.

2422.76

2422.77. London (*Londinium*). Iron ring ($\frac{1}{1}$), diameter 19 mm, with an oblong bezel measuring 11 by 6.4 mm into which an inscribed bronze plate has been inserted ($\frac{1}{1}$). Found at Lothbury in or shortly before 1868. Museum of London. Drawn by R.P.W., 1951.

EE iv 716. Price, *T. Lond. Middl. AS* iii part 9 (1868), 220 with fig. Watkin, *Arch. J.* xxxiii (1876), 263 (not xxxii (1875), 68 as cited in *EE*). RCHM, *Roman London* (1928), 176 No. 49. Henig, *T. Lond. Middl. AS* xxxv (1984), 17–18 with fig. T. Murdoch (ed.), *Treasures and Trinkets* (1991), 29, fig. 4.2.

engraved with niello filling on the bronze plate inserted in the bezel: VITAVOLO
vita(m) volo
'I wish for life' *or* 'I wish (you long) life'

Compare *RIB* 2422.74.

[VITAVOLO]

2422.77

(e) *RIB* 2422.78–80, jet rings

2422.78. South Shields (*Arbeia*), Tyne and Wear [Durham]. Jet ring, found in 1878. Now lost. Reprinted from *EE*.

EE vii 1176. Watkin, *Arch. J.* xxxvi (1879), 157. Charlesworth, *Arch. Ael.*[4] xxxix (1961), 25 No. A9.

engraved: CPS
Presumably *G(aius) P(...) S(...)*

2422.79. Chesterholm (*Vindolanda*), Northumberland. Part of a jet ring ($\frac{1}{1}$), diameter 19 by 17 mm, height 19 mm, with oval bezel. Found in 1970 during excavations in the bath-house of the *vicus*. Vindolanda Museum. Drawn by R.P.W., 1970.

Britannia ii (1971), 301 No. 73.

incised: GATNI | VS
   Probably *G(aius) At(i)nius* or for *Catinius*

2422.79

2422.80. (?) Chesters (*Cilurnum*), Northumberland. Jet ring ($\frac{2}{1}$), greatest diameter 24.5 mm, maximum width 21 mm, with a bezel at each end. The upper and lower faces are decorated with incised lines and the inscriptions are in relief in sunken panels. Found before 1903. Chesters Museum. Drawn by S.S.F. from photographs. See PL. IV.

Budge, *Cat.* (1903), 389 No. 1710. Charlesworth, *Arch. Ael.*[4] xxxix (1961), 25 No. A8 with pl. I.8. Wall, *Arch. Ael.*[4] xliii (1965), 223 with fig.

engraved:
(a)   retrograde on the bezel: X̂P
   'Chi-Rho'
(b)   retrograde on the minor bezel: QVIS·SEPA:
and on the hoop:
MEVMETTVVM | DVRANTEVITA
   quis sepa(rabit) meum et tuum durante vita?
   'Who shall separate mine and thine while life lasts?'

2422.80

(f) *RIB* **2422.81. ring of unrecorded material**

Note: for other rings of unrecorded material, carrying inscribed gems, see *RIB* 2423.12, 26, 29.

2422.81. Brough under Stainmore (*Verteris*), Cumbria [Westmorland]. Ring of unrecorded material, found before 1866, bearing 'the Christian monogram'. Now lost. Reprinted from Simpson.

JRS lii (1962), 196 No. 30. Simpson, *CW*[1] i (1866–74), 9. Birley, *CW*[2] (1961), 298. Henig, *Corpus* No. 796.

   X̂P
   'Chi-Rho'

FALSA

2422.82.* York (*Eboracum*). Jet ring with an ansate bezel ($\frac{1}{1}$), probably genuinely of Roman date, but with a clearly spurious modern inscription added. Yorkshire Museum, York. Drawn by R.P.W.

RCHM, *York* i (1962), 144.

(a)   incised retrograde on the bezel: IMA (drawn in *impression*)
(b)   carved in relief around the hoop:
IVLIA MAMAEA AVGVSTA

2422.82*

2422.83.* Leyland, Lancashire. Ring 'of base metal' (Watkin, *Arch. J.*) or 'of much-alloyed gold' (Watkin, *Lancs*), found before 1859 and formerly preserved at Worden Hall near Preston. Now lost. Inscription traced by R.P.W., 1952, from a drawing by Watkin in Chetham's Hospital Library: ring reproduced from Watkin, *Lancs*.

ffarington, *Arch. J.* xvi (1859), 362. Watkin, *Arch. J.* xxxv (1878), 74; *Lancs* (1883), 229 with fig.

engraved on the front of the hoop: SPQR

The ring produces a retrograde impression; it lacks a bezel, the inscription being engraved (very unusually for a Roman ring) on the curving surface of the widest part of the hoop. Its Roman date was doubted by Watkin (*Lancs*) and by K.S. Painter, P. Lasko, D. Strong and R. Higgins. (K.S.P. to R.P.W., 7 Jan. 1965).

2422.83*

2422.84.* (?) Richborough, Kent. Bronze ring (⅓) with gilding, diameter 27 mm, with oval bezel, 28.5 by 25.5 mm. Trinity College, Cambridge. Drawn by R.P.W., 1967.

CIL vii 24*. *EE* ix p. 681.

engraved, (a) on the bezel: FL F F̂L
(b) on the hoop: STIMIVΓAMATO | N

Although allegedly from Richborough, the object is accompanied by a label which states 'probably found in the de Freville property at Little Shelford, Cambridge, about 1860. ? Belonged to Robert de Freville (1529).' Huebner, *CIL*, and F.H., *EE*, both assign a medieval date.

RIB 2423. GEMSTONES, AMULETS AND CAMEOS

The great majority of gems found in Britain are uninscribed intaglii which once were, or are still, incorporated in finger-rings. An account of them has been published by M.E. Henig, *A Corpus of Roman Engraved Gemstones from British Sites* (1974; ed. 2, 1978). The present chapter contains only gemstones which are inscribed. Four of these (*RIB* 2423.1, 15, 16, 17) may be described as amulets, since they carry mystical invocations on the reverse side, concealed when set in a ring. There are three cameos (2423.10, 11, 19), but these, too, are of a size to suit a finger-ring. An unusual proportion (45%) of the inscribed gemstones carry Greek inscriptions.

Although drawings are provided of most of the inscriptions, one (*RIB* 2423.25, whose letters are distributed around a complicated design) is illustrated only by a photograph (PL. IX C), and in two other examples (2423.6 and 30) the inscriptions alone have been drawn, but the whole stones are shown in photographs (VII A, IX D).

Unless described as retrograde, the inscriptions are cut so as to be directly legible and were presumably intended to be ornamental rather than to be used as seals.

2423.1. Lockleys, Welwyn, Hertfordshire. Oval haematite amulet ($\frac{4}{1}$), 13.5 by 17 mm, by 2.4 mm thick. On the obverse, within a frame provided by a serpent devouring its tail (the Ouroboros, an Egyptian symbol for Eternity), stands Isis flanked on the left by Bes and on the right by a lioness. Below the goddess is a globular uterine symbol, and below this the representation of a key with its seven teeth pointing upwards and the handle rising on the right. On the reverse is a *scarabaeus* (sacred beetle) with an uncertain symbol above and a uterine symbol below. Found in 1963 with a coin of Gratian during excavation of a Roman site at Dicket Mead. Verulamium Museum. Drawn by Nicholas Griffiths. And see PL. V.

JRS liv (1964), 180 No. 18 with pl. XV.3 and 4. Wright, *Antiq. J.* xliv (1964), 143–6 with pl. XLII. Henig, *Corpus* No. 369 with pl.

obverse, (a) engraved clockwise inside the Ouroboros: ΛΕ[Η]ΙΟV (*for* Υ) Ω
(b) engraved in Greek letters outside the Ouroboros, a palindrome:

Λ[Ε]ΜΕΙΝΛΕ[ΒΑΡΩ]ΘΕΡΕΘΩΡΑΒΕΛΕΝΙΕΜΕΛ

reverse, engraved around the field:
ΟΡΩΡΙΟΥΘΙΛΗΩΙΛΩΛΩΙ

obverse (a) the seven Greek vowels; compare *RIB* 2423.17.
(b) is a palindrome used in invocations to Typhon (cf. Delatte, *Musée Belge* xviii (1914), 75–88), a monster typifying elemental force.

reverse: Ὀρωριουθ, a spirit giving protection in women's diseases, is invoked on many amulets. ΙΑΩ is frequently invoked in magical texts. Here the invocation occurs three times for extra force.

2423.2. London (*Londinium*). Onyx gem ($\frac{2}{1}$) with blue-grey upper face on a dark ground, 14 by 13 mm, thickness 1.5 mm, found in 1983 during excavations at Nos. 23–29 Eastcheap, in a pit dated *c*. A.D. 55–61. The gem depicts a *dextrarum iunctio* (clasped hands, the symbol of concord and betrothal) within an olive-wreath tied with ribbons. The inscription was first scratched below the hands retrograde and subsequently obliterated, to be replaced above them; but it was not cut more deeply than the marking-out stage before loss. Museum of London. Drawn by Emma Rigby. See also PL. VI.

Henig, *T. Lond. Middl. AS* xxxv (1984), 11–12 with fig. T. Murdoch (ed.), *Treasures and Trinkets* (1991), 34 No. 499(i) with fig.

scratched retrograde above the hands: ΛΛΒΛ

2423.1

2423.2

2423.3. Cirencester (*Corinium*), Gloucestershire. Blue nicolo gem ($\frac{2}{1}$), 10.5 by 7.5 mm, set in an iron ring. Found before 1892. Corinium Museum. Drawn by R.S.O.T. in *impression* from a photograph.

EE ix 1333. Haverfield, *Arch. J.* xlix (1892), 186. Henig, *Corpus* No. 586 with pl.

engraved retrograde above and in front of the figure of a horse:
ΛM | LS

AMA | L | E, R.P.W. As text, Henig.

2423.3

Possibly *Am(icu)l(u)s*, 'Dear Friend', Henig. An abbreviated *Tria nomina* is more probable: *L(ucius) S(...) Am(...)*, R.S.O.T.

2423.4. Chesterholm (*Vindolanda*), Northumberland. Red cornelian set in a gold ring ($\frac{2}{1}$ with sketch of detail not to scale), diameter 16 mm, height 14 mm, with a hexagonal bezel 8 mm wide by 5 mm high. The cornelian forms a truncated hexagonal pyramid bearing on the top an engraved cross and the inscription engraved on the six facets below. Found in 1970 during excavations in Building XXIV in the *vicus*. Vindolanda Museum. Drawing: Vindolanda Trust.

Britannia ii (1971), 301 No. 79. Henig, *Corpus* No. 746 with pl. R. Birley, *Vindolanda: A Roman Frontier Post on Hadrian's Wall* (1977), pl. 13.

carved in relief: ΛN|IM|ΛME|Λ
   anima mea
   'My soul' or 'My darling'

Compare *RIB* 2423.7 and 18 for similar gemstones.

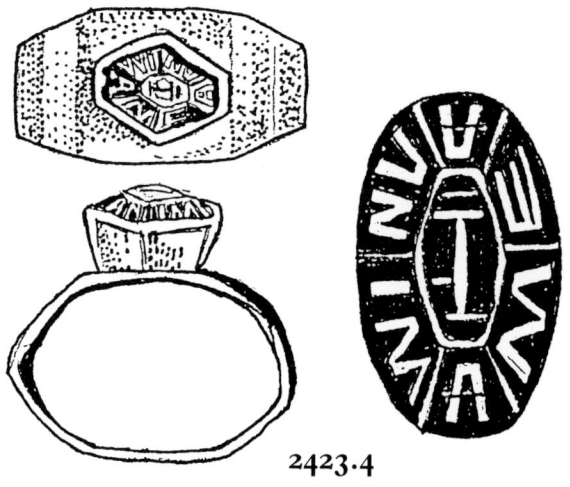

2423.4

2423.5. Thetford, Norfolk. Chalcedony intaglio set in a gold ring ($\frac{2}{1}$ and $\frac{3}{1}$), depicting the Tyche of Antioch seated on a rock and wearing a mural crown. Behind her is a small winged Victory with wreath, and below her feet is a small swimming figure representing the river Orontes. Found in 1979 with *RIB* 2423.15 in the Thetford Treasure (for which see *RIB* 2420.2). British Museum. Reproduced from Johns and Potter.

Britannia xii (1981), 393 No. 97. C. Johns and T. Potter, *The Thetford Treasure* (1983), 83 No. 4 with fig. 3.4.

engraved: ΔИT
   Ant(iochia)

When impressed YNΔ, Hassall *Britannia*. ΔNT, Johns and Potter. Δ has been cut by mistake for A

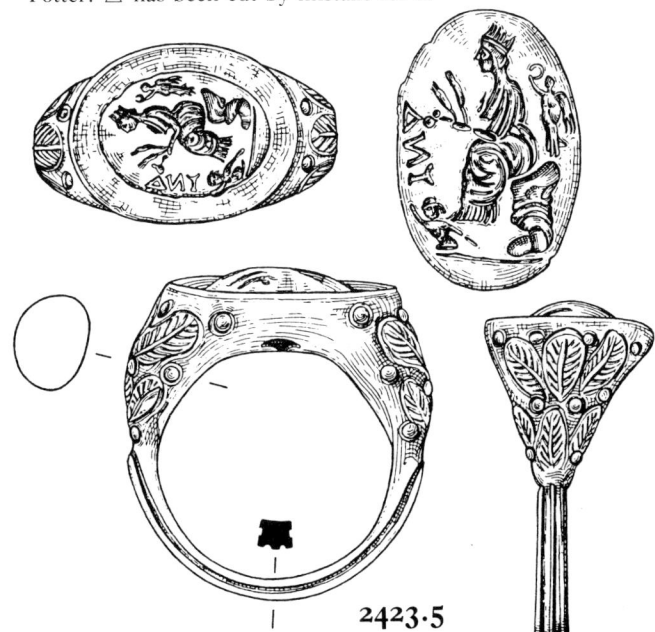

2423.5

2423.6. Braintree, Essex. Oval cornelian intaglio ($\frac{2}{1}$), 15 by 12 mm, thickness 5 mm, depicting Asclepius on the left (as seen in *impression*), leaning on a staff about which twines a serpent, and, on the right Hygieia. The inscription is cut to the left of Asclepius's legs (as seen in *impression*). Found in 1983 during excavations at The Fountain. Brain Valley Archaeological Society. Inscription drawn by S.S.F. from a photograph. For the gem see PL. VII A, B.

Britannia xvi (1985), 327 No. 20. Henig, *Britannia* xvi (1985), 241–2 with pl. XVII.

engraved retrograde to give a positive impression:
   APE
   Perhaps ἀρε(τή)
   'Virtue'

2423.6

2423.7. Ribchester (*Bremetennacum*), Lancashire. Hexagonal red cornelian intaglio with a white surface-layer, set in a gold ring, diameter 17 mm. The letters are in relief in white against a red background, cut on the facets on the sides of the stone; the centre carries the incised figure of a dove. Found before 1801. Present whereabouts unknown. Reproduced from Watkin.

CIL vii 1306. T. Pennant, *Tour from Downing to Alston Moor* (1801), 95–6. Whitaker, *Whalley* (1872), 30. Watkin, *Lancs.* (1883), 155 with fig. Henig, *Corpus* No. 745.

cut in relief around the stone: A | VE | ME | A | VI | TA
  Ave mea vita
  'Hail, my life'

Compare *RIB* 2423.4 and 18 for similar gemstones.

2423.7

2423.8. Caistor St Edmund (*Venta Icenorum*), Norfolk. Oval intaglio of red jasper ($\frac{2}{1}$), 12.5 by 16 mm, set in an iron ring, diameter 25.5 mm; it shows a *combination* design portraying three conjoined male heads in profile each with a letter in front. The principal head has a top-knot which may alternatively be taken as a poor rendering of the elephant's trunk grasping a palm-frond which is found on other similar combination gems. Found in 1964–5, when it was dredged from the bed of the river Tas. Norwich Castle Museum. Drawn by S.S.F.; and see PL. VII C.

JRS lvii (1967), 207 No. 25 with pl. XVIII.2. Ross, *Norfolk Arch.* xxxiv.3 (1968), 263–71 with pl. I and figs. Allen, *Britannia* i (1970), 24. Ross, *Britannia* iii (1972), 293–5. Frere, *Britannia* iii (1972), 295–6. Henig, *Corpus* No. 380 with pl.

engraved: CEΝ

The inscription may refer to the *Cenimagni* or *Iceni*, in whose territory it was found. However, a classical gem (J. Boardman, *Engraved Gems: The Ionides Collection* (1968) No. 50) inscribed NICE . . . (for the Greek NIKE, Victory) may suggest a similar reading on the Caistor gem, the I being combined with the eye of the principal face; but read from a different starting-point, ICEN could still be understood.

2423.9. Colchester (*Camulodunum*), Essex. Oval nicolo intaglio ($\frac{2}{1}$), 12 by 9 mm, 1.5 mm thick, depicting on the obverse a satyr seated on a rock, facing left (as seen in *impression*), with a tree behind. He holds a bunch of grapes in his right hand and a cup in his left. Found in 1985 during excavations in Culver Street. Colchester Museum. Drawn by R.S.O.T. from a photograph.

Britannia xvii (1986), 442 No. 44 with pl. XXXIII A and B (showing both faces).

graffito incised on the reverse of the stone: EYCE|BI
  Ἐυσεβί(ου) *or* Ἐυσεβί(ῳ)
  '(Property) of Eusebius' *or* 'For Eusebius'

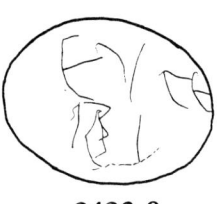

2423.9

2423.10. Keynsham, Avon [Somerset]. Sardonyx cameo ($\frac{2}{1}$) set in a gold ring, diameter 16 mm, with the hoop expanding from 3 to 4.75 mm and the bezel measuring 9.5 by 6.4 mm. Found before 1926 in a garden near the Roman villa. Bristol Museum. Drawn by R.P.W., 1947.

JRS xxxviii (1948), 102 No. 9. Henig, *Corpus* No. 743.

engraved, showing white letters on a brown ground:
  EYTYXI | OΦOPWN
  εὐτύχ(ε)ι ὁ φορῶν
  'May you, the wearer, prosper'

For similar legends see the parallels quoted under No. 38 in M. Henig, *The Content Family Collection of Ancient Cameos* (1990).

2423.8

2423.10

2423.11. North Wraxall, Wiltshire. Onyx cameo (²⁄₁), 13.5 by 9.5 mm, thickness 3.5 mm, depicting a *dextrarum iunctio* (clasped hands, the symbol of concord and betrothal), with a Greek inscription above and below. The upper level of the stone, *c.* 0.5 mm thick, in which the hands and letters are carved, is white; the middle layer *c.* 0.5 mm thick, is grey to brown; and the base layer *c.* 2.5 mm thick, is white. Found in 1972 at the Roman villa. Ashmolean Museum, Oxford. Drawn by S.S.F. from a photograph. See also PL. VII D.

Britannia iv (1973), 334 No. 37 with pl. XL c. Henig, *Antiq. J.* liii (1973), 76–7 with pl. XIX; *Corpus*, App. 30 with pl.

carved in relief: EYTYXωC | OMONOIA
εὐτύχως | ὁμόνοια
'With good fortune' *and* 'Harmony'

For the site, see *VCH* Wiltshire i (1957), 92. For parallels see those cited under Nos. 50 and 51 in M. Henig, *The Content Family Collection of Ancient Cameos* (1990).

Compare *RIB* 2423.19.

2423.11

2423.12. Castlesteads (*Camboglanna*), Cumbria [Cumberland]. Cornelian intaglio (fig. (a) below, size unrecorded), set in a ring of unrecorded material, depicting a bust of Jupiter Serapis facing right and flanked by two other busts facing inwards, perhaps of the Dioscuri. Found before 1745 'in a Roman urn' in the churchyard. The object is here identified with the very similar intaglio recorded by Gordon without provenance (fig. (b) below), in which case it was found before 1726. Now lost. Reproduced from *PSAN* and Gordon.

(a) *IG* xiv 2573, 2. *EE* vii 1175 (wrongly giving the date of discovery as *c.* 1780). Carlisle, *Arch.* xi (1808), 71 with pl. VI.25. W. Jackson (ed.), *Memoirs of Dr Richard Gilpin of Scaleby Castle . . .* (1879), 40–41. Blair, *PSAN*² ii (1886), 147. Watkin *Arch. J.* xliv (1887), 127. McCann, *Memoirs American Acad. Rome* xxx (1968), 55, 183 with pl. XCII.3. Henig, *Corpus* No. 358. Henig, *Antiq. J.* lxvi (1986), 378 with fig. 4.
(b) A. Gordon, *It. Sept.* (1726), No. 3 on pl. facing p. 146.

engraved below the busts: EZC
ε(ἷς) Ζ(εύς) Σ(άραπις)
'(There is) one Zeus Sarapis'

The acclamation is frequent on gemstones and in other media (O. Weinreich, *Ausgewählte Schriften* (1969) i, 430–2), but this is the only instance of abbreviation.

C.W. King (to Blair) identified the subsidiary busts as Isis and Horus. McCann identified the three figures as 'Severus in the guise of Sarapis between Caracalla and Geta as the Dioscuri'.

2423.13. Dover (*Dubris*), Kent. Sard intaglio (*c.* ¹⁄₁) set in a collet of gold on the bezel of a 'white metal, probably silver' ring. Found before 1864 'among the ruins of St Martin's Church'. Now lost. Reproduced from Astley.

EE iii p. 146. *IG* xiv 2573,7. Astley, *Arch. J.* xxi (1864), 263–4 with fig. Watkin, *Arch. J.* xxxi (1874), 355. Haverfield, Taylor and Wheeler, *VCH* Kent iii (1932), 44. Amos and Wheeler, *Arch. J.* lxxxvi (1930), 49. Henig, *Corpus* No. 585.

engraved above and below the figure of a horse facing right: HPAKΛI|ΔHC
Ἡρακλ(ε)ίδης
'Heraclides'

l.2. ΛΗΣ, Astley.

The 'heroic' name *Heraclides* may have been the horse's rather than the owner's.

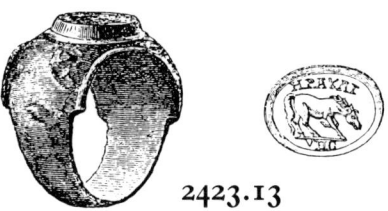

2423.13

2423.14. Wroxeter (*Viroconium*), Shropshire. Gem of (?) plasma or green paste (¹⁄₁), inscribed to give a retrograde impression, found shortly before 1828. Sought in vain by F.H. Now lost. Traced by S.S.F. from Leighton.

CIL vii 1326. Parkes, B.M. Ms Add. 21180 f. 66b. Leighton, *Gent. Mag.* (1828) i, 18 with fig. W.H., ibid. 98. Watkin, *T. Shrops. AS* ii (1879), 336 with pl. III.11. Haverfield, *VCH* Shropshire i (1908), 250 No. 21. Henig, *Corpus* No. 425.

engraved (*impression* illustrated):   FELIX

The personal name *Felix*, or the wish '(be) happy'.

Leighton states that the published drawing is from an impression.

2423.12

 2423.14

RIB 2423. GEMSTONES

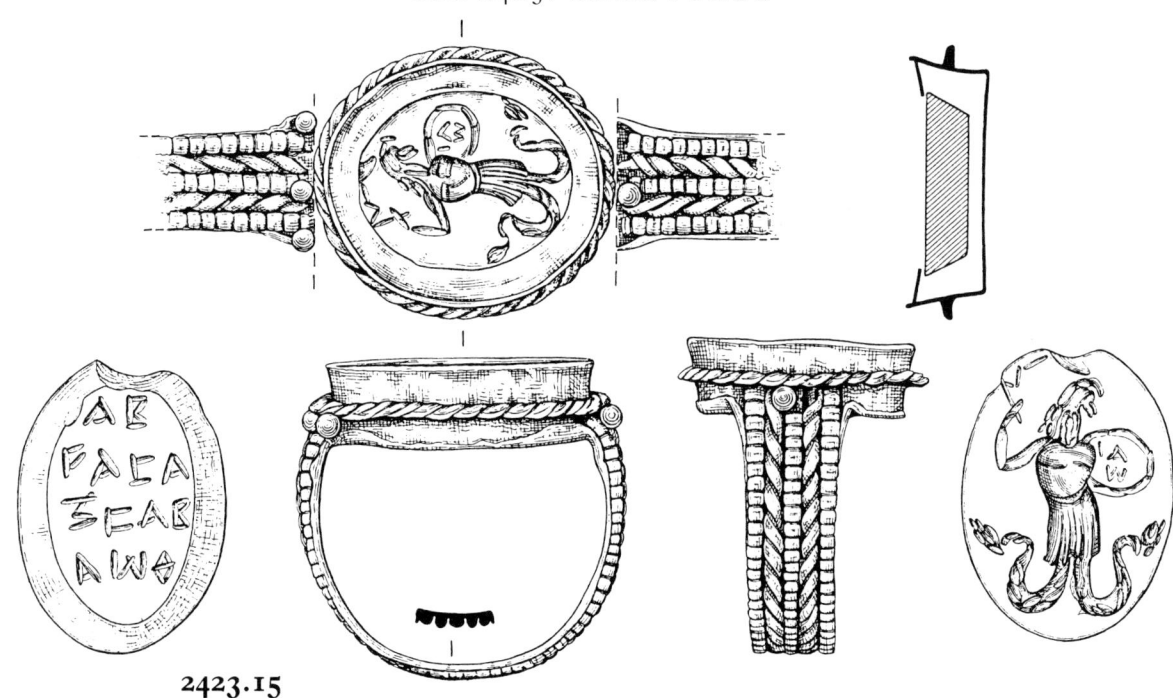

2423.15

2423.15. Thetford, Norfolk. Amulet of brown chalcedony (jasper), 13 by 9.5 mm, loosely set in a gold ring ($\frac{2}{1}$ and $\frac{3}{1}$) and depicting in intaglio a cock-headed, snake-legged deity with an inscribed shield; when removed from the ring the gem was found to be inscribed also on the back. Found in 1979 with *RIB* 2423.5 in the Thetford Treasure (for which see *RIB* 2420.2). British Museum. Reproduced from Johns and Potter.

Britannia xii (1981), 393 No. 98; xiii (1982), 421 Addendum (d). C. Johns and T. Potter, *The Thetford Treasure* (1983), 88 No. 13 with fig. 13.13.

(a) engraved on the shield on the obverse: IΛ | ω
    'Iaō'
(b) engraved on the reverse: AB|PACA|ΞCAB|ΛωΘ
    'Abrasax Sabaōth'

2423.16. Silchester (*Calleva*), Hampshire. Bloodstone amulet ($\frac{1}{1}$), 8.5 by 6 mm, showing on the obverse a cock-headed, snake-legged deity (Abrasax or Iaō) in intaglio and inscribed retrograde on the reverse. Found in 1899 during excavations. Reading Museum. Drawn by R.P.W., 1951, and see PL. VII E.

EE ix 1342. Hope and Fox, *Arch.* lvii (1900), 111 (repr. 25). Haverfield, *VCH* Hampshire i (1900), 254. Henig, *Corpus* No. 366 with pls.

engraved retrograde on the reverse (illustrated in *impression*): ωΔI
    i.e. IAω
    'Iaō'

2423.16

Δ has been cut by mistake for Λ.

G.C. Boon (in Henig) notes that the reverse retains more of the original polish than the obverse, suggesting that the invocation on the reverse had been concealed in a ring.

2423.17. (?) Colchester (*Camulodunum*), Essex. Lapis lazuli amulet ($\frac{2}{1}$), 11.75 by 9 mm, portraying on the obverse an intaglio of Harpocrates, nude, standing left; inscribed on the reverse. Found before 1928, when it was purchased by the Museum, and said to be from Colchester. Colchester Museum. Drawn by S.S.F. from a photograph; see also PL. VIII A, B.

Britannia iii (1972), 356 No. 22 with pl. XXXI B, C. Henig, *Corpus* No. 368 with pls.

engraved on the reverse: IωEH | AYO
    Iωεη | αυο

The seven Greek vowels; compare *RIB* 2423.1.

2423.17

2423.18. Gogmagog Hills, Cambridge. Hexagonal red cornelian with white surface (*c.* $\frac{1}{1}$ and $\frac{2}{1}$), set in a gold ring, diameter 25 mm, height 18 mm, width of bezel 10 mm. The letters are cut in relief in separate panels on the sides of the stone, on the centre of which is incised an anchor. Found in 1844 'at the seat of the late Lord F. Godolphin Osborne in the Gogmagog Hills' (Neville). British Museum. Drawn by R.P.W., and the ring reproduced from Marshall.

CIL vii 1303. Neville, *Arch. J.* xvii (1860), 75 with fig. F.H. Marshall, *Cat. of Finger-rings . . . in the BM* (1907), 109 No. 651 with fig. 97. Henig, *Corpus* No. 744 with pl.

cut in relief around the stone: M | IH | I | VI | VΛ | S
  mihi vivas
  'Live for me'

MIB(?)I, Marshall. The H has serifs which connect, R.P.W. MISCE VIVAS, Neville.

Compare *RIB* 2423.4 and 7 for similar gemstones.

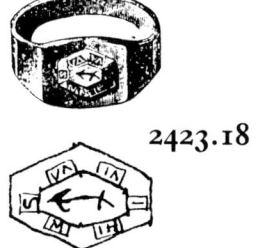

2423.18

2423.19. Bradwell (*Othona*), Essex. Onyx cameo ($\frac{2}{1}$), 11 by 7.5 mm, set in a gold ring. The cameo depicts a *dextrarum iunctio* (clasped hands, the symbol of concord and betrothal) with a wreath above and the inscription below in badly-cut lettering. British Museum. Drawn by S.S.F. from a photograph. See also PL. VIII C.

F.H. Marshall, *Cat. of Finger-rings . . . in the BM* (1907), No. 561 with pl. XVI. H.B. Walters, *Cat. of Engraved Gems and Cameos, Gk., Etr. and Rn., in the BM* (1926), No. 3696. Henig, *Corpus* No. 742 with pl.; *Antiq. J.* l (1970), 339 No. 7.

engraved: OMONOIΛ
  Ὁμόνοια
  'Harmony'

Compare *RIB* 2423.11. It is possible that the wreath above the joined hands is really a blundered inscription.

2423.19

2423.20. Oxfordshire, with no exact provenance. Oval nicolo intaglio ($\frac{1}{1}$), 14 by 11 mm, depicting on the obverse a semi-nude male (perhaps the Genius of Comedy), looking towards a theatrical mask held in his right hand and holding a *pedum* in the crook of his left arm. Found before 1982 'near Burford' and possibly therefore at the Roman villa at Asthall. Ashmolean Museum, Oxford. Drawn by S.S.F. from a photograph; and see PL. VIII D, E.

Britannia xv (1984), 345 No. 47. Henig and Wilkins, *Antiq. J.* lxii (1982), 380–1 with pl. LVI b, c.

engraved on the reverse: P

2423.20

2423.21. Kingsholm, Gloucestershire. Oval cornelian intaglio ($\frac{2}{1}$), 12 by 10 mm, depicting a cow standing on a ground-line in front of a haulm of wheat, with surrounding inscription. Found in 1979 at No. 117 Dean Way. In private possession. Drawn by S.S.F. from a photograph, and see PL. IX A.

Britannia xiii (1982), 413 No. 24 with pl; xiv (1983), 350 Corrigendum (d). Henig, *J. Roman Archaeology* i (1988), 147 with fig. 5.

engraved retrograde: PI | Q
  Presumably *P(ublius) I(. . .) Q(. . .)*

2423.21

2423.22. Dragonby, Humberside [Lincolnshire]. Yellow glass intaglio ($\frac{2}{1}$), 8.75 by 7 mm, with moulded retrograde legend on the underside to be read in positive form through the glass. Found in 1972 in a depression overlying a late Iron Age ditch during excavation of a settlement-site, and dated tentatively by M. Henig to the end of the first century B.C. Scunthorpe Museum. Drawing by courtesy of Jeffrey May.

moulded: ROSA
  'Rose'

2423.22

Compare E. Zwierlein-Diehl, *Die Antiken Gemmen des Kunsthistorischen Museums in Wien* ii (1979), No. 951 for a close parallel.

For *Rosa* as a personal name see Kajanto, *Cognomina* 33.

2423.23. Akenham, Suffolk. Amber-coloured cornelian intaglio (⅟₁), length 21 mm, width 16 mm, showing Victory walking left and surrounded by the inscription, which is not cut retrograde for a positive impression. Found before 1928, when it was acquired by Ipswich Museum. Drawn by R.P.W., 1951; and see PL. IX B.

Britannia iv (1973), 333 No. 31 with pl. XL B. Henig, *Corpus* No. 297.

engraved: RVBRIVS CARINVS ORIENTAL|IS
  Rubrius Carinus Oriental|is
  Presumably 'Rubrius Carinus the Oriental'

The engraver blundered the inscription, cutting a second E after ORIE and then changing it to N; no space was left for IS, which is placed in the field. *Rubrius* and *Carinus* are a common nomen and cognomen respectively, but *Orientalis* is virtually unknown as a cognomen and would seem to be descriptive.

2423.23

2423.24. Folkestone, Kent. Modern wax impression (²⁄₁), 12 by 10 mm, showing 'two storks above the head of (?) Octavian' (Henig). The impression, in the Ashmolean Museum, Oxford, has a label: 'ancient intaglio ring found at Folkestone, Kent, in the possession of H.H. Rolfe, Sandwich'. Drawn by S.S.F. from a photograph.

M. Henig, *Corpus* (ed. 2, 1978), 318 App. 213 with pl.

inscribed around the edge: SERI · FAVSTI
  '(seal) of Serius Faustus'

Compare M.L. Vollenweider, *Porträtgemmen*, pl. 147 Nos. 1 and 5 for gems showing Octavian with storks. The style of the Folkestone piece is of the first century B.C.; the apparent beard is the result of the wax bubbling.

For the nomen *Serius* (not in Mócsy, *Nomenclator*, but well-attested in *CIL* xi), see Schulze, 229.

2423.24

2423.25. Caerleon (*Isca*), Gwent [Monmouthshire]. Oval cornelian intaglio, 15 by 11 mm, depicting Diana shooting an arrow (to the right in *impression*) with a hound leaping at her feet. The three letters of the inscription are distributed around the field. Found in 1978 during excavation of the fortress baths. Caerleon Museum. See PL. IX C.

Britannia xiii (1982), 421 No. 85. J.D. Zienkiewicz, *The Legionary Fortress Baths at Caerleon* ii (1986), 140–1 No. 88 with pl. XVII Nos. 8a, 8b.

engraved retrograde: TEB
  Presumably *T(itus) E[...] B[...]*

2423.26. Colchester (*Camulodunum*), Essex. Gem of unrecorded material set in a ring also of unrecorded material, found at Colchester before 1853. Now lost. Reprinted from Neville.

EE iii p. 146. *IG* xiv 2573, 8. Neville, *Arch. J.* x (1853), 350. Watkin, *Arch. J.* xxxiv (1877), 79. Henig, *Corpus* No. 655.

engraved above the figure of a sphinx: ΘΕΡΜΙΑ
  Thermia

A personal name *Thermia*, of Greek etymology, is implied by the cognomina *Thermiola* and *Thermitanus* (*CIL* xiii 1676).

2423.27. Malton (*Derventio*), North Yorkshire. Red jasper intaglio (⅟₁ and ²⁄₁), 15.5 by 14 mm, set in an iron ring; it depicts the youthful Hercules with his lion-skin around the neck. Found in the 19th century in the cutting of the Thirsk railway. British Museum. Reproduced from Manning.

W.H. Manning, *Cat.* (1985), 78 No. J9 with pl. 33. F.H. Marshall, *Cat. of Finger-rings ... in the British Museum* (1907), No. 1467. H.B. Walters, *Cat. of Engraved Gems and Cameos, Gk., Etr. and Rn., in the British Museum* (1926), No. 1896. Kitson-Clark, *Gazetteer* (1935), 107. Henig, *Corpus* (ed. 2, 1978), App. 150 with pl.

incised retrograde, divided by the neck: VS
  Perhaps *v(oto) s(oluto)* or more probably a name, V...S...
  'A vow paid' *or* 'V...S...'

  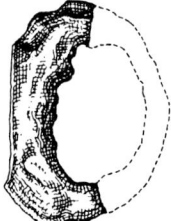

2423.27

2423.28. Southwark, south London. Bronze intaglio ($\frac{1}{1}$) set in a bronze ring, found in 1977 during excavation of a late Roman well below the Cathedral Crypt. Museum of London. Drawn by Alison Hawkins, 1990.

Britannia x (1979), 354 No. 35.

engraved: VTF
  ut(ere) f(elix)
  'Good luck to the user'

For this abbreviation compare *CIL* xiii 10024.97a, b, 158, and *CIL* xii 5692.7.

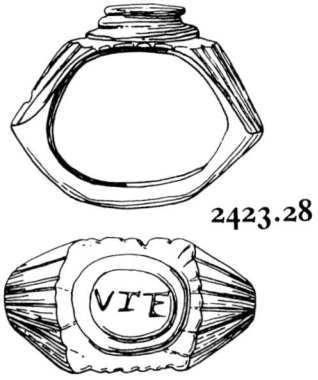

2423.29. Kilbride, Strathclyde Region [Lanarkshire]. Sard intaglio, dimensions unrecorded, set in a ring of unrecorded material, found before 1711 in a tumulus near the Kittock stream. Haverfield, *EE*, rightly identified the object described by Sibbald with *CIL* vii 1327, a gem recorded by Gordon without provenance. Now lost. Reproduced from Gordon.

CIL vii 1327. *EE* ix 1334. R. Sibbald, *Tractatus* (1711), 110 with pl. I.6. A. Gordon, *It. Sept.* (1726), No. 14 on pl. facing p. 146.

engraved: VTERE | FELIX
  'Good luck to the user'

2423.30. Caerleon (*Isca*), Gwent [Monmouthshire]. Oval intaglio in dark green prase ($\frac{2}{1}$), 11 by 5.3 mm; below the inscription are depicted (a) clasped hands (*dextrarum iunctio*); (b) below (a), a cornucopiae over a globe and surmounted by a raven on a pedestal; (c), to the left of (b) in the *impression*, a hippocamp swims to the right with an unidentified object below it. Inscription traced by S.S.F. from a photograph. For the gem, see PL. IX D, E.

Britannia xix (1988), 506 No. 103. J.D. Zienkiewicz, *The Legionary Fortress Baths at Caerleon* ii (1986), 129–30 No. 7, with pl. V, Nos. 7a, 7b. Henig, *Arch. J.* cxlv (1988), 423.

engraved above the field (to give a retrograde impression): ΧΑΡΑ
  χαρά
  'Joy'

ΧΑΡΑ, M. Henig, op. cit. ΑΙΑΧ retrograde to give a positive impression, G.C. Boon in Zienkiewicz.

2423.31. Silchester (*Calleva*), Hampshire. Onyx intaglio, found before 1789. Now lost. Reprinted from *EE*.

EE iv 718. Gough's *Camden* (1789) i, 142. Watkin, *Arch. J.* xxxiii (1876), 263. Haverfield, *VCH* Hampshire i (1900), 284 No. 14. Henig, *Corpus* No. 365.

engraved: ZACP

Boon, in Henig, suggests Z(EYC) CAP(AΠIC) 'Zeus Sarapis', whose cult is attested at Silchester.

ALIENA

2423.32.* Reculver (*Regulbium*), Kent. Crystal intaglio mounted in the binding of a Gospel. Now lost. Reprinted from Leland.

CIL vii 1325. Leland, *Itinerary* (ed. 1), vii (1711), 111. Philpott, *Villare Cantianum*, 270, quoting Leland. W. Somner, *A Treatise of the Roman Ports and Forts in Kent* (1693), 82. Gough's *Camden* (1789), 235; (1806) i, 343. Henig, *Corpus* No. M 31.

engraved: CLAVDIA ATEPICCVS

'In the Chirch is a very auncient Boke of the Evangelyes *in majusculis literis* Ro. and yn the Bordes thereof ys a Christal Stone thus incribid: CLAVDIA. ATEPICCVS' Leland, loc. cit. Whether the stone had been found in Britain must remain uncertain.

2423.33. * Canterbury Cathedral, Kent. Plasma intaglio ($\frac{1}{1}$ and $\frac{2}{1}$), 17 by 13 mm, depicting a lion-headed serpent above the inscription, set in a thirteenth-century gold ring and found in 1890 on opening the tomb of an archbishop; the ring was on the index finger of the right hand. Canterbury Cathedral Library. Ring reproduced from Hope, intaglio drawn by R.S.O.T. from a photograph. See PL. X A.

W.H. St J. Hope, *Vetusta Monumenta* vii (1893), 6 with fig. 2. Henig, *Corpus* No. M 20; *JBAA* cxxxv (1983), 57 No. 1, 59, with pl. I A.

engraved: XNOYBIC
  Χνοῦβις
  'Chnoubis'

2423.33

This pagan magical invocation is a surprising ornament on an archiepiscopal ring. It was originally an amulet against stomach ailments: see works cited by Henig, *JBAA*, 58 note 10.

He notes that, on the analogy of other examples, the back may have been inscribed with three Ss bisected by a bar; but the back here has been cut away. There can be no certainty that the intaglio was originally found in Britain.

FALSA

2423.34. * Kirmington, Humberside [Lincolnshire]. Red jasper intaglio showing a combination design of the heads of Silenus and Minerva. In front of the former is an incised L interpreted by Ross as an angular C; Henig shows that this is part of the plume of the helmet worn by Minerva. Not illustrated.

Ross quoted by RPW, *JRS* lviii (1968), 211 No. 39 with pl. XVIII.2. Henig, *Corpus* No. 373.

2423.35. * Dringhouses near York. Glass intaglio ($\frac{1}{1}$) in an iron seal. Found before 1877. Colchester Museum. Drawn in *impression* by R.P.W.

EE iii 26.*

obverse, surrounding a laureate bust facing left:
  FLAVI VSDOMIT
  Flavius Domit(ianus)

reverse, surrounding a horseman facing right holding a whip: HOMO ET EQVS
  homo et eq(u)us

F.H. considered it to be 18th-century work. Martin Henig agrees

2423.35*

RIB 2424. BRACELETS

2424.1–2. Castlethorpe, Buckinghamshire. Two penannular silver bracelets ($\frac{1}{1}$ and $\frac{2}{3}$) of snake-head type. No. 1, oval, diameters 70 and 57 mm, width 19 mm with a graffito on the flat inner surface at one end. No. 2, oval, diameters 73 and 57 mm, width 20.6 mm, with a graffito at either end of the inner surface. Found c. 1827 during ploughing on Burtles Hill, contained in a black urn together with a silver ring and coins of A.D. 138–69. The graffiti were detected by Miss G. Woodhouse in 1964. British Museum. No. 2424.2 drawn by R.P.W., 1965; the bracelets reproduced from B.M. *Guide* (1922).

JRS lv (1965), 225 No. 19. Pretty, *JBAA* ii (1847), 352. Way, *Arch.* xxxiii (1849), 348. *Reliquary* xiii (1872–3), pl. XVIII. *VCH* Buckinghamshire ii (1908), 5 with fig. B.M. *Guide Rom. Brit.* (1922), 64 with fig. 81; (1952), 13 No. 1 with fig. 6.1.

2424.1. graffito: VIIRNICO O
Vernico

2424.2. graffito: VIIRNIC[.], VIIRNICO
Vernico

The final letter of the first word of No. 2 is damaged by wear. The I in the second word is placed horizontally. The personal name *Vernico* seems to be unattested, but like *Vernio* probably derives from *verna* (Kajanto, *Cognomina*, 34).

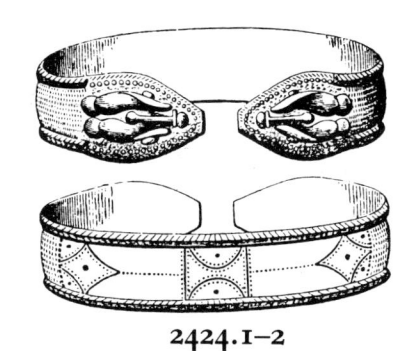

2424.1–2

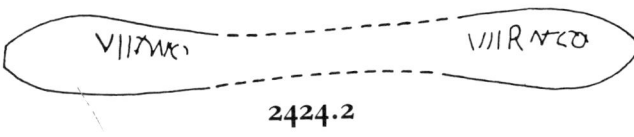

2424.2

RIB 2425. HELMETS

This chapter contains examples of both legionary helmets and cavalry 'parade' helmets, together with one of native Iron Age manufacture and one considered to be gladiatorial. Only the last carries a maker's stamp; the inscriptions on the others are graffiti naming the owners, sometimes successive, from which it is seen that such items of equipment were often handed in for re-issue or sold to a colleague at the end of service. On this see Macmullen, *AJA* lxiv (1964), 21–40.

2425.1. Unknown provenance, probably in Britain. Conical bronze helmet (⅟₁), of La Tène III type and pre-Roman British manufacture. The neck-guard carries a bold repoussé curvilinear pattern of Celtic art, in which are set two flat domed bosses, grooved for enamel. Acquired in 1872 by the British Museum as part of the Meyrick collection. Drawn by R.P.W., 1953.

JRS liv (1964), 181 No. 19. BM, *Guide to Early Iron Age Antiquities* (1925), 107 with fig. 65; *Guide to Later Prehistoric Antiquities* (1953), 68 with pl. XVIII.2. C. Fox, *Pattern and Purpose* (1958), 119 with pl. 62 c (neck-guard only).

scored behind the right ear-guard: II

'It may have been a captured piece and have received the number II, which is carefully incised in Roman manner, for a temple-inventory, or as an item of booty', E.M. Jope to R.P.W., 1963.

2425.2. London (*Londinium*). Bronze helmet (²⁄₁) of mid first-century legionary ('Coolus') type, diameters 190.5 by 295 mm (including the neck-guard), height 140 mm. It has a movable brow-guard pinned at either end, and on either side a plume-holder and two rivets for a cheek-piece. A solder-mark on the top indicates the position of the crest. Found some years before 1940 in the Walbrook or Thames and acquired in 1950 by the British Museum. Drawn by R.P.W., 1950. See also PLS. XII, XIII.

JRS xli (1951), 142 No. 11. Brailsford, *Illus. Lond. News*, 26 Aug. 1950, 306 with pl; *BMQ* xvi (1951), 18 with fig. and pl. VIII A. BM, *Guide Rom. Brit.* (1951), 67 No. 5 with pl. XXV.5. H.R. Robinson, *The Armour of Imperial Rome* (1975), 32 with pl. 54.

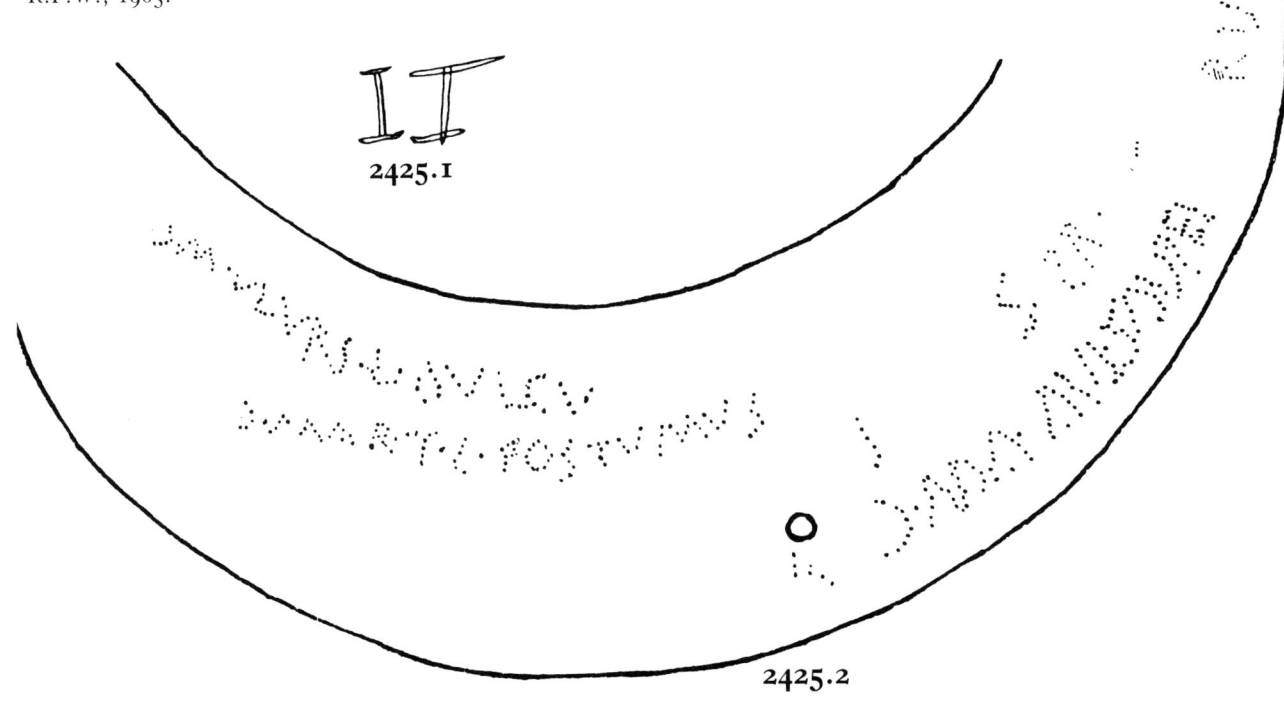

punched graffiti on the neck-guard:

(a) >·M·V̂AL·VRS·L·DVLCI·
(centuria) M(arci) Val(erii) Urs(i) L(uci) Dulci
'(Property) of Lucius Dulcius in the century of Marcus Valerius Ursus'

(b) ↄ·MART·L·POSTVMVS·
(centuria) Mart(ialis?) L(ucius) Postumus
'In the century of Martialis, Lucius Postumus'

(c) >·SCR·RVFI
(centuria) Scr(iboni) Rufi
'(Property) of Rufus in the century of Scribonius'

(d) ↄ·MA·AVL·SAVFEI
c(enturia) Ma(rtialis ?) Aul(i) Saufei
'(Property) of Aulus Saufeius in the century of Martialis'

(b) >·MARCI, R.P.W.
(d) SAVPEI, R.P.W.

Some other names have been deleted: in (a) three letters before >; in (c) traces of a previous text appear, especially before RVFI, and >SCR may not belong to the same text as RVFI; in (d) a letter like L or F precedes the extant line, which has been deeply punched. Thus, apart from deletions, there have been four owners of the helmet, attached to at least two centuries.

The nomen *Dulcius* seems to be unattested, but can be inferred from the place-name *Dulciacum* (see Holder s.v.); it is 'manufactured' from *dulcis*.

Saufeius is a common Italian nomen and should be read here: compare the P of *Postumus* and the F of *Rufi* for the difficulty of distinguishing F from P in this script. R.S.O.T.

2425.3. St. Albans (*Verulamium*), Hertfordshire. Bronze helmet (¼) of mid first-century legionary ('Coolus') type with neck-guard; diameter 216 mm, length including neck-guard 266.5 mm; over each ear two holes indicate where the brow-guard should hinge and above this is the mark of a plume-holder, now missing. On the top is an attachment for the crest. The neck-guard carries traces of three inscriptions: (b) was first recorded by R.G.C., and (c) by R.P.W. (1943). Found in the nineteenth century; between 1862 and 1870 it entered the Colchester Museum and was transferred to the Verulamium Museum in 1965. Drawn by S.S.F. from tracings by R.G.C. and R.P.W.

EE vii 1166; ix p. 665. Colchester Museum *Cat.* (ed. 2, 1870), 40 No. 734. Franks, *PSA*² v (1872), 362. Watkin, *Arch. J.* xli (1884), 185. Page, *VCH* Hertfordshire, iv (1914), pl. I a. Webster, *Arch. J.* cxv (1958), 90 No. 196. H.R. Robinson, *The Armour of Imperial Rome* (1975), 33 pl. 58.

graffiti in punched dots on the neck-guard; (a) and (c) are set in relationship, but (b) is set separately.

(a) deeply hammered in: PP·[.]·PΛPIRI | A
(Centuria) p(rimi) p(ili) [.] Papiri <A>
'(Property) of [.] Papirius (in the century) of the primus pilus'

(b) ↄVICTORSI M·VS[.]R[...]
(centuria) Victoris M(arci) ...
'(Property) of Marcus ... in the century of Victor'

(c) in the same line as (a) but in the reverse direction: >[...] \
(centuria [...])

(a) PETRONI Huebner, *CIL* vii 1296 (see next entry). PAPIRIVS Franks, Watkin.
Three unexplained dots conclude l.1, and A is repeated below in l.2.

(b) The sequence of S and I in VICTORIS was reversed.

Corrosion has damaged the inscriptions, particularly (c).

CIL vii 1296, a helmet said to have been found at Colchester and to be in the British Museum, is shown by Haverfield, *EE* ix p. 665 to be a confusion with *EE* vii 1166, now *RIB* 2425.3, a helmet once in the Colchester Museum but found at St. Albans, which is omitted from *CIL* vii.

2425.3

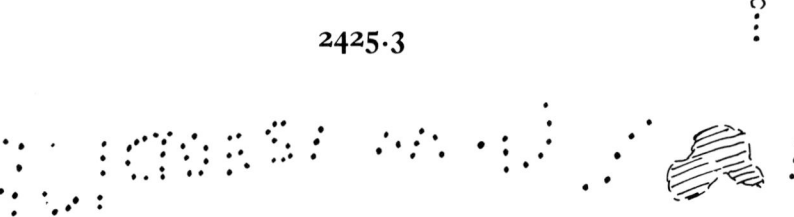

2425.4. Newstead (*Trimontium*), Borders Region [Roxburghshire]. Iron cavalry helmet of 'parade' or 'sports' type and Flavian date, found in 1906 during excavation of Pit XXII in the South Annexe of the fort with *RIB* 2425.5 and 2427.4–12 and 21–24. The inscriptions were first noted by Mr. J. Scott in 1983 but are not readily drawable. National Museums of Scotland, Queen Street, Edinburgh. Not illustrated.

Britannia xv (1984), 348 No. 62. For the helmet see J. Curle, *Newstead* (1911), 168–70 with pl. XXIX. J. Garbsch, *Römische Paraderüstungen* (1978), 57.

On the underside of the rim are two graffiti:

(a) in punched dots: MI[c. 4]VCI·T ATINIA
Mị[. . .]uci t(urma) Atinia(na?)
'(Property) of Mi[. . . .]ucus in the *Atinia* troop'

(b) cut with a chisel: IIX X
Perhaps 'eighteen'

The command of the *turma* was temporarily vacant, so it was named adjectivally from its last decurion (*Atinius?*). The numeral(s) were apparently cut this way up (not XXII), with a space between the Xs.

2425.5. Ibid. Bronze cavalry helmet ($\frac{2}{3}$) of 'parade' or 'sports' type and Flavian date; the crown carries decoration in high relief, including a nude winged figure driving a chariot left, drawn by two leopards. Found in 1906 with *RIB* 2425.4 and 2427.4–12, 21–24 during excavation of Pit XXII in the South Annexe of the fort. National Museums of Scotland, Queen Street, Edinburgh. Drawn by R.G.C., 1936.

EE ix 1320. J. Curle, *Newstead* (1911), 166–8 with fig. 15 and pls. XXVII, XXVIII. J.M.C. Toynbee, *Art in Roman Britain* (1962), No. 98 with pl. 106. H.R. Robinson, *The Armour of Imperial Rome* (1975), 112–13 with pls. J. Garbsch, *Römische Paraderüstungen* (1978), 57 with Taf. 12.2.

graffito in punched dots on the rim at the back:
VFFI·T GES
Uffi t(urma) Ges(. . .)
'(Property) of Uffus (?) in the troop of Ges(. . .)'

VFFI·T GES·S, Curle

The name *Uffus* (?) seems to be unparalleled. The decurion's name was probably *Gesatius* or *Gessius*.

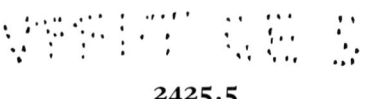

2425.5

2425.6. Ribchester (*Bremetennacum*), Lancashire. Bronze cavalry helmet ($\frac{2}{3}$) of 'parade' or 'sports' type and probably Flavian, with vizor-mask; height 280 mm; the crown is embossed with combat scenes. Found in 1796 with *RIB* 2415.31. The inscriptions were first observed by Dr. H. Klumbach. British Museum. Drawn by R.P.W., 1960.

JRS l (1960), 240 No. 21. For the helmet itself see Towneley, *Vet. Mon.* iv (1799), pl. I–III. Watkin, *Lancs* (1883), 152 with pl. BM, *Guide Rom. Britain* (1922) 80 with pl. V; (1951), 67 No. 4 with pl. XXV.4. J.M.C. Toynbee, *Art in Roman Britain* (1962), 167 No. 101 with pl. 108. H.R. Robinson, *The Armour of Imperial Rome* (1975), 112–13 with pls. J. Garbsch, *Römische Paraderüstungen* (1978), 58 with Taf. 12.1.

graffiti in punched dots:

(a) on the underside of the neck-guard: CARAVI

(b) on the underside of the flange below the left ear of the vizor: CARAV followed by two setting-out dots for the top and bottom of an I.

CARINI, R.S.O.T. by conjecture. (The cognomen *Carinus* is well attested, whereas *Caravus* is unique; R.P.W. compares the Spanish place-name *Caravis*, see Holder s.v.)

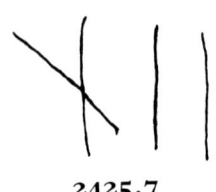

2425.6

2425.7. Worthing, Norfolk. Brass cavalry-helmet ($\frac{1}{1}$) of 'parade' or 'sports' type and third-century date, with traces of gilding; height 251 mm, width 202 mm. The crest, with an eagle-head terminal, is engraved with standing feathers, on either side of which is an embossed sea-dragon facing forwards. The front is formed of a false upturned peak, triangular in shape, whose sides are decorated with bird-headed snakes. Found in 1947 in the river Wensum. Norwich Castle Museum. Drawn by R.P.W., 1951.

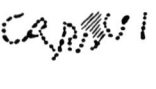

2425.7

JRS xli (1951), 143 No. 12. Toynbee and Clarke, *JRS* xxxviii (1948), 20–27. Clarke, *Norfolk Arch.* xxx (1947–50), 145 with pls. I, II. H.R. Robinson, *The Armour of Imperial Rome* (1975), 130–1 with pls. J.M.C. Toynbee, *Art in Roman Britain* (1962), 167–8 with pl. 109. J. Garbsch, *Römische Paraderüstungen* (1978), 74 No. 61 with Taf. 30.1.

graffito scored near the right-hand end of the upper side of the neck-guard: XII
   'Twelve'

The numeral has been taken to refer to a twelfth *turma* (Toynbee, *JRS*, R.P.W., *JRS*); but *turmae* were normally named after their commanders (compare *RIB* 2425.4 and 5), and numbers unrelated to units are found on other pieces of military equipment: compare *RIB* 2425.4, 8 and 2427.21–24.

2425.8. Chesterholm (*Vindolanda*), Northumberland. Iron reinforcing-peak from a helmet, found in 1986 in a context dated *c.* 120–30 or a little later. Vindolanda Museum. Drawing: The Vindolanda Trust.

Britannia xix (1988), 502 No. 71.

incised: XXXVII
   'Thirty-seven'

Compare *RIB* 2425.7, with note.

2425.9. Hawkedon, Suffolk. Bronze helmet ($\frac{1}{1}$), width 441 mm including the neck-guard, height 197 mm, diameter of the cap 254 mm, weight 2280 gm. The width of the neck-guard and the weight of the object (over twice the weight of a legionary helmet) suggest a gladiatorial context. Found in 1965 during harrowing. British Museum. Drawn by S.S.F. from a draft by R.P.W.

JRS lvi (1966), 221 No. 20 with pl. X.4 and 5. Painter, *Antiq. J.* xlvii (1967), 286–7 with pl. LXII; *BMQ* xxxiii (1968–9), 121–9 with figs. and pls. LVII–LX.

stamped in a panel on the upper surface of the neck-guard at the back: [. . .]O?

This inscription is much weathered.

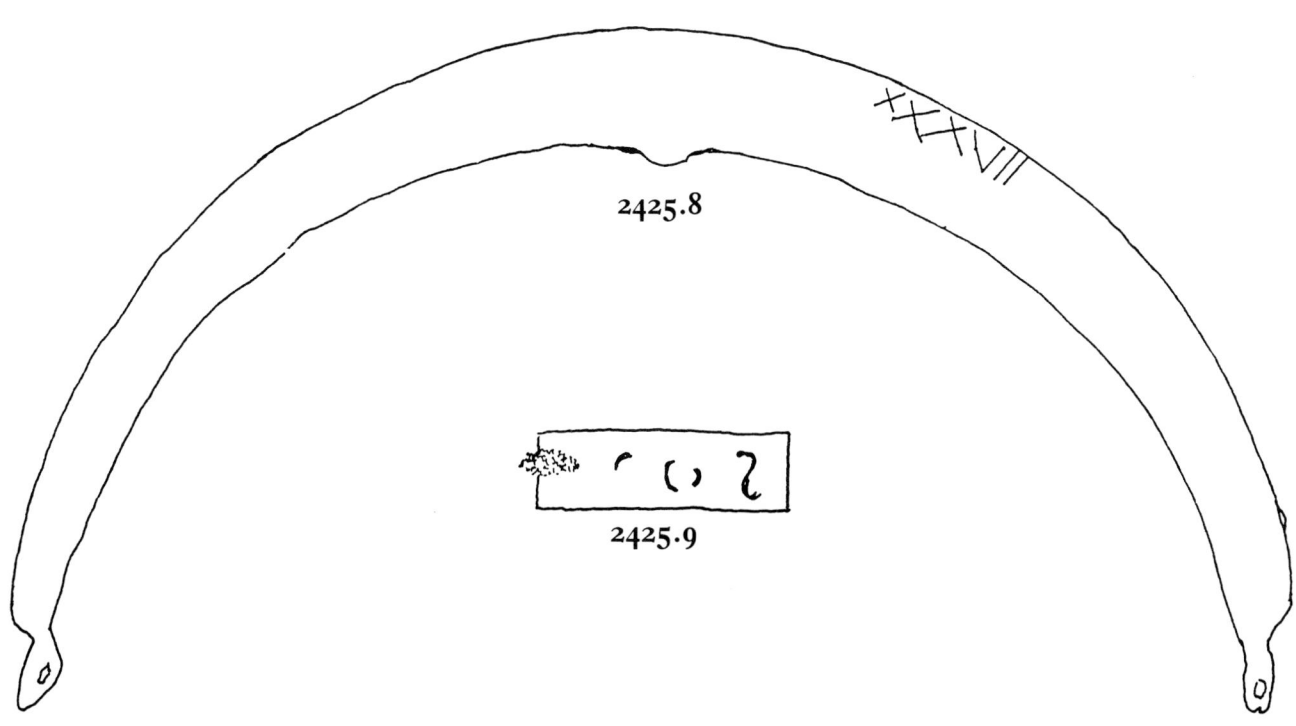

RIB 2426. SHIELDS AND ARMOUR

2426.1. River Tyne, Tyne and Wear. Bronze shield-plate (³⁄₇ and ²⁄₃) in the form of a legionary shield, with raised central circular boss, decorated with scenes reserved against a niello background. Flanking the boss, which bears the figure of an eagle, are two standards; the remaining panels show the Four Seasons at the corners; Mars (centre, top); and a bull (emblem of Legion VIII Augusta) with moon and stars (representing the Constellation *Taurus*) above it (centre bottom). Found in 1867 in the bed of the river Tyne near its mouth. British Museum. Drawing of the whole plate by courtesy of the Trustees of the British Museum; details drawn by R.P.W., 1960. See also PL. XI.

CIL vii 495. Bruce, *LS* 106. *NCH* viii, 278 with fig. B.M. *Guide Rom. Britain* (1922), 77 with fig. 98; (1951), 67 No. 8 with fig. 35. J.M.C. Toynbee, *Art in Britain under the Romans* (1964), 299 with pl. LXIX a.

2426.1

Two inscriptions in punched dots:

(a) interrupted by the central boss, set in reserved spaces: LEG VIII AVG
leg(io) VIII Aug(usta)
'The Eighth Legion Augusta'

(b) vertically along the left margin:
⊃ IVLI·MAGNI IVNI DVBITATI
(Centuria) Iuli Magni Iuni Dubitati
'(Property) of Iunius Dubitatus in the century of Iulius Magnus'

Legion VIII Augusta was stationed at Strasbourg from A.D. 69. A vexillation of the legion is known to have been despatched to Britain in the reign of Hadrian (*CIL* x 5829= *ILS* 2726), and this may have been the occasion of the loss.

2426.2. Matfen, Northumberland. Bronze shield-boss ($\frac{1}{1}$), diameter 203 mm, found about 1825 in a field near Matfen. Present whereabouts unknown. Reproduced from Franks.

CIL vii 570. Chambers, *PSAN*[1] i (1856), 192. Franks, *Arch. J.* xv (1858), 55–8 with fig. Charlton, *Arch. Ael.*[2] ii (1858), 49–50. Bruce, *LS* 105. Haverfield, *NCH* x (1914), 472 No. 13.

graffito in punched dots:
⊃ VIIRI QVINTI
(centuria) Veri Quinti
'(Property) of Quintus in the century of Verus'

⊃ RVSPI QVINTI, Franks (rejecting DON SP IOVINTI).
⊃·APIRLOVINCTI, R.P.W. As text, R.S.O.T.

Franks notes that the shield boss was corroded and had been regularly scoured since discovery, so that some of the 'dots' were probably pitting. In the absence of the original, any reading is somewhat conjectural.

2426.3. London (*Londinium*). Bronze shield-boss ($\frac{1}{2}$ and $\frac{2}{1}$), diameter 192 mm, diameter of dome 115 mm, thickness of the flange 1–3 mm, of the dome 0.5–1 mm. Found some years before 1940 'between Fenchurch Street and Gracechurch Street', in or near the Forum. British Museum. Drawn by Philip Compton.

Britannia xvi (1985), 328 No. 28. Jackson, *Britannia* xv (1984), 246–50 with fig.

stamped near the rim: COCILLVS F
Cocillus fecit
'Cocillus made (this)'

COGILLVS, M.W.C.H., *Britannia*. COCILLVS, Compton.

The stamp partly obliterates the outermost engraved circle of decoration. The boss may have been discarded before use, since there are no rivet-holes for fixing it to the shield.

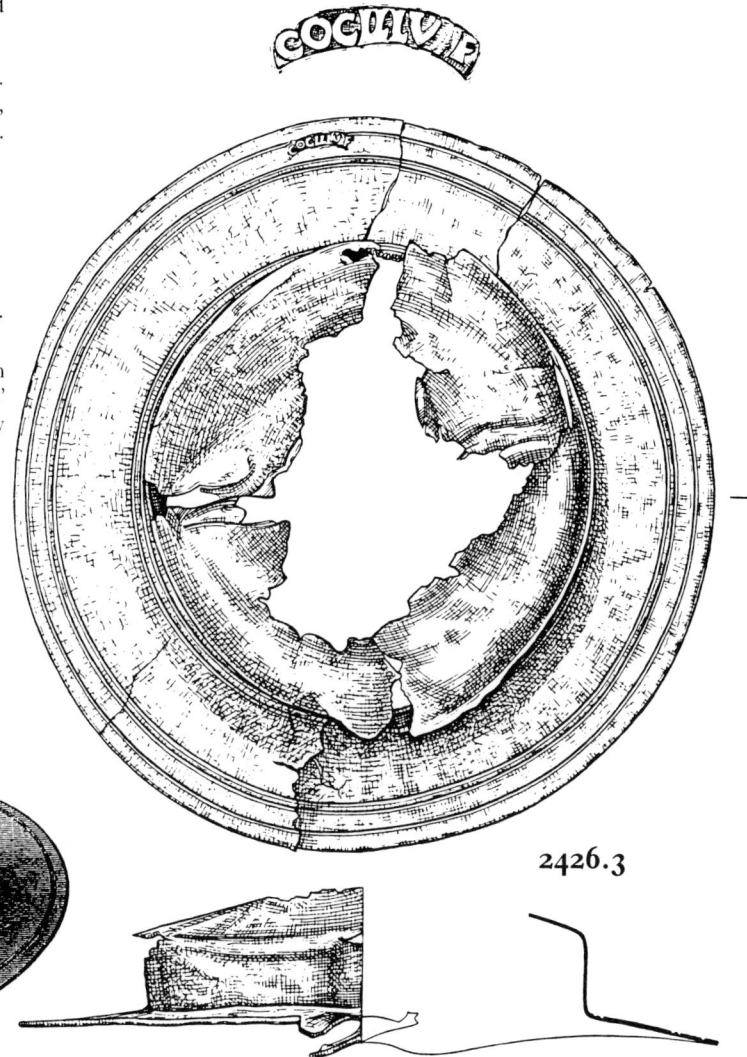

2426.2

2426.3

2426.4. Corbridge (? *Coria*), Northumberland. Part of the left-hand leaf ($\frac{1}{1}$ and $\frac{1}{3}$) from a pair of panels of bronze armour plate, 62 by 46 mm, decorated with an incised figure of Victory facing right, with a stole over the right arm, and a wreath and punched garland in her right hand. A stud on the left is riveted to its counterpart on the underside, and still retains a small portion of another bronze sheet. Found probably before 1949 during excavation at Corbridge, but the inscription was first observed by Dr. H. Klumbach in 1959. Corbridge Museum. Inscription drawn by R.P.W., 1966; the whole leaf by S.S.F., 1990, from a photograph by J.P. Gillam.

JRS lvii (1967), 207 No. 26 with pl. XX.2. Klumbach, *Aus Bayerns Frühzeit* lxii (1962), 193. Wright, *Arch. Ael.*[4] xlvi (1968), 1–2 with pl. I.1.

inscription in punched dots vertically along the right margin: LARS[. . .] | A[. . .]

    Lars[. . .] | A[. . .]

    '(Property) of Lars[. . .] A[. . .]'

For the rare nomen see in masculine or feminine form *Larsidius* (*CIL* xi 5242), *Larsinius* (*CIL* iii 12663; vi 29027) or *Larsius* (*CIL* ix 5874).

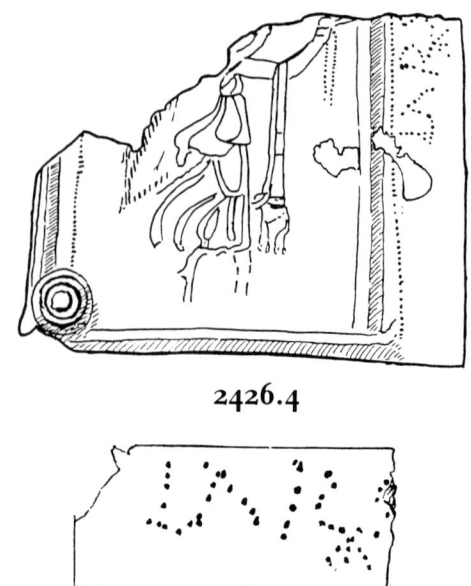

2426.4

Klumbach, loc. cit., shows that these leaves were used in pairs on breast-plates and were curved at the top to fit below the neck. From 29 examples he shows that eight are repoussé, twenty are embossed and the present example is the only one with incised decoration.

RIB 2427. WEAPONS AND OTHER MILITARY EQUIPMENT

This chapter contains a miscellaneous collection of weapons and other objects with military inscriptions or associations:

No. 1: an iron sword
Nos. 2–3: iron spearheads
Nos. 4–17: bronze *phalerae* and other discs
Nos. 18–20: bronze plates
Nos. 21–24: bronze saddle-stiffeners
No. 25: a bronze spatula
No. 26*: a bronze roundel

For some iron tools with military inscriptions or associations see *RIB* 2428.

2427.1. Silchester (*Calleva*), Hampshire. Part of an iron sword ($\frac{1}{1}$), length 292 mm (including a tang of 63.5 mm), found in 1890 in Pit N to the south of Insula I, House 2. The inscription was first noted by G.C. Boon. Reading Museum. Drawn by R.P.W., 1953.

JRS xliv (1954), 108 No. 28.

stamped on the blade when hot, 12.5 mm from the tang: VXI

Perhaps a blundered numeral, XIV or XVI, R.P.W.; but a maker's name might be expected on a stamped sword-blade: compare *CIL* xiii 10028.9, 18; 10036.64, 67–9, 84 for such makers' stamps.

2427.2. London (*Londinium*). Iron spearhead ($\frac{2}{3}$), length 247.5 mm, width 41 mm, found in 1954 in a late first-century well in the north-western corner of the Bucklersbury House site. Museum of London. Drawn by R.P.W., 1956. See also PL. XVI C.

JRS xlvi (1956), 149 No. 16.

graffito in punched dots above the rib: ƆVER·VICT
(centuria) Ver(i) Vict(oris)
'(Property) of Victor in the century of Verus'

2427.3. Newstead (*Trimontium*), Borders Region [Roxburghshire]. Iron spearhead ($\frac{1}{2}$), length 270 mm, found in 1906 with four others uninscribed and *RIB* 2428.3 and 4 in Pit XVI (which is of Flavian date) in the South Annexe of the fort. National Museums of Scotland, Queen Street, Edinburgh. Drawn by R.P.W.

EE ix 1328. J. Curle, *Newstead* (1911), 188 with fig. 20 and pl. XXXVI.5.

inscribed on both sides in punched dots:

(a)   ..TIVN | TBΛ
      Perhaps *t(urma) Iun(i) | t(urma) Ba(...)*

(b)   X

(a) T IVN BA for *turma Iuni Bassi*, F.H., *EE*. The inscriptions perhaps indicate successive owners. Side (a) may carry two superimposed inscriptions. Other names than *Bassus* are possible.

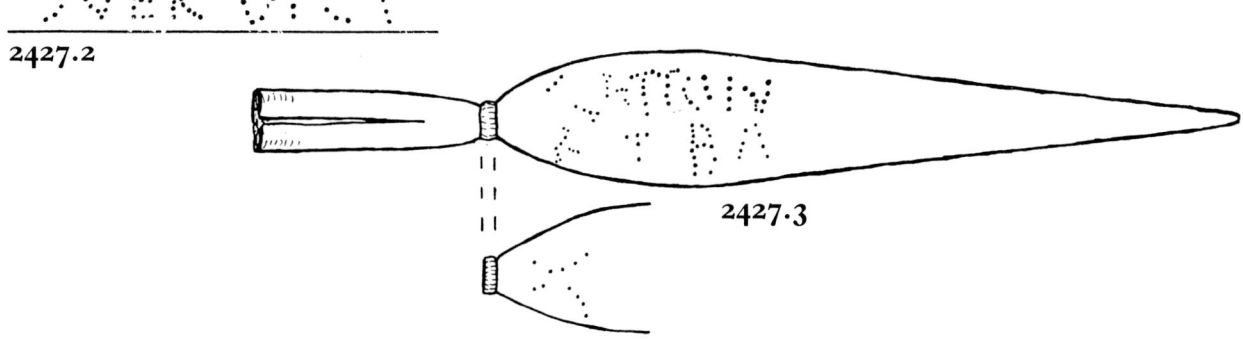

2427.4–12. Ibid. Nine bronze discs (½), eight of them circular, one lenticular; around the circumference are rivet-holes, some still retaining bronze rivets furnished with washers. Found in 1906 all together in Pit XXII of Flavian date in the South Annexe, with another parade helmet (uninscribed), *RIB* 2425.4 and 5 and *RIB* 2427.21–24. National Museums of Scotland, Queen Street, Edinburgh. Drawn by R.P.W.

EE ix 1321. J. Curle, *Newstead* (1911), 174 with pl. XXII. V.A. Maxfield, *The Military Decorations of the Roman Army* (1981), 91.5 with fig. 11 and pl. XVI a.

4. Diameter 110 mm. Six rivet-holes.
   Scratched graffito: DOMIITI | ATTICI
   Dometi Attici
   '(Property) of Dometius Atticus'

5. Greater diameter 83 mm. Five rivet-holes.
   Inscription as No. 4.

6. Diameter 116 mm. Six rivet-holes.
   Inscription as No. 4.

7. Diameter 98 mm. Six rivet-holes.
   Inscription as No. 4.

8. Diameter 99 mm. Four rivet-holes.
   Inscription as No. 4.

9. Diameter 104 mm. Six rivet-holes.
   Inscription as No. 4.

10. Diameter 104 mm. Six rivet-holes.
    Scratched graffito: DMIITI | ATTICI
    D(o)meti Attici
    '(Property) of Dometius Atticus'

11. Diameter 106 mm. Six rivet-holes.
    Scratched graffito: DOMIITI ATICI
    Dometi At(t)ici
    '(Property) of Dometius Atticus'

12. Diameter 101 mm. Four rivet-holes.
    Scratched graffito: DOMIITI
    Dometi
    '(Property) of Dometius'

Dometius for *Domitius* is an instance of the frequent 'Vulgar' confusion between medial *ĕ* and *ĭ*.

These objects are the backing-plates of *phalerae*, a type of military decoration often awarded in sets of nine, the front plates of which, now missing, probably carried either central bosses surrounded by circles in relief or more elaborate iconographic ornament, as surviving examples and representations on tombstones attest: see Maxfield, op. cit., 91–5. The inscriptions are all on the same side of the objects as the washers and so were normally invisible against their leather mounting. This, as Maxfield shows, was a system of straps worn over the chest.

2427.4

2427.5

2427.6

2427.7

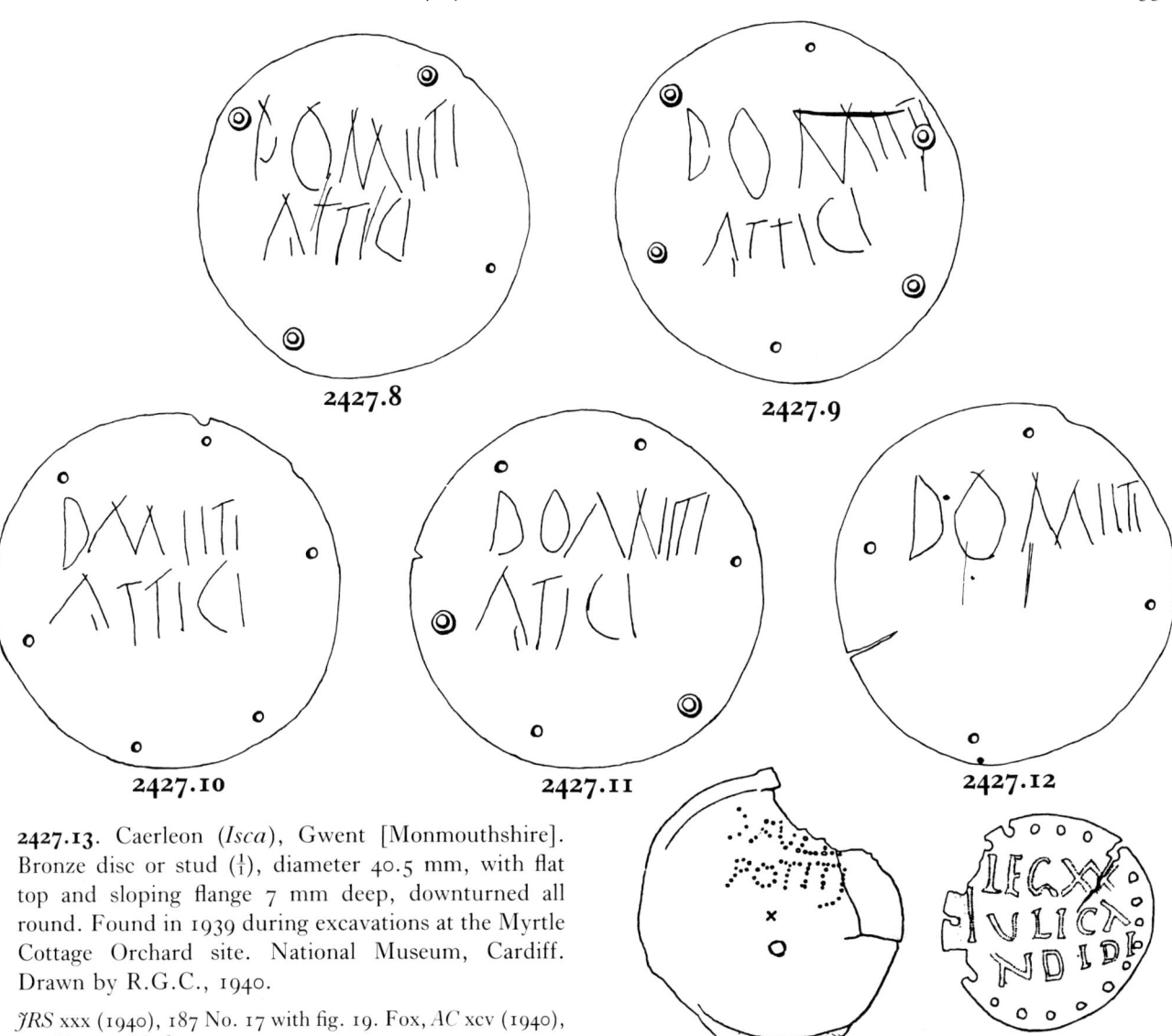

2427.13. Caerleon (*Isca*), Gwent [Monmouthshire]. Bronze disc or stud (⅟₁), diameter 40.5 mm, with flat top and sloping flange 7 mm deep, downturned all round. Found in 1939 during excavations at the Myrtle Cottage Orchard site. National Museum, Cardiff. Drawn by R.G.C., 1940.

JRS xxx (1940), 187 No. 17 with fig. 19. Fox, *AC* xcv (1940), 127 No. 2 with fig. 5.2.

graffito in punched dots: ƆFVL[1–2]|POTITỊ

(centuria) Ful[vi] Potiti

'Century of Fulvius Potitus'

Understand *(centuria)*, not *(centurionis)*, since for the latter the symbol would have followed the centurion's name. However, this object can hardly have been the property of a *centuria*, and we must suppose that the owner's name was inscribed on another disc.

The central shank (indicated by X) is still 12.5 mm long, but has been bent and broken. After fracture a small hole was punched from the back for re-attachment. The shank appears over-long for fitting to leather, and the object is probably not a *phalera* but a stud fastened to woodwork such as a shield.

2427.14. Chester (*Deva*). Silvered bronze disc (⅔), diameter 47.5 mm, edged with a series of holes, some of which have broken away. Found in 1923 during excavations in the Deanery Field. Grosvenor Museum, Chester. Drawn by R.G.C., 1925.

JRS xiv (1924), 246. Droop and Newstead, *Liv. Ann.* xi (1924), 75 with pl. V 3, 3a.

inscribed in letters formed of double lines of punched dots: LEGXX | IVLICA | NDIDI

Leg(ionis) XX Iuli Candidi

'(Property) of Iulius Candidus of the Twentieth Legion'

Possibly Iulius Candidus is identical with the centurion, legion unknown, recorded in *RIB* 1632, 1646 and 1674 on Hadrian's Wall near Housesteads; but the combination of names is not uncommon.

2427.15. Ibid. Bronze disc (1.5:1), diameter 44 mm, with a loop at the back for attachment, found in 1976 in a late or post-Roman context at the back of the fortress rampart at Abbey Green. Grosvenor Museum, Chester. Drawn by S.S.F. from a rubbing by R.P.W., 1976.

Britannia viii (1977) 434 No. 37. McPeake et al., *JCAS* lxiii (1980), 25.

graffito in punched dots: L·VN·ABENI
 Perhaps *L(uci) (I)un(i) Abeni*
 '(Property) of Lucius Iunius Abenus'

The cognomen is unmatched.

2427.15

2427.16. Stanwix (*Uxelodunum*), Cumbria [Cumberland]. Bronze disc ($\frac{1}{1}$), diameter 48.25 mm with central hole 5 mm in diameter, found in 1930 with *RIB* 2427.17 and 20 during excavation of a sewer trench in Kings Meadow, south of the fort. Tullie House Museum, Carlisle. Drawn by R.G.C., 1930.

2427.16

JRS xxi (1931), 248 No. 4. Collingwood, CW^2 xxxi (1931), 74 No. 13 with fig. 4; *Antiq. J.* xi (1931) 39 with fig. 4.

in punched dots around the circumference:
 T SVPIIRI GIICI
 t(urma) Superi Geci
 '(Property) of Gecus in the *turma* of Super'

The name *Gecus* seems to be unparalleled.

2427.17. Ibid. Bronze disc ($\frac{1}{1}$), diameter 33 mm, with a shank attached to the middle of the back; found in 1930 with *RIB* 2427.16 and 20, during excavation of a sewer trench in Kings Meadow, south of the fort. Tullie House Museum, Carlisle. Drawn by R.G.C., 1930.

JRS xxxi (1931), 248 No. 5. Collingwood, CW^2 xxxi (1931), 78 with fig. 5; *Antiq. J.* xi (1931), 39 with fig. 5.

in punched dots around the circumference:
 [. . .]TIHILARIO
 [. . .]ti Hilario
 Presumably 'Hilario [in the *turma* of . . .]tus'

For the cognomen *Hilario* compare *RIB* 1562, 2003.

2427.17

2427.18. Kirkby Thore (*Bravoniacum*), Cumbria [Westmorland]. Bronze ansate plate ($\frac{1}{2}$), found 'long since' before 1927. Tullie House Museum, Carlisle. Drawn by R.G.C., 1927.

JRS xvii (1927), 216 No. 22.

in punched dots: ƆPRISCI | ITOSI
 (centuria) Prisci Itosi
 '(Property) of Itosus in the century of Priscus'

The name *Itosus* seem to be unique, but compare *Etosa* (*CIL* xiii 4336).

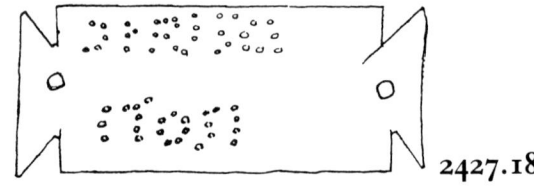

2427.18

2427.19. Wall (*Letocetum*), Staffordshire. Very thin bronze plate ($\frac{2}{3}$), 38 by 32 mm, with a shank 2.5 by 2.5 mm brazed on to the middle of the back; this had been passed through a backing *c*. 6 mm thick and bushed out at the end to hold it in place. Found before 1925. Wall Museum. Drawn by R.P.W., 1951.

W.F. Blay, *Letocetum: Wall* (1925), 27. *Cat*. (ed. 2, 1947), 9.

inscribed in punched letters: ƆVITA|LIS | PRIMẸ
 (*centuria*) Vitalis Primẹ
 '(century) of Vitalis . . .'

The final letter is E or, less probably, F, R.P.W.

PRIME may be an error for PRIMI, giving the meaning '(property) of Primus in the century of Vitalis'; it probably does not stand for (*cohortis*) *prim(a)e*, 'of the first cohort', which would seem to be unparalleled.

2427.19

2427.20. Stanwix (*Uxelodunum*), Cumbria [Cumberland]. Bronze plate ($\frac{1}{1}$), 65 by 18 mm, with two shanks braised on at the back, length 6 mm to the expanded head, found in 1930 with *RIB* 2427.16 and 17 during excavation of a sewer trench in Kings Meadow south of the fort. Tullie House Museum, Carlisle. Drawn by R.G.C., 1930.

JRS xxi (1931), 248 No. 6. Collingwood, *CW*² xxxi (1931), 75 No. 14 with fig. 4; *Antiq. J.* xi (1931), 39-40 with fig. 4.

in punched dots: T·G·SABINIPRISCI
 t(urma) G(. . .) Sabini Prisci
 '(Property) of Priscus in the *turma* of G(. . .) Sabinus'

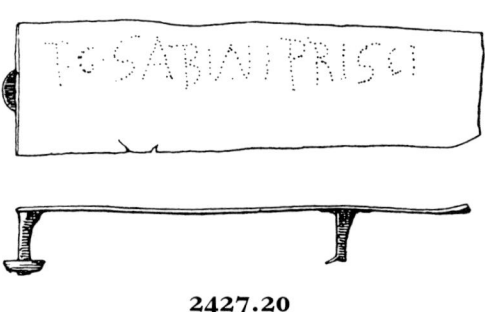

2427.20

2427.21–24. Newstead (*Trimontium*), Borders Region [Roxburghshire]. Four bronze pommel-stiffeners forming a set from a saddle ($\frac{1}{2}$); a series of small holes along the edges for stitching shows that they were formerly covered on the outside with leather, of which traces remained on another (uninscribed) set of four from Pit XXVII. Found in 1906 with *RIB* 2425.4 and 5 and 2427.4–12 during the excavation of Pit XXII, of Flavian date, in the South Annexe of the Fort. National Museums of Scotland, Queen Street, Edinburgh. Reproduced from Curle and see PL. XIV.

EE ix 1322 a-d. J. Curle, *Newstead* (1911), 177 with fig. 17 and pl. XXXII.

21. graffito on one of two L-shaped stiffeners
 (a) in punched dots: XV
 (b) scratched with a point: SIINIICIO
  Senecio
 (c) similarly scratched but in the reverse direction: CRIISCIIS
  Cresce(n)s

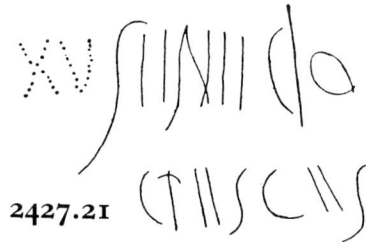

2427.21

22–24. graffito on the other three stiffeners
 (a) in punched dots: XII
 (b) scratched with a point: SIINIICIONIS
  Senecionis
  '(Property) of Senecio'

The numerals are unlikely to represent *turma* numbers, for *turmae* were normally named after their commanders (compare *RIB* 2425.4 and 5, 2427.3, 16 and 20); moreover there are two different numbers here on the same set without indication of alteration. For numbers unrelated to units on other pieces of military equipment, see *RIB* 2415.39, 2425.4, 7 and 8.

For a reconstruction of the Roman military saddle, see Connolly in M. Dawson (ed.), *Roman Military Equipment* (1987), 7–27.

2427.22–24

2427.25. Caerleon (*Isca*), Gwent [Monmouthshire]. Bronze spatula ($\frac{2}{1}$), length 79.4 mm tapering from 6.4 mm to a point, thickness 3 mm; the side bearing the inscription is convex, the other flat. Found in 1939 during excavations at the Myrtle Cottage Orchard site. National Museum, Cardiff. Drawn by R.P.W., 1960.

JRS xxx (1940), 186 No. 16. Fox, *AC* xcv (1940), 127 with fig. 5.1.

graffito in punched dots: ƆCV . . . MⱯLLVI

ƆCV. . . .ᴧⱯIL[I. . .] R.G.C., *JRS*

ALIENUM

2427.26.* Unknown provenance, almost certainly Continental. Bronze roundel ($\frac{1}{1}$), diameter 117 mm, with an engraved scene at the top showing an eagle flanked by *vexilla* and emblems of two legionary vexillations (on the left the *vexillum* and boar of *legio xx Valeria Victrix*, on the right the *vexillum* and capricorn of *legio ii Augusta*). Below are representative groups of soldiers, five in each group facing inwards, carrying oval shields. The lower half of the roundel is occupied by a *venatio* in the arena, featuring hounds, a lion, stag and hare, with two peacocks below, that on the right pecking a flower. Cabinet des Medailles, Paris. Reproduced from Brushfield. See also PL. X B.

F. Buonarrotti, *Osservazioni istoriche sopra alcuni Medaglioni antichi all' Altezza Serenissima di Cosmo III Granduca di Toscana* (1698), pp. xvii–xviii with pl. before p. 1. Brushfield, *JCAS*[1] iii (1885), 7 with fig. E. Babelon and A. Blanchet, *Cat. des Bronzes* (1895), 557–8, No. 1363. Cagnat, *Rev. arch.* 1895.1, 213–20. Jarrett, *AC* cxvii (1968), 88–9. Tomlin in *Encyclopaedia of Warfare* (1991), 49 with colour plate.

obverse, engraved:
(a) LEG XX | VV
    leg(io) xx V(aleria) V(ictrix)
(b) LEG SE | CVNDA | AVGVS
    leg(io) secunda Augus(ta)
(c) AVRELIVS | CERVIANVS
(d) VTEREFELIX
    utere felix
    'Good luck to the user'

reverse: blank

The owner, Aurelius Cervianus, is otherwise unattested. He was perhaps an officer in, or in command of, a vexillation from the two legions of third-century Upper Britain, sent on a Continental expedition (as is attested under Gallienus, *CIL* xiii 6780, iii 3228 bis (= *ILS* 546); compare *RIB* 369. A third-century date is also suggested by the use of oval shields by the legionaries and by the nomen *Aurelius*.

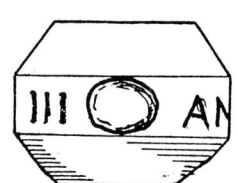

2427.27*

FALSA

2427.27.* Colchester (*Camulodunum*), Essex. Cheese-shaped jasper pommel ($\frac{1}{2}$), diameter 57 mm, height 40.5 mm, with oval perforation. A flat central zone round the circumference is inscribed; above and below this the top and bottom of the truncated cones are incised, the obverse with a head of Antoninus Pius, the reverse with a boat carrying the wolf and twins in the centre, together with a head of Faustulus (left) facing right and (right) a head of Roma or Mars facing left; above is a tree with two birds in the branches. To the right of the boat is a second inscription. Found before 1863. Colchester Museum. Drawn by S.S.F. from a rubbing by R.P.W., 1954. See also PL. XVI A, B.

EE vii 1189. Colchester Museum *Cat.* (1863), 33 No. 651.

(a) engraved around the circumference:
ANTOOINVS AVS PIVS PPTRPCOS III
Anto[n]inus Au[g](ustus) Pius p(ater) p(atriae) tr(ibunicia) p(otestate) co(n)s(ul) III
'Antoninus Augustus Pius, Father of his Country (holder of) tribunician power, three times consul'
(b) engraved on the reverse: COMMVNIS

A.D. 140–144

(b) F.H., *EE*, has printed COMMVNIS retrograde as if from an impression.

The object was condemned as a *falsum* by both F.H. and R.P.W. For *falsa* collected in Colchester in the mid nineteenth century see *RIB* 2439, Introduction. The design on the reverse is not derived from the coinage, but (as Dr. Martin Henig informs us) is copied from the impression of an ancient intaglio, for which see A. Furtwängler, *Die antiken Gemmen* i (1900), pl. XXVIII No. 58; ii, 142 No. 58.

2427.28.* Exeter (*Isca*), Devon. Bronze hilt of a sword or dagger, found in 1834 in South Street. Now lost. Reprinted from Shortt.

EE iii 134. Shortt, *Gent. Mag.* 1836 Aug., p. 156.

interpreted by Shortt as: Σ.MEFITI.T.EQ.FRIS.
  S(ervii) Mefiti t(ribuni) eq(uitum) Fris(iorum)
  '(Property) of Servius Mefitius, tribune of the Frisian Horse'

The sigma cannot stand for Servius, but in reverse might indicate *centuria*. *Mefitius* is unrecorded as a nomen although *Mefitis* is the name of a goddess. T should stand for *turma*; *tribunus* should be abbreviated *trib*.

The find was made during a period when many Falsa and Aliena were recorded at Exeter, sometimes reported as having been recovered from the digging of main sewers. See *RIB* 2409.38*; P.T. Bidwell, *Roman Exeter: Fortress and Town* (1980), 87 note 6; M. Todd, *The South-West to A.D. 1000* (1987), 214–16. However, the possibility remains that the object is genuine but the inscription totally misunderstood.

RIB 2428. IRON TOOLS

In addition to four heavy tools from military contexts (Nos. 1, 3, 4 and 18) this chapter lists eight knives (including one probably imported example, (No. 17), three chisels, two *stili* and two awls, all stamped by their makers. Twelve of these objects were found in London, suggesting by the number of the names concerned (eight) that the city was a thriving centre of retail manufacture; Basilius, indeed, used three different stamps, and Martialis two. But the notable absence of the products of any of these smiths from well-excavated sites elsewhere in the province implies that the market was restricted and that there were other centres of local manufacture where products were not stamped. The remaining sites where stamped iron knives have been found are Colchester, Catterick and Chesterholm (one each). The facts strongly suggest that the knife found at Catterick (2431.17), stamped by Victor of Vienne, if correctly identified, was imported as a personal possession rather than as an object of trade.

The only heavy tools carrying stamps or graffiti came from the forts at Bar Hill (No. 1) and Newstead (two *dolabrae*, Nos. 3 and 18, and an axe, No. 4).

2428.1. Bar Hill, Strathclyde Region [Dunbartonshire]. Iron socketed hammer ($\frac{1}{2}$), length 135 mm, double-ended with one end blunted by use. Found in 1902 during excavation of a well in the *principia* of the Antonine Wall fort. Hunterian Museum, Glasgow. Reproduced from Robertson *et al*.

EE ix 1329. G. Macdonald and A. Park, *The Roman Forts on the Bar Hill* (1906), 113–14. A. Robertson, M. Scott and L. Keppie, *Bar Hill: A Roman Fort and its Finds* (1975), 100 No. 22 with fig. 33.22.

graffito on the upper face of the blunted end: >IIBVTI

> (centuria) (A)ebut(i)i
> 'Century of Aebutius'

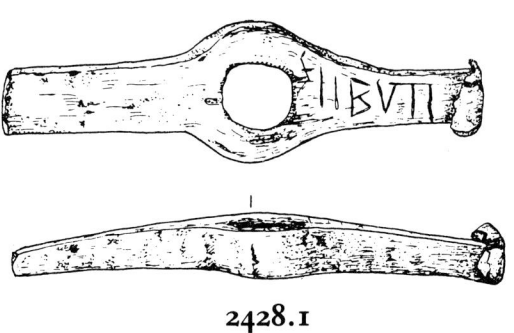

2428.1

2428.2. London (*Londinium*). Iron chisel ($\frac{2}{3}$), length 184 mm, width 19 mm, with a stamp running towards the tang. Found before 1892. Museum of London. Drawn by R.P.W., 1953.

EE vii 1163. Guildhall Museum *Cat*. (ed. 2, 1908), 53 No. 72. RCHM *Roman London* iii (1928), 176 No. 48.

stamped: APRILISF

> Aprilis f(ecit)
> 'Aprilis made (this)'

APRILISF 2428.2

2428.3. Newstead (*Trimontium*), Borders Region [Roxburghshire]. Iron mattock (*dolabra*) ($\frac{1}{1}$), length 425 mm, found in 1906 with *RIB* 2427.3 and 2428.4 during excavation of Pit XVI of Flavian date, in the South Annexe of the fort. National Museums of Scotland, Queen Street, Edinburgh. Drawn by R.G.C., 1936.

EE ix 1326. J. Curle, *Newstead* (1911), 279 with pl. LVII.3.

stamped on the upper surface: ATTICVS

ATTICVS 2428.3

2428.4. Ibid. Iron axe ($\frac{1}{1}$ and $\frac{1}{2}$), length 253 mm, found in 1906 with *RIB* 2427.3 and 2428.4 during excavation of Pit XVI of Flavian date, in the South Annexe of the fort. National Museums of Scotland, Queen Street, Edinburgh. Graffiti reproduced from Curle; stamp drawn by R.G.C., 1936.

EE ix 1327. J. Curle, *Newstead* (1911) 283 with fig. 41 and pl. LXI.4.

(a) stamped on the lower side of the square end (¹⁄₁):
L·G·R
L(uci) G(...) R(...)
'(Product) of Lucius G... R...'

(b) in punched dots along the upper edge (½):
⊃ BARRI | COMPITALICI
(centuria) Barri Compitalici
'(Property) of Compitalicius of the century of Barrus'

The name *Compitalicius* (from *Compitalia*) is unmatched, but *Competalis* (*CIL* v 1142) is also known: Kajanto, *Cognomina*, 220.

2428.4

2428.5. London (*Londinium*). Iron knife (¹⁄₁) with integral handle, length 132 mm. The inscription is divided by a small human figure. Found before 1923 in Moorgate Street. Museum of London. Drawn by R.G.C., 1923.

RCHM *Roman London* (1928), 175 No. 43. R.E.M. Wheeler, *London in Roman Times* (1930), 78 with fig. 19.2. Collingwood, *Antiq. J.* x (1930), 400; in Tenney Frank, *ESAR* iii, 94.

stamped in the centre of the blade:
.BΛƧ (figure) ILI.
[P(...)] *Basili (servus) [f(ecit)]*
'P(...), (slave) of Basilius, made (this).'

Compare *RIB* 2431.6 (with note) and 7–8.

2428.5

2428.6. Ibid. Iron knife (¼ and ²⁄₁), length 93 mm, with portion of wooden handle formerly surviving. The inscription is divided by a small human figure. Found before 1854 when it was in the Roach Smith collection. British Museum. Reproduced from Manning.

CIL vii 1298 b. Roach Smith, *Cat. London Antiquities* (1854), 79; *Roman London* (1859), 140 with pl. XXXVII.10. RCHM *Roman London* (1928), 175 No. 44. W.H. Manning, *Cat.* (1985), 110 No. Q4 with pl. 53, Q4.

stamped on the blade: P. BΛS (figure) ILIF
P(...) Basili (servus) f(ecit)
'P(...), (slave) of Basilius, made (this).'

Compare *RIB* 2431.5 and 7–8. The four stamps differ in detail, but evidently carried the same text; this is the only one to be complete. The expansion of P. BASILI is unclear: it could be the maker's abbreviated nomen and cognomen (e.g. *Pompeius Basilides*), but it seems best to follow R.G.C. in taking it to refer to the slave P(...) (not necessarily *Publius*) of a manufacturer called Basilius.

2428.6

2428.7. Ibid. Iron knife (¹⁄₁), length 128 mm, with a rivet surviving at the end of the tang. The inscription is divided by a small human figure. Found before 1929 at Lothbury. Museum of London. Drawn by R.G.C., 1929.

R.E.M. Wheeler, *London in Roman Times* (1930), 78.

stamped on the blade: PBΛ (figure) SILIF
P(...) Basili (servus) f(ecit)
'P(...), (slave) of Basilius, made (this).'

Compare *RIB* 2421.5–6 (with note) and 8.

2428.7

2428.8. London (*Londinium*). Iron knife (¼ and ²⁄₁), length 100 mm, with ring handle similar to *RIB* 2428.14 but smaller. Found before 1930 in the Walbrook valley near the Mansion House. Museum of London. Drawn by S.S.F. from a rubbing by R.P.W.

R.E.M. Wheeler, *London in Roman Times* (1930), 79 with pl. XXXVI.1.

stamped on the blade: perhaps BASILIF

Compare *RIB* 2428.5–7.

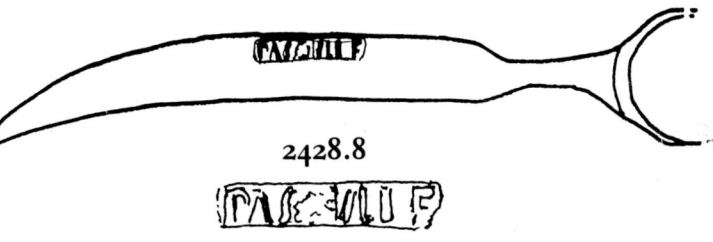

2428.8

2428.10

2428.9. Ibid. Iron *stilus* ($\frac{1}{1}$), length 143 mm, diameter 8 mm, found in 1929 at the Midland Bank site in Princes Street, Poultry. Museum of London. Drawn by R.P.W., 1971.

Britannia iii (1972), 359 No. 31. R.E.M. Wheeler, *London in Roman Times* (1930), 58 No. 10 with fig. 10 (without reading).

stamped near the butt and reading towards it:
  BONOS·FE
  Bonos(us) fe(cit)
  'Bonosus made (this).'

BONOS·FE
2428.9

2428.10. Colchester (*Camulodunum*), Essex. Iron knife ($\frac{1}{1}$ and $\frac{2}{1}$), length 120 mm, width 15 mm, with broken remains of the bronze handle riveted on either side at one end. Colchester Museum. Drawn by R.G.C.

stamped on the blade: LVCCVSF
  Luccus f(ecit)
  'Luccus made (this).'

For the Celtic name *Luccus* compare the Dobunnian *Lucco* (*CIL* xiv 49) and *Tab. Sulis* 30, *Lucillus Lucciani*.

2428.11. Corbridge (? *Coria*), Northumberland. Iron quarry-wedge ($\frac{1}{2}$), length 178 mm, maximum width 51 mm, thickness 25.5 mm. Found in c. 1936. Corbridge Museum. Drawn by R.P.W., 1945.

JRS xxxvi (1946), 148 No. 5. Wright, *PSAN*[4] x (1945), 270.

inscribed: MΛ or ΛM

2428.12. London (*Londinium*). Iron chisel ($\frac{2}{1}$), length 171.5 mm including a tang of 47.5 mm, found in 1955 in the bed of the Walbrook on the Bucklersbury House site. Museum of London. Drawn by R.P.W., 1956.

JRS xlvi (1956), 149 No. 17.

stamped: M̂ARTIAL
  Martial(is)
  '(Product) of Martialis.'

M̂ARTIAL
2428.12

2428.13. Ibid. Carpenter's iron paring chisel ($\frac{1}{3}$ and $\frac{1}{1}$), length 228.5 mm, in section 22 by 22 mm, found in or shortly before 1934 in the bed of the Walbrook. British Museum. Reproduced from Manning.

JRS xlv (1955), 148 No. 17. W.H. Manning, *Cat.*, 21–2 No. B25 with pl. 10, B25.

stamped: M̂ARTALISF
  Mart(i)alis f(ecit)
  'Martialis made (this).'

M̂AENALIS.F, R.P.W., *JRS*. M̂ARTIALIS, R.P.W., Manning.

I seems to have been omitted in error, but it may have been ligatured above T (whence Mart(i)alis), R.S.O.T.

2428.11

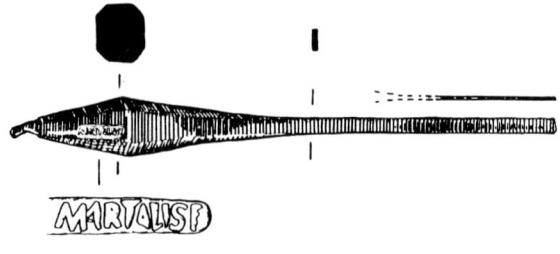

2428.13

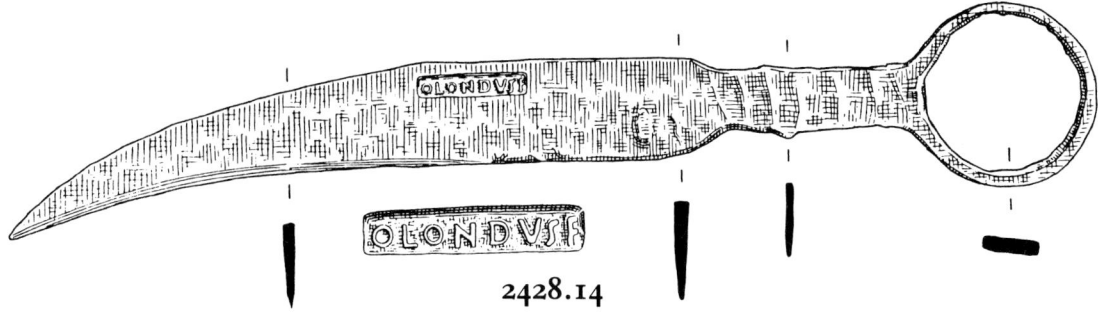

2428.14

2428.14. Ibid. Iron knife or razor ($\frac{1}{1}$ and $\frac{2}{1}$), length 150 mm, with ring-handle. Found before 1842. British Museum. Reproduced from Manning.

CIL vii 1298 a. Roach Smith, *Arch.* xxix (1842), 270; *Cat.* (1854), 73 No. 326; *Roman London* (1859), 140 with pl. XXXVII.9. RCHM, *Roman London* (1928), 175 No. 45. W.H. Manning, *Cat.* (1985), 111 No. Q11 with pl. 53 Q.11.

stamped on the blade: OLONDVS·F

Olondus f(ecit)

'Olondus made (this)'

The name, presumably Celtic, seems to be otherwise unattested. Mócsy, *Nomenclator*, cites the nomen *Olondius* in Gallia Narbonensis, but perhaps by confusion with *Mars Olloudius* (*CIL* xii 166).

2428.15. Ibid. Iron *stilus* ($\frac{1}{3}$ and $\frac{2}{1}$), length 142 mm, found in 1934 in the bed of the Walbrook. British Museum. Reproduced from Manning.

JRS xlix (1959), 137 No. 10. Smith, *BMQ* ix (1934–5), 96 with pl. XXXI.7. BM *Guide Rom. Brit.* (1951), 48 No. 3 with fig. 22.3. W.H. Manning, *Cat.* (1985), 86 No. N7 with pl. 35.N7.

stamped on the shaft below the eraser: REGNF

Reg(i)n(us) f(ecit)

'Reginus made (this).'

The name *Reginus* is frequent in *CIL* xiii and is presumably Celtic; compare the Catuvellaunian *Regina* (*RIB* 1065).

2428.15

2428.16. Ibid. Leatherworker's iron awl ($\frac{1}{1}$), length 136 mm, of Manning's Type 2 with a diamond-shaped head (here stamped), having a small tang at the top and a long tapering point. Found before 1923 at London Wall. Museum of London. Drawn by R.G.C., 1923.

RCHM *Roman London* (1928), 175 No. 46. R.E.M. Wheeler, *London in Roman Times* (1930), 76 with pl. XXXII 10. W.H. Manning, *Cat.* (1985), 40.

stamped on the head: TITVLI M

Tituli m(anu)

'By the hand of Titulus.'

2428.16

Titulus is probably a variant of the common cognomen *Titullus*.

2428.17. Catterick (*Cataractonium*), North Yorkshire. Iron knife-blade ($\frac{1}{1}$ and $\frac{2}{1}$), length 55.5 mm, width 27 mm, with tang 36.5 mm long, found in 1958 in Building VII.5. Yorkshire Museum, York. Drawn by S.S.F. from a rubbing by R.P.W.

JRS lix (1969), 240 No. 29.

stamp: VICTORV·F

Victor V(iennae) f(ecit)

'Victor of Vienne made (this).'

V(IENNAE) is expanded by analogy with *CIL* xii 5701.36, 37 and 54, lead pipes at Vienne carrying a personal name followed by VF. That V indicates the place-name is confirmed by *CIL* xii 5701.7 inscribed AREL(ATE)F. The suggestion, at first surprising, that the knife is an import is strengthened by the fact that no knives stamped by manufacturers working in Britain carry a similar indication of origin (see *RIB* 2428.5–8, 10, 14).

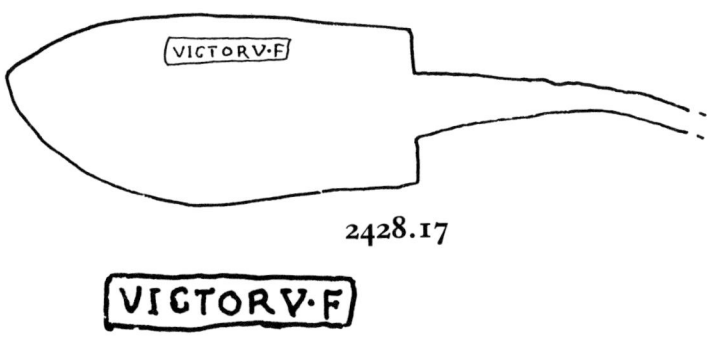

2428.17

2428.18. Newstead (*Trimontium*), Borders Region [Roxburghshire]. Iron *dolabra* (mattock) ($\frac{1}{1}$), length 336 mm, found in 1908 during excavation of Pit LXI, of Flavian date, to the north of the fort. National Museums of Scotland, Queen Street, Edinburgh. Drawn by R.P.W., 1956.

J. Curle, *Newstead* (1911), 278 with pl. LVII.1 (without reading).

deep semicircular stamp on the lower surface of the axe blade: VINDISSI
   '(Product) of Vindissus'

This Celtic name is not recorded by Holder, but is clearly cognate with *Vindius* (etc).

2428.18

2428.19. Chesterholm (*Vindolanda*), Northumberland. Part of the blade of an iron knife or razor ($\frac{2}{1}$), length 73 mm, width 10 mm, thickness up to 2 mm, found in 1976 in the *vicus* of the fort in a context dated *c.* A.D. 115/25. Vindolanda Museum. Drawn by R.S.O.T., 1990.

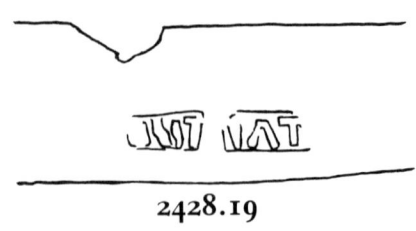

2428.19

Britannia ix (1978), 481 No. 64.

stamped in two panels:
[. . .] RITIAT[. . .]

2428.20. London (*Londinium*). Leatherworker's iron awl ($\frac{1}{1}$), length 171 mm, of Manning's Type 3 with a diamond-shaped head and no tang. Found before 1923 in Moorgate. Museum of London. Drawn by R.P.W., 1957.

RCHM *Roman London* (1928) 176 No. 47. R.E.M. Wheeler, *London in Roman Times* (1930), 76 with pl. XXXII.11. For the type see W.H. Manning, *Cat.* (1985), 40.

stamped on the head: [. . .]INI.[. . .]

The stamp has been struck twice.

2428.20

RIB 2429. BRONZE BALDRIC- AND BELT-FITTINGS

Except perhaps for 2429.10, which is from Brettenham, Norfolk, a site unlikely to have a military connection, all the objects listed in this chapter may be classified as pieces of military equipment, despite the discovery of three of them at civitas-capitals and one at a temple-site. Nine objects (2429. 1–9) are from the decoration of the baldric (*balteus*), a leather strap from which the sword was suspended, and which hung diagonally across the chest from the shoulder. All are of a rare, probably third-century, type, only 16 other examples of which are attested (see note to *RIB* 2429.1). Seven objects (2429. 11–17) are metal fittings of the belt (*cingulum*), and these too are also probably of third-century date.

2429.1. High Rochester (*Bremenium*), Northumberland. Bronze circular openwork attachment (¼) from a *balteus* (baldric), diameter 66.5 mm, with central eagle perched on a thunderbolt over a globe, and openwork letters in an outer circle; there is a stud for attachment at the back. Found in 1852. Alnwick Castle. Drawn by R.P.W., 1945.

CIL vii 1290. *EE* ix 1366 a. Bruce, *Wall* (ed. 2, 1853), 463; *LS* 578. Haverfield, *Arch. J.* xlix (1892), fig. facing p. 183; *PSAN*³ iv (1910), 225.

cast openwork letters: OPTIMEMAXIMECON
  Optime Maxime con(serva)
  'Best (and) Greatest, preserve'

Understand *Iuppiter*.

In a complete specimen the legend was continued on a separate fitting composed of a rectangular and a curved triangular part hinged together, with the words NVMERVM OMNIVM MILITANTIVM ('the number of all those serving') (see *RIB* 2429.7). Although formerly considered (Collingwood and Richmond, *The Archaeology of Roman Britain* (1969), 309) to be pendants for streamers of standards, or (Jacobi, *Saalburg Jahrb.* i (1910), 48) as part of a horse-trapping, Oldenstein has shown (*BRGK* lvii (1976), 226–34) that these objects were worn on the military *balteus* or baldric: see also Allason-Jones, *Saalburg Jahrb.* xlii (1986), 68–9).

In addition to *RIB* 2429. 1–8, examples have been found at three forts on the Upper German *limes* (Zugmantel (five), Saalburg (three) and Osterburken: see Oldenstein, Nos. 1092–1101); at Königshofen near Strasbourg (R. Forrer, *Strasbourg-Argentorate* ii (1927), 554–6 with Taf. 78A); at Weingarten bei Euskirchen (Klein, *BJ* xc (1891), 29–30 with fig. 8); at Lauriacum (RLÖ xiii (1919), 263 Abb. 102; Gahais, *BJ* cxlii (1937), 354–5 with Abb. 1 b); at Carnuntum (Abramić, *Osterreichische Jahreshefte* xii (1900), Abb. 88); St. Valentin bei Albing (Abramić, Abb. 87); Mainz (*ORL* B No. 8 (Zugmantel), 86 Abb. 9); and at Thamusida in Morocco (Ruhlmann, *Académie des*

2429.1

Inscriptions et Belles-Lettres (1935), 67; J.P. Callu *et al.*, *Thamusida* (1965), pl. 133. 1–2).

Allason-Jones (loc. cit.) shows that many examples were products of a single workshop (whether in Britain or on the Continent), and that flaws in the casting, together with the close-spacing of the letters EC, suggest the use of a single mould – at least for the examples from Carlisle (*RIB* 2429.2), High Rochester and (probably) Thamusida.

The legends suggest that those objects were a special issue, perhaps on the occasion of a campaign, rather than normal items of infantry equipment, and their comparative rarity makes it likely that they were worn only perhaps by officers. What dating evidence there is (Allason-Jones, op. cit., 69) suggests a context in the first half of the third century, a period when troops from Britain and Germany are known to have taken part together in at least two expeditions (*CIL* iii 3228; xiii 6780). As for the example from Thamusida, it may be explained by a personal transfer to the fort there, which was occupied until the second half of the third century.

See now also a new study by L. Petculescu of examples from Dacia in V.A. Maxfield and M.J. Dobson, *Roman Frontier Studies 1989* (1991), 392–6.

2429.2. Carlisle (*Luguvalium*), Cumbria [Cumberland]. Bronze circular openwork attachment ($\frac{1}{1}$) from a *balteus* (baldric), as *RIB* 2429.1, *q.v.* for details and discussion. Found in 1983 by metal-detector on the south bank of the river Eden, some yards east of Stanwix Bridge, in an area named the Swifts. Tullie House Museum, Carlisle. Reproduced from Allason-Jones.

Allason-Jones, *Saalburg Jahrb.* xlii (1986), 68–9 with figs. 1–2.

cast openwork letters: OPTIMEMAXIMECON
  Optime Maxime, con(serva)
  'Best (and) Greatest, preserve'

Understand *Iuppiter*.

See note to *RIB* 2429.1.

2429.3. Silchester (*Calleva*), Hampshire. Bronze circular openwork attachment ($\frac{1}{1}$) from a *balteus* (baldric), as *RIB* 2429.1, *q.v.* for details and discussion. Found in 1891 during excavation of Pit V in Insula III. Reading Museum. Drawn by R.P.W., 1951.

EE ix 1316 b. Haverfield, *Arch. J.* xlix (1892), 182 with fig. Fox, *Arch.* liii (1892), 268 (repr. p.6) with fig. G.C. Boon, *Roman Silchester* (1957), 90 with fig. 11.1; *Silchester, The Roman Town of Calleva* (1974), 66 with fig. 8.3.

cast openwork letters: OPTIME[. . .]IMECON
  Optime [Max]ime con(serva)
  'Best (and) Greatest, preserve'

Understand *Iuppiter*.

See note to *RIB* 2429.1.

2429.3

2429.4. Uley, Gloucestershire. Part of a bronze circular openwork attachment ($\frac{1}{1}$) from a *balteus* (baldric), similar to *RIB* 2429.1, *q.v.* for details and discussion. Diameter originally 60 mm, thickness 4 mm. Found in 1977 during excavation of demolition-debris south of Building I at the temple site on West Hill. British Museum. Drawn by Joanna Richards.

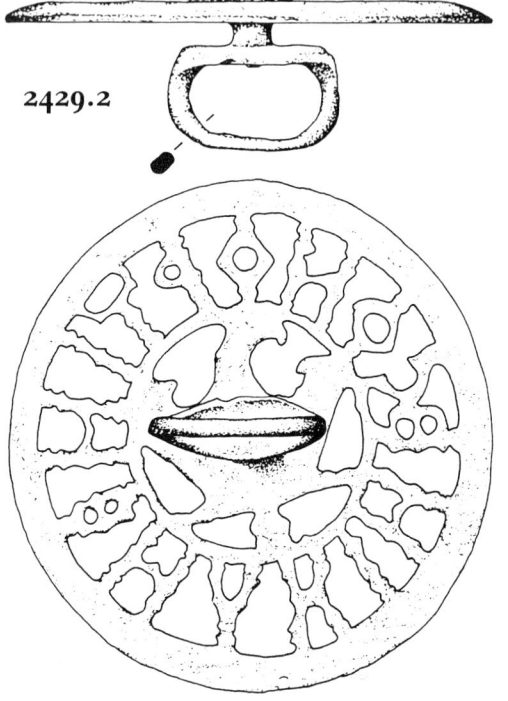

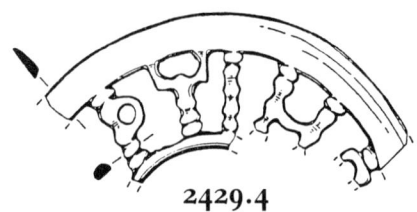

2429.4

Britannia x (1979), 349 No. 24.

cast openwork letters: [.]PTIM[. . . . .]
   [O]ptim[e Maxime con(serva)]
   'Best (and) Greatest, preserve'

Understand *Iuppiter*.

See note to *RIB* 2429.1.

2429.5. Corbridge (? *Coria*), Northumberland. Part of a bronze circular openwork attachment ($\frac{1}{1}$) from a *balteus* (baldric), as *RIB* 2429.1, *qv* for details and discussion. Found in 1910 during excavations at Site XI. Corbridge Museum. Drawn by R.P.W., 1945.

EE ix 1316 d. Haverfield, *Arch. Ael.*³ vii (1911), 178 (repr. p. 36) with pl. IV.8.

cast openwork letters: [.]PTI[. . . . .]N
   [O]pti[me Maxime co]n(serva)
   'Best (and) Greatest, preserve'

Understand *Iuppiter*.

See note to *RIB* 2429.1.

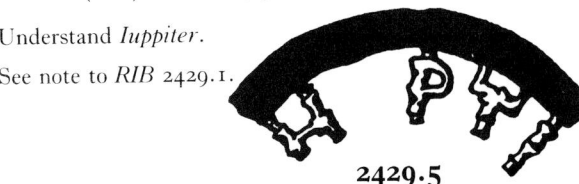

2429.5

2429.6. York (*Eboracum*). Central portion of a bronze circular openwork attachment ($\frac{1}{1}$) from a *balteus* (baldric), as *RIB* 2429.1, *q.v.* for details and discussion. Found before 1877. Yorkshire Museum, York. Drawn by S.S.F. from a photograph. See also PL. XV A.

EE vii 1161; ix 1316 c. Haverfield, *Arch. J.* xlvii (1890), 260, No. 59; *PSAN*³ iv (1910), 225.

cast openwork letters: [. . .] I [. .] M [. . .]
   [Opt]i[me] M[axime con(serva)]
   'Best (and) Greatest, preserve'

Understand *Iuppiter*.

See note to *RIB* 2429.1.

This example is from a mould different from that of *RIB* 2429.1–3.

2429.7. Aldborough (*Isurium*), North Yorkshire. Two fragments from the lower part of a bronze openwork attachment ($\frac{1}{1}$), once hinged together, from a *balteus* (baldric) of the type described under *RIB* 2429.1, *q.v.* for details and discussion. Found before 1910. Aldborough Museum. Drawn by R.P.W., 1952. See also PL. XV B.

EE ix 1317 a, b. Haverfield, *Arch. Ael.*³ vii (1911), 179 (repr. p. 37) with fig. 10 a.

cast openwork letters:
   (a) [. . .]OMNI|VM
   (b) MILIT|ANTI|VM
   [numerum] | omni|um | milit|anti|um

The first part of the text can be restored from an example found at Zugmantel (Oldenstein, *BRGK* lvii (1976), Taf. 83 No. 1099).

2429.6

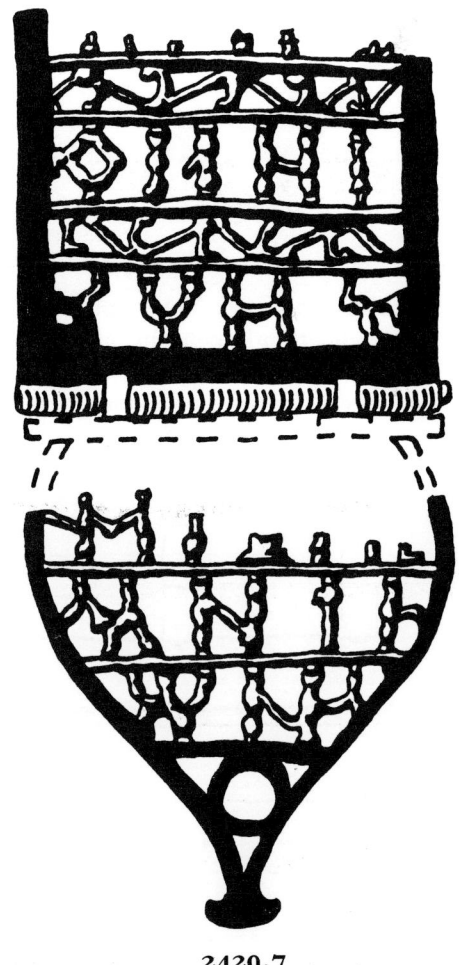

2429.7

2429.8. Ibid. Fragment of the bottom portion of a bronze openwork attachment ($\frac{1}{1}$) from a *balteus* (baldric). See *RIB* 2429.7 and note to 2429.1. Found before 1910. Aldborough Museum. Drawn by R.P.W., 1952. See also PL. XV B.

EE ix 1317 c. Haverfield, *Arch. Ael.*³ vii (1911), 179 (repr. p. 37) with fig. 10 a.

cast openwork letters: MILIT|AN[. .]|V[.]
 milit|an[ti]|u[m]
 'of those serving'

See note to *RIB* 2429.1.

2429.9. Corbridge (? *Coria*), Northumberland. Heart-shaped bronze openwork pendant or terminal ($\frac{1}{1}$), possibly of the type represented by *RIB* 2429.7 but with a different text. Found in 1909 during excavations. Corbridge Museum. Drawn by R.P.W.

EE ix 1317 d. Haverfield, *Arch. Ael.*³ vii (1911), 175–9 (repr. p. 37) with fig. 9 a.

cast openwork letters: OMNIA | VOS
 omnia vos
 'everything . . . you'

The earlier part of the text was presumably on a separate missing plate.

2429.10. Brettenham, Norfolk. Part of a bronze belt ($\frac{2}{3}$), formed of hinged rectangular plates 3 mm thick and ranging in size from 47 by 33 mm to 41 by 29 mm; five conjoining plates survive from an estimated twenty-four. Each originally carried a silver disc on the other side. Found in 1979 by metal-detector at the Roman settlement in Money Field. In private possession. Drawn by A.K. Gregory.

Britannia xi (1980), 415 No. 55 with fig. 27. Gregory, *Norfolk Arch.* xxxvii.3 (1980), 343–5 with fig.

incised capitals: [. . .]SECVN[. . .]
 [. . .] *Secun[d. . .]*

The owner's name was *Secundus* or possibly *Secundinus*, his cognomen being preceded by nomen and (?) praenomen, now lost.

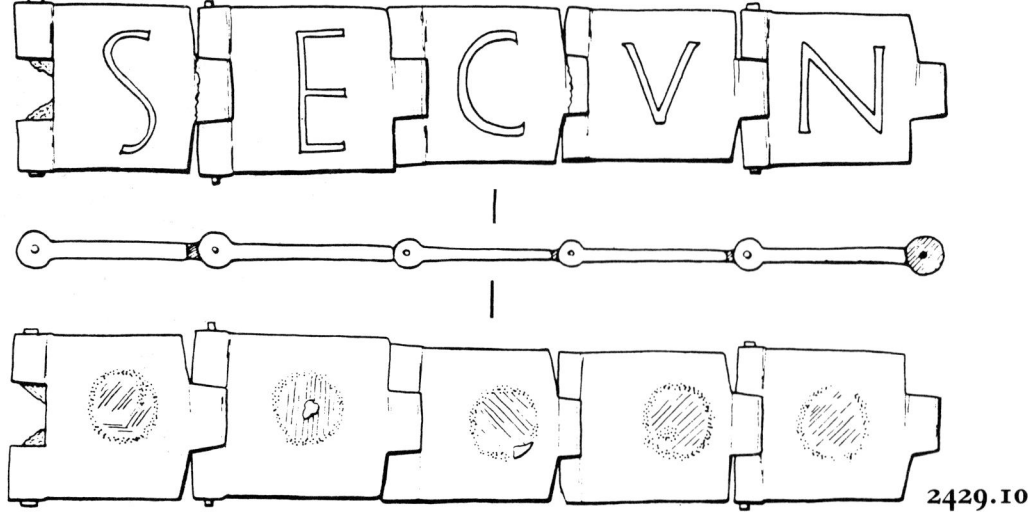

2429.11. Brampton, Cumbria [Cumberland]. Bronze openwork plate ($\frac{1}{1}$), perhaps for a belt, with a stud at each end of the back. Found before 1789. Formerly at Lazonby Hall; present whereabouts unknown. Reproduced from Bruce.

Rooke, *Arch.* ix (1789), 222 with fig. (g). Hutchinson, *Cumb.* i (1794), 125 note. Bruce *LS* 453.

cast openwork letters: IOVIS
    'of Jupiter'

2429.11

2429.12. Kirkby Thore (*Bravoniacum*), Cumbria [Westmorland]. Part of a bronze openwork plate ($\frac{2}{3}$), perhaps for a belt, with one stud at the back surviving. Found in 1838 when the bridge was rebuilt at Kirkby Thore and in 1951 bequeathed by Miss E. Cumpston to Tullie House Museum, Carlisle. Drawn by R.P.W., 1952.

JRS xliii (1953), 130 No. 12.

cast openwork letters: SERV.[. . .]
    Perhaps *serv[a]* or, if this plate is one of a series, [. . .con]serv[a. . .]
    'Preserve'

SERVI, R.P.W., *JRS*

The text is presumably similar to *RIB* 2429.1–6, but is not from a similar circular attachment.

2429.12

2429.13. South Shields (*Arbeia*), Tyne and Wear [Durham]. Bronze strap- or belt-terminal ($\frac{1}{1}$) of triangular cross-section now in two pieces, length 61 mm. The loop at the end is broken; for the shape of this see *RIB* 2429.14. Found in 1880 at the fort. Museum of Antiquities, Newcastle upon Tyne. Drawn by R.P.W., 1941.

EE vii 1169. Blair, *JBAA*[1] xxxvi (1880), 237. Lewis, *P. Camb. Antiq. Soc.* iv (1876–80), 340 with fig. Watkin, *Arch. J.* xxxviii (1881), 280. Anon., *PSAN*[2] i (1882–4), 331. Hodgkin, *PSAN*[2] iv (1891), 291 with fig. on p. iii. Bruce, *Arch. Ael.*[2] x (1885), 260 with fig. Anon., *Arch. Ael.*[3] xvii (1920), 12. Cowen and Richmond, *Arch. Ael.*[4] xii (1935), 325 with fig. 2. L. Allason-Jones and R. Miket, *Cat* (1984), 214 No. 3.726 with fig.

engraved letters filled alternately with red and green enamel: VTERE crescent | FELIX crescent
    'Good luck to the user'

Compare *RIB* 2429.14–16. Cowen and Richmond show that the letters and crescents closely resemble those of the Rudge Cup (*RIB* 2415.53) and suggest the same workshop.

See now also a new study of examples from Dacia by L. Petculescu in V.A. Maxfield and M.J. Dobson, *Roman Frontier Studies 1989* (1991), 392–6.

2429.13

2429.14. Ibid. Bronze strap- or belt-end ($\frac{1}{1}$) of triangular cross-section, with a flattened loop at one end. Found before 1935 at the fort. Museum of Antiquities, Newcastle upon Tyne. Drawn by R.P.W., 1941.

Cowen and Richmond, *Arch. Ael.*[4] xii (1935), 325 with fig. 2. L. Allason-Jones and R. Miket, *Cat.* (1984), 214 No. 3.726.

engraved letters filled alternately with red and green enamel: VTER[.]|FELI[.]
    uter[e] feli[x]
    'Good luck to the user'

See note to *RIB* 2429.13.

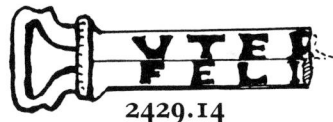

2429.14

2429.15. Chester (*Deva*). Bronze strap- or belt-terminal ($\frac{1}{1}$), probably from the same mould as *RIB* 2429.13–14, found in 1898 in Eastgate Street North, on the west side of Godstall Lane. Grosvenor Museum, Chester. Drawn by R.P.W., 1954.

EE ix 1318 a. Taylor, *PSA*[2] xviii (1899–1901), 93. Newstead, *Reliquary*[3] vi (1900), 112. Haverfield, *Cat.* = *JCAS* vii (1900), 89 No. 205. Newstead, *JCAS* viii (1902), 85 with fig.

engraved letters filled alternately with red and green enamel: VTER[.]|FELI[.]
    uter[e] feli[x]
    'Good luck to the user'

See note to *RIB* 2429.13.

2429.15

2429.16. Chesters (*Cilurnum*), Northumberland. Part of an openwork bronze belt-plate (1/1), length 54 mm, with a stud having a flat head for attachment at the back. Found in 1895. Chesters Museum. Drawn by R.P.W., 1943. See also PL. XV C.

EE ix 1318 c. Anon., *PSAN*² vii (1895–6), 234. Budge, *Cat.* (1903), 375, No. 627.

openwork cast letters: VTER
 uter(e felix)
 'Good luck to the user'

The text was probably continued by a second plate, now lost. The style of lettering closely resembles that of *RIB* 2429.1–9.

2429.17

2429.16

2429.17. Ibid. Thin pierced bronze belt-plate (1/2) with rivet-holes at the two surviving corners, found in or before 1891. Chesters Museum. Drawn by R.P.W., 1946. See also PL. XV C.

EE ix 1318 b. Hodgkin, *PSAN*² iv (1891), 291 with fig. Budge, *Cat.* (1903), 375 No. 628.

openwork cut letters: VTE[. . .]
 ute[re felix]
 'Good luck to the user'

'The plate is pierced, not cast', R.G.C., 1926.

FALSVM

2429.18.* Mancetter (*Manduessedum*), Warwickshire. Bronze belt-buckle of fourth-century type with attached belt-plate, on which are two lines of what appear to be letters, cut with a chisel and inverted with respect to each other; they are, however, probably ornamental rather than epigraphic. Found unstratified in 1976. In private possession. Drawn by Diana Webster.

Britannia ix (1978), 481 No. 68.

cut with a chisel, two lines mutually inverted:
 ΛIIVMVIIΛ
 VIIΛWΛIIV

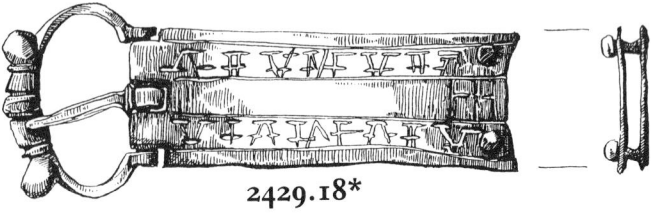

2429.18*

RIB 2430. VOTIVE OBJECTS AND AN AMULET IN GOLD

The objects described in this chapter belong to a class hitherto classified under Monumental Inscriptions, presumably because they were usually affixed to the walls of temples; compare *RIB* 436, a gold amulet from Caernarvon; 706, a gold amulet from York; and 1077, a gold plaque from Lanchester. It has been thought more logical, however, to include them here among moveable objects, together with comparable votive plaques in Silver (*RIB* 2431) and Bronze (*RIB* 2432), rather than to retain them for eventual publication in *RIB* iii.

2430.1. Stonea, Cambridgeshire. Gold plaque ($\frac{2}{1}$) in the form of a leaf or feather, width of base 21 mm, height 35 mm, formerly rolled up, found in 1979 by metal detector. British Museum. Reproduced from Johns.

Britannia xi (1980) 403–4 No. 2. Johns, *Britannia* xii (1981), 101–3 with fig. 10.1; Hassall ibid., 104.

repoussé letters: DEΛ | MIR | VΛD
 Probably *Dea(e) Mi(ne)rva(e) d(onum))*
 'A gift to the goddess Minerva'

2430.1

Additional vertical strokes at the end of lines 1 and 2 are taken by Hassall, loc. cit., to be vestiges of a bungled attempt to define the right-hand margin of the panel.

2430.2. Wood Eaton, Islip, Oxfordshire. Fragment of an amulet in gold leaf ($\frac{1}{1}$), 25 by 19 mm, formerly rolled up, found in or before 1968 at the site of the temple. On loan to the Ashmolean Museum, Oxford. Drawn by R.P.W., 1969.

Britannia i (1970), 305 No. 1, with fig. 11.

incised: [...] Θ Θ [...] | [...]Δ ΟΝΛ [...] |
 [...] Λ ΔΟΝΛΕΜ [...] | [...] Θ ΥΙSSSS
 ΤΤΤ [...] | [...] Θ EEEE [...] | [...].
 [...]

2430.2

Adona(i)e, the vocative of the Hebrew word for 'Lord' occurs twice (compare *RIB* 436), and certain Greek letters have been repeated up to four times for magical effect.

For two votive bronze plaques from this site see *RIB* 236, 237.

2430.3. Chesterton (*Durobrivae*), Cambridgeshire [Huntingdonshire]. Gold disc ($\frac{1}{1}$), diameter 49 mm, with a central hole for attachment, found in 1975 within the Roman town as part of a hoard revealed by ploughing. The remainder of the hoard consisted of twenty-seven silver objects including four inscribed silver vessels (*RIB* 2414.1–4) out of a total of nine, and nine inscribed silver plaques (*RIB* 2431.1 and 4–11) out of a total of seventeen. British Museum. Drawn by S.S.F. from a photograph.

Britannia vii (1976) 386 No. 34 with pl. XXXIII C. K.S. Painter, *The Water Newton Early Christian Silver* (1977), 17 No. 11 with pl. 11.

in relief: A X͡P ω
 'Alpha Chi-Rho Omega'

The omega is inverted.

2430.3

RIB 2431. VOTIVE OBJECTS IN SILVER

All but one of the objects in this chapter are triangular plaques with leaf-decoration. Presumably because these were usually affixed to the walls of temples, they have been included hitherto among Monumental Inscriptions and some examples were published in *RIB* i. It has been thought more logical, however, to include them here among moveable objects, together with comparable votive plaques in Gold (*RIB* 2430) and Bronze (*RIB* 2432), rather than to retain them for eventual publication in *RIB* iii.

Some examples carry suspension-holes, but orientation could be variable; the direction of the inscriptions shows that the 'tip' of the leaf could sometimes be at the top, sometimes at the bottom. For six other silver votive leaf-decorated plaques see *RIB* 215, 218–220 and 986–7, and for one in bronze see *RIB* 2432.4. For two silver dedicatory tablets see *RIB* 216 and 582. See also the discussion of silver plaques in J.M.C. Toynbee, *Art in Britain under the Romans* (1964), 328–31, and compare the Hagenbach hoard, which contained 128 plaques (Landesmuseum Trier, *Trier Kaiserresidenz und Bischofssitz* (1984), 84–6 with pls.).

2431.1. Chesterton (*Durobrivae*), Cambridgeshire [Huntingdonshire]. Part of a triangular silver votive plaque (⅔), length 87 mm, width 100 mm, with embossed decoration. Above the roundel (diameter 55 mm) is a small hole pierced from the front for suspension. Found in 1975 within the Roman walled town after ploughing which revealed a hoard of one gold roundel (*RIB* 2430.3) and twenty-seven silver objects. Of the nine silver vessels four were inscribed (*RIB* 2414.1–4) as were nine of the seventeen plaques (2431.1 and 4–11). British Museum. Drawn by P.C. Compton.

Britannia vii (1976), 386 No. 35; viii (1977), 448 corrigendum (e). K.S. Painter, *Rivista di Archeologia Cristiana* li (1975), 336–8 with fig. 10; *The Water Newton Early Christian Silver* (1977), 17 No. 12 with fig. 8 and pl. 12.

(a) in relief below the top edge:
[. . .]IAMCILLAVOTVMQVO[. . .]|[. . .?]
PROMISITCONPLEVIT[. . .]
(?) *Iamcilla votum quo[d] | promisit conplevit*
(?) 'Iamcilla fulfilled the vow that she promised'

ANICILLA, Painter (as drawing). IAMCILLA, R.P.W.

(b) in relief in the roundel : ω X͡P A
'Omega Chi-Rho Alpha'

The silversmith reversed Q and one N and inverted ω in error as a result of embossing the letters from behind.

The initial I (not drawn) depends on R.P.W.'s autopsy (*Britannia* vii). A personal name *Iamcilla* is unknown, and a name in *-amcus*, of which it would be a diminutive, is improbable, but compare *Iamius* (*CIL* ii 767). Painter's *Anicilla* (compare *CIL* ii 3361), presumably a diminutive of *Anicius*, is plausible but faces two objections: the initial letter read by R.P.W., and the difficulty of reading M as N͡I.

The site lies in Chesterton, not Water Newton, parish, but is often referred to under the latter name.

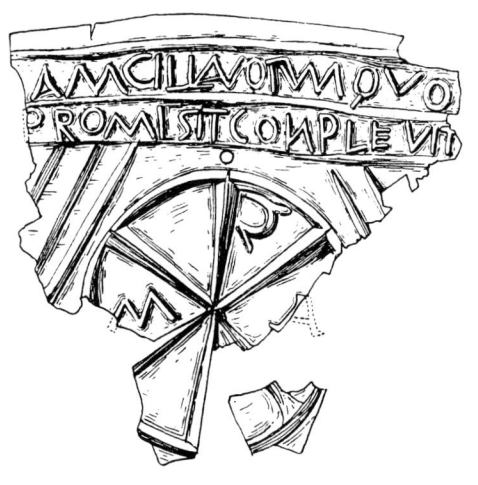

2431.1

2431.2. Chesterholm (*Vindolanda*), Northumberland. Silver pendant in the form of a crescent (¹⁄₁), width 27 mm, height 20 mm, thickness 1 mm, found in 1970 above the flagstones on Site XXII in the *vicus*. Vindolanda Museum. Drawn by S.S.F. from a draft by R.P.W., 1971.

Britannia ii (1971), 291 No. 12.

incised: DEO MAPONO
  deo Mapono
  'To the god Maponus'

The final letter has corroded.

2431.2

2431.3. Thistleton, Leicestershire [Rutland]. Part of a silver votive plaque (¹⁄₁ and ²⁄₁), 46 by 142 mm, thickness 0.5 mm, found in 1961 during excavation of an aisled temple. In store with English Heritage: destined for Oakham Museum. Drawn by A. Maclaren, 1990.

JRS lii (1962), 192 No. 6. For the site see S.S. Frere and J.K. St. Joseph, *Roman Britain from the Air* (1983), 222–3.

in dotted letters punched from the back within an incised ansate panel:
DE·VE|TE·MO|CVX̣|[.]O|MA·PA
  De(o) Vete(ri) Mocux[s]oma pa(ngit)
  'To the god Veteris Mocuxsoma affixes (this)'

Possibly DE·VE|TERI 1–2 | CV.[.]O|MA·FA, *de(o) Veteri [ ]cu[ ]oma fa(cit)*, R.S.O.T. As text, R.P.W.

The back of the plaque is illustrated because after discovery the object was glued face-downwards to a support. The drawing of the inscription itself has accordingly been reversed. The text was read by R.P.W. in 1961 before this conservation occurred.

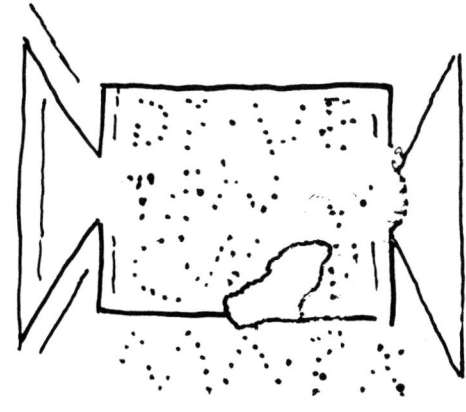

2431.3

2431.4–11. Chesterton (*Durobrivae*), Cambridgeshire [Huntingdonshire]. Eight triangular silver votive plaques (¼), found in 1975 with *RIB* 2431.1, *q.v.* for details. British Museum. Drawn by S.S.F. from photographs.

Britannia vii (1976), 389 No. 34. K.S. Painter, *Rivista di Archeologia Cristiana* li (1975), 336–8; *The Water Newton Early Christian Silver* (1977) (hereafter *Water Newton*).

4. length 80 mm, width 64 mm, with embossed leaf-decoration in the upper part and a roundel demarcated only by a line incised in the back. In the lower corners are two fronds; beaded borders accompany the edges of the plaque near the roundel.

   Water Newton, 19 No. 22 with pl. 22.

   embossed within the roundel: A X͡P ω
   'Alpha Chi-Rho Omega'

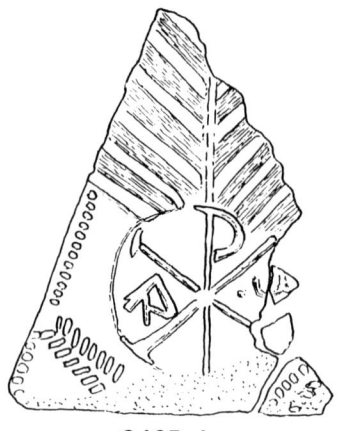

2431.4

5. length 49 mm, width 35 mm, diameter of roundel 25 mm.

   Water Newton, 19 No. 19 with pl. 19.

   embossed within the roundel: A X͡P ω
   'Alpha Chi-Rho Omega'

2431.5

6. length 60 mm, width 45 mm, diameter of roundel 28 mm. A border of small beads accompanies the edges of the plaque near the roundel, in which the Chi-Rho is in intaglio but the Alpha and Omega are in relief.

   Water Newton, 19 No. 21 with pl. 21.

   inscribed within the roundel: A X͡P ω
   'Alpha Chi-Rho Omega'

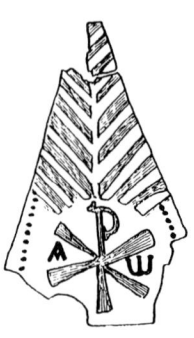

2431.6

7. length 67 mm, width 59 mm, diameter of roundel 38 mm; no suspension-hole.

   Water Newton, 18 No. 14 with pl. 14.

   embossed within the roundel: A X͡P ω
   'Alpha Chi-Rho Omega'

2431.7

8. length 157 mm, width 113 mm, with gilt roundel (diameter 70 mm).

   Water Newton, 18 No. 18 with pl. 18.

   embossed within the roundel: A X͡P ω
   'Alpha Chi-Rho Omega'

RIB 2431. VOTIVES IN SILVER

2431.8

9. length 112 mm, width 105 mm, diameter of roundel 55 mm, with holes for suspension in the centre of the roundel and near the lower angle.

   Water Newton, 18 No. 13 with pl. 13.

   embossed retrograde within the roundel: A $\widehat{XP}$ ω
   'Alpha Chi-Rho Omega'

2431.9

10. length 68 mm, width 52 mm, diameter of roundel 25 mm. A small hole in the centre is pierced from the back.

    Water Newton, 18 No. 16 with pl. 16.

    embossed within the roundel: $\widehat{XP}$
    'Chi-Rho'

2431.10

11. length 131 mm, width 90 mm, diameter of roundel (which is demarcated by small repoussé beads) 48 mm; in the centre of the roundel is a small hole for attachment, punched from the front.

    Water Newton, 16 No. 10 with pl. 10.

    embossed within the roundel: A $\widehat{XP}$ ω
    'Alpha Chi-Rho Omega'

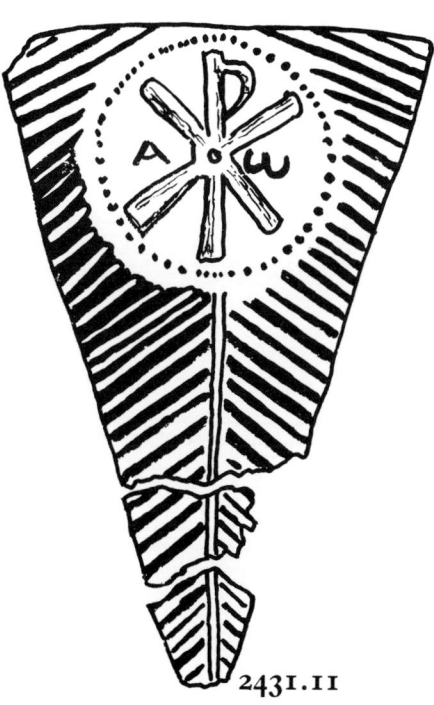

2431.11

RIB 2432. VOTIVE OBJECTS IN BRONZE

This chapter contains ten miscellaneous votive objects in bronze. For a votive bronze vessel see *RIB* 2415.55. Other votive vessels, in silver and pewter respectively, will be found under *RIB* 2414.33, 34, 36, 37 and 2417.5–9. For other bronze plaques see *RIB* 191, 194–5, 197, 217, 236–7, 241, 305, 307 and 662–3.

2432.1. London (*Londinium*). Miniature bronze warship's prow with ram and figurehead of a swan ($\frac{2}{3}$), overall length 81 mm. Found before 1854; acquired by The British Museum in 1856. Drawn by R.G.C., 1927.

EE ix 1319. Roach Smith, *Cat. London Antiquities* (1854), 10 with pl. III.1. Read and Haverfield, *PSA*² (1895–7), 306–8 with fig. B.M. *Guide Rom. Britain* (1922), 90 with fig. 110; (1951), 71.1. with fig. 37.1. RCHM *Roman London* (1928), 175 No. 40 with fig. 86.

engraved letters filled with niello, on one side, retrograde: AMMILLA | AVG FELIX

 Ammilla | Aug(usta) felix

 'Ammilla Augusta, the Fortunate'

The reference is obscure. The title *Augusta* is appropriate to a goddess, but none is known of this name. R.G.C. understands it as an imperial warship, its name transliterated from Greek ἅμιλλα ('contest'), but there is no name of this kind among the known names of Roman warships; they were usually named after gods or ideal qualities: see M. Reddé, *Mare Nostrum* (1986), 665–72. In form the name is a diminutive of the nomen *Ammius*, but there may have been a Celtic homonym, since it tends to occur in *CIL* xiii; note especially *Amilla* with a Celtic patronymic at Sens (xiii 2960) and *Ammillusima* (*RIB* 2029).

2432.1

2432.2. Caister-on-Sea, Norfolk. Bronze tablet ($\frac{1}{1}$), originally *c.* 33 by 23 mm, now broken, found in 1986 with third- to fourth-century pottery in a large depression *c.* 100 m west of the Roman walled site. The edges of the letters have been finely nicked to provide a key for blue enamel, some of which survives. When found the back retained a lump of solder around a small bronze stud used for attachment to a metal object. Norwich Castle Museum. Drawing: Norfolk Archaeological Unit.

Britannia xix (1987), 485 No. 1.

incised:

A[.]R̂ÂT̂T̂ICI | A[.]VS | M̂ER̂ĈV̂RIO | VSLM

 A[u]r(elius) Atticia[n]us Mercurio v(otum) s(olvit) l(ibens) m(erito)

 'Aurelius Atticianus willingly and deservedly fulfilled his vow to Mercury'

2432.2

2432.3. Nettleton, West Kington, Wiltshire. Bronze plaque ($\frac{1}{1}$), height 107 mm, maximum width 76 mm, worked in repoussé and showing traces of an iron backing behind, to which it was soldered; a rivet was placed near the bottom. The plaque shows a bust of Apollo under an *aedicula* composed of an arch in cable pattern supported on two balusters. Found in 1958 during excavations at the Shrine of Apollo at Nettleton Scrubb. Bristol Museum. Reproduced from Wedlake.

2432.3

JRS lii (1962), 191 No. 3. W.J. Wedlake, *The Excavation of The Shrine of Apollo at Nettleton, Wiltshire, 1956–71* (1982), 143–5 with fig. 61 and frontispiece.

in punched dots: D·A·POL | DECIMIVS
  D(eo) Apol(lini) Decimius
  'Decimius (dedicated this) to the god Apollo'

2432.4. Godmanchester, Cambridgeshire [Huntingdonshire]. Lower part of a bronze votive plaque ($\frac{1}{1}$) in the form of a feather with an inscribed and decorated roundel, diameter 55 mm, found in 1971 rolled up with at least three other repoussé feathers in rubbish deposited in the late third century in the disused aqueduct of the baths of the *mansio*. Museum of Archaeology and Anthropology, Cambridge. Drawn by S.S.F. from a photograph.

Britannia iv (1973), 325 No. 4 with pl. XL A.

2432.4

letters impressed at the foot of the feather within two circles of decoration:

DEO | ABAND|[.]NOVAT|IAVCVS | DSD
  deo Aband[i]no Vatiaucus d(e) s(uo) d(edit)
  'To the god Abandinus, Vatiaucus gave (this) at his own (expense)'

The names of the deity and his worshipper both seem to be unique, but compare *deus Abianius* (*CIL* xii 6034 and *deus Abinius* (*CIL* v 7865 = *ILS* 4664).

2432.5. Brancaster (*Branodunum*), Norfolk. Ansate bronze tablet ($\frac{1}{1}$), width 55 mm (originally 60 mm), height 20 mm, found in 1972 during field-walking west of the fort. The left-hand *ansa* is missing. Norwich Castle Museum. Reproduced from Hinchliffe and Green.

Britannia v (1974), 461 No. 2 with pl. XLII A. J. Hinchliffe and C.S. Green, *Excavations at Brancaster, 1974 and 1977* (East Anglian Archaeology No. 23, (1985)), 213 No. 59 with fig. 60.59.

incised: DEO | HER
  deo Her(culi)
  'To the god Hercules'
Traces of solder on the back suggest former attachment to a metal object.

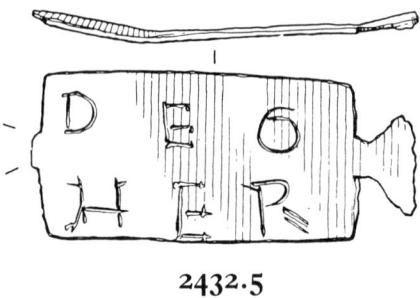

2432.5

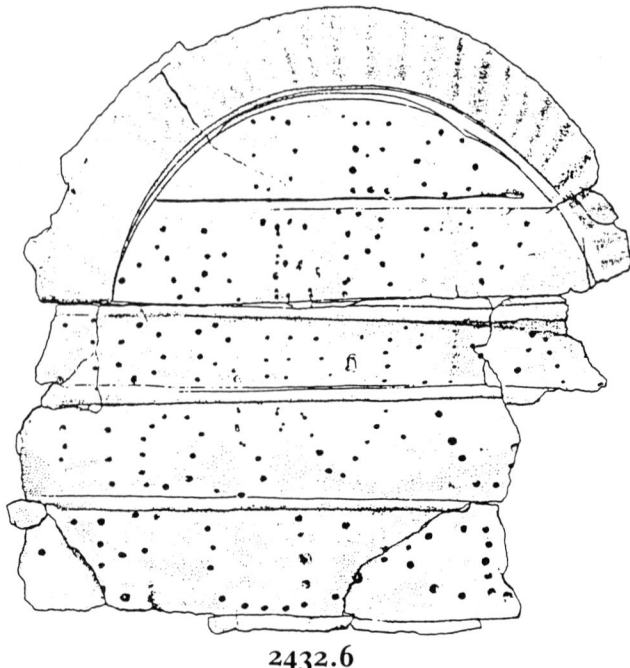

2432.6

2432.6. Uley, Gloucestershire. Part of a plaque with arched top ($\frac{1}{1}$) in thin bronze sheet, 80 by 80 mm overall, now broken into two large and six small pieces probably as the result of folding in antiquity. Found in 1977 in a residual context during excavations at the temple. British Museum. Drawn by Joanna Richards.

Britannia xvii (1986), 429 No. 4.

inscribed in punched dots:
DEO | MERCV|RIOSEVERA[?]|.IOSV.. [?]| .FELIXE(or L) [?]|[. . .]
  Deo | Mercu|rio Severa [?] |.IOSVL . .[?]| Felix E (or L) [. . .]
  'To the god Mercury Severa ... Felix ... [dedicated (this)]'
l.3. SIIVERA, M.W.C.H. l.4. PIOSVS Ellison; IIOSVL[. . .], M.W.C.H.

Compare a similar arched plaque in silver, figured but uninscribed, from Niederbieber: W. Dorow, *Römische Altertümer in und um Neuwied* (1827), 14; La Baume, *BJ* 177 (1977), 566–8 with Abb. 2; Toynbee in J. Bird *et al*, *Collectanea Londiniensia* (1978), 136–7 with fig. 5.2.

2432.7. Ibid. Bronze fragment ($\frac{1}{1}$), 15 by 38 mm, thickness 2 mm. There are two nail-holes and the object terminates with a broken hinge; it was perhaps part of the hinged clasp of a box. Found in 1977 during excavations at the temple site. British Museum. Drawn by Joanna Richards.

Britannia xvii (1986), 443 No. 50.

incised below the hinged: MER
  Mer(curio)
  'For Mercury'

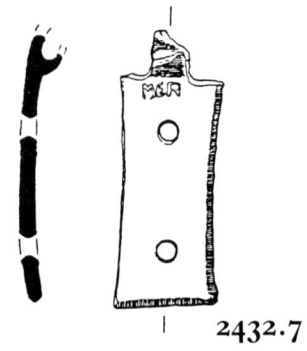

2432.7

2432.8. Colchester (*Camulodunum*), Essex. Ansate bronze tablet (¼), 58 by 25 mm, found in 1976 during building-work at St. Helena's School, which lies within the temenos of a Romano-Celtic temple (Temple 2) at Sheepen Farm, north-west of the *colonia*. The right-hand *ansa* was broken away in antiquity. Colchester Museum. Drawn by S.S.F. from a photograph.

Britannia viii (1977), 427 No. 7 with pl. XXVII C. N. Crummy, *Small Finds* (1983), 145 No. 4284. For the temple, M.R. Hull, *Roman Colchester* (1958), 224–33 and M.J. Lewis, *Temples in Roman Britain* (1966), 'Colchester 2'.

in punched letters: P ORANIVS· | FACILIS·IOVI | SIGILLVM· EX· TESTA

P(ublius) Oranius Facilis Iovi sigillum ex testa(mento)

'P(ublius) Oranius Facilis (dedicated) the statuette to Jupiter in his will'

For other votive tablets from Colchester see *RIB* 191, 194–5. For the nomen *Oranius* see *CIL* ix 4686; x 4262.

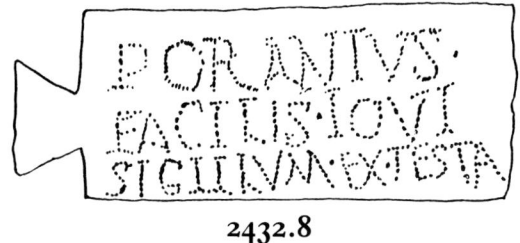
2432.8

2432.9. Silchester (*Calleva*), Hampshire. Fragment of thin bronze sheet (¹⁄₁), 24 by 30 mm, found before 1910 during excavations. The inscription was first noted by G.C. Boon in 1955. The inscription is punched from the back, but at the foot a dotted decoration has been punched from the front. Reading Museum. Drawn by S.S.F. from a draft by R.P.W., 1955.

JRS xlvi (1956), 146 No. 2.

in punched letters:
[. . .].[. . .] | [. . .]ECILLA | [. . .]TVI[. . .]

l.2 may contain part of a personal name like *Senecilla* of diminutive form.

2432.9

2432.10. Uley, Gloucestershire. Piece of sheet bronze (¹⁄₁), 32 by 23 mm, from the right-hand end of an oblong mounting; a series of closely-spaced nail-holes runs along the three original edges, and a central nail-hole is surrounded by a repoussé ring. Found in 1977 in a late fourth-century context at the site of the temple. British Museum. Drawn by Joanna Richards.

Britannia xi (1980), 411 No. 36.

inscription in repoussé along the top and bottom edge: [. . .]ORV[.] | [. . .]VMFECERVNT

'. . . (they) made'

The first line probably began with the name of the deity, presumably *deo Mercurio*, and probably ended with the name of one dedicator, *[Fl]oru[s]* or a name of Greek etymology in *-dorus* or *-phorus*. The second line added the name of another dedicator and ended with *[sacr]um fecerunt* (cf. *RIB* 151), *[vot]um fecerunt* (cf. *RIB* 759), or similar.

2432.10

RIB 2433. MISCELLANEOUS OBJECTS IN BRONZE

This chapter contains a somewhat mixed collection of objects which fall outside such major categories as *RIB* 2401 (Diplomata), 2415 (Bronze Vessels), 2412 (Weights) or 2432 (Votives). It includes two strigil-handles, a knife, a bell, a joiner's square, a seal-box and a number of inscribed scraps. *RIB* 2433.8 is now accepted as a weight, and should have been included in *RIB* 2412.

2433.1. Waddon Hill, Stoke Abbot, Dorset. Fragment of bronze ($\frac{1}{1}$), 33 by 33 mm, with no margin intact. Found in 1959 during excavation of the Roman fort. Bridport Museum. Reproduced from Webster.

JRS lii (1962), 191 No. 5. Webster, *P. Dorset NH & AS* lxxxii (1960), 104 No. 45 with fig. 9.45.

in letters embossed from the back, between lines of dots similarly embossed: AL[. . .]

Compare *RIB* 2435.1.

2433.1

2433.2. Chilgrove, West Sussex. Part of a bronze openwork fitting ($\frac{1}{1}$), length 40 mm, found in 1963–75 during excavation of the bath-suite at the Chilgrove I Roman Villa. Chichester Museum. Reproduced from Down.

A. Down, *Chichester Excavations* iv (1979), 151 No. 13 with fig. 45.13.

Cast openwork letters: AQV[. . .]
    Aqu[is . . .]

Compare *CIL* xiii 10027.204 a–f, six very similar objects, of which the complete text reads AQVIS H̄EC GEMELLIANVS F(ECIT): 'Gemellianus made these at Aquae'.

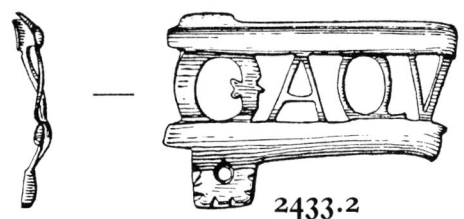

2433.2

2433.3. East Winterslow, Wiltshire. Bronze handle ($\frac{2}{3}$) decorated with niello, octagonal in section, length 67 mm; traces of iron on one side of the tang suggest the former presence of some kind of iron blade or other utensil. Found in 1955 on a Roman site at Broomhill, East Winterslow. Salisbury Museum. Drawn by R.P.W., 1956.

JRS xlvii (1957), 232 No. 25.

Two inscriptions in engraved letters filled with niello:
(a) on two bevelled edges: AVSONI | AVITI
    '(Property?) of Ausonius Avitus'
(b) around the top of the handle: VTI FẸL
    uti fel(ix)
    'Good luck to the user'

A variant using the infinitive *uti* for the imperative *utere*. Compare *RIB* 2420.52, with note.

2433.3

2433.4. Catterick (*Cataractonium*), North Yorkshire. Bronze ansate plaque ($\frac{1}{1}$ and $\frac{2}{1}$), 63.5 by 20.5 mm; on the upper edge one of two hinges survives, and on the lower edge three portions of openwork remain. Found in 1959 during excavations below Building VII.3. Yorkshire Museum, York. Drawn by S.S.F. from a rubbing by R.P.W.

JRS l (1960), 240 No. 22.

stamped in raised letters in an ansate label: DVBNVS

For *dubno-* as a Celtic name-element see D. Ellis Evans, *Gaulish Personal Names* (1967), 196–7.

2433.4

Britannia v (1974), 464 No. 18. D.S. Neal, *The Excavation of the Roman Villa in Gadebridge Park, Hemel Hempstead, 1963–8* (1974), 129 No. 41, with fig. 55.41.

incised below a horizontal line: I[. . .] | NII[. . .]

As text, R.P.W. NI[. . .], Neal (drawing).

2433.7. Caerleon (*Isca*), Gwent [Monmouthshire]. Bronze strigil ($\frac{2}{1}$), inlaid with silver and gold, overall length 250 mm. The underside is engraved for inlay (none surviving) with a median straight wreath and an undulating vine-scroll on either side flanked by a wave-pattern at the edges. The square-looped handle is decorated on each side with three of the labours of Hercules. Found in 1979 in the upper levels of the *frigidarium* drain in the fortress baths. Caerleon Museum. Reproduced from Zienkiewicz.

Britannia xiii (1982), 420 No. 84. Boon in J.D. Zienkiewicz, *The Legionary Fortress Baths at Caerleon* ii (1986) 157–66 with pls I, XVIII C, and fig. 51.

engraved on the butt of the handle: ΚΑΛѠC | ΕΛΟΥCΕ

καλῶς | ἔλουσε

'It washed (you) well'

2433.5. London (*Londinium*). Leatherworker's bronze knife ($\frac{1}{1}$ and $\frac{2}{1}$), length 147 mm, maximum width 60 mm, found in 1974 in a late first- to early second-century context during excavations at Billingsgate Buildings. Museum of London. Drawn by D. Parfitt.

Britannia ix (1978), 479 No. 48. D.M. Jones, *Excavations at Billingsgate Buildings 'Triangle' . . . 1974* (Lond. Middl. AS Special Paper No. 4, 1980), 88 No. 466 with fig. 52 and pl. 2.

stamp on the blade near the handle: GERMA[. . .]

Ġerma[nus . . .?]

'Germanus (made this)'.

The name is preceded by an unidentifiable symbol.

For stamps on iron knives see *RIB* 2428.5–8, 10, 14, 17 and 19.

2433.6. Hemel Hempstead, Hertfordshire. Bronze strip ($\frac{1}{1}$), 18 by 8 mm, found in 1965 at Gadebridge Park Roman Villa. Verulamium Museum, St Albans. Drawn by D.S. Neal.

Boon (loc. cit.) shows that the labours depicted correspond to Nos. 4–9 in the canon established by the second century A.D., and suggests that this implies the former existence of a second strigil to form a pair, the missing one depicting the three first and last labours, and probably carrying the inscription καλῶς λούσει: 'It will wash (you) well'.

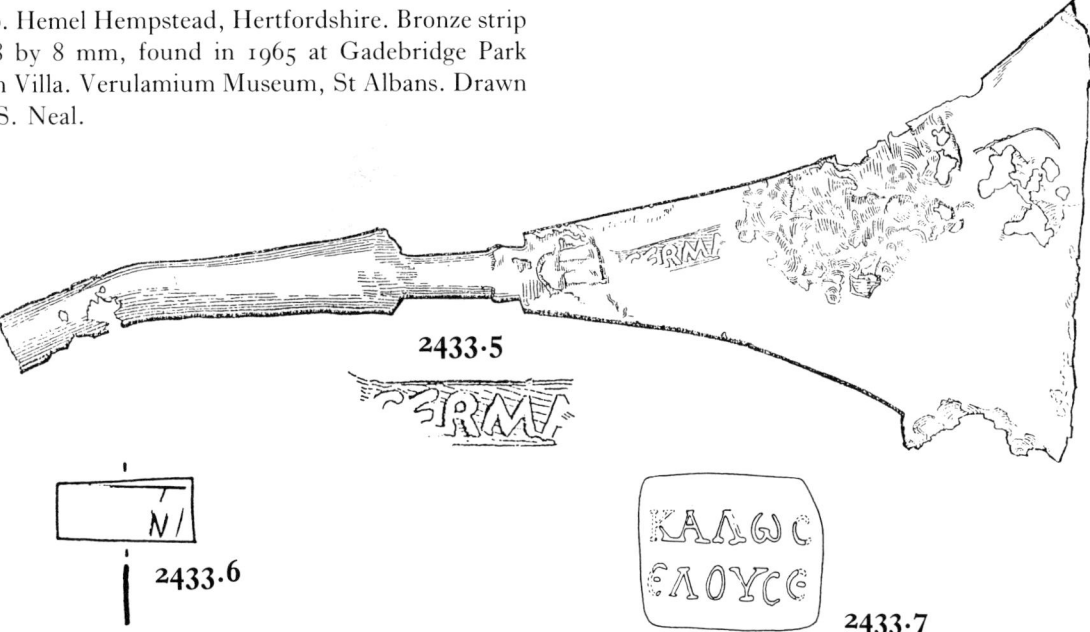

2433.8. Colchester (*Camulodunum*), Essex. Bronze weight in the form of a disc ($\frac{1}{1}$), diameter 17 mm, thickness 1.5 mm, weight 1.9 gm, found in 1973 at Lion Walk in a late-Roman context. Colchester Museum. Reproduced from Crummy.

Britannia ix (1978), 477 No. 31. N. Crummy, *Cat.* (1983), 101 No. 2511 with fig.

incised: <
punched: two dots
 'Two (*scripula*)'

L, *Britannia*
We follow Crummy in accepting this as a weight of two scruples; it is 0.37 gm underweight (16%) It should have been included under *RIB* 2412, where it would follow No. 47.

2433.8

2433.9. London (*Londinium*). Bronze bell, found before 1873. Formerly in Liverpool Museum but destroyed during an air raid in 1941. Not illustrated.

CIL vii 1295. RCHM *Roman London* (1928), 175 No. 38.

engraved: MARTINVS

2433.10. Chichester (*Noviomagus*), West Sussex. Bronze seal-box ($\frac{2}{3}$), found in 1959–64 during excavations in the Central Car Park. Chichester Museum. Reproduced from Down.

A. Down, *Chichester Excavations* ii (1974), 141 No. 30 with fig. 8.16 No. 30.

incised on the outer surface of the lid: MEL | ELP

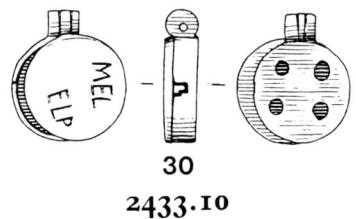

2433.10

2433.11. Chester (*Deva*). Fragment of bronze sheet ($\frac{1}{1}$), 25 by 25 mm, thickness 0.5 mm, somewhat curved in section; found in 1979 during excavations in Princess Street. Grosvenor Museum, Chester. Drawn by M.W.C.H., 1984.

Britannia xv (1984), 342 No. 15.

graffito in punched dots: [. . .]NT[. . .]

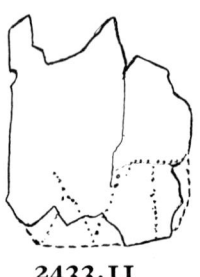

2433.11

2433.12. Richborough (*Rutupiae*), Kent. Thin fragmentary strip of bronze, length 63.5 mm, width 6.3 mm, thickness 2.5 mm, found in 1924 unstratified during excavation. In store at Dover Castle. Reprinted from *JRS*.

JRS xvi (1924), 247 No. 15. J.P. Bushe-Fox, *Richborough* ii (1928), 97 No. 5.

inscribed: OVIÑEI·EI·ILII[. . .]

The first letter might be D or Q. All letters are worn away at the top, hence I might be T or the like, R.G.C., *JRS*.

2433.13. (?) Canterbury (*Durovernum*), Kent. Bronze strigil handle ($\frac{1}{1}$), length 146 mm, formerly in the Brent collection and so presumably a local find of the 19th century. Royal Museum, Canterbury. Drawn by R.P.W.

stamped on the handle: ΤΑΡΑΝΤΙΦΑΝΕΟΣ
 Probably for παρ' Ἀντιφάνεος
 'From Antiphanes'

For makers' stamps of this form compare *CIL* xi 6718.14 (where π is also incomplete) and 17.

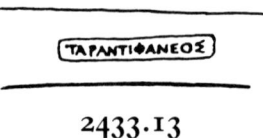

2433.13

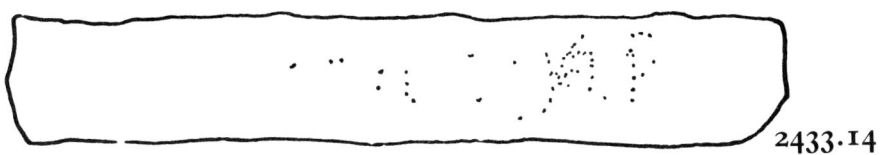

2433.14

2433.14. Usk (*Burrium*), Gwent [Monmouthshire]. Piece of bronze (⅟₁), 214 by 16 mm, thickness 2 mm, folded in half to make a strip 107 mm long; found in 1974 in a pre-Flavian pit in the fortress. National Museum, Cardiff. Reproduced from Hassall.

Britannia x (1979), 355 No. 47. M. Hassall in W.H. Manning (ed.), *The Coins, Inscriptions and Graffiti (Report on the Excavations at Usk 1965–76)* (1982), 51 No. 2 with fig. 4.2.

graffito in punched dots: [*c*.4] AP

2433.15. Springhead (*Vagniacis*), Kent. Part of a bronze headstall for a horse, formed by an L-shaped frame comprising part of the vertical check-piece and horizontal side element. The loop at the angle is missing; above it is the maker's stamp (³⁄₁), set diagonally but very corroded. Gravesend Museum. Traced by S.S.F. from a photograph.

Britannia xv (1984), 343 No. 32.

stamp: perhaps I.OVI.

2433.15

2433.16. Canterbury (*Durovernum*), Kent. Bronze fragment (⅔), 65 by 53 mm, thickness 2 mm, found in 1976 at Nos. 77–9 Castle Street with third-century material in a drain flanking the south-east side of the temenos of the temple. Canterbury Museum. Drawing: Canterbury Archaeological Trust.

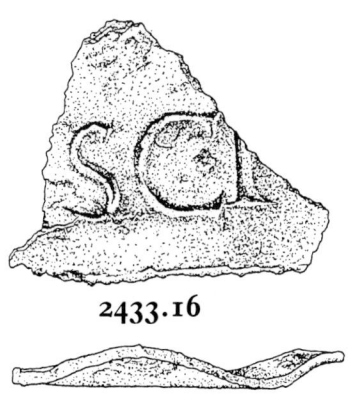

2433.16

Britannia viii (1977), 426 No. 3; xv (1984), 343 No. 31.

engraved: [. . .]SC·P[. . .]

[. . .]SC·R[. . .], *Britannia* viii.

The spacing of the letters casts doubt upon the medial point, and from the drawing at least it appears that [. . .SCI[. . .] could be read. The quality of the lettering suggests that it belongs to a monumental inscription. R.S.O.T.

2433.17. Covesea, Highland Region [Morayshire]. Strip of bronze (⅟₁), broken at each end and divided into two at one end; length 30 mm, cross-section 3 by 2 mm. Found in 1929 with Roman material in Sculptor's Cave. National Museums of Scotland, Queen Street, Edinburgh. Drawn by R.P.W., 1966.

JRS lvi (1966), 221 No. 21.

moulded in recessed letters (P and L reversed):
[. . .]SPILV[. . .]

Alternatively, [. . .]VLIPS[. . .] could be read retrograde, with S reversed. Neither reading admits of restoration.

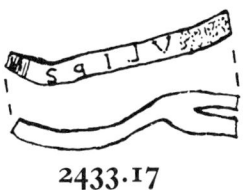

2433.17

2433.18. Rockbourne, Hampshire. The right-hand end of a thin bronze plate (⅟₁), 19 by 17.5 mm, found in 1957 in Room III at the West Park Roman Villa. Hampshire Museum Service. Drawn by S.S.F. from a rubbing by R.P.W., 1963.

JRS liii (1963), 164 No. 25.

in letters embossed from the back: [. . .]VII

Presumably [. . .]*ve*, an imperative or a vocative, rather than a numeral.

2433.18

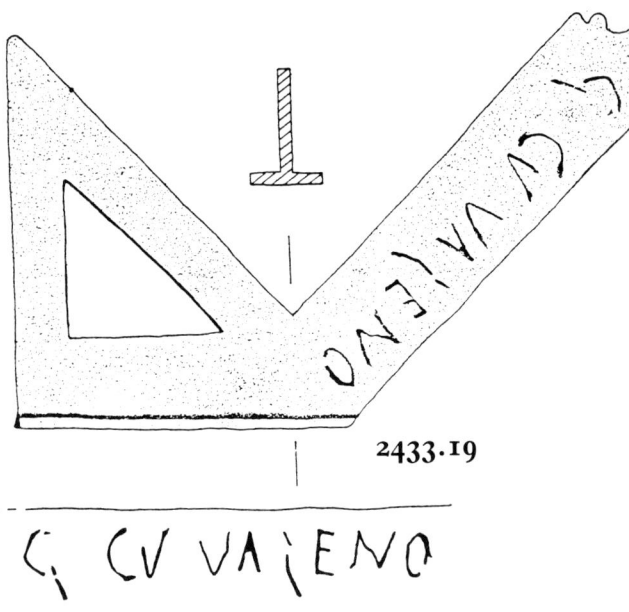

2433.19

ALIENVM

2433.21.* Unknown provenance. Convex bronze disc with flat reverse (¼), diameter 79.5 mm, with four concentric moulded rings on the obverse, forming the setting of a *sestertius* of Nero, diameter 33 mm. Now separate (but formerly attached to the back of the disc, where there are traces of solder at points corresponding to its three loops) is a bronze ring, diameter 73.5 mm, width 7.5 mm, to which are attached three equidistant projecting loops giving a total height of 12.5 mm. The obverse of the coin, on the reverse of the disc, carries the laureate head of Nero, facing left. On the obliterated reverse of the coin, on the obverse of the disc, is an engraved *quadriga* in niello, with gold for the charioteer's head, wreath and palm-branch, and for the body of the chariot and its reins, and with silver for the charioteer's robe and for the two wheels of the chariot.

2433.19. Canterbury (*Durovernum*), Kent. Joiner's bronze try and mitre square (½), overall width 162 mm, height 90 mm, thickness 1.5 mm with the oblique arm terminating in a series of mouldings and pierced by a suspension-hole 3.5 mm in diameter. A base-plate 17 mm wide, presumably soldered on, enables the square to stand vertically. Found in 1978 in a second-century context during excavations at No. 16 Watling Street. Canterbury Museum. Reproduced from Chapman.

Britannia x (1979), 350 No. 32 with fig. 25. Chapman, *Antiq. J.* lix (1979), 403–7 with fig. 2. Ball and Ball, *Antiq. J.* lxviii (1988), 294–301 with fig. 1.3. *The Archaeology of Canterbury* v (1991), forthcoming.

incised: G CV VALENO
  G(aio) Cu(. . .) Valeno
  'For Gaius Cu(. . .) Valenus'.

There are several possible nomina (*Curius*, *Curtius*, etc); the cognomen seems to be unattested.

2433.20. Colchester (*Camulodunum*), Essex. Bronze strip (1/1), 31 by 7 mm, thickness *c*. 0.2 mm, found in 1981 in a probably fourth-century context during excavations in Culver Street. Colchester Museum. Drawing: Colchester Archaeological Trust.

Britannia xv (1984), 343 No. 25.

graffito in punched dots: XVII
  '17'

2433.20

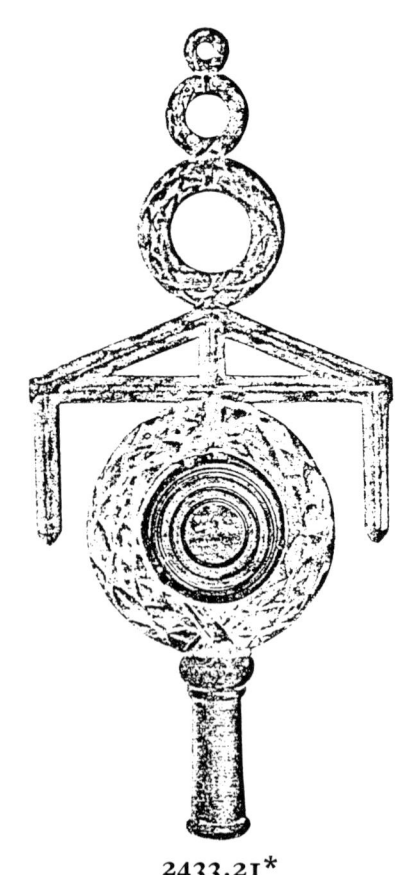

2433.21*

Formerly in the collection of C.T. Seltman, whose father bought it about 1900 from the early nineteenth-century Forman collection, which contained objects from Colchester as well as from abroad. Present location unknown. Reproduced from *Numismatic Circular*.

EE ix 1360. Anon., *Numismatic Circular* (April, 1908) colls. 10508–10 with pl. and figs. *Bull. Soc. des Antiq. de France* (1907), 168–70.

Coin-legend on the obverse of the sestertius: NERO CLAVDIVS CAESAR AVG IMP TR POT PP

The object has been made to resemble a military standard by being placed in a circular bronze fitting decorated with laurel leaves, and by the addition of a triangular framework 203 mm wide with dependent side-pieces, carrying at the top three open circles vertically arranged in diminishing sizes and similarly decorated with laurel leaves.

J.M.C. Toynbee and I.A. Richmond (to R.P.W.) dismissed the identification as a standard and considered the disc and its fitting to be a horse-trapping, possibly intended for good luck in racing, and assembled in the post-Constantinian period. The additional fittings to resemble a standard are presumably a much later antiquarian fiction.

The central disc, with its obverse portrait of Nero and reverse type of a charioteer driving a *quadriga* resembles a 'contorniate', and may indeed be one with precious-metal heightening. (See A. and E. Alföldi, *Die Kontorniat-Medaillons* (1976).) It would thus be of fourth-century date and originally from Rome, presumably a modern import. R.S.O.T.

FALSA

2433.22.* Bath, Avon [Somerset]. Oval bronze relief or medallion ($\frac{3}{1}$), depicting a woman's head facing right. Found in the 18th century in digging the foundation of the Pump Room. Reproduced from Scarth.

Warner, *Hist.* (1801), 123. Scarth, *Aquae* (1864), 84 pl. XXXIV.

engraved: POMPEIA·I·C·V
  presumably *Pompeia I(ulii) C(aesaris) u(xor)*
  'Pompeia, wife of Julius Caesar'

Late 18th century, R.G.C.

2433.22*

2433.23.* South Shields (*Arbeia*), Tyne and Wear [Durham]. Flat square bronze plaque ($\frac{1}{1}$) 19 by 19 mm, thickness 1 mm, with incised parallel grooves and traces of lettering above. Not certainly Roman. Museum of Antiquities, Newcastle upon Tyne. Reproduced from Allason-Jones and Miket.

L. Allason-Jones and R. Miket, *Cat.* 220 No. 3.750 with fig.

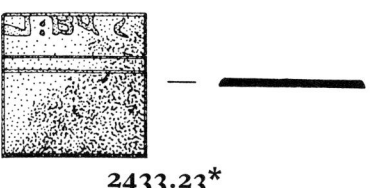

2433.23*

2433.24.* Dorchester (*Durnovaria*), Dorset. A pair of bronze compasses ($\frac{1}{1}$ and $\frac{3}{1}$) found in the late 19th century at Somerleigh Court. Dorchester Museum. Reproduced from Henig.

Henig, *P. Dorset NHAS* cv (1983), 159 with fig.

stamped: a six-pointed star within a circle

Stars are not infrequently found as ownership marks on pottery. This stamp has been claimed (loc. cit.) as a loopless Chi-Rho, but the surrounding circle suggests a wheel-symbol.

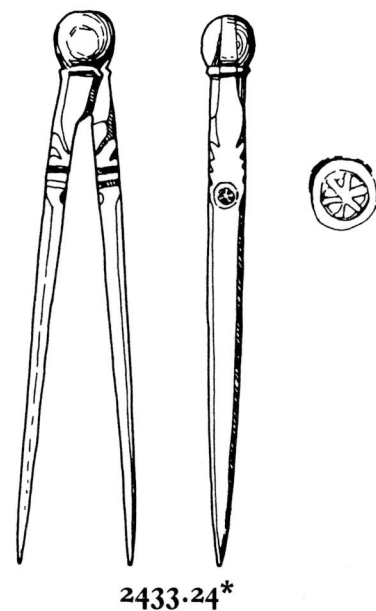

2433.24*

RIB 2434. LEAD WATER-PIPES

Virtually every bathing establishment, whether in town or villa, made use of lead pipes even if often only to drain a bath through the adjacent wall; remarkably few carry inscriptions. In this chapter only five inscribed pipes are recorded. Three of these come from the extensive systems laid down in Chester in A.D. 79 during construction of the fortress there; they carry lengthy abbreviated texts indicating the official character of the work. Of the remaining two, *RIB* 2434.5 from Bath suggests the work of a private contractor, while the other, 2434.4, from Chester once again, is a secondary graffito possibly indicating repair work. When the enormous weight of lead used in the thermal establishment at Bath is remembered (8½ tons on the floor of the Great Bath alone (B.W. Cunliffe, *Roman Bath* (1969), 126), it is perhaps curious that epigraphic evidence is so scarce. The nearness of the Mendip lead-field no doubt facilitated liberal use of the metal at Bath, and at Chester too a source was nearby in the Flintshire field; but at the majority of Romano-British sites water-mains were formed of hollowed lengths of timber joined together with iron collars, and drains too were usually lined with timber planks. Lead pipes, however, may often have been used in above-ground internal ducts in bath-buildings: the evidence has normally been destroyed with the demolition or post-Roman robbing of the walls.

IMP·VESP·VIIII·T·IMP·VII COS·CN·IVLIO·AGRICOLA·LEG·AVG·PR·PR 2434.1

2434.1–2. Chester (*Deva*). Lead water-pipes ($\frac{1}{10}$), 76 mm in diameter; a length of 5029 mm was uncovered and cut into four lengths by workmen. There were three joints in the section exposed, dividing lengths of 2489 and 2134 mm respectively, each carrying a moulded inscription on a panel measuring 1194 by 51 mm. Found in 1899, running east–west in the central range of the fortress, c. 23 m north of Eastgate Street and 45 m west of Northgate Street. Grosvenor Museum, Chester. Drawn by R.P.W.

EE ix 1039. *ILS* 8704a. Haverfield, *Westdeut. Zeitschr.* (1899) *Korrespondenzbl.*, col. 185 No. 103. Taylor, *PSA*[2] xviii (1899–1901), 98 with fig. Newstead *JCAS*[2] viii (1902), 88 pl. 12; *Reliquary*[2] vi (1900), 114 with figs. 1–3; vii (1901), 45 with figs. 1–2. R.P. Wright and I.A. Richmond, *Cat.* (1955) 48 No. 199 with pl. XLIV.199. F.H. Thompson, *Roman Cheshire* (1965), 29–30 with pl. 3.

1. moulded: IMP·VESP·VIIII·T·IMP·VII COS·CN·IVLIO·AGRICOLA·LEG·AVG·PR·PR
2. moulded: text as 2434.1 from the same mould (not illustrated)
   Imp(eratore) Vesp(asiano) VIIII T(ito) Imp(eratore) VII co(n)s(ulibus) Gn(aeo) Iulio Agricola leg(ato) Aug(usti) pr(o) pr(aetore)

'(Made) in the ninth consulship of the emperor Vespasian and the seventh of the emperor Titus, in the governorship of Gnaeus Julius Agricola'.

A.D. 79.

2434.3. Ibid. Lead water-pipe ($\frac{1}{10}$), 2690 mm long and 100 mm in diameter at the joint. Found in 1969 south-west of the monument in the centre of the courtyard of the elliptical building which lies in the rear part of the central range of the fortress, north-west of the *principia*. The pipe ran east–west until it turned north to join the monument. The first 19 mm of the inscribed panel had been cut off and the remaining length of pipe had been soldered to an uninscribed section, 79 mm long. Grosvenor Museum, Chester. Drawing: Grosvenor Museum.

Britannia ii (1971), 292 No. 17.

moulded: [. . .]VIIII·T·IMP·VII COS·CN·IVLIO·AGRICOLA·LEG·AVG·PR·PR

[*Imp(eratore) Vesp(asiano)*] *VIIII T(ito) Imp(eratore) VII co(n)s(ulibus) Gn(aeo) Iulio Agricola leg(ato) Aug(usti) pr(o) pr(aetore)*
'(Made) in the ninth consulship of the emperor Vespasian and the seventh of the emperor Titus, in the governorship of Gnaeus Julius Agricola'.

A.D. 79.

VIIII T·IMP VII COS CN·IVLIO·AGRICOLA LEG AVG PR·PR 2434.3

Both inscriptions (Nos. 1 and 3) show identical differences between the C of *cos* and the C of *Agricola*, between all three As and between the R of *Agricola* and the Rs of PR PR, showing that more than one stamp for each letter was in use during mould-manufacture. Slight differences in the spacing of letters may suggest that Nos. 1 and 3 were made in distinct moulds; but the same letter-stamps were used in both moulds and in the same order, slight differences of outline between the Gs and Cs in the two examples of AGRICOLA being no more than might be accounted for by differences of application.

2434.4. Ibid. Section of flattened lead water-pipe (⅓), length 165 mm, external diameter 114 mm, internal diameter 96 mm. A small area of the patina has been cut away with a knife to make a smooth surface for the graffiti. Found in 1976 unstratified at No. 76 Lower Bridge Street, south of the fortress. Grosvenor Museum, Chester. Drawn by M.W.C.H.

Britannia viii (1977), 435 No. 39.

Two graffiti inverted in respect to each other:
PRIVIS | ATICVRTO

2434.4

2434.5. Bath (*Aquae Sulis*), Avon [Somerset]. Lead water-pipe, diameter *c*. 57 mm carrying a label (½), 159 by 57 mm, with cabled border and raised letters, soldered to it. Found in 1825 near the junction of York

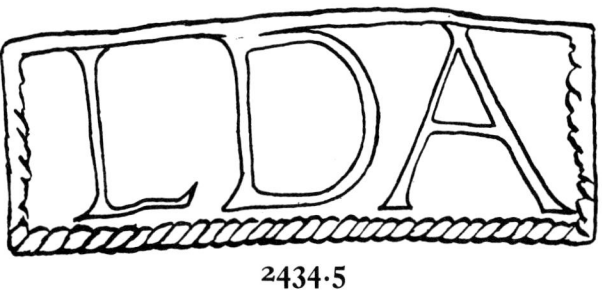
2434.5

Street and Stall Street, within the south-west corner of the Roman Baths complex. Roman Baths Museum, Bath. Drawn by R.G.C.

CIL vii 1266. Haverfield, *VCH Somerset* i (1906), 283 No. 48. B.W. Cunliffe, *Roman Bath* (1969), 128 with pl. XXV C.

moulded letters: LDA
 L(ucius) D(...) A(...)

Probably the initials of the *tria nomina* of the maker.

ALIENVM

2434.6.* Unknown provenance. Portion of a lead pipe. Museum of Archaeology and Anthropology, Cambridge. Drawn by R.G.C., 1923.

moulded: [...]RVATVS·PLVMB·FECIT
 [? Se]rvatus plumb(arius) or plumb(um) fecit
 'Servatus (?) the lead-worker made (this)' *or* 'made the lead'.

2434.6*

RIB 2435. LEAD ROUNDELS

The objects classified here as lead roundels may have served a variety of purposes. Two are pierced at the centre (2435.4 and 7), and resemble spindle-whorls, although a very similar object (*RIB* 2410.4) has been classified as a label. Others, also of regular circular form, in size resemble gaming counters (which are normally made of bone, or sometimes of pottery see *RIB* 2439, 2440), and carry similar inscriptions or numerals (2435.1, 6, 10, 11, 12), while others are merely discs of irregular outline and very varied size (2435.2, 5, 8, 9, 13). All, however, are complete objects and differ from the pieces cut from sheet lead which are catalogued under *RIB* 2436.

2435.1. Waddon Hill, Dorset. Lead roundel of irregular shape ($\frac{1}{1}$), diameter 16 mm, thickness 2 mm, found in 1964 in the Roman fort. Bridport Museum. Drawn by R.P.W., 1967.

JRS lix (1969), 237 No. 10. G. Webster, *P. Dorset NH and Arch S.* ci (1979), 73 No. 114 and fig. 34.

obverse: ΛL
reverse: blank

Compare *RIB* 2433.1.

2435.1

2435.2. Brough on Humber (*Petuaria*), Humberside [Yorkshire]. Lead roundel ($\frac{1}{1}$), diameter 57 mm, thickness 1.6 mm. The obverse carries a scratched rectangle with rays inside a circle, with the inscription below. Found in 1958 during excavations near the north-west corner of the Roman town. Drawn by R.P.W., 1969.

JRS lix (1969), 240 No. 30 with fig. 44. J.S. Wacher, *Excavations at Brough on Humber 1958–61* (1969), 100 No. 4 with fig. 44.

obverse, inscribed from left to right (as illustrated) in cursive letters (?): ΛMICΛVIMI *or* perhaps ΛMICΛVOM

As text, R.P.W. Other readings are possible, and all are uncertain. R.S.O.T.

2435.3. Charterhouse on Mendip, Somerset. Lead roundel ($\frac{1}{1}$), diameter 25.5 mm. Found in the late nineteenth century and formerly in the A.C. Pass collection. Bristol Museum. Drawn by R.P.W., 1953.

EE ix 1300. Haverfield, *VCH* Somerset i (1906), 344 with fig.

stamped: CATV

F.H., *VCH*, considered that the lettering might have been transferred from a samian stamp, but B.R. Hartley (to S.S.F.) writes that no samian stamps are similar.

2435.3

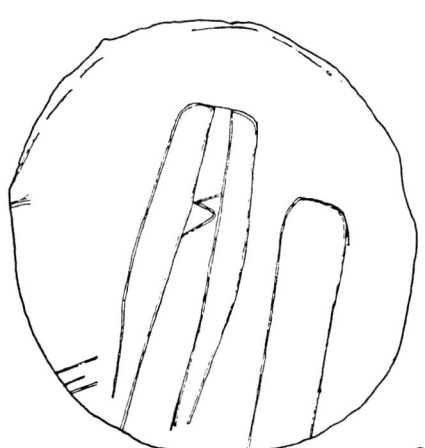

2435.2

2435.4. Caerleon (*Isca*), Gwent [Monmouthshire]. Pierced lead roundel (1/1), diameter 32 mm, thickness 4 mm, weight 31.4 gm, with central hole 3 mm in diameter punched from the reverse and forming a raised rim on the obverse. Found in 1981 during excavation at Roman Gates, Backhall Street in the *latera praetorii* of the fortress near the *porta principalis dextra*. Caerleon Museum. Drawn by M.W.C.H.

Britannia xix (1988), 506 No. 105.

graffito, lightly incised before the hole was pierced:
 CIRVDE | M | IX

Perhaps a tag or label; compare *RIB* 2410.4 from the same site.

2435.5. Chesters (*Cilurnum*), Northumberland. Thin irregular lead roundel (1/1), maximum diameter 44 mm, found before 1903 at the fort. Chesters Museum. Drawn by S.S.F. from a draft by R.G.C., 1927.

EE vii 1150. *JRS* xviii (1928), 214 No. 7. Budge, *Cat.* (1903), 366 No. 67.

graffito: PRIMVS
 'Primus'

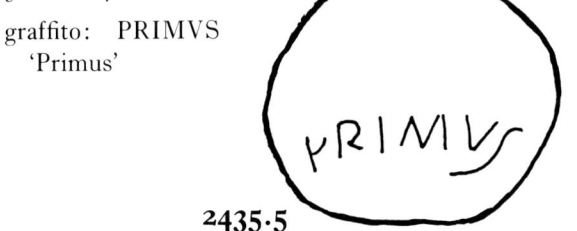

IBIMVS, Haverfield, *EE*. IANNIEI (?), Budge. PRIMVS, R.G.C., *JRS*.

2435.6. Waddon Hill, Dorset. Lead roundel (1/1), diameter 16 mm, thickness 6 mm. Found in 1967 at the Roman fort. Bridport Museum. Drawn by S.S.F. from a rubbing by R.P.W.

JRS lix (1969), 237 No. 13. Webster, *P. Dorset NH and Arch. S.* ci (1979), 73 No. 108 with fig. 34.

obverse: R
reverse, retrograde: R

The weight, 11.6 gm, does not correspond to any Roman weight.

2435.7. Binchester (*Vinovia*), Durham. Pierced lead roundel (1/1), diameter 48 mm, thickness 4.75 mm, diameter of hole 6 mm. The edges of the obverse have been formed into a flange by hammering, possibly during use; the reverse is flat. Found in 1929 near the Roman fort. Bowes Museum, Barnard Castle. Drawn by R.G.C.

obverse, incised: TAMVI
 Perhaps *Tam(...) VI*

The last two letters are less deeply incised and may be by another, perhaps earlier, hand.

2435.8. Richborough (*Rutupiae*), Kent. Irregular lead roundel (1/1), 40 by 30 mm, thickness 3 mm, reverse flat. Found in 1932 during excavations in Area XVII. In store in Dover Castle. Drawn by R.P.W., 1948.

stamped: IXN (?)

A hole pierced after the punch was made has damaged the (?) letters. A piece of lead (unpublished) from Chesterholm (*Vindolanda*) carries a similar impression, better preserved, which is clearly decoration, not letters.

The object is not certainly epigraphic: compare *RIB* 2436.7 (with note) and especially 11.

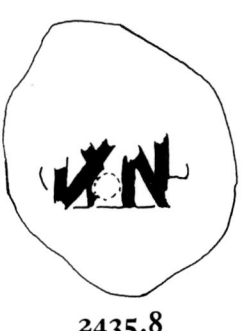

2435.9. Caerhun (*Canovium*), Gwynedd [Caernarvonshire]. Irregular lead roundel ($\frac{7}{8}$) with flat obverse and the reverse slightly convex; maximum diameter 90 mm, maximum thickness 8 mm, weight 278.19 gm. Found in 1926–36 during excavations in Building XV at the Roman fort. Llandudno Museum. Reproduced from Reynolds.

Baillie Reynolds, *AC* xci (1936), 222 with fig. 51.2.

obverse, in roughly incised strokes: IIII

The object is not considered to be a weight since the inscription bears no relation to the weight of four *unciae* in any of their possible variants (see *RIB* 2412, Introduction).

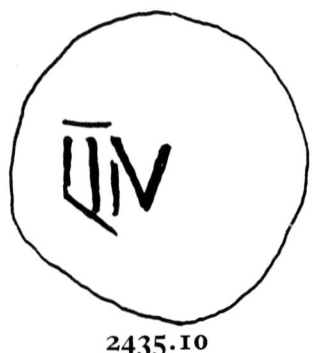

2435.10

2435.11. Wroxeter (*Viroconium*), Shropshire. Lead roundel ($\frac{1}{1}$), diameter 25 mm, weight 72.77 gm. Found probably about 1859. Rowley's House Museum, Shrewsbury. Drawn by S.S.F. from a sketch by R.P.W., 1953.

obverse: X, deeply grooved
reverse: blank

The weight falls far short of ten *unciae* (272.8 gm).

2435.11

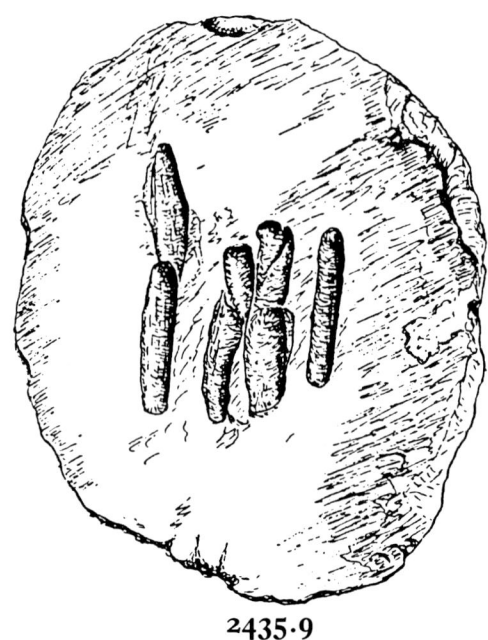

2435.9

2435.10. Nettleton, Wiltshire. Lead roundel ($\frac{1}{1}$), diameter 38 mm, thickness 4 mm, found in 1962 at the shrine of Apollo, Nettleton Scrubb, West Kington, Wilts. in a third-century level near Building X. Reproduced from Wedlake.

JRS lvii (1967), 206 No. 22. W.J. Wedlake, *Excavation of the Shrine of Apollo at Nettleton, Wilts., 1956–71* (1982), 177, 235 and fig. 92.4.

obverse: V (primary), LII (secondary)

2435.12. South Shields (*Arbeia*), Tyne and Wear [Durham]. Lead roundel ($\frac{1}{1}$), diameter 19 mm, thickness 7 mm, found about 1877 on The Lawe, at or near the Roman fort. Museum of Antiquities, Newcastle upon Tyne. Reproduced from *Cat*.

JRS xxxii (1942), 117 No. 11 d. *PSAN*⁴ iv (1929), 106 No. 73; x (1942), 17 No. 4. L. Allason-Jones and R. Miket, *Cat.* (1984), 330 No. 8.52 with fig.

obverse: blank
reverse: X

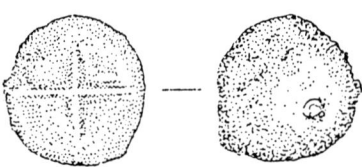

2435.12

2435.13. Caerhun (*Canovium*), Gwynedd [Caernarvonshire]. Irregular lead roundel ($\frac{7}{8}$), maximum diameter 25 mm, thickness 4 mm, found in 1927–34 at the Roman fort. Llandudno Museum. Reproduced from Reynolds.

Baillie Reynolds, *AC* xci (1936), 222 with fig. 51.2.

obverse: X
reverse: eleven parallel scratches crossed by another

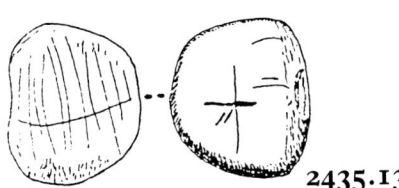
2435.13

FALSVM

2435.14.* Hylton, Tyne and Wear [Durham]. Lead roundel found in 1865 in the bed of the river Wear. Now lost. Reprinted from *EE*.

EE vii 987. Watkin *Arch. J.* xl (1883), 141. Hooppell, *PSAN*² i (1884), 19, 24, 134. Haverfield, *PSAN*² iv (1890), 230.

incised in a circle: IMD AVG
incised in the middle: SC

IM D AVG, Watkin. *S(trator) C(onsularis)*, Watkin. 'A wholly corrupt inscription', F.H., *PSAN*; 'lectio incerta', F.H., *EE*.

RIB 2436. LEAD SHEETS, EXCEPT *DEFIXIONES*

Pieces of lead sheet were convenient media for graffiti of various types. This chapter excludes labels (published under *RIB* 2410) and curse-tablets (*defixiones*)(including lists of names), which are reserved for later publication, and so contains only die-impressions and graffiti of unknown purpose. Some die-impressions may well be decorative rather than epigraphic (Nos. 7, 8, 11). For a lead votive plaque see *RIB* 306, from Lydney Park.

2436.1. Lydney Park, Gloucestershire. Piece of sheet lead (½), 76 by 38 mm, thickness 5 mm, inscribed with part of an alphabet; later it was damaged by being violently forced against a coin, apparently of the fourth century, which left an impression on which only the letters AVG are legible. Found during the nineteenth century. Lydney Park. Reproduced from Wheeler.

EE ix 1299. Haverfield, *Arch. J.* xlix (1892), 189. Collingwood in Wheeler, *Lydney* (1932), 101 No. 5 with fig. 28.5.

incised between guide-lines: ABCDEFG[. . .]

ABCDEFG[HIK]I, R.G.C.

Perhaps compare *RIB* 2437.1. Part of an alphabet scratched on lead sheet was also found with *defixiones* at Bath: see *Tab. Sulis* 1

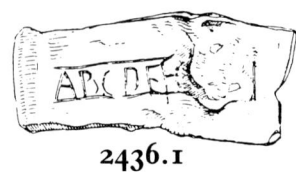

2436.1

2436.2. Sea Mills (*Abona*), Avon [Gloucestershire]. Fragment of sheet lead (⅔), 42 by 26 mm, found in or before 1924. Bristol Museum. Drawn by R.G.C., 1924.

JRS xiv (1924), 246 No. 13.

incised: [. . .]AVET

AVEI R.G.C. *JRS*: 'the last letter might be T'.

2436.2

2436.3. Lydney Park, Gloucestershire. Piece of lead (1/1), 42 by 24 mm, found sometime between 1805 and 1817 at the temple site. Lydney Park. Drawn by R.G.C.

CIL vii 1218. *EE* ix p. 643. Lysons, *Rel. Brit. Rom.* ii pl. XXIX 7. Bathurst and King (1879), 67 with pl. XXX.5. Haverfield, *Arch. J.* xlix (1892), 190. Collingwood in Wheeler, *Lydney* (1932), 101 No. 4 with fig. 28.4.

stamped twice: DOCCIVSF
   Doccius f(ecit)
   'Doccius made (this).'

Collingwood, loc. cit., claimed that the stamp had been moulded from a stamp of the Lezoux samian potter Doccius. B.R. Hartley (to S.S.F.) states that it is not modelled from a Lezoux stamp, but possibly on one from Toulon-sur-Allier. It is difficult, however, to see why the stamp should have been thus moulded rather than made independently, with the resemblance coincidental.

The name is adapted from the Celtic *Docca* (see *Tab. Sulis* 34.1).

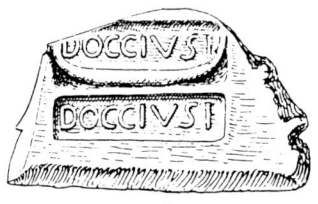

2436.3

2436.4. Malton (*Derventio*), North Yorkshire. Irregular rectangle of sheet lead (⅔), 36 by 27 mm, thickness 4 mm, inscribed on both sides with a sharp point. A strip is almost detached, but without affecting the text, which seems to be complete. The clumsily inscribed 'letters' resemble Roman cursive, but no satisfactory transcript has yet been made. The tablet's purpose is unknown. It is not a label, since it is not pierced for attachment and no names or numerals can be discerned; nor does it resemble a curse tablet (*defixio*).

2436.4

Found in 1969 during excavations in the *vicus* of the fort. Malton Museum. We print here R.P.W.'s transcript, but for a letter-by-letter criticism, see Tomlin, op. cit. Drawn by R.S.O.T., 1987.

Britannia ii (1971), 302 No. 87, with fig. 20. Tomlin, in B. Heywood (ed.), Malton final report, forthcoming.

obverse: ISΛRSES | COVIS | ΛEEO | CECEX
reverse: ISVXOSIS

R.P.W. draws and reads the reverse the other way up, at the cost of transcribing from left to right a text inscribed from right to left. Our drawing assumes the text was inscribed from left to right.

2436.5. Alcester, Warwickshire. Strip of lead (⅔), 90 by 25 mm, cut from a sheet. It was inscribed on both sides in capital letters and later folded several times with damage to the inscription. Found in 1983 unstratified during excavations at Stratford House, Stratford Road. Warwick Museum. Drawn by R.S.O.T., 1985.

Britannia xvii (1986), 449 No. 78. Tomlin in S. Cracknell, final report (forthcoming).

obverse: MARIV.
  perhaps *Mariu[s]*
reverse: *c*.6CE*c*.4

2436.6. Watercrook (? *Alauna*), Cumbria [Westmorland]. Fragment of lead sheet found in 1974. Present whereabouts unknown. Not illustrated.

Britannia xix (1988), 500 No. 55. Shotter, CW^2 lxxvi (1976), 42 No. 15.

incised in capitals: [. . .]MVV[. . .]

2436.7. Caerhun (*Canovium*), Gwynedd [Caernarvonshire]. Fragment of lead (⅓), 63 by 19 mm, thickness 5 mm, found in 1927 in the *praetorium* of the fort. Llandudno Museum. Reproduced from Reynolds, 1938.

Baillie Reynolds, *AC* lxxxii (1927), 303; xci (1936), 224 with fig. 52.3; xciii (1938), 265–6 with fig. 1.

stamped: N͡N

ΛΛI or ΛΛL, Reynolds 1927; N͡N, Reynolds 1936, 1938.

Compare *RIB* 2436.8 for a similar but not identical stamp. Neither is certainly epigraphic, and they may merely be trial strikes of an embossing tool for making ornament.

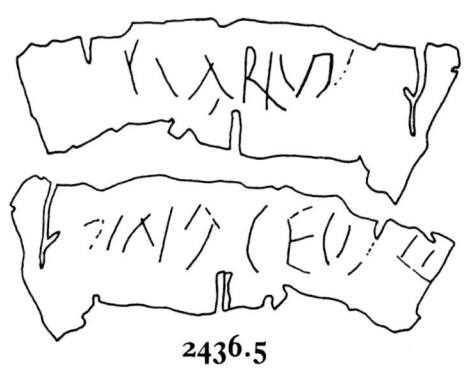

2436.5

2436.7

2436.8. Wroxeter (*Viroconium*), Shropshire. Small lead plate (¼), 63 by 44.5 mm, thickness 9.5 mm, with another plate 63 by 19 mm, thickness 4.75 mm, attached to one of its sides and once set at right angles to it, but now bent flat. Found in or before 1938 on the surface of the site excavated in 1859–61 to the south-west of the Baths. Wroxeter Museum. Reproduced from Reynolds 1938.

Baillie Reynolds, *AC* xci (1936), 224; xciii (1938) 265 with fig. 2.

obverse, stamped: NN NN(?), the first stamp inverted
reverse, stamped: XX(?)

Perhaps not epigraphic. Compare *RIB* 2436.7, with note.

2436.9. London (*Londinium*). Rectangular piece of sheet lead (½), 57 by 39 mm, thickness 2 mm, inscribed on both sides in a mixture of capitals and cursive letters. Found in 1984 during excavations at Billingsgate Lorry Park. Museum of London. Drawn by R.S.O.T., 1985.

Britannia xvii (1986), 445 with figs. 10, 11.

obverse: VICOIOVIO | MITTIVCTRILIORII | ..FERDARĪ ĪĪ
  'At *Vicus Iovius* . . . two'
reverse: X. . . . IIF.VVI V | A. . . .NIE. . .

The object is not a curse tablet or label (with pierced hole), but its purpose is unknown: see further, loc. cit. *Vicus Iovius* is an unidentified place, perhaps but not necessarily in Britain. The rest of the text is obscured by corrosion and especially by being inscribed over many small casting blemishes.

2436.10. Lincoln (*Lindum*). Fragment of lead sheet (⅔), 46 by 35.5 mm, clipped along the right-hand edge, stamped in relief with a die not fully impressed in the lower right-hand corner. Found in 1957 under Surface 4 of the Roman street at Cottesford Place, James Street. Lincoln Museum. Drawn by S.S.F. from a cast by R.P.W.

JRS xlviii (1958), 153 No. 18.

stamped: XEF[. . .]

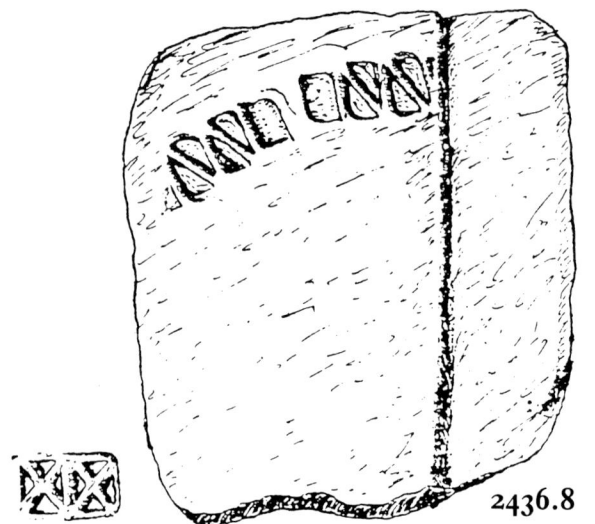
2436.8

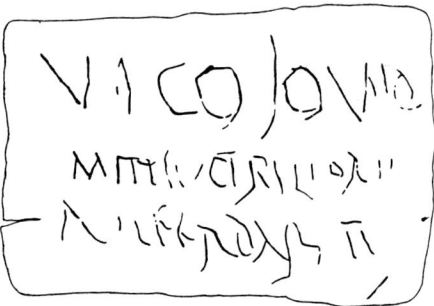
2436.9

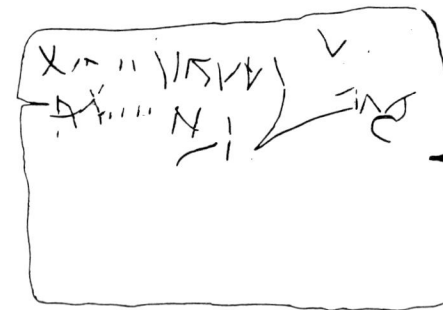

2436.10

2436.11. Box, Wiltshire. Rectangular piece of lead ($\frac{1}{1}$), 42 by 18 mm, thickness 5 mm, found in 1982 with late first- to mid second-century material in a shallow ditch 100 yards south of the Roman villa. Devizes Museum. Drawn by M.W.C.H.

Britannia xv (1984), 348 No. 61.

stamped: XNXI or XNXN(?)

The stamp is overstruck and difficult to read. Perhaps XIVXI. The object in any case is not certainly epigraphic: compare *RIB* 2436.7 (with note) and 2435.8 (with note).

2436.11

2436.12. Richborough (*Rutupiae*), Kent. Fragment of lead ($\frac{1}{1}$), 25.5 by 19 mm, reverse flat. Found in 1930 during excavations in Area XVII at the fort. In store at Dover Castle. Drawn by S.S.F. from a cast by R.P.W.

obverse stamped: XX[1–2]

The first X has a recessed field, the second is vestigial. Perhaps not epigraphic: compare *RIB* 2436.7 (with note).

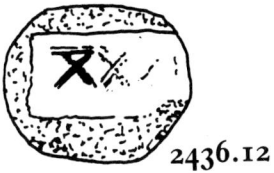

2436.12

2436.13. Wall (*Letocetum*), Staffordshire. Small fragment of sheet lead ($\frac{1}{1}$), 31.75 by 25.5 mm, thickness 4 mm, found in 1964–6 in the filling of the punic ditch on the north-western side of the second-century fort. Wall Museum. Drawn by R.S.O.T. from a cast by R.P.W.

JRS lviii (1968), 211 No. 40.

double-stamped: XX (?)

Perhaps not epigraphic: compare *RIB* 2436.7 (with note).

2436.13

RIB 2437. MISCELLANEOUS LEAD OBJECTS

This chapter contains five lead objects of diverse types, which have been grouped together under the heading 'Miscellaneous' because each is the sole example of its class. For a lead burial-canister, see *RIB* 691.

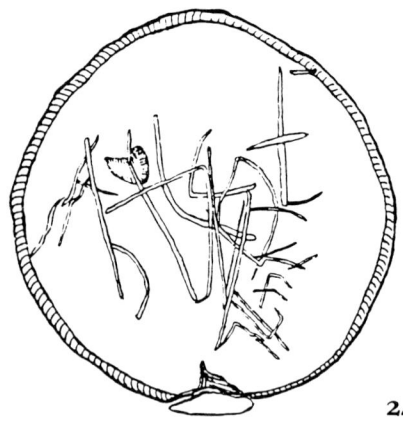

2437.1

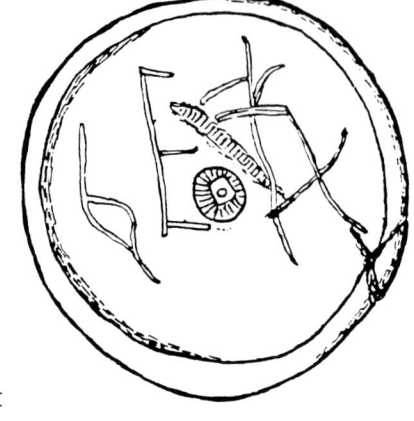

2437.2

2437.1. Holt (? *Bovium*), Clwyd [Denbighshire]. Lead cap (1/1), diameter 53 mm, flange 3 mm deep, with central socket on the reverse for a pin. Found in 1907–15 at Hilly Field, Holt. The inscriptions were first noted by G.C. Boon, 1965. National Museum, Cardiff. Drawn by R.P.W., 1965.

JRS lvi (1966), 221 No. 22.

obverse: the first part of an alphabet has been cut mostly in cursive style, here printed in italics, and repeated in larger letters, here printed in roman:
A ABC CBDEFG DEFGH
reverse: SEX with X recut
Sex(ti)
'(Property) of Sextus'

The reading of the obverse is by no means certain. Perhaps compare *RIB* 2436.1 (with note).

2437.2. Poundbury, Dorchester, Dorset. Part of the lead lining of the broad end of a tapering wooden coffin-lid (1/5), 970 by 670 mm, found in 1972, orientated east–west, during excavation of one of the fourth-century mausolea in the Roman cemetery. Drawn by R.S.O.T. from photographs, 1990.

Britannia iv (1973), 330 No. 17. Tomlin in DIE Farwell et al., *Excavations at Poundbury ii: The Cemeteries* (forthcoming).

moulded, retrograde: END IN

NI and retrograde DEO, D.E. Johnston. Retrograde END IN, M.W.C.H., R.S.O.T.

'The first two letters, NI, have probably been inverted and the inscription was intended to read I(N) N(OMINE TVO) D(OMI)NE, "in thy name, O Lord," ' M.W.C.H., *Britannia*. These contractions seem medieval rather than Roman. A blundered signature of the mould-maker is perhaps more likely, R.S.O.T.

2437.3. Slack (? *Camulodunum*), West Yorkshire. Lead lamp-stand with handle (2/3), overall length *c.* 190 mm, found in 1915 in the drain running along the south side of the *praetentura*. Tolson Memorial Museum, Huddersfield. Drawn by S.S.F. from a rubbing by J.P. Wild, 1990.

Dodd and Woodward, *YAJ* xxvi (1920), 79 with pl. XXV (fig. 48), not showing the inscription. I.A. Richmond *Huddersfield* (1925), 41 with fig. 38 (not showing the inscription).

graffito on the base: FVR
'Thief'

FVR, Richmond. VK, Dodd and Woodward.

Except for the right-hand stroke of the V, the letters are extremely hard to distinguish among other scratches on the surface, and the F, indeed, may be illusory.

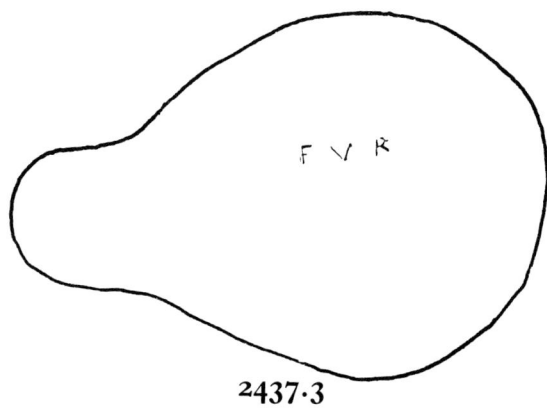

2437.4. Meols, Cheshire. Piece of lead ($\frac{1}{1}$), 30 by 13.5 mm, thickness 6 mm, with letters 1.5 mm deep punched with a die into the obverse, leaving their tops level with the surrounding surface, thus forming a rough retrograde die. Found before 1899, washed out with other Roman and medieval material on the foreshore at the end of the Wirral peninsula. Grosvenor Museum, Chester. Drawn by S.S.F. from a cast by R.P.W.

obverse, stamped: IIV
reverse, graffito: VII

The first I on the obverse has a small tail suggesting L retrograde. But the graffito on the reverse confirms that VII is intended.

There is some distortion above the right-hand end of the obverse from a U-shaped dent.

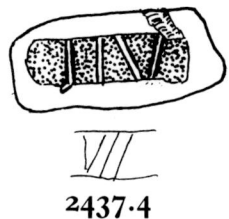

2437.5. Upchurch Marshes, Kent. Lead dome-shaped object ($\frac{1}{1}$), diameter 30 mm, maximum height 9.5 mm, weight 54.77 gm, having a small depression in the centre of the obverse seemingly unintentional. Found c. 1951 on Burntwick Island on the right bank of the river Medway. In private possession. Drawn by R.S.O.T. from a sketch and cast by R.P.W., 1953.

obverse: incised, figures probably not letters
reverse (dome): incised, three semi-circles, two having radii, the other parallel chords (*not drawn*)

The object is not certainly Roman, but was found in association with Roman coins and sherds. It weighs two *unciae* (54.58 gm), but does not appear to be a weight.

ALIENUM

2437.6.* Minster, Kent. Oval sling-bullet of lead ($\frac{2}{3}$), length 38 mm, width 19 mm, found before 1926. Margate Public Library from the Dr Arthur Rowe collection. Drawn by R.P.W., 1964.

JRS liv (1964), 185.

obverse: FERI
reverse: POMP
feri Pomp(eium)
'Strike Pompeius'

This is another example of those found at *Asculum* (Ascoli Piceno): see Zangermeister, *CIL* ix 6086 ix 16 with fig; *EE* vi p. 21 No. 9, 15 with pl. IV 3. Cn. Pompeius Strabo besieged Asculum in the Marsic War, 90–89 B.C.

RIB 2438. STONE ROUNDELS

The stone roundels listed here (five in number) are far less common than those of pottery (*RIB* 2439 (eighteen)), and both are greatly outnumbered by roundels in bone (*RIB* 2440 (three hundred and eighty-one)). Two examples (*RIB* 2438.4 and 5) are similar in shape and size to the bone examples and like them may have been employed as gaming counters (see the Introduction to *RIB* 2440). But 2438.1 and 2 resemble the majority of the pottery roundels in being twice the size of the bone roundels; if used for gaming (as indeed the inscriptions suggest) they would have required a much larger gaming board.

2438.1. Ashby de la Launde, Lincolnshire. Roundel ($\frac{2}{3}$) of limestone, diameter 70 mm, thickness 14.3 mm, found in 1965 on a Roman site east of the village. Lincoln Museum. Drawn by S.S.F. from a rubbing by R.P.W., 1966.

JRS lvi (1966), 220 No. 11.

obverse, (a) primary text, deeply cut: ADALMA
        (b) secondary text, inverted in relation to (a) and placed above and below it: DONA|TVS·L. . | FELICITER
reverse: LOPISCALLVS | SATVRNI|NO

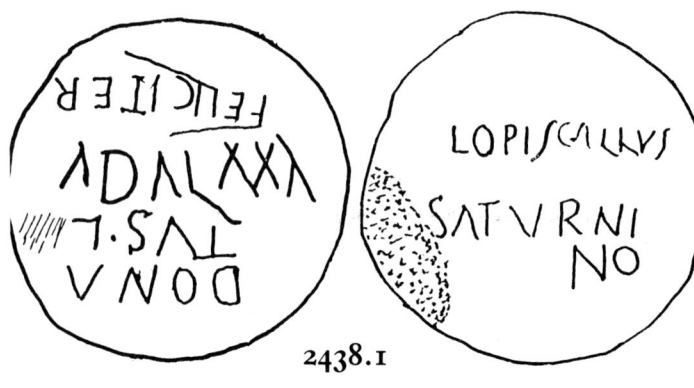

2438.2. Neath (*Nidum*), West Glamorgan. Slate roundel ($\frac{1}{1}$), diameter 38 mm, found in 1949 at the fort. National Museum, Cardiff. Drawn by S.S.F. from a rubbing by R.P.W., 1953.

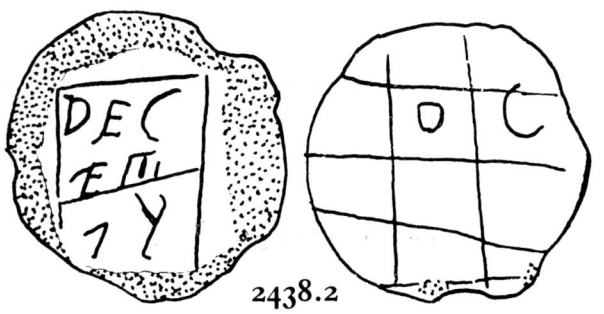

JRS xli (1951), 142 No. 9. Nash-Williams, *BBCS* xiii (1950), 242 fig. 9.

obverse: DEC|EM | IV (enclosed in a frame)
reverse: OC (in a grid)

2438.3. Dorchester (*Durnovaria*), Dorset. Shale roundel ($\frac{1}{1}$), diameter *c.* 48 mm, thickness 5 mm, with broken edges cut down from a larger piece. Found in 1970 on the site of Dorchester Prison. Drawn by R.P.W., 1970.

Britannia ii (1971), 295 No. 34 with fig. 16.

graffito (first line): LACTABPVSA[. . .]. .

B and S are retrograde. The remaining five lines are largely repetitive and seem to be part of a writing exercise. In l.4 a horned animal is depicted.

2438.4. London (*Londinium*). Stone roundel ($\frac{1}{1}$), diameter 22 mm, thickness 2.4 mm. Said to be from the bed of the Walbrook, London. In 1933 it was bought by Lt. Col. L.A.D. Montague (for whom see note to *RIB* 2422.74). Exeter Museum. Drawn by R.P.W., 1954.

JRS xliv (1954), 106 No. 22.

obverse: countersunk, VENTINVS
reverse: blank

The cognomen *Ventinus* (*CIL* ii 1176) and derived nomen *Ventinia* (v 7100) are attested, perhaps cognate with the (Celtic) spring-name *Ventina* (ix 3351) and thus *Coventina*.

2438.5. Usk (*Burrium*), Gwent [Monmouthshire]. Thin oval pebble (¼), presumably used as a gaming piece, diameters 20 and 14 mm, thickness 1 mm, found in 1974 in a pre-Flavian pit. National Museum, Cardiff. Reproduced from Boon and Hassall.

Britannia x (1979), 355 No. 48. G.C. Boon and M.W.C. Hassall, in W.H. Manning (ed.), *The Coins, Inscriptions and Graffiti* (*Report on the Excavations at Usk 1965–76*) (1982), 53 No. 3 with fig. 4.3.

obverse: X
reverse: blank

FALSA

2438.6.* Richborough (*Rutupiae*), Kent. Chalk roundel (¼), diameter 18 mm, thickness 4.75 mm, with a letter left in relief on each side after the field had been cut away. Found in 1928–31 in the 'stone fort road-metal'. In store at Dover Castle. Drawn by S.S.F. from a sketch by R.P.W., 1953.

J.P. Bushe-Fox, *Richborough* iv (1949), 125 No. 83 with pl. XXXIV.83.

obverse, carved in relief: D
reverse, carved in relief: GE

As with *RIB* 2412.123*, the material, the relief letters and the character of the inscription on the reverse combine to throw doubt on the Roman date of this object.

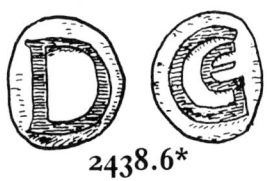

2438.7.* Colchester (*Camulodunum*), Essex. Slate roundel (⅔), diameter 57 mm, thickness 3 mm, found 'at Colchester' in 1843. Colchester Museum. Drawn by S.S.F. from a rubbing by R.P.W., 1954.

Colchester Museum *Cat.* (ed. 1, 1863), 31 No. 601.

obverse, incised: ˅ETKERON over the figure of an elephant

Compare *RIB* 2439.20, where ETKR< is preceded by an X.

For the reasons for rejecting this object as genuine see the Introduction to *RIB* 2439.

RIB 2439. POTTERY ROUNDELS

Five of the pottery roundels are made from sherds of samian (*terra sigillata*) and twelve of coarse pottery. In addition there is a group of 13 roundels of coarse pottery or tile from Colchester (to which should be added *RIB* 2438.7 in slate) which are here classified as *Falsa*. Although they are made from Roman pottery or tile, and although some, e.g. *RIB* 2439.24*, cannot be rejected with assurance, the group as a whole shows suspicious features. All were found around or before the middle of the 19th century, a period when several collectors were at work in Colchester (M.R. Hull, *Roman Colchester* (1958), 250); some of the roundels carry exotic – even meaningless – legends but which seem designed to catch the eye of an undiscriminating collector, together with some unparalleled figures possibly similarly intended. Some carry unusually elaborate incised frames, and the style of lettering is often heavy. Such characteristics tend to justify regarding them as a group of forgeries. On the other hand, it must be admitted that Colchester has also yielded an unusual number of undoubtedly genuine inscribed pottery roundels (only three in the chapter come from elsewhere in Britain), some of which bear inscriptions in equally heavy style (though lacking the elaborate ornament): compare *RIB* 2439.8, 10 and 11.

Although pottery roundels are normally at least twice the size of bone roundels (*RIB* 2440), they were probably used in the same games (but on larger boards). This suggestion is supported by the legend on 2439.12.

2439.1. (?) Colchester (*Camulodunum*), Essex. Roundel of coarse pottery ($\frac{1}{1}$), diameter 41 mm, thickness 13 mm, found before 1892 at an unknown provenance, probably at Colchester. Colchester Museum (Jarmin collection). Drawn by R.G.C., 1928.

May, *Cat.*, 247 No. 16 with fig. 9 No. 16.

incised: AGRI

A.P. May; AGRI R.G.C., R.P.W.

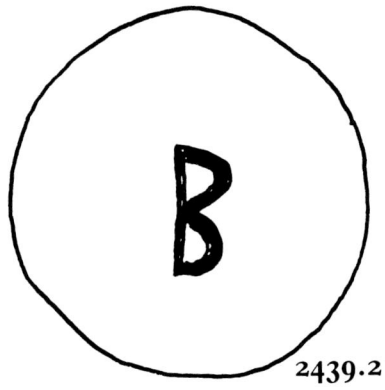

2439.2

2439.1

2439.2. (?) Ibid. Pottery roundel in white ware ($\frac{1}{1}$), diameter 49 mm. No provenance, but probably somewhere in Colchester. Colchester Museum. Drawn by R.P.W., 1943.

incised: B

2439.3. Ibid. Roundel ($\frac{1}{1}$) made from a samian sherd (*terra sigillata*), diameter *c*. 50 mm, found before 1892 at Colchester. Now lost. Reprinted from *EE*.

EE vii 1147 d.

incised: B

2439.4. Ibid. Roundel of grey pottery ($\frac{1}{1}$), diameter 39 mm, one of seven, varying in diameter from 34 to 43 mm, found in 1967 in a Roman pit in the garden of St Mary's Rectory. Two were uninscribed; for the others see *RIB* 2439.5, 8, 10 and 11. Colchester Museum. Drawn by R.P.W., 1967.

JRS lviii (1968), 210 No. 33 a. Dunnett, *T. Essex AS*³ iii.1 (1971), 71 and fig. 27.14.

obverse: DRA
reverse: blank

2439.4

2439.5. Ibid. Roundel of grey pottery (¼), diameter 30 mm, found with *RIB* 2439.4 (*q.v.* for circumstances and location). Drawn by R.P.W., 1967.

JRS lviii (1968), 210 No. 33 b. Dunnett, *T. Essex AS*³ iii. 1 (1971), 71 and fig. 27.14.

obverse: DRA
reverse: blank

2439.5

2439.6. Chesterholm (*Vindolanda*), Northumberland. Roundel (¼) of black pottery, diameter 32 mm, thickness 5 mm, found in 1971 in Room II of the *mansio* in the *vicus*, in a floor of Period I. Vindolanda Museum. Drawn by R.P.W., 1971.

Britannia iii (1972), 360 No. 45.

obverse: blank
reverse: M and (inverted) M

2439.6

2439.7. Nettleton, West Kington, Wiltshire. Irregular roundel of coarse grey pottery, maximum diameter 35 mm, thickness 7.5 mm, found in 1967 in a third- to fourth-century level on Site E at the Shrine of Apollo at Nettleton Scrubb. Bristol Museum. Drawn by S.S.F. from a rubbing by R.P.W., 1968.

JRS lix (1969), 237 No. 12.

obverse: central hole
reverse: M above central hole

2439.7

2439.8. Colchester (*Camulodunum*), Essex. Roundel of grey pottery (¼), diameter 42 mm, one of seven, varying in diameter from 34 to 43 mm, found in 1967 in a Roman pit in the garden of St Mary's Rectory. Two were uninscribed; for the others see *RIB* 2439.4, 5, 10 and 11. Colchester Museum. Drawn by S.S.F. from a rubbing by R.P.W., 1967.

JRS lviii (1968), 210 No. 33 c. Dunnett, *T. Essex AS*³ iii.1 (1971), 71 and fig. 27.14.

obverse: MILITIA
reverse: blank

2439.8

2439.9. Ibid. Roundel of black pottery ($\frac{1}{1}$), diameter 67 mm, thickness 9.5 mm, found probably in the 19th century at Colchester. Colchester Museum. Drawn by R.P.W., 1943.

JRS xxxiv (1944), 89 No. 10.

incised: PARATVS

2439.9

2439.10. Ibid. Roundel of grey pottery ($\frac{1}{1}$), diameter 35 mm, one of seven, varying in diameter from 34 to 43 mm, found in 1967 in a Roman pit in the garden of St Mary's Rectory. Two were uninscribed; for the others see *RIB* 2439.4, 5, 8 and 11. Colchester Museum. Drawn by S.S.F. from a rubbing by R.P.W., 1967.

JRS lviii (1968), 210 No. 33 d. Dunnett, *T. Essex AS*[3] iii.1 (1971), 71 with fig. 27.14.

obverse: (first hand) PCI
(second hand) VI

2439.10

2439.11. Ibid. Roundel in grey pottery ($\frac{1}{1}$), diameter 40 mm, one of seven found in 1967 as above. Colchester Museum. Drawn by S.S.F. from a rubbing by R.P.W., 1967.

JRS lviii (1968), 210 No. 33 e. Dunnett, *T. Essex AS*[3] iii.1 (1971), 71 with fig. 27.14.

obverse: POLLI
reverse: blank

2439.11

2439.12. Ibid. Roundel of grey pottery ($\frac{1}{1}$), diameter 32 mm, thickness 6 mm, found in or before 1905 at Goojerat Barracks, Colchester. Colchester Museum. Drawn by S.S.F. from a rubbing by R.P.W., 1943.

May, *Cat.*, 247 fig. 9.14.

obverse: PREMI|ATOR

The inscription is an anagram of IMPERATOR. For this as the winning throw in *ludus latrunculorum* see *HA, Proculus* xiii.2.

2439.12

2439.13. Bar Hill, Strathclyde Region [Dumbartonshire]. Large roundel (⅔), made from the base of a red-ware jar, diameter 79 mm, found in 1902–5 at Bar Hill fort on the Antonine Wall. Hunterian Museum, Glasgow. Reproduced from Robertson, Scott and Keppie.

G. Macdonald and A. Park, *Bar Hill* (1906), 71; *PSAS*[4] iv (1905–6), 473. A. Robertson, M. Scott and L. Keppie, *Bar Hill: A Roman Fort and its Finds* (1975), 122 No. 12 with fig. 43.

obverse: ƧEN
 Sen(. . .)

2439.13

2439.14. Colchester (*Camulodunum*), Essex. Roundel (¹⁄₁) made from a sherd of grey ware, diameter 40 mm, thickness 12 mm, found in 1972 in a medieval pit at Lion Walk. Colchester Museum. Drawing: Colchester Archaeological Trust.

Britannia viii (1977), 438 No. 64. N. Crummy, *Small Finds* (1983), 95 No. 2319 with fig. 96.

obverse: SVPER
reverse: blank

2439.14

2439.15. Traprain Law, Lothian Region [East Lothian]. Roundel (¹⁄₁) made from the base of a samian vessel stamped D[EVIXT]VS, found in 1920 in excavations at Traprain Law. National Museums of Scotland, Queen Street, Edinburgh. Drawn by S.S.F. from a photograph.

Cree, *PSAS* lv (1920–21), 180, fig. 14 No. 58.

reverse: TB (twice)

2439.15

2439.16. Colchester (*Camulodunum*), Essex. Roundel (¹⁄₁) made from a samian sherd (*terra sigillata*) of Drag. 37; diameter 31 mm, found before *c*. 1890 at the Lexden Road kiln site (Joslin Collection). Colchester Museum. Drawn by R.G.C., 1928.

EE vii 1147 a. May, *Cat.*, 247 No. 15 with fig. 9.

incised: VAK

2439.16

2439.17. Ibid. Roundel made from a sherd of samian (*terra sigillata*), diameter *c*. 25 mm. Found before *c*. 1890. Colchester Museum (Joslin Collection), but not seen by R.P.W., 1954. Reprinted from *EE*.

EE vii 1147 d.

obverse: I
 'One'

2439.18. Ibid. Roundel made from a sherd of samian (*terra sigillata*), found before 1877 at Colchester. Reprinted from *EE*.

EE vii 1147 c.

obverse: X
          'Ten'

FALSA
(See Introduction to this chapter)

2439.19.* Colchester (*Camulodunum*), Essex. Pottery roundel (⅔), diameter 35 mm, thickness 4.75 mm. Colchester Museum. Drawn by S.S.F. from rubbings by R.P.W., 1954.

obverse, incised: CHO below the figure of a (?) bird
reverse, incised: SPΩHD around a rough human bust

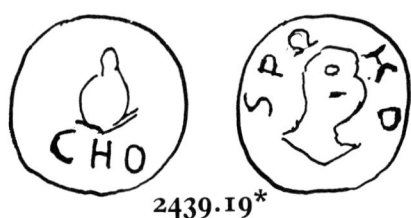

2439.20.* Ibid. Roundel of buff pottery (⅔), diameter 47.5 mm, thickness 6 mm, found before 1863. Colchester Museum. Drawn by S.S.F. from a rubbing by R.P.W., 1954.

Colchester Museum *Cat.* (ed. 1, 1863), 32 No. 610.

obverse: X | ETKR< | dot Ω dot
reverse: blank

2439.21.* Ibid. Roundel of grey pottery (⅔) with traces of glaze on the reverse, diameter 51 mm, thickness 6 mm, found before 1863. Colchester Museum. Drawn by S.S.F. from rubbings by R.P.W., 1954.

Colchester Museum *Cat.* (ed. 1, 1863), 32 No. 608.

obverse: EQVVS III REKESH
reverse: dot | L'NC

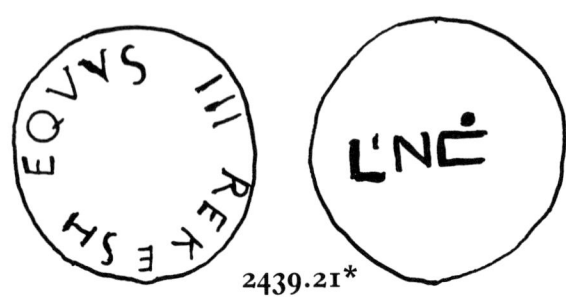

2439.22.* Ibid. Roundel of red pottery, found before 1863. Colchester Museum, but not seen by R.P.W., 1954. Not illustrated. Reprinted from *Cat.*

Colchester Museum *Cat.* (ed. 1, 1863), 31 No. 652.

obverse: ETV with the figure of a stag
reverse: 'a circular ornament'

2439.23.* Ibid. Roundel of grey pottery, found before 1863. Colchester Museum, but not seen by R.P.W., 1954. Not illustrated. Reprinted from *Cat.*

Colchester Museum *Cat.* (ed. 1, 1863), 32 No. 609.

obverse: FOWSTRA–N PΛSVIK
reverse: blank

2439.24.* Ibid. Pottery roundel (⅔), diameter 41 mm, thickness 9.5 mm. Colchester Museum. Drawn by S.S.F. from a rubbing by R.P.W., 1954.

obverse, incised: L surrounded by five dots

Compare *RIB* 2439.27.*

2439.25.* Ibid. Roundel of red tile ($\frac{2}{3}$), diameter 60.5 mm, thickness 6 mm, found 'at Colchester' before 1863. Colchester Museum. Drawn by S.S.F. from a rubbing by R.P.W., 1954.

Colchester Museum *Cat.* (ed. 1, 1863), 31–2 No. 606.

obverse, incised: RAPEDVE within a frame of lines and dots
reverse: nine dots within a grid

2439.28.* Colchester (*Camulodunum*), Essex. Roundel of red pottery ($\frac{2}{3}$), diameter 54 mm, thickness 6 mm, found before 1863. Colchester Museum. Drawn by S.S.F. from a rubbing by R.P.W., 1954.

Colchester Museum *Cat.* (ed. 1, 1863), 32 No. 612.

obverse, incised within an incised wreath: VII
reverse: nine dots (*not illustrated*)

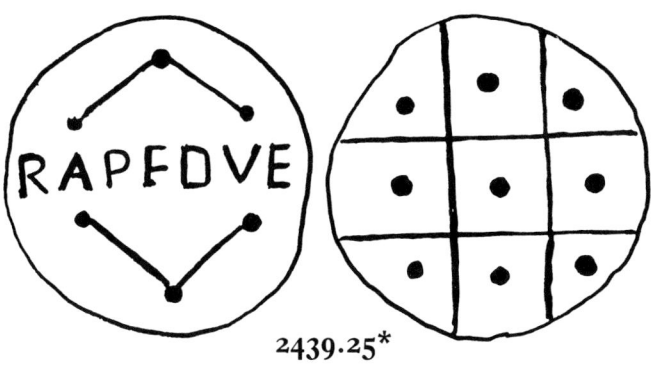

2439.25*

2439.28*

2439.26.* Ibid. Roundel of grey pottery, found before 1863. Colchester Museum, but not seen by R.P.W., 1954. Not illustrated. Reprinted from *Cat.*

Colchester Museum *Cat.* (ed. 1, 1863), 32 No. 607.

obverse: RAPEDVE
reverse: blank

Compare *RIB* 2439.25.

2439.29.* Ibid. Pottery roundel, found before 1863. Colchester Museum, but not seen by R.P.W., 1954. Not illustrated. Reprinted from *Cat.*

Colchester Museum *Cat.* (ed. 1, 1863), 31 No. 651.

obverse: XVI with the figure of a galley with rowers
reverse: an incised square

2439.27.* Ibid. Pottery roundel ($\frac{2}{3}$), diameter 40 mm, thickness 4.75 mm, found 'at Colchester in 1845'. Colchester Museum. Drawn by S.S.F. from a rubbing by R.P.W., 1954.

obverse, incised: five dots and TH below two inclined lines
reverse: blank

Compare *RIB* 2439.24.

2439.30.* Ibid. Roundel of grey pottery ($\frac{2}{3}$), diameter 62 mm, thickness 9 mm, found before 1863 'at Colchester'. Colchester Museum. Drawn by S.S.F. from rubbings by R.P.W., 1954.

Colchester Museum *Cat.* (ed. 1, 1863), 31 No. 605.

obverse, incised: dot | XIX | dot within a frame like that on 2439.31*
reverse: incised lines

2439.27*

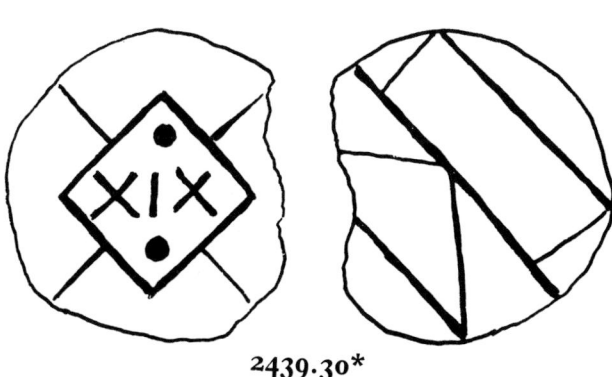

2439.30*

2439.31.* Colchester (*Camulodunum*), Essex. Roundel of red tile (⅔), diameter 51 mm, thickness 6 mm, found before 1863. Colchester Museum. Drawn by S.S.F. from a rubbing by R.P.W., 1954.

Colchester Museum *Cat.* (ed. 1, 1863), 32 No. 611.

obverse, incised within an incised frame like that on 2439.30*:   LXVII

2439.31*

RIB 2440. BONE ROUNDELS

Bone roundels, usually between 17 and 25 mm in diameter and between 2 and 5 mm thick, are frequent finds on excavations. The shapes were classified by K.M. Kenyon, (*Excavations at the Jewry Wall site, Leicester* (1948), 266) and have recently been discussed afresh by S. Greep (*The Archaeology of Canterbury* v (*The Marlowe Car Park*, 1991, forthcoming)). There are three principal forms: (i) plain with dished or countersunk obverse (Kenyon, Type A); (ii) the obverse having a varying number of concentric rings (Kenyon, Type B); and (iii) plain, with flat obverse and reverse (Kenyon, Type C). On all types a central sunken dot is often apparent, the chuck-mark which is caused by manufacture on a lathe. Greep has shown that Kenyon Type C is the earliest, occurring in the first century; Type A occurs from early in the second century, while Type B is found at all periods. A. MacGregor has demonstrated (*Finds from a Roman Sewer System . . . in Church Street, York* (The Archaeology of York xvii fasc. 1 (1976)) that the bevel or bevels frequently found on the reverse, and sometimes on both sides, are caused not by wear or function (e.g. 'as for tiddlywinks', Kenyon, loc. cit., 266), but by manufacture from long bones whose curvation did not allow a totally flat surface. For this reason neither bevels nor chuck-marks are normally noted in the descriptions below.

Although the great majority of bone roundels are uninscribed, a significant number do bear letters or numerals scratched on one or other of the main surfaces and even sometimes around the edge. Because of the toughness of the material these marks are often faint or roughly incised and thus are difficult to read, particularly when successive inscriptions occur on the same face. In the present chapter numerals form the principal inscriptions on 231 examples, and letters on only 150; but the preponderance of numerals is partly due to the exceptionally large group of 119 roundels recovered at the fort of Ravenglass (see *RIB* 2440.42), of which 79 carried numbers. Very occasionally drilled dots, presumably substituting for numerals, are found (*RIB* 2440.33, 62, 122, 168–172, 185, 203, 207–208, 232, 291, 321, 372, 378 and 380). They recall similar indications on some of the Weights (*RIB* 2412). Notable are two roundels which express fractions (*RIB* 2440.358 and 369).

Bone roundels may have been used in two main ways. There is evidence for their employment in calculation: as true counters, in fact. The younger Pliny (*Ep.* vi 33.9) describes an occasion when there arose 'a frequent need of calculation and almost of calling for counters and a board' (*frequens necessitas computandi ac paene calculos tabulamque poscendi*). S.F. Bonner (*Education in Ancient Rome* (1977), 183) discusses and illustrates the use of the *abacus*, a wooden reckoning-board with raised edges, on which counters (*calculi*) were manipulated in computation. More elaborate *abaci* also existed, not dissimilar from the modern variety, in which small knobs were moved in a series of slots (ibid., 184). Illustrations of *abaci* are also found in Kretzchmer and Heinsius, *Trierer Zeitschr.* xx (1951), 96–108. If used on such boards, the value of each counter would depend upon the line in which it stood, since successive lines represented digits, tens, hundreds, and so on; it would not be necessary to mark the counters themselves.

But perhaps the chief use was as gaming pieces in board-games. This conclusion is supported by the sets of marked pieces which have been found: twenty-three and at least twenty-four pieces from two burials at Chichester (see *RIB* 2440.27 and 52 respectively), a set of twenty from Corbridge (see 2440.35) and the sets of twelve each at Colchester and Bermondsey (see 2440.33 and 123) or nine at Ewell (2440.20) and Wroxeter (Atkinson, *Wroxeter* (1942), 252). The group of 119 at Ravenglass, already mentioned, was associated with seven glass roundels, and had evidently once been contained in a bag. A group of forty-six accompanied a cremation at York (2440.310).

Association with board-games is perhaps also supported by the frequent occurrence of numerals. For the types of game see R.G. Austen, 'Roman Board-Games', *Greece and Rome* iv (1934), 24–34, 76–82; R.C. Bell, *Board and Table Games from many Civilizations* (1960); A. MacGregor, op. cit., and R.C. Turner in T.W. Potter, *Romans in North-West England* (1979), 76–9.

It should be noted, however, that four of the nine bone roundels found together at Ewell (see *RIB* 2440.20) carried the graffito VX or XV, perhaps standing for 'five denarii' two of them also with the words *remi(ttam) l(ibenter)*, 'I will gladly repay' (but see the note to 2440.20). This suggests occasional use as gambling tokens.

Thirty-five other roundels (*RIB* 2440.327–352 and eight others) carry the symbol ✕ or ✶, depending on the orientation. The symbol in its latter form was taken by R.P. Wright (*RIB* archive) as indicating XI; and since examples of XI distinctly inscribed occur only eleven times (see *RIB* 2440.322–326 with note), this view is perhaps not implausible. Yet TABLE I shows that individual numbers vary very widely in the frequency of their occurrence on the roundels: XVI and XVIII do not appear at all, and numbers over 20 are extremely sporadic. Moreover the symbol ✶ is the normal sign for *denarius* and may occur in this sense on *RIB* 2440.20, 109, 188 and 335), despite the crudity of rendering, which may account for X rather than ✶ in the appropriate place on No. 107. Indeed R. Eggers was of the opinion (*Ausgrabungen auf dem Magdalensburg, 1954 und 1955* (1956), 155–62) that the symbol X itself stood for *denarii*. He also suggested that A stood for *aureus*, N for *nummus* and V for *quinarius*; but in view of the many other single letters which occur (TABLE II), these last are unlikely expansions. It is wiser to take such letters as owners' marks. Owners' names occur in more recognizable form on *RIB* 2440.38–40, 68–71, 93, 97–98, 123–132, 138, 144–147, 149 and 198.

As may be seen from TABLE I, X (135 examples) far outnumbers all other numerals; V (with only 31) follows next, and I (with 24); few of the rest exceed single figures. The symbol ✶ (35 examples) therefore seems statistically unlikely to represent XI, at least in the majority of instances, and more probably either indicates '*denarius*' (as a gambling token), or else is really only a simple star used as a personal mark or to invoke luck. The extraordinary preponderance of X may perhaps be explained if, as Eggers thought, it too represents '*denarius*' (it possibly does this on *RIB* 2440.107), or if it indicated the start of a new decimal series on the gaming-board. But in many instances it, too, is probably only an owner's mark.

Pairs of letters, of which the occurrences are shown in TABLE III, rarely appear in the same combination more than once. This suggests that they are more likely to represent marks of ownership than to relate, for instance, to the details of a game or to the furtherance of calculations.

The distribution of inscribed bone roundels is illustrated in TABLE IV. Inevitably to a large extent the actual numbers found are the result of the varying scale of excavation at different sites and of the care and observation of their excavators. Nevertheless, it is a striking fact that the vast majority derive from urban or military centres, less than 5 per cent having been found on rural sites. In this they reflect the normal distribution of inscriptions.

Gaming pieces or counters were also sometimes made of glass. The material is usually either opaque white or blue-black in colour. Naturally glass counters are uninscribed, but they are occasionally decorated with marvered spots in a different colour: see the discussion by H.E.M. Cool and J. Price in G.W. Meates, *The Roman Villa at Lullingstone, Kent* ii (1987), 123–5.

Stone and Pottery roundels (*RIB* 2438 and 2439 respectively) may also have been used in games, although they are often of a much larger size than the bone roundels and would have needed a larger board.

TABLE I
Bone Roundels: Occurrences of numerals

Numeral		On Face		On Edge	Total
I	sixteen	: Nos. 23(?), 45, 152–163, 197(?), 341.	eight	: Nos. 85, 151, 222, 223, 237, 298, 299, 329	24
II	five	: Nos. 158, 164, 165, 166(?), 252	nine	: Nos. 26, 134, 141, 167, 221, 223, 237, 329, 347	14
Two dots	four	: Nos. 62, 168, 169(?), 207	–		4
III	four	: Nos. 170, 173, 175, 176	six	: Nos. 5, 149, 151, 174, 304, 347	10
Three dots	nine	: Nos. 122, 169(?), 171, 172, 207, 208, 232, 291, 372	–		9

RIB 2440. BONE ROUNDELS

Numeral		On Face		On Edge	Total
IV	eight	: Nos. 158, 177–183	one	: No. 222	9
IIII	two	: Nos. 23, 39	nine	: Nos. 141, 184, 199, 202, 223, 224, 237, 329, 348	12
Four dots	two	: No. 185, 380	–		2
V	twenty-six	: Nos. 20, 38, 39, 107, 109, 179, 187–195, 197–8, 200–202, 230, 244–246 260(?), 335	five	: Nos. 196, 199(?), 221, 222, 347	31
IIIII			one	: No. 186	1
Five dots	two	: No. 203, 378	–		2
VI	six	: Nos. 140, 204–206, 262(?), 289	five	: Nos. 105, 199, 209, 336, 366	11
Six dots	one	: No. 170	–		1
VII	one	: No. 40	two	: Nos. 26, 207	3
IIIIIII	–		one	: No. 208	1
VIII	one	: No. 243(?)	two	: Nos. 222, 381	3
IX	three	: Nos. 140, 264(?), 329	–		2
VIIII	one	: No. 210	seven	: Nos. 209, 222, 297, 336, 347, 364, 366	8
X	one hundred and thirty	: Nos. 27, 31, 32, 42, 75, 82(?), 90, 91, 103, 104, 107, 134, 143, 150, 155, 180, 201(?), 210–308, 310–320, 337, 354, 372	five	: Nos. 26, 161, 198, 199, 309	135
Ten dots	one	: 321			1
XI	seven	: Nos. 197(?), 249, 322–326	four	: Nos. 76(?), 198, 220, 354	11
✶	thirty-five	: Nos. 68, 140, 142, 207, 223, 241, 271(?), 322, 327–352, 378	–		35
XII	three	: Nos. 354(?), 355–356	four	: Nos. 220, 353, 357, 359	7
Twelve dots	one	: No. 33	–		1
XIII	one	: No. 244(?)	one	: No. 220	2
XIIIS	one	: No. 358	–		1
XIIII	–		two	: Nos. 220, 365(?)	2
XV	three	: Nos. 359–361	two	: Nos. 220, 357	5
15 digits			one	: No. 236	1
XVI	–		–		–
XVII	one	: No. 73	–		1
XVIII	–		–		–
XVIIII	–		two	: Nos. 57(?), 362	2
XX	seven	: Nos. 224, 363–368	two	: Nos. 26, 76(?)	9
XXS	one	: No. 369	–		1

TABLE I, continued

Numeral	On Face		On Edge		Total
XXIIII	–		one	: No. 365(?)	1
XXV	one	: No. 370	–		1
XXVI	one	: No. 371	–		1
XXVIIII	one	: No. 372	–		1
XXX	one	: No. 373	two	: No. 365, 374(?)	3
XXXIIII	–		one	: No. 365(?)	1
XLV	one	: No. 375	–		1
XLIIX	one	: No. 376	–		1
L	two	: Nos. 97, 197(?)	–		1
LII	one	: No. 377	–		1
LX	one	: 378(?)			1
XCI	one	: No. 379	–		1

TABLE II

Bone Roundels: Occurrences of single letters

A	eight	: Nos. 1–3, 7–9, 137(?), 140	M	nineteen	: Nos. 33, 48–63, 210, 292
Λ	ten	: Nos. 4–6, 10, 11, 91, 198(?), 199(?), 221, 362	N	seven	: Nos. 80–85, 183(?)
			O	one	: No. 33
B	one	: No. 122	P	six	: Nos. 90–92, 103(?), 123, 264(?)
C	–		Q	one	: No. 99
D	two	: Nos. 27, 28	R	six	: Nos. 100–102, 103(?), 105, 270
E	five	: Nos. 29–32, 147	S	nine	: Nos. 113–121
F	two	: No. 41(?), 165(?)	T	three	: Nos. 134–136
G	two	: Nos. 35, 36	V	see TABLE I	
H	three	: Nos. 37, 82(?), 137(?)	X	one	: No. 150 (perhaps here not a numeral, although listed in TABLE I)
K	one	: No. 46			
L	three	: Nos. 97, 109, 197			

TABLE III

Bone Roundels: Occurrences of pairs of letters

AE	: No. 12	LK	: No. 47	PR	: Nos. 74, 95
AM	: No. 14	LM	: No. 25(?)	RI or RV	: No. 106
AN	: No. 9	MA	: Nos. 64, 65, 66, 67	RT	: No. 111
AS	: No. 18	MR	: No. 78	SS	: No. 133
AT	: No. 19	MV	: Nos. 9, 79	TN	: No. 141
AV	: No. 221	NI	: Nos. 86, 87, 88	VA	: No. 143
AX	: Nos. 21, 150(?)	NN	: No. 83	VN	: No. 347
CM	: No. 25(?)	NV	: Nos. 79(?), 198	VV	: No. 189 (if not M)
EI	: No. 197	OB	: No. 89	VX	: No. 360
LB	: No. 108(?)	PE	: Nos. 94, 263		
LE	: No. 30(?)	PP	: No. 104		

TABLE IV
Inscribed bone roundels: Occurrences by type of site
(For identifications, consult the index to this fascicule)

A. Urban		B. Military and Urban		C. Military		D. Rural	
Aldborough	6	Brough on Humber	1	Binchester	1	Bishop's Stortford	1
Bath	2	Corbridge	14	Brecon	9	Ewell	9
Bermondsey	10	York	18	Caerleon	12	Margate	2
Caerwent	14			Chesterholm	10	Marshfield	2
Caistor St Edmund	2			Chesters	2	North Warnborough	1
Canterbury	1			Hod Hill	1	Ospringe	2
Chichester	32			Housesteads	1	Springhead	1
Cirencester	1			Malton	3		
Colchester	26			Ravenglass	89		
Dorchester	4			Richborough	11		
Great Chesterford	2			South Shields	6		
Leicester	5						
London	6						
St Albans	20						
Silchester	30						
Wall	1						
Wroxeter	22						
TOTAL	184(48.4%)		33(8.7%)		145(38.1%)		18 (4.7%)

(a) Nos. 1–150. Letters

2440.1. Caerleon (*Isca*), Gwent [Monmouthshire]. Bone roundel (1/1), diameter 19 mm, thickness 4.5 mm, found in 1964–69 at the fortress baths. Caerleon Museum. Reproduced from Zienkiewicz.

J.D. Zienkiewicz, *The Legionary Baths at Caerleon* ii (1986), 205 No. 16 with fig. 71.

obverse, flat: A
reverse: blank

2440.1

2440.2. Chesters (*Cilurnum*), Northumberland. Bone roundel (1/1), diameter 20 mm, found before 1890. Chesters Museum. Drawn by R.P.W., 1941.

JRS xxxii (1942), 117 No. 11 c. Budge, *Cat.*, No. 198 p. 368. Wright, *PSAN*[4] x (1942), 16.

obverse: concentric rings
reverse: A

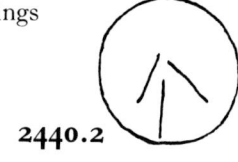

2440.2

2440.3. Colchester (*Camulodunum*), Essex. Bone roundel (1/1), diameter 22 mm, thickness 5 mm, found in 1937 in the grounds of the Union House, now St Mary's Hospital. Colchester Museum. Drawn by S.S.F. from a rubbing by R.P.W., 1943.

JRS xxxiv (1944), 89 No. 9 f.

obverse: countersunk
reverse: blank
edge: A

2440.3

V, R.P.W., *JRS*. A, R.P.W. from rubbing.

2440.4. Housesteads (*Vercovicium*), Northumberland. Bone roundel (1/1), diameter 16 mm, found probably in 1895. Museum of Antiquities, Newcastle upon Tyne. Drawn by R.P.W., 1941.

JRS xxxii (1942), 117 No. 11 f. Wright, *PSAN*[4] x (1942), 17.

obverse: countersunk
reverse: Λ

2440.4

2440.5. Leicester (*Ratae*). Bone roundel ($\frac{1}{1}$), diameter 22 mm, thickness 3 mm, found in 1936–39 during excavation of Level VI or VII at the Baths. Leicester Museum. Drawn by S.S.F. from a rubbing by R.P.W., 1951.

K.M. Kenyon, *Leicester* (1948), 266.

obverse: countersunk
reverse: Λ with small A above,
edge: III

κ could also be read.

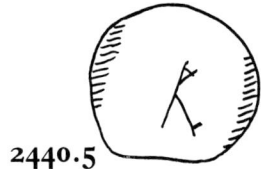

2440.5

2440.6. Ospringe, Kent. Bone roundel ($\frac{1}{1}$), diameter 19 mm, thickness, 3 mm, found in 1924 with *RIB* 2440.122 in Burial Group XXXVII inside a samian bowl, Dr. 31, stamped PRIMVLI. Maison Dieu Museum, Ospringe. Drawn by S.S.F. from a rubbing by R.P.W., 1961.

Whiting, *Arch. Cant.* xxxvii (1925), 95.

obverse: countersunk
reverse: Λ

2440.6

2440.7. Richborough (*Rutupiae*), Kent. Bone roundel ($\frac{1}{1}$), diameter 17.5 mm, thickness 1.6 mm, found in 1929 west of Section 47. In store at Dover Castle. Drawn by S.S.F. from a rubbing by R.P.W., 1948.

obverse: three concentric rings
reverse: A

2440.7

2440.8. Ibid. Bone roundel ($\frac{1}{1}$), diameter 19 mm, thickness 2.5 mm. In store at Dover Castle. Drawn by S.S.F. from a rubbing by R.P.W., 1948.

obverse: three concentric rings
reverse: A

2440.8

2440.9. St Albans (*Verulamium*), Hertfordshire. Bone roundel ($\frac{1}{1}$), diameter 20 mm, thickness 2.5 mm, found in 1932. Verulamium Museum. Drawn by R.P.W., 1942.

JRS xxxii (1942), 118 No. 11 g. Wright, *PSAN*[4] x (1942), 17 (g) No. 1.

obverse: countersunk
reverse: A
edge: ΛN M̂V

M̂V cut twice, *JRS*.

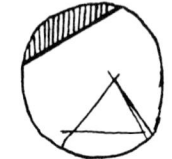

2440.9

2440.10–11. Wroxeter (*Viroconium*), Shropshire. Two bone roundels ($\frac{1}{1}$). Rowley's House Museum, Shrewsbury. Drawn by S.S.F. from rubbings by R.P.W., 1953.

10. diameter 25.5 mm.
    obverse: Λ
    reverse: blank

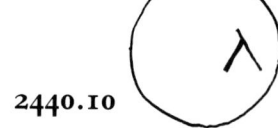

2440.10

11. diameter 19 mm.
    obverse: countersunk
    reverse: Λ

2440.11

For other examples of A see *RIB* 2440.91, 137(?), 140, 198(?), 199(?), 221 and 362.

2440.12. London (*Londinium*). Bone roundel ($\frac{1}{1}$), diameter 22 mm, thickness 3 mm, found in 1924–34 in excavations on the site of the Bank of England, Princes Street, E.C.2. Bank of England Museum. Drawn by S.S.F. from a rubbing by R.P.W., 1953.

obverse: countersunk
reverse: Λ⸸E

2440.12

2440.13. Chesterholm (*Vindolanda*), Northumberland. Bone roundel (¹⁄₁), diameter 19 mm, thickness 4 mm, found in excavations directed by R.E. Birley. Vindolanda Museum. Drawing: The Vindolanda Trust.

obverse: AIIILX
reverse: blank

Perhaps ANILA was intended.

2440.14. Ibid. Bone roundel (¹⁄₁), diameter 19 mm, thickness 4 mm, found in 1973 on Site III in the *vicus*, in a layer dated *c*. A.D. 90–100. Vindolanda Museum, Drawing: The Vindolanda Trust.

Britannia xv (1984), 345 No. 44.

obverse: ΛM
reverse: blank

reverse: a trident, *Britannia*. This is a confusion with *RIB* 2440.53, *q.v.*

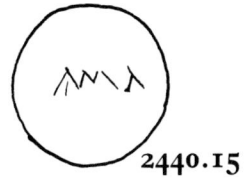

2440.15. Chichester (*Noviomagus*), West Sussex. Bone roundel (¹⁄₁), diameter 20 mm, thickness 3 mm, one of five found in 1937 in a pre-Flavian layer at the amphitheatre. Two were uninscribed; for the others see *RIB* 2436.51 and 68. Chichester Museum. Drawn by S.S.F. from a rubbing by R.P.W., 1941. See also PL. XVI D.

JRS xxxii (1942), 118 No. 11 h. Wright, *PSAN*⁴ x (1942), 17 (h) No. 1.

obverse: countersunk
reverse: AMΛ
  ama
  'Love (me)'

2440.16. Leicester (*Ratae*). Bone roundel (¹⁄₁), diameter 17.5 mm, thickness 4.8 mm, found in 1939 during excavations at the Baths. Leicester Museum. Drawn by S.S.F. from a rubbing by R.P.W., 1951.

obverse: ΛMΛ
  ama
  'Love (me)'
reverse: blank

2440.17. South Shields (*Arbeia*), Tyne and Wear [Durham]. Bone roundel (¹⁄₁), diameter 22 mm. Found in 1877 on the Lawe. Museum of Antiquities, Newcastle upon Tyne. Drawn by R.P.W., 1941.

JRS xxxii (1942), 117 No. 11 d. Wright, *PSAN*⁴ x (1942), 17 (d) No. 1 L. Allason-Jones and R. Miket, *Cat.*, 58 No. 2.160.

obverse: slightly countersunk
reverse: ΛRI

2440.18. Brecon (? *Cicucium*), Powys [Brecknockshire]. Bone roundel (¹⁄₁), diameter 19 mm, one of a set of eight of which six are inscribed S and one SS (see *RIB* 2440.113–118, 133). Found in 1924–5 in the conduit of the latrine during excavations at the fort. The inscriptions were not noted by Wheeler. Brecon Museum. Drawn by S.S.F. from a rubbing by R.P.W., 1953.

R.E.M. Wheeler, *The Roman Fort near Brecon* (1926), 120; see fig. 62 for the obverse.

obverse: four concentric rings
reverse: (first hand) A
  (second hand) S

2440.19. Chichester (*Noviomagus*), West Sussex. Bone roundel (¹⁄₁), diameter 19.5 mm, thickness 5 mm, one of a group of twenty-three found in 1965 in Burial Group 66 in the Roman cemetery at St Pancras. For the group, see *RIB* 2440.27. Chichester Museum. Drawn by R.P.W., 1965.

JRS lvi (1966), 220 No. 14 a. Wright in A. Down and M. Rule, *Chichester Excavations* i (1971), 83 No. 11 with fig. 5.15.

obverse: countersunk
reverse: ΛT

For an example of ΛV see *RIB* 2440.221 and for ΛVR see 2440.198.

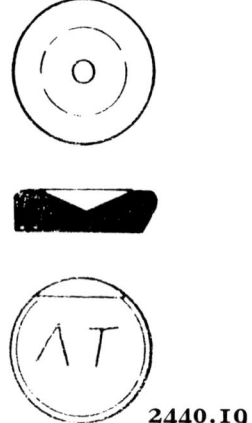

2440.19

2440.20. Ewell, Surrey. Bone roundel (¹⁄₁), diameter 23 mm, thickness 3.5 mm, one of nine found in 1946 in association with a cremation in the grounds of the lodge of 'The Looe'. For the others see *RIB* 2436.107–110, 188–190 and 335. Bourne Hall Museum, Ewell. Drawn by J. Cotton, 1976.

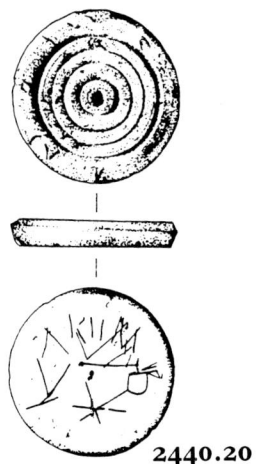

2440.20

Britannia viii (1977), 445 No. 104 c, with fig. 30.

obverse: compass-scribed concentric circles
reverse: (first hand) ΛVV
(second hand) RIIM LB | V ✶

Perhaps *rem(ittam) l(i)b(enter) quinque denarios* 'I will gladly repay five denarii'(?)

The expansion *rem(ittam)* or *remi(ttam)* is also offered in *RIB* 2440.107–10 and 188, but remains conjectural. The reading LB here and in *RIB* 2440.108–9 is uncertain, and in particular the expansion *l(i)b(enter)*. A six-pointed 'star' is common as a mark of identification on pottery and is not necessarily a *denarii* symbol (see the Introduction to this chapter, pp. 105–6); and where the symbol is used, the numeral *follows* it. Although the phrase *remittere denarios* occurs in an unpublished writing-tablet from Carlisle, its occurrence here in such an abbreviated form must be questioned. Since words inscribed on bone roundels are usually personal names, it may be that RIIM and RIIMI should be understood as *Rem(i)* and *Remi*, '(Property) of Remus'. The name *Remus* is well attested in *CIL* xiii. R.S.O.T.

2440.21. Wroxeter (*Viroconium*), Shropshire. Bone roundel (¹⁄₁), diameter 17.5 mm. Rowley's House Museum, Shrewsbury. Drawn by S.S.F. from a rubbing by R.P.W., 1953.

obverse: blank
reverse: ΛX

2440.21

For an example of B see *RIB* 2440.122.

2440.22. Silchester (*Calleva*), Hampshire. Bone roundel (¹⁄₁), diameter 20.5 mm. Reading Museum. Drawn by S.S.F. from a rubbing by R.P.W., 1955.

obverse: four concentric rings
reverse: BII

2440.22

2440.23. Wroxeter (*Viroconium*), Shropshire. Bone roundel (⅟₁), diameter 23 mm, thickness 2.4 mm, found in 1967 in the *praefurnium* of the baths. Wroxeter Museum. Drawn by S.S.F. from a rubbing by R.P.W., 1967.

JRS lviii (1968), 210 No. 32.

obverse: central hole and casual scorings
reverse: (first hand) CALIID
Perhaps *Cale(n)d(ae)*
(second hand) I III
'The Kalends' 'Four'

For the omission of *n* in *Calendae* see *ILCV* 2572, 3572, 4455. Another possibility is the abbreviated personal name *Caledius* (*RIB* 764) or *Caledonius* (*RIB* 1679, 1854). R.S.O.T.

2440.23

2440.24. Richborough (*Rutupiae*), Kent. Bone roundel (⅟₁), diameter 20.5 mm, thickness 4 mm, found in 1930–31 in Pit 212, dated to the first half of the third century. In store at Dover Castle. Reproduced from Bushe-Fox.

J.P. Bushe-Fox, *Richborough* iv (1949), 124, 255 No. 10 with pl. XXXIV No. 82.

obverse, flat: CAM|PVS
An abbreviated nomen and cognomen (e.g. *Camerius Pusillus*) or *Campus*, 'field'
reverse: blank

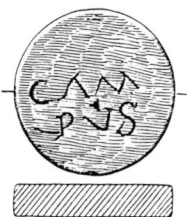

2440.24

2440.25. Silchester (*Calleva*), Hampshire. Bone roundel (⅟₁), diameter 19 mm, thickness 3 mm. Reading Museum. Drawn by S.S.F. from a rubbing by R.P.W., 1953.

obverse: countersunk
reverse: (first hand) L
(second hand) M

C̄M, R.P.W.

2440.25

2440.26. Ibid. Bone roundel (⅟₁), diameter 22 mm, thickness 3 mm. Reading Museum. Drawn by S.S.F. from a rubbing by R.P.W., 1953.

obverse: central hole
reverse: CVR
edge: II VII XX X (not illustrated)

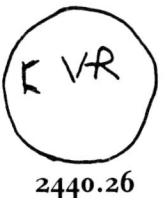

2440.26

2440.27. Chichester (*Noviomagus*), West Sussex. Bone roundel (⅟₁), diameter not recorded, one of a group of twenty-three varying in diameter from 16 to 25.5 mm and in thickness from 2 to 5 mm, found in 1965 in Burial Group 66 in the St Pancras Roman cemetery. Six are uninscribed: for the remainder see *RIB* 2440.19, 74, 106, 151, 170, 199, 204, 207, 220–223, 329–331 and 357. Chichester Museum. Not illustrated.

JRS lvi (1966), 220 No. 14 (l). Wright in A. Down and M. Rule, *Chichester Excavations* i (1971), 83 No. 3.

obverse: incision which may be casual or perhaps intended for D
reverse: X

2440.28. Richborough (*Rutupiae*), Kent. Bone roundel ($\frac{1}{1}$), diameter 19 mm, thickness 2.5 mm, found, presumably in 1930, in the bottom of the innermost of the three ditches of the earth fort. In store at Dover Castle. Drawn by S.S.F. from a rubbing by R.P.W., 1948.

obverse: three concentric rings
reverse: D

2440.28

2440.29. Silchester (*Calleva*), Hampshire. Bone roundel ($\frac{1}{1}$), diameter 19 mm, found in or before 1909. Reading Museum. Drawn by S.S.F. from a rubbing by R.P.W., 1953.

obverse: central hole
reverse: E

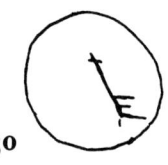
2440.29

2440.30. Ibid. Bone roundel ($\frac{1}{1}$), diameter 19 mm, thickness 4.75 mm, found in or before 1909. Reading Museum. Drawn by S.S.F. from a rubbing by R.P.W., 1955.

obverse: countersunk
reverse: cross | E
or perhaps L͡E

2440.30

2440.31. Brough on Humber (*Petuaria*), Humberside [Yorkshire]. Bone roundel ($\frac{1}{1}$), diameter 22.5 mm. Hull Museum. Drawn by S.S.F. from a rubbing by R.P.W., 1951.

obverse: countersunk
reverse: (first hand) X
(second hand) E

2440.31

2440.32. Colchester (*Camulodunum*), Essex. Bone roundel ($\frac{1}{1}$), diameter 20 mm, thickness 2.5 mm, found in 1936 in the grounds of the Union House, now St Mary's Hospital. Colchester Museum. Drawn by S.S.F. from a rubbing by R.P.W., 1943.

JRS xxxiv (1944), 89 No. 9 a.

obverse: three concentric rings
reverse: (first hand) X
(second hand) E

2440.32

2440.33. Ibid. Bone roundel ($\frac{1}{1}$), diameter 21 mm, thickness 4 mm, one of twelve ranging in diameter from 16 to 21 mm and in thickness from 2.5 to 5.5 mm, found in 1975 in a pit containing third- to fourth-century material at Balkerne Lane. Nine are uninscribed; for the others see *RIB* 2440.197 and 228. Colchester Museum. Drawing: Colchester Archaeological Trust.

Britannia ix (1978), 477 No. 34 b. N. Crummy, *Small Finds* (1983), 91 No. 2243 with fig. 34.

obverse: EIR crossing the perimeter of a scratched oval
reverse: an oval with a series of twelve dots marking the long axis. To the left of this line, O. To right, M.

The letters EI also appear on *RIB* 2440.197, found with this piece.

2440.33

For examples of F(?) see *RIB* 2440.41 and 165.

2440.34. Ibid. Bone roundel (⅟₁), diameter 18 mm, thickness 2.5 mm, found in the nineteenth century (Acton collection). Colchester Museum. Drawn by S.S.F. from a rubbing by R.P.W., 1943.

obverse: three rings
reverse reading clockwise around the disc: FVIOV

2440.35–36. Corbridge (? *Coria*), Northumberland. Two bone roundels (⅟₁), both 23 mm in diameter, found in 1941 in a group of twenty at a depth of three feet in an upper level of the Stanegate road. All but one belong to a well-turned set with a deep depression on the obverse, the inscribed examples having diameters of between 20 and 23 mm and thicknesses of between 4.75 and 6.3 mm; the exception (*RIB* 2440.233) is thinner and has concentric rings on the obverse. Twelve are uninscribed. For the remainder see *RIB* 2440.79–80, 120, 145–146 and 233. Corbridge Museum. Drawn by R.P.W., 1942.

JRS xxxii (1942), 117 No. 11 a. Wright, *PSAN*⁴ x (1942), 16.

obverse: countersunk
reverse: G

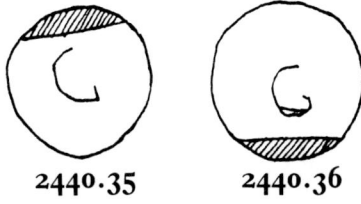

2440.37. South Shields (*Arbeia*), Tyne and Wear [Durham]. Bone roundel (⅟₁), diameter 20 mm, thickness 3 mm. Found at some date before 1956 at the fort. Museum of Antiquities, Newcastle upon Tyne. Not illustrated.

L. Allason-Jones and R. Miket, *Cat.*, 61 No. 2.221.

obverse: concentric groove and central depression; notched decoration round the edge
reverse, lightly scratched: H

2440.38. Wroxeter (*Viroconium*), Shropshire. Bone roundel (⅟₁), diameter 22 mm, thickness 2.4 mm, found in 1963 in layers below the Baths. Wroxeter Museum. Drawn by S.S.F. from a rubbing by R.P.W., 1963.

JRS liv (1964), 179 No. 9.

obverse (countersunk and bevelled), on level area: V
reverse: IAN
             Probably *Ian(uarius)*

Compare *RIB* 2436.39.

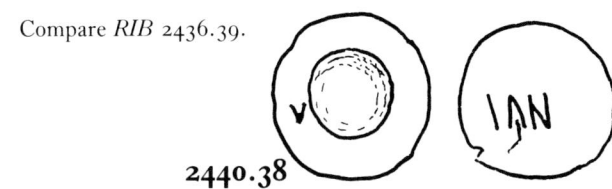

2440.39. St Albans (*Verulamium*), Hertfordshire. Bone roundel (⅟₁), diameter 23 mm, thickness 2.5 mm, found in 1933. Verulamium Museum. Drawn by R.P.W., 1942.

JRS xxxii (1942), 118 No. 11 g. Wright, *PSAN*⁴ x (1942), 17 (g) No. 2.

obverse: countersunk
reverse: (first hand) V
              (second hand) IANVA | IIII
              Probably *Ianua(rius)* | IIII

Compare *RIB* 2440.38.

2440.40. Caerleon (*Isca*), Gwent [Monmouthshire]. Bone roundel (⅟₁) with bevelled rim, diameter 18 mm, thickness 4 mm. Found in 1965 in the fortress baths. Caerleon Museum. Reproduced from J.D. Zienkiewicz.

JRS lvi (1966), 220 No. 12. J.D. Zienkiewicz, *The Legionary Fortress Baths at Caerleon* ii (1986), 203 No. 11 with fig.

obverse: flat, blank
reverse: ILLAI | ILL(AI) VII

For *Illaus* see *CIL* xiii 477. Perhaps, however, a blundered rendering of ILLIV(S) 'his', *Britannia* xiii (1982), 421 n. 93.
  Another possibility is that the text should be read the other way up as XIIS | *Mari* R.S.O.T.

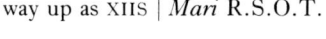
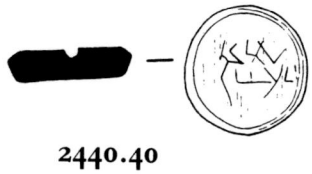

2440.41. Caerwent (*Venta Silurum*), Gwent [Monmouthshire]. Bone roundel (⅟₁), diameter 22 mm, thickness 2.5 mm, found in 1899–1912. Newport Museum. Drawn by S.S.F. from a rubbing by R.P.W., 1947.

obverse: six concentric rings
reverse: IMI | F̣

2440.41

For an example of IM͡V see *RIB* 2440.121.

2440.42–44. Ravenglass (*Glannoventa*), Cumbria [Cumberland]. Three bone roundels (⅟₁), found in 1975–77, as part of a group of 119 bone and seven glass roundels discovered together in a burnt deposit of *c.* A.D. 190–210, during excavations at the fort. Thirty were uninscribed. Ten are inscribed with letters (*RIB* 2440.42-44, 69, 90–92, 94, 103–104) and three with both letters and numerals (263, 264 and 270). The remaining seventy-five carry numerals only (*RIB* 2440.152–160, 165–166, 175–182, 201, 243–262, 265–269, 271–291, 337–343 and 355–356). Tullie House Museum, Carlisle. Drawn by T.W. Potter, 1978.

T.W. Potter, *Romans in North-West England* (1979), 75–87.

42. diameter 23 mm, thickness 2 mm. Potter, op. cit., 81 No. 21.

obverse: three concentric rings
reverse: (first hand) INCIḌIṾ|VS
(second hand) X̶

2440.42

43. diameter 18 mm, thickness 1.5 mm. Potter, op. cit., 85 No. 61.

obverse: two concentric rings
reverse: INC [. . .?]

2440.43

44. diameter 18 mm, thickness 2 mm. Potter, op. cit., 83 No. 46.

obverse: four concentric rings
reverse: (first hand) IN
(second hand) four cross-scorings and II

2440.44

2440.45. Chesterholm (*Vindolanda*), Northumberland. Bone roundel (⅟₁), diameter 18 mm, thickness 4 mm, found in excavations directed by R.E. Birley. Vindolanda Museum. Drawing: The Vindolanda Trust.

obverse: INỌ
reverse: I with symbols

2440.45

For examples of IVNIII see *RIB* 2440.123–127.

2440.46. Caerwent (*Venta Silurum*), Gwent [Monmouthshire]. Bone roundel (⅟₁), diameter 16 mm, thickness 2 mm, found in 1899–1912. Newport Museum. Drawn by S.S.F. from a rubbing by R.P.W., 1947.

obverse: countersunk
reverse: K

2440.46

2440.47. Cirencester (*Corinium*), Gloucestershire. Bone roundel (¹⁄₁), diameter 19 mm, thickness 3 mm. Corinium Museum, Cirencester. Drawn by S.S.F. from a rubbing by R.P.W., 1952.

obverse: hole in centre
reverse (the whole circuit bevelled): LK

2440.48. Bath (*Aquae Sulis*), Avon [Somerset]. Bone roundel (¹⁄₁), diameter 20.5 mm. Roman Baths Museum, Bath. Drawn by S.S.F. from a rubbing by R.P.W., 1951.

obverse: M
reverse: blank

2440.49. Caerwent (*Venta Silurum*), Gwent [Monmouthshire]. Bone roundel (¹⁄₁), diameter 19 mm, thickness 2 mm, found in 1899–1912. Newport Museum. Drawn by S.S.F. from a rubbing by R.P.W., 1947.

obverse: five concentric rings
reverse (badly cut): M

2440.50. Ibid. Bone roundel (¹⁄₁), diameter 19 mm, thickness 3 mm, found in 1899–1912. Newport Museum. Drawn by S.S.F. from a rubbing by R.P.W., 1947.

obverse: four concentric rings
reverse: M

2440.51. Chichester (*Noviomagus*), West Sussex. Bone roundel (¹⁄₁), diameter 20 mm, thickness 5 mm, one of five found in 1937 in a pre-Flavian layer at the amphitheatre. Two were uninscribed; for the others see *RIB* 2440.15 and 68. Chichester Museum. Drawn by S.S.F. from a rubbing by R.P.W., 1941. See also PL. XVI E.

JRS xxxii (1942), 118 No. 11 h. Wright, *PSAN*⁴ x (1942), 17 (h) No. 2.

obverse: countersunk, with radiating lines
reverse: M

2440.52. Ibid. Bone roundel (¹⁄₁), diameter 18 mm, one of a group of at least twenty-four, only twelve of which were sufficiently well-preserved for examination. These varied in diameter from 19 to 24 mm and in thickness from 2.3 to 4.7 mm. Of the twelve, one carried only a hole of uncertain significance. For the other inscribed roundels see *RIB* 2440.67, 86, 169, 171, 185, 200, 224, 325, 326 and 359. Found in 1968 in Burial Group 250 in the Roman cemetery at St Pancras. Chichester Museum. Drawn by S.S.F. from a rubbing by R.P.W., 1968.

JRS lix (1969), 237 No. 11. Wright in A. Down and M. Rule, *Chichester Excavations* i (1971), 88 No. 250.G.

obverse: countersunk
reverse: M

2440.53. Chesterholm (*Vindolanda*), Northumberland. Bone roundel (¹⁄₁), diameter 20 mm, thickness 5 mm, found in excavations directed by R.E. Birley. Vindolanda Museum. Drawing: The Vindolanda Trust.

obverse: M
reverse: a trident (?)

see note to *RIB* 2440.14.

 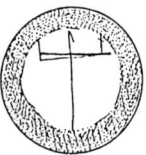

2440.54. Colchester (*Camulodunum*), Essex. Bone roundel (¼), diameter 22 mm, thickness 3 mm, found in 1975 in the fill of a road-ditch, with late third- to early fourth-century material, at Balkerne Lane. Colchester Museum. Drawing: Colchester Archaeological Trust.

Britannia ix (1978), 477 No. 32. N. Crummy, *Small Finds*, 91 No. 2282 with fig. 4.

obverse: notched decoration around the perimeter
reverse (with casual scratches):   M

2440.55. Corbridge (? *Coria*), Northumberland. Bone roundel (¼), diameter 16 mm, thickness 3 mm, found in 1934, south of Site XI. Corbridge Museum. Drawn by S.S.F. from a rubbing by R.P.W., 1941.

JRS xxxii (1942), 117 No. 11 b. Wright, *PSAN*[4] x (1942), 16 (b) No. 1.

obverse: slightly countersunk
reverse: M

2440.56. Leicester (*Ratae*), Bone roundel (¼), diameter 20.5 mm, found in 1938, unstratified. Leicester Museum. Drawn by S.S.F. from a rubbing by R.P.W., 1951.

obverse: five concentric rings
reverse: M

2440.57. Margate, Kent. Bone roundel (¼), diameter 22 mm, thickness 3 mm, Found in 1963 with *RIB* 2440.198 in a Roman ditch at Drapers Mills School, associated with late first- to second-century pottery. Present whereabouts unknown. Drawn by S.S.F. from a rubbing by R.P.W., 1963.

JRS liv (1964), 179 No. 10 a.

obverse: five concentric rings
reverse (with casual scorings): M
edge: XIIIIV

Perhaps 'Nineteen', wrongly ordered.

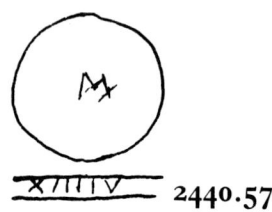

2440.58. Richborough (*Rutupiae*), Kent. Bone roundel (¼), diameter 23 mm, thickness 3 mm. In store at Dover Castle. Drawn by S.S.F. from a rubbing by R.P.W., 1948.

obverse: six concentric rings
reverse: M

2440.59. Ibid. Bone roundel (¼), diameter 22 mm, thickness 3 mm. In store at Dover Castle. Drawn by S.S.F. from a rubbing by R.P.W., 1948.

obverse: countersunk
reverse: probably M

2440.60. Silchester (*Calleva*), Hampshire. Bone roundel (1/1), diameter 20.5 mm, thickness 3 mm, found in or before 1909. Reading Museum. Drawn by S.S.F. from a rubbing by R.P.W., 1955.

obverse: four concentric rings
reverse: M

2440.61. Ibid. Bone roundel (1/1), diameter 19 mm, thickness 2 mm, found in or before 1909. Reading Museum. Drawn by S.S.F. from a rubbing by R.P.W., 1955.

obverse: many scorings
reverse: Ṃ

v, G.C. Boon (to R.P.W.).

2440.62. South Shields (*Arbeia*), Tyne and Wear [Durham]. Bone roundel (1/1), diameter 22 mm, thickness 4 mm, found in 1877 on the Lawe. South Shields Museum. Drawn by R.P.W., 1941.

JRS xxxii (1942), 117 No. 11 d. Wright, *PSAN*[4] x (1942), 17 (d) No. 2. L. Allason-Jones and R. Miket, *Cat.*, 58 No. 2.156.

obverse: slightly countersunk with central lathe-hole and two slight depressions to one side
reverse: M

2440.63. (?) York (*Eboracum*). Bone roundel (1/1), diameter 22 mm, thickness 3 mm. Yorkshire Museum, York (no provenance). Drawn by S.S.F. from a rubbing by R.P.W., 1946.

obverse: four concentric rings
reverse: M (twice)

For other examples of M see *RIB* 2440.33, 210 and 292.

2440.64. Aldborough (*Isurium*), North Yorkshire. Bone roundel (1/1), diameter 20.5 mm, thickness 1.5 mm. Aldborough Museum. Drawn by S.S.F. from a rubbing by R.P.W., 1952.

obverse: small recess
reverse: MΛ

2440.65. St Albans (*Verulamium*), Hertfordshire. Bone roundel (1/1), diameter 23 mm, thickness 2.5 mm, found in 1933. Verulamium Museum. Drawn by R.P.W., 1942.

JRS xxxii (1942), 118 No. 11 g. Wright, *PSAN*[4] x (1942), 17 (g) No. 3.

obverse: slightly countersunk
reverse: perhaps ṾIV | Ṭ
edge: MΛ

2440.66. Silchester (*Calleva*), Hampshire. Bone roundel (1/1), diameter 20.5 mm, thickness 4 mm, found in or before 1909. Reading Museum. Drawn by S.S.F. from a rubbing by R.P.W., 1955.

obverse: countersunk
reverse: blank
edge: MΛ

The second stroke of Λ has been cut three times.

2440.67. Chichester (*Noviomagus*), West Sussex. Bone roundel, diameter 18 mm, one of a group of at least twenty-four, only twelve of which were sufficiently well preserved for examination. Found in 1968 in Burial Group 250 in the Roman cemetery at St Pancras. For the group see *RIB* 2440.52. Chichester Museum. Drawn by S.S.F. from a rubbing by R.P.W., 1968.

JRS lix (1969), 237 No. 11. Wright in A. Down and M. Rule, *Chichester Excavations* i (1971), 88 No. 250.H.

obverse: five concentric rings
reverse: MΛ

MΛ *JRS*. MΛ, Wright, 1971.

2440.67

2440.68. Ibid. Bone roundel (¹⁄₁), diameter 18 mm, thickness 4 mm, one of five found in 1937 in a pre-Flavian layer at the amphitheatre. Two were uninscribed; for the others see *RIB* 2440.15 and 51. Chichester Museum. Drawn by S.S.F. from a rubbing by R.P.W., 1941. See also PL. XVI F, G.

JRS xxxii (1942), 118 No. 11 h. Wright, *PSAN*⁴ x (1942), 117 (h) No. 3.

obverse (around an indentation): MΛSCIILLIO
reverse: X

MACCIILLIO, R.G.C., R.P.W., citing *Macellio, CIL* v 5669, xii 2664. For MASCIILIO as a samian potter's stamp see *CIL* vii 1336.665 and Oswald, *Index* s.v. *Mascellio*.

2440.68

For the legend MAII see *RIB* 2440.298, and for MAI I͡MV see 2440.121.

2440.69. Ravenglass (*Glannoventa*), Cumbria [Cumberland]. Bone roundel (¹⁄₁), diameter 14 mm, thickness 1.5 mm, found in 1975–77 during excavations at the fort as one of the group of 119 described under *RIB* 2440.42–44, *q.v.*. Tullie House Museum, Carlisle. Drawn by T.W. Potter, 1978.

T.W. Potter, *Romans in North-West England* (1979), 83 No. 48.

obverse: three concentric rings
reverse: MAR
          Mar(tialis) or similar

rev. either M or VVV with P or R, Potter.

2440.69

2440.70. Silchester (*Calleva*), Hampshire. Bone roundel (¹⁄₁), diameter 20.5 mm, diameter 3 mm, found in 1900. Reading Museum. Drawn by S.S.F. from a rubbing by R.P.W., 1953.

EE ix 1344 b.

obverse: five concentric rings
reverse: MAR
          Mar(tialis) or similar

MΛR, *EE*.

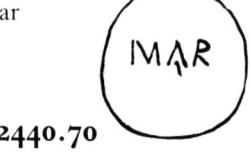

2440.70

2440.71. Caerleon (*Isca*), Gwent [Monmouthshire]. Bone roundel (¹⁄₁), diameter 16 mm, thickness 3 mm. National Museum, Cardiff. Drawn by S.S.F. from a rubbing by R.P.W., 1947.

obverse: MAVR with a casual stroke below the V
          Maur(i)
          '(Property) of Maurus'
reverse: blank

2440.71

2440.72. Ibid. Bone roundel (¹⁄₁), diameter 22 mm, thickness 5 mm, found in 1978 in a medieval deposit at the fortress baths. Caerleon Museum. Reproduced from Zienkiewicz.

Britannia xiii (1982), 421, No. 86. J.D. Zienkiewicz, *The Legionary Baths at Caerleon* ii (1986), 205 No. 53 with fig. 72.53.

obverse: countersunk
reverse: MII
          perhaps *me(um)*, 'mine'

Compare *RIB* 2440.73.

2440.72

2440.73. Ibid. Bone roundel (1/1), diameter 21 mm, thickness 2 mm, found in 1979 in the upper levels of the frigidarium drain of the legionary baths and dated to the second or early third century. Caerleon Museum. Reproduced from Zienkiewicz.

Britannia xiii (1982), 421 No. 87. J.D. Zienkiewicz, *The Legionary Baths at Caerleon* ii (1986), 205 No. 36 with fig. 72.

obverse: countersunk
reverse: (a) XVII,
'Seventeen'
(b) inverted in respect to (a): SIC (or casual scorings)
edge: MIIVM
meum
'mine'

Compare *RIB* 2440.72.

edge, NVLLVM, Zienkiewicz (as drawing). None of these readings is certain. R.S.O.T.

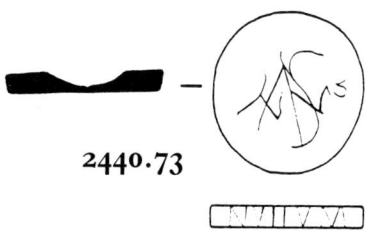

2440.73

2440.74. Chichester (*Noviomagus*), West Sussex. Bone roundel (1/1), diameter 25.5 mm, thickness 4 mm, one of a group of twenty-three found in 1965 in Burial Group 66 in the Roman cemetery at St Pancras. For the group see *RIB* 2436.27. Chichester Museum. Drawn by R.P.W., 1965.

2440.74

JRS lvi (1966), 220 No. 14 b. Wright in A. Down and M. Rule, *Chichester Excavations* i (1971), 83 No. 8 with fig. 5.15.

obverse: countersunk
reverse: MINI | PR

See *RIB* 2440.95 for another example of PR.

2440.75. Bishop's Stortford, Essex. Bone roundel (1/1), diameter 22 mm. Found in 1960 in a Roman rubbish-pit. Now lost. Reprinted from *Britannia*.

Britannia i (1970), 311 No. 22.

obverse: countersunk
reverse: MIT | MIITI intersected by a large X
Perhaps *Meti* cut twice
'(Property of) Metius'

The nomen *Metius* (for *Mettius*?) occurs in *RIB* 483 and *CIL* xiii 7288.

2440.76. Colchester (*Camulodunum*), Essex. Bone roundel (1/1), diameter 25 mm, thickness 3 mm, found before 1939 at Colchester. Colchester Museum. Drawn by S.S.F. from a rubbing by R.P.W., 1943.

JRS xxxiv (1944), 89 No. 9 b.

obverse: countersunk
reverse: blank
edge: MNMIV X̂I or XX

2440.76

2440.77. St Albans (*Verulamium*), Hertfordshire. Bone roundel (1/1), diameter 22 mm, thickness 3 mm. Found in 1931 in the west tower of the Chester Gate. Verulamium Museum. Drawn by R.P.W., 1942.

JRS xxxii (1942), 118 No. 11 g. Wright, *PSAN*[4] x (1942), 17 (g) No. 4.

obverse: countersunk
reverse: blank
edge: MNNII

2440.77

2440.78. Springhead, Kent. Bone roundel (⅟₁), diameter 21 mm, thickness 1.6 mm, found in 1960 in the area of Temple V. Gravesend Museum. Reproduced from Penn.

JRS li (1961), 194 No. 14. Penn, *Arch. Cant.* lxxvii (1962), 131 with fig. 6.4.

obverse: four concentric rings
reverse: MR

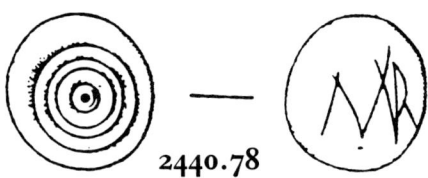

2440.79–80. Corbridge (? *Coria*), Northumberland. Two bone roundels (⅟₁), found in 1941 with eighteen others at a depth of three feet in an upper layer of the Stanegate road. All but one belong to a well-turned set with a deep depression on the obverse, the inscribed examples having diameters of between 20 and 23 mm, and thicknesses of between 4.75 and 6.3 mm; the exception (*RIB* 2440.233) is thinner and has concentric rings on the obverse. Twelve are uninscribed. For the remainder see *RIB* 2440.35–36, 120, 145–146 and 233. Corbridge Museum. Drawn by R.P.W., 1942.

JRS xxxii (1942), 117 No. 11. Wright, *PSAN*⁴ x (1942), 16.

79. diameter 23 mm, thickness 6.3 mm.

obverse: countersunk
reverse: M̂V

NV, R.S.O.T.

80. diameter 23 mm, thickness 6 mm

obverse: countersunk
reverse: N

For another example of M̂V see *RIB* 2440.9 and of NV see 2440.198.

2440.81. Aldborough (*Isurium*), North Yorkshire. Bone roundel (⅟₁) with bevelled edges, diameter 19 mm, thickness 3 mm. Aldborough Museum. Drawn by S.S.F. from a rubbing by R.P.W., 1952.

obverse: small recess
reverse: N̄

2440.82. Caerwent (*Venta Silurum*), Gwent [Monmouthshire]. Bone roundel (⅟₁), diameter 22 mm, thickness 2.5 mm, found in 1899–1912. Newport Museum. Drawn by S.S.F. from a rubbing by R.P.W., 1947.

obverse: countersunk with two concentric rings
reverse: N | H or X̂X

X, R.P.W.

The lower line is less heavily cut than the N.

2440.83. Malton (*Derventio*), North Yorkshire. Bone roundel (⅟₁), diameter 19 mm, found in the north-east angle of the fort. Malton Museum. Drawn by S.S.F. from a rubbing by R.P.W., 1951.

obverse: countersunk
reverse: NN

The first N is faintly cut.

2440.84. Silchester (*Calleva*), Hampshire. Bone roundel (⅟₁), diameter 19 mm, found in or before 1909. Reading Museum. Drawn by S.S.F. from a rubbing by R.P.W., 1953.

obverse: central hole
reverse (crossed by two horizontal lines): N

2440.85. Ibid. Bone roundel ($\frac{1}{1}$), diameter 20.5 mm, thickness 3 mm, found in or before 1909. Reading Museum. Drawn by S.S.F. from a rubbing by R.P.W., 1955.

obverse: countersunk
reverse (with random scorings): N
edge: I

2440.85

2440.86. Chichester (*Noviomagus*), West Sussex. Bone roundel ($\frac{1}{1}$), diameter 18 mm, one of a group of at least twenty-four found in 1968 in Burial Group 250 in the Roman cemetery at St Pancras. For the group see *RIB* 2440.52. Chichester Museum. Drawn by R.P.W., 1968.

JRS lix (1969), 237 No. 11. Wright in A. Down and M. Rule, *Chichester Excavations* i (1971), 88 No. 250.E with fig. 5.15.

obverse: five concentric rings
reverse: NI

2440.86

2440.87–88. Wroxeter (*Viroconium*), Shropshire. Two bone roundels ($\frac{1}{1}$), diameters 19 mm and 16 mm respectively. Rowley's House Museum, Shrewsbury. Drawn by S.S.F. from rubbings by R.P.W., 1953.

87. obverse: central hole
    reverse: NI

2440.87   **2440.88**

88. obverse: three concentric rings
    reverse: NI

For an example of N(?) see *RIB* 2440.183, and of NIIA see *RIB* 2440.366; for NV see 2440.79(?) and 198.

2440.89. Caerwent (*Venta Silurum*), Gwent [Monmouthshire]. Bone roundel ($\frac{1}{1}$), diameter 22 mm, thickness 3 mm, found in 1899–1912. Newport Museum. Drawn by S.S.F. from a rubbing by R.P.W., 1947.

obverse: countersunk
reverse: OB

For an example of O see *RIB* 2440.33.

2440.89

2440.90–92. Ravenglass (*Glannoventa*), Cumbria [Cumberland]. Three bone roundels ($\frac{1}{1}$), found in 1975–77, as part of a group of 119 bone and seven glass roundels discovered together in a burnt deposit of *c.* A.D. 190–210, during excavations at the fort. Thirty were uninscribed; ten are inscribed with letters (*RIB* 2440.42–44, 69, 90–92, 94, 103–104 (and three with both letters and numerals (263, 264, 270). The remaining seventy-five carry numerals only (*RIB* 2440.152–160, 165–166, 175–182, 201, 243–262, 265–269, 271–291, 337–343 and 355–356). Tullie House Museum, Carlisle. Drawn by T.W. Potter.

T.W. Potter, *Romans in North-West England* (1979), 75–87.

90. diameter 17 mm, thickness 2 mm. Potter, op. cit., 82 No. 25.

   obverse: two concentric rings
   reverse: P overlying X

2440.90

91. diameter 18 mm, thickness 2.5 mm. Potter, op. cit., 86 No. 84.

   obverse: plain
   reverse: P overlying X(?); Λ

2440.91

92. diameter 20 mm, thickness 3 mm. Potter, op. cit., 83 No. 58.

2440.92

obverse: three concentric rings
reverse: P partly overlaid by a Y-shaped symbol; another Y-shape with crossbars lies horizontal.

For further examples of P see *RIB* 2440.103(?), 123 and 264(?).

2440.93. London (*Londinium*). Bone roundel (⅟₁), diameter 20 mm, thickness up to 3 mm, found in 1984 in excavations at the Billingsgate Lorry Park. Museum of London. Drawn by Christine Jones.

Britannia xvi (1985), 329 No. 30.

obverse: countersunk with central hole plugged by an iron rivet. Around this, reading clockwise, PAIIIRNVS.
Paternus
reverse: radial scored lines

I has been scratched in error for T.

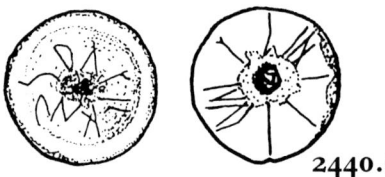
2440.93

2440.94. Ravenglass (*Glannoventa*), Cumbria [Cumberland]. Bone roundel (⅟₁), diameter 18 mm, thickness 2 mm, found in 1975–77 as one of a group of 119, for which see *RIB* 2440.90–92. Tullie House Museum, Carlisle. Drawn by T.W. Potter.

T.W. Potter, *Romans in North-West England* (1979), 85 No. 77.

obverse: countersunk
reverse: PE

See *RIB* 2440.263 for another example of PE from this group.

2440.94

2440.95. Chesterholm (*Vindolanda*), Northumberland. Bone roundel (⅟₁), diameter 18 mm, thickness 5 mm, found in excavations directed by R.E. Birley. Vindolanda Museum. Drawing: The Vindolanda Trust.

obverse: PR
reverse: blank

See *RIB* 2440.74 for another example of PR.

2440.95

2440.96. Caistor St Edmund (*Venta Icenorum*), Norfolk. Bone roundel found in 1929 in Pit 8 on the west side of the street bounding the west side of Insula VI (which contained two temples). Present whereabouts unknown. Not found by R.P.W. in Norwich Castle Museum, 1971. Not illustrated.

Britannia ii (1971), 300 No. 65.

reverse: PRI

2440.97. Silchester (*Calleva*), Hampshire. Bone roundel (⅟₁), diameter 13 mm, found in 1900. Reading Museum. Drawn by S.S.F. from a rubbing by R.P.W., 1953.

EE ix 1344 a

obverse: PRIM|VS
reverse: L

2440.97

2440.98. Hod Hill, Dorset. Bone roundel (⅟₁), diameter 16 mm, thickness 3 mm, found before 1892 unstratified in the Roman fort. British Museum. Drawn by S.S.F. from a rubbing by R.P.W., 1966.

JRS lvi (1966), 220 No. 13. J.W. Brailsford, *Hod Hill* i (1962), 22, pl. XIV A.

obverse: PRISCI
Prisci
'(Property) of Priscus'
reverse: blank

PRIS|CI erroneously, *JRS*.

2440.98

2440.99. Corbridge (? *Coria*), Northumberland. Bone roundel (⅟₁), diameter 23 mm, thickness 3 mm, found in 1934 on Site XI. Corbridge Museum. Drawn by R.P.W., 1942.

JRS xxxii (1942), 117 No. 11 b. Wright, *PSAN*⁴ x (1942), 16 (b) No. 2.

obverse: four concentric rings
reverse: Q

2440.99

2440.100. South Shields (*Arbeia*), Tyne and Wear [Durham]. Bone roundel ($\frac{1}{1}$), diameter 22 mm, found in 1877 on the Lawe. In 1941 it was in the Black Gate Museum, Newcastle upon Tyne. Drawn by S.S.F. from a rubbing by R.P.W., 1941.

JRS xxxii (1942), 117 No. 11 d. Wright, *PSAN*[4] x (1942), 17 (d) No. 3. Not in Allason-Jones and Miket, *Cat.*

obverse: blank with central hole
reverse (with central hole): R

2440.101. Ibid. Bone roundel ($\frac{1}{1}$), diameter 19 mm, thickness 1.6 mm. South Shields Museum. Drawn by S.S.F. from a rubbing by R.P.W., 1946.

obverse: plain with central hole
reverse (with central hole): R

2440.102. Colchester (*Camulodunum*), Essex. Bone roundel ($\frac{1}{1}$), diameter 19 mm, thickness 2.5 mm, found sometime between 1840 and 1888. Colchester Museum (Acton collection). Drawn by S.S.F. from a rubbing by R.P.W., 1943.

JRS xxxiv (1944), 89 No. 9 c.

obverse: three concentric rings
reverse: R

2440.103–104. Ravenglass (*Glannoventa*), Cumbria [Cumberland]. Two bone roundels ($\frac{1}{1}$), found in 1975–77 as part of a group of 119, for which see *RIB* 2440.90–92. Tullie House Museum, Carlisle. Drawn by T.W. Potter, 1978.

T.W. Potter, *Romans in North-West England* (1979), 75–87.

103. diameter 20 mm, thickness 2.5 mm. Potter, op. cit., 83 No. 47.

obverse: three concentric rings
reverse: 'R or P deeply cut, with X overlying successive attempts (?) to cut D'

104. diameter 21 mm, thickness 2.5 mm. Potter, op. cit., 81 No. 22.

obverse: three concentric rings
reverse: (first hand) X
(second hand) PP (one P inverted)

2440.105. York (*Eboracum*). Bone roundel ($\frac{1}{1}$), diameter 22.5 mm, thickness 4 mm, found in 1972–3 in the Roman sewer, Church Street, in the fortress. Yorkshire Museum. Reproduced from MacGregor.

A. MacGregor, *Finds from a Roman Sewer System ... in Church Street*, The Archaeology of York xvii fasc. 1 (1976), 22 No. 84 with fig. 3.

obverse: countersunk
reverse: R retrograde
edge: VI within single vertical lines

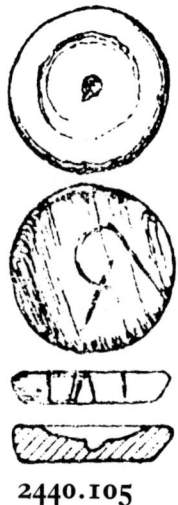

For a further example of R see *RIB* 2440.270.

2440.106. Chichester (*Noviomagus*), West Sussex. Bone roundel, one of a group of twenty-three (for which see *RIB* 2440.27) found in 1965 in Burial Group 66 in the Roman cemetery at St Pancras. Chichester Museum. Not illustrated.

JRS lvi (1966), 220 No. 14 c. Wright in A. Down and M. Rule, *Chichester Excavations* i (1971), 83 No. 19.

obverse: countersunk
reverse: R͡I or R͡V

2440.107–110. Ewell, Surrey. Four bone roundels (¹⁄₁), part of a group of nine found in 1946 associated with a cremation in the grounds of the lodge of The Looe. For the others see *RIB* 2440.20, 188–190 and 335. Bourne Hall Museum, Ewell. Drawn by J. Cotton, 1976.

Britannia viii (1977), 445 with fig. 30.

107. diameter 21 mm, thickness 4 mm. *Britannia*, loc. cit., No. 104 b.

obverse: six concentric rings
reverse: RIIMI | X | V
Perhaps *remi(ttam) (denarios ?) quinque*
'I will repay five (denarii ?)' (?)

For RIIMI as *remi(ttam)* see *RIB* 2440.20 with note and 110.

The X has no cross-bar, but it is taken to indicate *denarios* on the analogy of *RIB* 2440. 20 and 109.

108. diameter 21 mm, thickness 3.5 mm. *Britannia*, loc. cit., No. 104 d.

obverse: four concentric rings
reverse: RIIM L͡B
Perhaps *rem(ittam) l(i)b(enter)*
'I will repay gladly' (?)

For RIIM as *rem(ittam)* see *RIB* 2440.20 with note and 188.

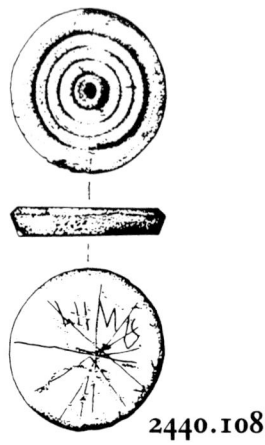

2440.108

109. diameter 22.5 mm, thickness 3.5 mm. *Britannia*, loc. cit., No. 104 e.

obverse: four concentric rings
reverse: RIIM L | VX̶
Perhaps *rem(ittam) l(ibenter) | quinque (denarios)*
'I will gladly repay five (denarii)' (?)

For RIIM as *rem(ittam)* see *RIB* 2440.20 with note and 188.

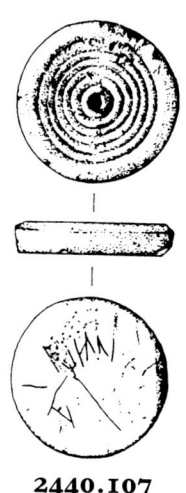

2440.107

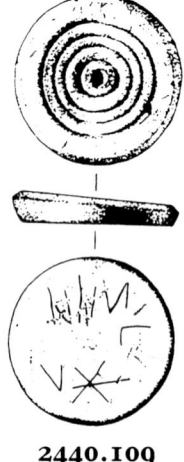

2440.109

110. diameter 23 mm, thickness 3.5 mm. *Britannia*, loc. cit., No. 104 g.

obverse: seven concentric rings
reverse: RIIMI
Perhaps *remi(ttam)*
'I will repay' (?)

For RIIMI as *remi(ttam)* see *RIB* 2440.20 with note.

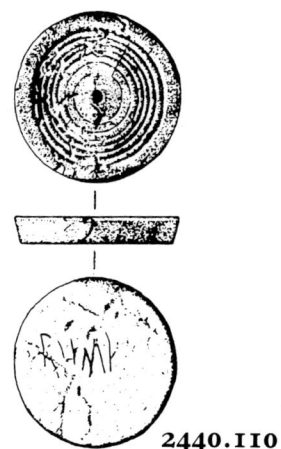

2440.110

2440.111. Richborough (*Rutupiae*), Kent. Bone roundel (¹⁄₁), diameter 19 mm, thickness 3 mm, found in 1929–30 outside the north wall of the fort. In store at Dover Castle. Drawn by S.S.F. from a rubbing by R.P.W., 1948.

obverse: three concentric rings
reverse: RT

2440.111

For a roundel inscribed RVFINVS see *RIB* 2440.128.

2440.112. Number not used.

2440.113–118. Brecon (? *Cicucium*), Powys [Brecknockshire]. Six bone roundels (¹⁄₁), forming with *RIB* 2440.18 and 133 a set of eight. Found in 1924–5 in the conduit of the latrine during excavations at the fort. The inscriptions were not noted by Wheeler. Brecon Museum. Drawn by S.S.F. from rubbings by R.P.W., 1953.

R.E.M. Wheeler, *The Roman Fort near Brecon* (1926), 120; see fig. 62 for the obverses.

113. diameter 19 mm.

obverse: three concentric rings
reverse: S

2440.113

114. diameter 19 mm.

obverse: four concentric rings
reverse: S

2440.114

115. diameter 17.5 mm.

obverse: four concentric rings
reverse: S

2440.115

116. diameter 16 mm.

obverse: four concentric rings
reverse: S

2440.116

117. diameter 14.3 mm.

obverse: four concentric rings
reverse: S

2440.117

118. diameter 14.3 mm.

obverse: three concentric rings
reverse: S

2440.118

2440.119. Chesters (*Cilurnum*), Northumberland. Bone roundel (¹⁄₁), diameter 19 mm, found before 1890 at the fort. Chesters Museum. Drawn by R.P.W., 1941.

JRS xxxii (1942), 117 No. 11 c. Budge, *Cat.*, 368 No. 189. Wright, *PSAN*⁴ x (1942), 16.

obverse: blank
reverse: S

2440.119

2440.120. Corbridge (? *Coria*), Northumberland. Bone roundel (¹⁄₁), diameter 23 mm, thickness 6 mm, found in 1941 with nineteen others in an upper level of the Stanegate road. For details, association and references see *RIB* 2440.79–80. Corbridge Museum. Drawn by R.P.W., 1942.

obverse: countersunk
reverse: S

There is a chance scratch at the tail.

2440.120

For an example of SIC (?), see *RIB* 2440.73.

2440.121. Great Chesterford, Essex. Bone roundel (¹⁄₁), diameter 20.5 mm, thickness 3 mm. Museum of Archaeology and Anthropology, Cambridge. Drawn by S.S.F. from a rubbing by R.P.W., 1951.

obverse: countersunk
reverse: S
edge: M{A̤}I IM̂V̤

For an example of IMI see *RIB* 2440.41.

2440.121

2440.122. Ospringe, Kent. Bone roundel (¹⁄₁), diameter 22 mm, thickness 3 mm, found in 1924 with *RIB* 2440.6 in Group XXXVII inside a samian bowl, Dr. 31, stamped PRIMVLI. Maison Dieu Museum, Ospringe. Drawn by S.S.F. from a rubbing by R.P.W., 1961.

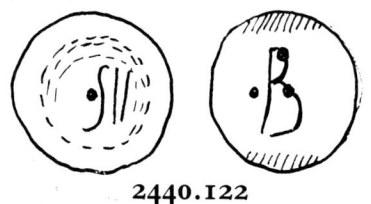

2440.122

Whiting, *Arch. Cant.* xxxvii (1925), 95.

obverse (countersunk): SII
reverse: three dots, B

2440.123–132. Bermondsey, south London. Ten bone roundels (¹⁄₁) found in 1971 as part of a group of twelve during excavation of a late first-century building at Toppings Wharf, Tooley Street. They vary in diameter from 16 to 18 mm and in thickness from 2 to 6 mm, and have bevelled edges on both sides. The two others are uninscribed. Nos. 123–128 have a dark patina and have been neatly inscribed with a sharp point on both sides in the same hand. Some have been decorated with figures. Incised lines which continue some of the letter-strokes encircle the legends or otherwise occupy the field. From these lines project a series of short strokes which, like the letters, are provided with serifs. Nos. 129–132 are inscribed on one side only, by a different hand. They are somewhat thicker than the others and lack the dark patina; the letters lack serifs and the mark left by the lathe has not been polished away from the reverse. Of the two uninscribed roundels, one is similar in thickness and patina to the first group. Museum of London. Drawn by I. Schwab.

Britannia iii (1972), 357 No. 30 with fig. 21. Sheldon, T. *Lond Middl. AS* xxv (1974), 100 with fig. 47.

123. diameter 16 mm, thickness 2.5 mm. *Britannia*, loc. cit., No. 30 a.

obverse: SIIXTIII with P retrograde beneath the last two letters
reverse: IVNIII

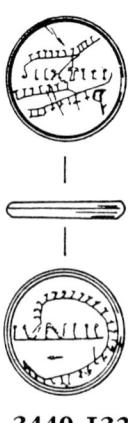

2440.123

124. diameter 18 mm, thickness 2 mm. *Britannia*, loc. cit., No. 30 b.

obverse: SIIXTIII
reverse: IVNIII·F with a figure facing right with crested helmet, loin-cloth and shield

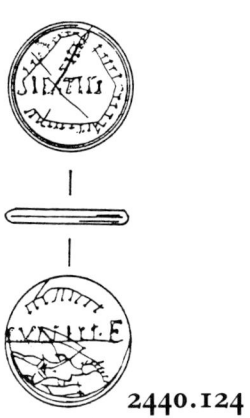

2440.124

125. diameter 17 mm, thickness 3 mm. *Britannia*, loc. cit., No. 30 c.

obverse: SIIXTIII
reverse: IVNIII

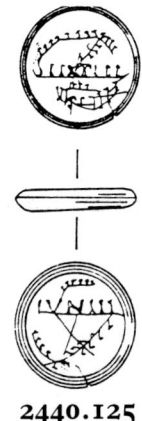

2440.125

126. diameter 16 mm, thickness 2.5 mm. *Britannia*, loc. cit., No. 30 e.

obverse: SIIXTIII
reverse: IVNIII

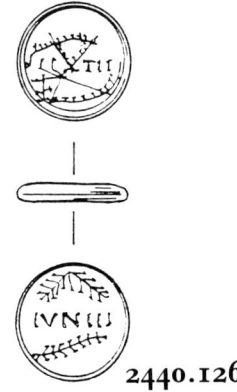

2440.126

127. diameter 17 mm, thickness 2 mm. *Britannia*. loc. cit., No. 30 f.

obverse: SIIXTIII
reverse: IVNIII

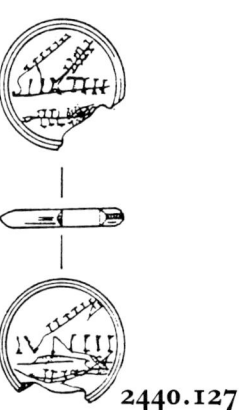

2440.127

128. diameter 16 mm, thickness 2.5 mm. *Britannia*, loc. cit., No. 30 d.

obverse: SEIXTIII over a sinuous quadruped facing right
reverse: RVFINVS

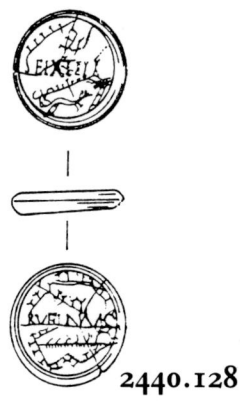

2440.128

(Bermondsey, continued)

129. diameter 18 mm, thickness 4 mm. *Britannia*, loc. cit., No. 30 g.

obverse: SEXTI
reverse: blank

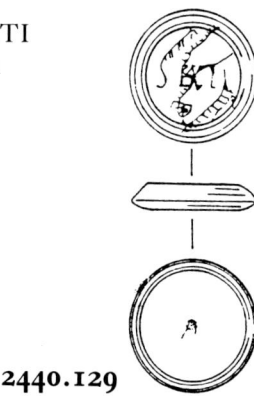

2440.129

130. diameter 17 mm, thickness 5 mm. *Britannia*, loc. cit., No. 30 h.

obverse: SEXTI
reverse: blank

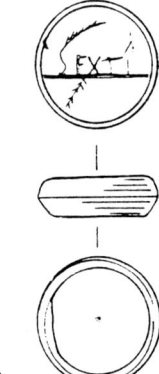

2440.130

131. diameter 18 mm, thickness 5 mm. *Britannia*, loc. cit., No. 30 i.

obverse: SEXTI
reverse: blank

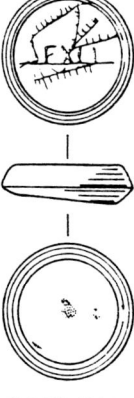

2440.131

132. diameter 17 mm, thickness 4 mm. *Britannia*, loc. cit., No. 30 j.

obverse: SEXTI
reverse: blank

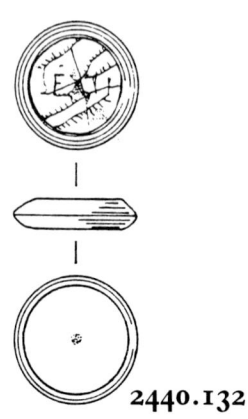

2440.132

2440.133. Brecon (? *Cicucium*), Powys [Brecknockshire]. Bone roundel (1/1), diameter 19 mm, one of a set of eight found in 1924–5 in the conduit of the latrine during excavations at the fort. The inscription was not noted by Wheeler. For the others see *RIB* 2440.18 and 113–118. Brecon Museum. Drawn by S.S.F. from a rubbing by R.P.W., 1953.

R.E.M. Wheeler, *The Roman Fort near Brecon* (1926), 120; see fig. 62 for the obverse.

obverse: four concentric rings
reverse: SS

2440.133

2440.134–135. St Albans (*Verulamium*), Hertfordshire. Two bone roundels (1/1), found in 1931. Verulamium Museum. Drawn by R.P.W., 1942.

JRS xxxii (1942), 118 No. 11 g. Wright, *PSAN*⁴ x (1942), 17 (g) Nos. 5, 6.

134. diameter 20 mm, thickness 2.5 mm.

obverse: five concentric circles
reverse: (first hand) X
(second hand) T
edge: II

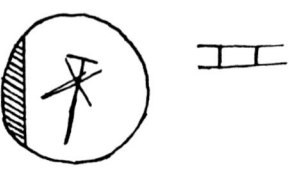

2440.134

135. diameter 20 mm, thickness 2.5 mm.

obverse: countersunk
reverse: T

T with bottom-stroke, not H, R.P.W.

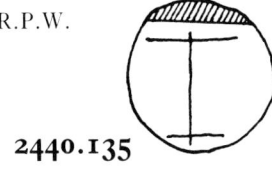
2440.135

2440.136–137. Caerleon (*Isca*), Gwent [Monmouthshire]. Two bone roundels (⅟₁), found in 1964–9 in the fortress baths. Caerleon Museum. Reproduced from Zienkiewicz.

J.D. Zienkiewicz, *The Legionary Baths at Caerleon* ii (1986), 205.

136. diameter 20 mm, thickness 3 mm. Zienkiewicz, loc. cit., No. 39 with fig. 72

obverse: countersunk
reverse (cut in wide strokes): T

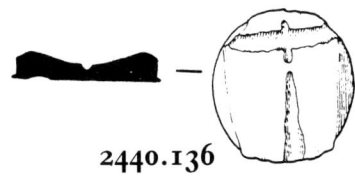
2440.136

137. diameter 18 mm, thickness 5 mm. Zienkiewicz, loc. cit., No. 14 with fig. 71

obverse: flat
reverse: three strokes lightly incised, perhaps A or H

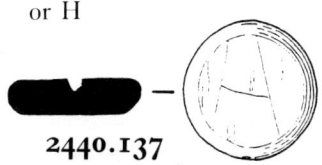
2440.137

2440.138. London (*Londinium*). Bone counter (⅟₁), diameter 15 mm, found in 1940 unstratified at a depth of eighteen feet in All Hallows churchyard, Lombard Street. Museum of London. Drawn by R.P.W., 1940.

JRS xxxi (1941), 146. For the site see *Antiq. J.* xx (1940), 510.

TIIRT|IVS
Tert|ius

2440.138

2440.139. St Albans (*Verulamium*), Hertfordshire. Bone roundel (⅟₁), diameter 23 mm, thickness 3 mm, found in 1931 at the London Gate. Verulamium Museum. Drawn by R.P.W., 1942.

JRS xxxii (1942), 118 No. 11 g. Wright, *PSAN*[4] (1942), 17 (g) No. 7.

obverse: slightly countersunk
reverse: TIT

2440.139

2440.140. Chesterholm (*Vindolanda*), Northumberland. Bone roundel (⅟₁), diameter 19 mm, thickness 3 mm, bevelled on obverse and reverse and also on two arcs. Found in 1973 below Site LXXVI in a layer dated c. A.D. 80–90 in the *vicus*. Vindolanda Museum. Not illustrated.

Britannia xv (1984), 345 No. 45.

obverse: TIIT
reverse: A star VI, IX

2440.141. Silchester (*Calleva*), Hampshire. Bone roundel (⅟₁), diameter 24 mm, thickness 2 mm, found in or before 1909. Reading Museum. Drawn by S.S.F. from a rubbing by R.P.W., 1955.

obverse: six concentric rings
reverse (with some miscut strokes): TN
edge: II IIII

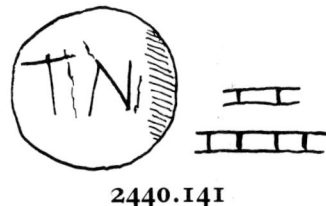
2440.141

2440.142. Leicester (*Ratae*). Bone roundel ($\frac{1}{1}$), diameter 25.5 mm, thickness 1.5 mm, found in 1937 during excavations at the Baths. Leicester Museum. Drawn by R.P.W., 1951.

obverse: six concentric rings
reverse: VNAT around ✕
          Possibly *una t(essera)*, R.P.W.
          'one counter'

CA|LF could also be read. R.S.O.T.

2440.142

2440.143. Caistor St Edmund (*Venta Icenorum*), Norfolk. Bone roundel ($\frac{1}{1}$), diameter 20.5 mm. Norwich Castle Museum. Drawn by S.S.F. from a rubbing by R.P.W., 1951.

obverse: countersunk with parts of X on the rim
reverse: VA

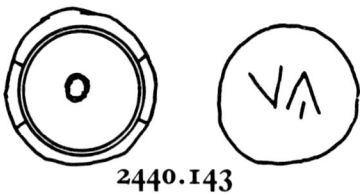
2440.143

2440.144. Colchester (*Camulodunum*), Essex. Bone roundel ($\frac{1}{1}$), diameter 25 mm, thickness 3 mm, found in 1976 at the Butt Road Roman cemetery. Colchester Museum. Drawing: Colchester Archaeological Trust.

Britannia ix (1978), 477 No. 33. N. Crummy, *Small Finds* (1983), 91 No. 2277 with fig. 94.

obverse: six concentric mouldings
reverse: VAL
          Val(ens) or *Val(erius)*

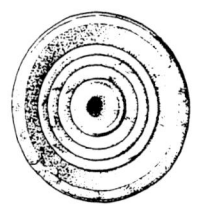 
2440.144

2440.145–146. Corbridge (? *Coria*), Northumberland. Two bone roundels ($\frac{1}{1}$), found in 1941 with eighteen others at a depth of three feet in an upper level of the Stanegate road. All but one belong to a well-turned set with a deep depression on the obverse, the inscribed examples having diameters of between 20 and 23 mm and thicknesses of between 4.75 and 6.3 mm; the exception (*RIB* 2440.233) is thinner and has concentric rings on the obverse. Twelve are uninscribed. For the remainder see *RIB* 2440.35–36, 79–80, 120 and 233. Corbridge Museum. Drawn by R.P.W., 1942.

JRS xxxii (1942), 117 No. 11 a. Wright, *PSAN*[4] x (1942), 16.

145. diameter 20 mm, thickness 6 mm.

    obverse: countersunk
    reverse: VIILI
              Veli
              '(Property) of Velius'

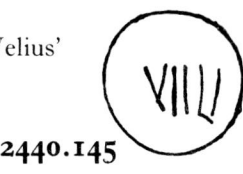
2440.145

146. diameter 20 mm, thickness 6 mm.

    obverse: countersunk
    reverse: VIILI
              Veli
              '(Property) of Velius'

Compare *RIB* 2440.147.

2440.146

2440.147. Wroxeter (*Viroconium*), Shropshire. Bone roundel ($\frac{1}{1}$), diameter 18 mm. Rowley's House Museum, Shrewsbury. Drawn by S.S.F. from a rubbing by R.P.W., 1953.

obverse: (a) VIIL | M
          Perhaps *Vel(i) m(anu)* '(Made) by the hand of Velius'. But the many occurrences on counters of M without this meaning makes the interpretation uncertain. See TABLE II.
        (b) secondary, deeply cut, E

For *Velius* compare *RIB* 2440.145–6.

2440.147

2440.148. Colchester (*Camulodunum*), Essex. Bone roundel (¼), diameter 23 mm, thickness 3 mm, found in 1935 during excavations in the High Street. Colchester Museum. Drawn by S.S.F. from a rubbing by R.P.W., 1943.

JRS xxxiv (1944), 89 No. 9 d.

obverse: five concentric rings
reverse: blank
edge: VIMIM

2440.148

2440.149. St Albans (*Verulamium*), Hertfordshire. Bone roundel (¼), diameter 23 mm, thickness 3 mm, found in 1930–34. Verulamium Museum. Drawn by R.P.W., 1942.

JRS xxxii (1942, 118 No. 11 g. Wright, *PSAN*⁴ x (1942), 17 (g) No. 8.

obverse: slightly countersunk
reverse: VITÂL
Vital(is)
'(Property) of Vitalis'
edge: M with III imposed later.

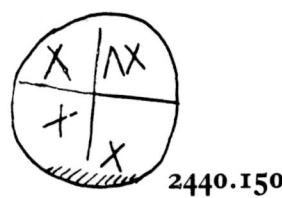

2440.149

For an example of VIV (?), see *RIB* 2440.65; for VN see 2440.347 and VX see 2440.360.

2440.150. Caerwent (*Venta Silurum*), Gwent [Monmouthshire]. Bone roundel (¼), diameter 25 mm, thickness 2 mm, found in 1899–1912 during excavations. Newport Museum. Drawn by S.S.F. from a rubbing by R.P.W., 1947.

obverse: six concentric circles
reverse: large cross with X | ΛX | X | X in the quadrants

X repeated: no other certain letters, R.P.W.

2440.150

For examples of XVV see *RIB* 2440.361 and 366.

(b) Nos. 151–381. Numerals

2440.151. Chichester (*Noviomagus*), West Sussex. Bone roundel (¼), dimensions not recorded. One of a group of twenty-three found in 1965 in Burial Group 66 in the Roman cemetery at St Pancras. For the group see *RIB* 2440.27. Chichester Museum. Not illustrated.

JRS lvi (1966), 220 No. 14 d. Wright in A. Down and M. Rule, *Chichester Excavations* i (1971), 83 No. 13.

edge: I III

2440.152–160. Ravenglass (*Glannoventa*), Cumbria [Cumberland]. Nine bone roundels (¼), found in 1975–77 as part of a group of 119 bone and seven glass roundels, in a burnt deposit of *c*. A.D. 190–210, during excavations at the fort. For other details of the group see *RIB* 2440.42–44. Tullie House Museum, Carlisle. Drawn by T.W. Potter.

T.W. Potter, *Romans in North-West England* (1979), 75–87.

152. diameter 21 mm, thickness 1.5 mm. Potter, op. cit., 81 No. 23.

obverse: three concentric rings
reverse: I

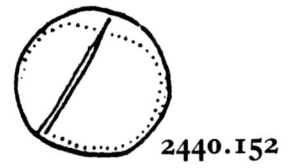

2440.152

153. diameter 17 mm, thickness 2 mm. Potter, op. cit., 83 No. 51.

obverse: two concentric rings
reverse: I

154. diameter 13 mm, thickness 1.5 mm. Potter, op. cit., 85 No. 66

obverse: three concentric rings
reverse: I (?)

2440.154

(Ravenglass, continued)

155. diameter 20 mm, thickness 2 mm. Potter, op. cit., 83 No. 43

    obverse: four concentric rings
    reverse: I over X and $\overline{X}$ (?)

156. diameter 14 mm, thickness 1.5 mm. Potter, op. cit., 83 No. 49.

    obverse: two concentric rings
    reverse: $\overline{I}$ or $\overline{II}$ (?)

157. Oval. Diameters 18 and 13 mm, thickness 2 mm. Potter, op. cit., 85 No. 73.

    obverse: two concentric rings
    reverse: I

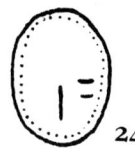

158. diameter 14 mm, thickness 1.5 mm. Potter, op. cit., 86 No. 87.

    obverse: plain
    reverse: I II IV (?)

159. diameter 16 mm, thickness 2 mm. Potter, op. cit., 86 No. 101.

    obverse: slightly concave
    reverse: I

160. diameter 18 mm, thickness 2 mm. Potter, op. cit., 86 No. 109.

    obverse: plain
    reverse: I, not certainly intentional

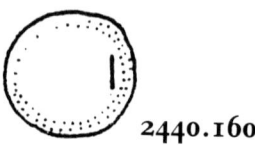

2440.161. Silchester (*Calleva*), Hampshire. Bone roundel ($\frac{1}{1}$), diameter 16 mm, thickness 3 mm, found in or before 1909. Reading Museum. Drawn by S.S.F. from a rubbing by R.P.W., 1955.

    reverse: I
    edge: X

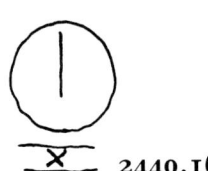

2440.162. Wroxeter (*Viroconium*), Shropshire. Bone roundel ($\frac{1}{1}$), diameter 20.5 mm. Rowley's House Museum, Shrewsbury. Drawn by S.S.F. from a rubbing by R.P.W., 1953.

    obverse: central hole
    reverse: I

2440.163. Ibid. Black bone roundel ($\frac{1}{1}$), diameter 22 mm. Rowley's House Museum, Shrewsbury. Drawn by S.S.F. from a rubbing by R.P.W., 1953.

    obverse: central hole
    reverse: I

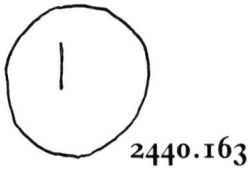

For further examples of I see *RIB* 2440.23(?), 45, 85, 197(?), 222, 223, 237, 298, 299, 329 and 341.

2440.164. Chesterholm (*Vindolanda*), Northumberland. Bone roundel (¼), diameter 17 mm, thickness 4 mm, found in excavations directed by R.E. Birley. Vindolanda Museum. Drawing: The Vindolanda Trust.

obverse, scratched partly on the bevelled edge: II
reverse: blank

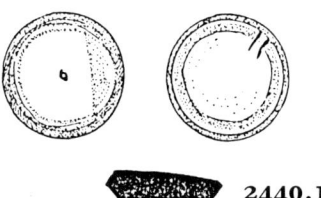

2440.165–166. Ravenglass (*Glannoventa*), Cumbria [Cumberland]. Two bone roundels (¼), found in 1975–77 in the group of 119 noted under *RIB* 2440.152–160 (for full details see *RIB* 2440.42–44). Tullie House Museum, Carlisle. Drawn by T.W. Potter, 1978.

T.W. Potter, *Romans in North-West England* (1979), 75–87.

165. diameter 17 mm, thickness 2 mm. Potter, op. cit., 82 No. 28.

obverse: ringed
reverse: II (?), or F (?)

rev. V (?), Potter.

166. oval, diameters 16 and 20 mm, thickness 2 mm. Potter, op. cit., 86 No. 98.

obverse: countersunk
reverse: II, probably intentional

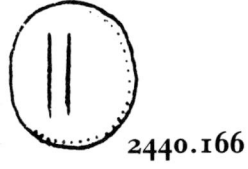

2440.167. Silchester (*Calleva*), Hampshire. Bone roundel (¼), diameter 20.5 mm, thickness 3 mm, found in or before 1909. Reading Museum. Drawn by S.S.F. from a rubbing by R.P.W., 1955.

obverse: countersunk
reverse: blank
edge: II

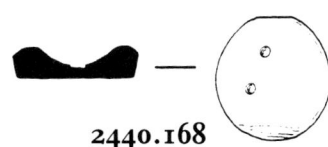

2440.168. Caerleon (*Isca*), Gwent [Monmouthshire]. Bone roundel (¼), diameter 16 mm, thickness 4 mm, found in 1979 in the frigidarium drain of the legionary baths. Caerleon Museum. Reproduced from Zienkiewicz.

J.D. Zienkiewicz, *The Legionary Baths at Caerleon* ii (1986), 205 No. 40 with fig. 72.40.

obverse: countersunk
reverse: two slight depressions
'Two'

2440.169. Chichester (*Noviomagus*), West Sussex. Bone roundel (¼), diameter 19 mm, one of a group of at least twenty-four, only twelve of which were sufficiently well-preserved for examination. Found in 1968 in Burial Group 250 in the Roman cemetery at St Pancras. For the group see *RIB* 2440.52. Chichester Museum. Drawn by S.S.F. from a rubbing by R.P.W., 1968.

JRS lix (1969), 237 No. 11. Wright in A. Down and M. Rule, *Chichester Excavations* i (1971), 88 No. 250 J.

obverse: three concentric rings
reverse: two (or perhaps three) dots
'Two' (*or* 'Three')

For further examples of II see *RIB* 2440.26, 134, 141, 158, 221, 223, 237, 252, 329, 347; and for two dots see 62, 168, 169(?) and 207.

2440.170. Chichester. Bone roundel (⅔), diameter 25.5 mm, thickness 4.5 mm, one of a group of twenty-three found in 1965 in Burial Group 66 in the Roman cemetery at St Pancras; for the group see *RIB* 2440.27. Chichester Museum. Drawn by R.P.W., 1965.

JRS lvi (1966), 220 No. 14 e. Wright in A. Down and M. Rule, *Chichester Excavations* i (1971), 83 No. 21 with fig. 5.15.

obverse: countersunk
reverse: III surrounded by six drilled holes

2440.171. Ibid. Bone roundel (1/1), diameter 17 mm, one of a group of at least twenty-four, only twelve of which were sufficiently well-preserved for examination. Found in 1968 in Burial Group 250 in the Roman cemetery at St Pancras. For the group see *RIB* 2440.52. Chichester Museum. Drawn by R.P.W., 1968.

JRS lix (1969), 237 No. 11. Wright in A. Down and M. Rule, *Chichester Excavations* i (1971), 88 No. 250 K with fig. 5.15.

obverse: four concentric rings
reverse: three dots
'Three'

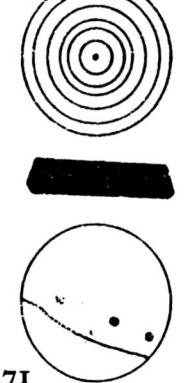

2440.172. St Albans (*Verulamium*), Hertfordshire. Oval bone roundel (1/1), diameters 13 and 11 mm, thickness 2 mm, found in an Antonine deposit in Insula XIV. Verulamium Museum. Drawn by M.G. Wilson.

S.S. Frere, *Verulamium Excavations* i (1972), 152 No. 212 with fig. 56.212.

obverse: countersunk
reverse: three dots
'Three'

2440.173–174. Silchester (*Calleva*), Hampshire. Two bone roundels (1/1), found in or before 1909. Reading Museum. Drawn by S.S.F. from rubbings by R.P.W., 1955.

173. diameter 20.5 mm, thickness 3 mm.

obverse: countersunk
reverse (with casual scratches): III

174. diameter 22 mm, thickness 3 mm.

obverse: countersunk
reverse: blank
edge: III

2440.175–182. Ravenglass (*Glannoventa*), Cumbria [Cumberland]. Eight bone roundels (1/1), found in 1975–77 as part of a group of 119 noted under *RIB* 2440.42–44. Tullie House Museum, Carlisle. Drawn by T.W. Potter, 1978.

T.W. Potter, *Romans in North-West England* (1979), 75–87.

175. diameter 14 mm, thickness 1 mm. Potter, op. cit., 79 No. 6.

obverse: two concentric rings
reverse: III

176. diameter 16 mm, thickness 1.5 mm. Potter, op. cit., 86 No. 91.

    obverse: countersunk
    reverse: III

2440.176

For further examples of III see *RIB* 2440.5, 149, 151, 304 and 347. For three dots see 122, 169(?), 171, 172, 207, 208, 232, 291 and 372.

177. diameter 16 mm, thickness 1.5 mm. Potter, op. cit., 83 No. 67.

    obverse: two concentric rings
    reverse: IV or IIV or III (?)

2440.177

178. diameter 16 mm, thickness 1.5 mm. Potter, op. cit., 85 No. 69.

    obverse: traces of circles
    reverse: IV

2440.178

179. diameter 18 mm, thickness 1.5 mm. Potter, op. cit., 85 No. 78.

    obverse: blank
    reverse: IV and V

2440.179

180. diameter 17.5 mm, thickness 2 mm. Potter, op. cit., 86 No. 88.

    obverse: (first hand) X
    (second hand) IV

2440.180

181. diameter 13 mm, thickness 2 mm. Potter, op. cit., 81 No. 18.

    obverse: three concentric rings
    reverse: IV

2440.181

182. diameter 19 mm, thickness 2 mm. Potter, op. cit., 82 No. 34.

    obverse: three concentric rings
    reverse: I | V
    Presumably 'Four'

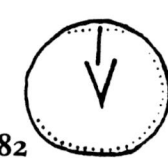
2440.182

2440.183. Marshfield, Avon [Gloucestershire]. Bone roundel (⅟₁), diameter 19.5 mm, thickness 3 mm, found in 1982 at Ironmonger's Piece. Bristol Museum. Reproduced from Blockley.

Britannia xiv (1983), 343 No. 13. K. Blockley, *Marshfield, Ironmonger's Piece, Excavations 1982–3* (B.A.R. No. 141) (1985), 189 No. 4 with fig. 60.

    obverse: countersunk
    reverse: IV or N

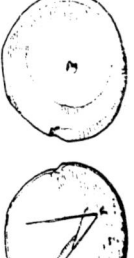
2440.183

2440.184. Silchester (*Calleva*), Hampshire. Bone roundel, diameter 22 mm, thickness 2 mm, found in or before 1909. Reading Museum. Not illustrated.

obverse: three concentric rings
reverse: blank
edge: IIII

2440.185. Chichester (*Noviomagus*), West Sussex. Bone roundel (¹⁄₁), diameter 19 mm, one of a group of at least twenty-four, only twelve of which were sufficiently well-preserved for examination. Found in 1968 in Burial Group 250 in the Roman cemetery at St Pancras. For the group see *RIB* 2440.52. Chichester Museum. Drawn by S.S.F. from a rubbing by R.P.W., 1968.

Wright in A. Down and M. Rule, *Chichester Excavations* i (1971), 88 No. 250. L.

obverse: countersunk
reverse: four dots
          'Four'

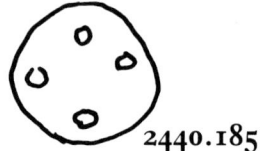
2440.185

For further examples of IV see *RIB* 2440.158, 222; and for four dots see 80.

For further examples of IIII see *RIB* 2440.23, 39, 141, 199, 202, 223, 224, 237, 329, 336 and 348.

2440.186. St Albans (*Verulamium*), Hertfordshire. Bone roundel (¹⁄₁), diameter 20 mm, thickness 3 mm, found in 1931 during excavation of Wheeler's Site A. Verulamium Museum. Drawn by R.P.W., 1942.

JRS xxxii (1942), 118 No. 11 g. Wright, *PSAN*⁴ x (1942), 17 (g) No. 9.

obverse: slightly countersunk
reverse: blank
edge: IIIII

IIII
2440.186

2440.187. Chesterholm (*Vindolanda*), Northumberland. Bone roundel (¹⁄₁), diameter 13 mm, thickness 3.5 mm, found in excavations directed by R.E. Birley. Vindolanda Museum. Drawing: The Vindolanda Trust.

obverse (with other marks): V
reverse: an arrow

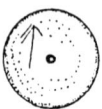

2440.187

2440.188–190. Ewell, Surrey. Three bone roundels (¹⁄₁), found in 1946 in a group of nine associated with a cremation in the grounds of the lodge of 'The Looe'. For the others see *RIB* 2440.20, 107–110, and 335. Bourne Hall Museum, Ewell. Drawn by J. Cotton, 1976.

Britannia viii (1977), 445 No. 104 with fig. 30.

188. diameter 20 mm, thickness 4 mm. *Britannia*, loc. cit., No. 104 f.

obverse: four concentric rings
reverse: X̶V̶ | RI[.]M
          Perhaps]X̶ v | rem(ittam)
          'I will repay five denarii' (?)

For RIIM as *rem(ittam)* see *RIB* 2440.20 with note.

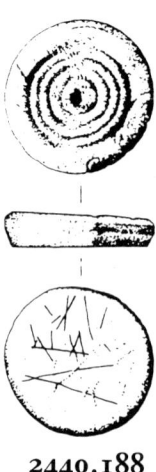
2440.188

189. diameter 21.5 mm, thickness 3 mm. *Britannia*, loc. cit., No. 104 h.

obverse: five concentric rings
reverse: VV
          'Five' (*twice*)

M could also be read.

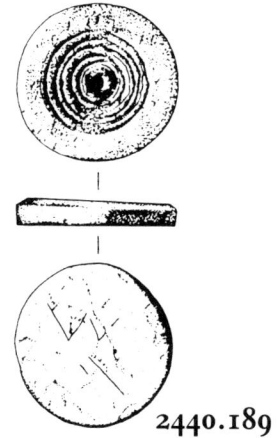

190. diameter 23 mm, thickness 3 mm. *Britannia*, loc. cit. No. 104 a.

obverse: six concentric rings
reverse: V

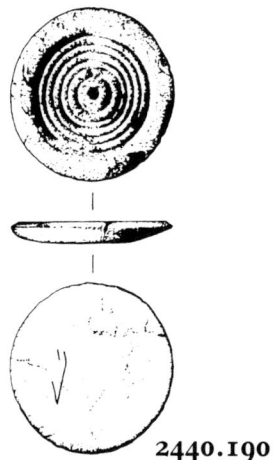

2440.191. St Albans (*Verulamium*), Hertfordshire. Bone roundel (1/1), diameter 23 mm, thickness 2.5 mm, found in or before 1935. Verulamium Museum. Drawn by R.P.W., 1942.

JRS xxxii (1942), 118 No. 11. Wright, *PSAN*[4] x (1942), 17 (g) No. 10.

obverse: six concentric rings
reverse: V

2440.192. Ibid. Bone roundel (1/1), diameter 23 mm, thickness 3 mm, found in 1930 during excavation of Building I. Verulamium Museum. Drawn by R.P.W., 1942.

JRS xxxii (1942), 118 No. 11. Wright, *PSAN*[4] x (1942), 17 (g) No. 11.

obverse: countersunk
reverse: V

2440.193. Ibid. Bone roundel (1/1), diameter 20 mm, thickness 3 mm, found in 1930–34 at Site A. Verulamium Museum. Drawn by R.P.W., 1942.

JRS xxxii (1942), 118 No. 11. Wright, *PSAN*[4] x (1942), 17 (g) No. 12.

obverse: countersunk
reverse: V

2440.194. Colchester (*Camulodunum*), Essex. Bone roundel (1/1), diameter 21 mm, thickness 2.5 mm, found before 1939. Colchester Museum. Drawn by R.P.W., 1943.

JRS xxxiv (1944), 89 No. 9 f.

obverse: countersunk with central perforation, V
reverse: blank

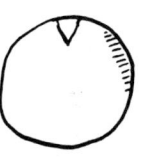

2440.195–196. Colchester. Two bone roundels (¼), found in 1935 and 1937 respectively in the grounds of the Union House, now St Mary's Hospital. Colchester Museum. No. 195 drawn by R.P.W., 1943.

JRS xxxiv (1944), 89 No. 9.

195. diameter 19 mm, thickness 3 mm. *JRS*, loc. cit., No. 9 g.

    obverse: countersunk, with one ring
    reverse: V

2440.195

196. (Not illustrated) diameter 18 mm, thickness 5 mm. *JRS*, loc. cit., No. 9 h.

    obverse: countersunk
    reverse: blank
    edge: V

2440.197. Ibid. Bone roundel (¼), diameter 18 mm, thickness 3 mm, one of a group of twelve ranging in diameter from 16 to 21 mm and in thickness from 2.5 to 5.5 mm, found in 1975 in a pit with third- to fourth-century material at Balkerne Lane. Nine were uninscribed; for the others see *RIB* 2440.33 and 228. Colchester Museum. Drawing: Colchester Archaeological Trust.

Britannia ix (1978), 477 No. 34 a. N. Crummy, *Small Finds* (1983), 91 No. 2242 with fig. 94.

    obverse: Ṿ with superimposed I *or* L with superimposed XI
    reverse (very faintly incised): EỊ

The letters EIR appear on *RIB* 2440.33, found with this piece.

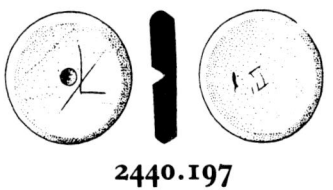

2440.197

2440.198. Margate, Kent. Bone roundel (¼), diameter 22 mm, thickness 3 mm, found in 1963 with *RIB* 2240.57 in a Roman ditch at Drapers Mills School, associated with late first- to second-century pottery. Present whereabouts unknown. Drawn by S.S.F. from a rubbing by R.P.W., 1963.

JRS liv (1964), 179 No. 10 b.

    obverse: countersunk
    reverse: V or Λ
    edge: ΛVR X XI NV
    Aur(elius)

2440.198

2440.199. Chichester (*Noviomagus*), West Sussex. Bone roundel (¼), diameter 26 mm, thickness 6 mm, one of a group of twenty-three found in 1965 in Burial Group 66 in the Roman cemetery at St Pancras. For the group see *RIB* 2440.27. Chichester Museum. Drawn by R.P.W., 1965.

JRS lvi (1966), 220 No. 14 f. Wright in A. Down and M. Rule, *Chichester Excavations* i (1971), 83 No. 10 with fig. 5.15.

    obverse: slightly countersunk
    reverse: blank
    edge: Λ *or* V (*inverted*) IIII X VI

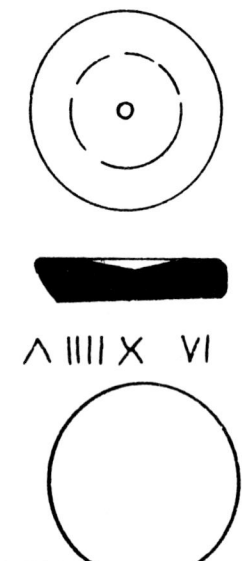

2440.199

2440.200. Ibid. Bone roundel (¼), diameter 25.5 mm, thickness 4.5 mm, one of a group of at least twenty-four (for which see *RIB* 2440.52) found in 1968 in Burial Group 250 in the Roman cemetery at St Pancras. Chichester Museum. Drawn by S.S.F. from a rubbing by R.P.W., 1968.

JRS lix (1969), 237 No. 11. Wright in A. Down and M. Rule, *Chichester Excavations* i (1971), 88 No. F with fig. 5.15.

obverse: countersunk
reverse: V

2440.200

2440.201. Ravenglass (*Glannoventa*), Cumbria [Cumberland]. Bone roundel (¼), diameter 18 mm, thickness 2.5 mm, found in 1975–77 in the group of 119 described under *RIB* 2440.90–92, (*q.v.* for further details). Tullie House Museum, Carlisle. Drawn by T.W. Potter.

T.W. Potter, *Romans in North-West England* (1979), 79 No. 7.

obverse: three concentric rings
reverse (with other marks): V overlying X

2440.201

2440.202. Silchester (*Calleva*), Hampshire. Bone roundel (¼), diameter 24 mm, thickness 2 mm, found in or before 1909. Reading Museum. Drawn by S.S.F. from a rubbing by R.P.W., 1955.

obverse: five concentric rings
reverse: V
edge: IIII IIII

2440.202

2440.203. Wroxeter (*Viroconium*), Shropshire. Bone roundel (¼), diameter 22 mm. Rowley's House Museum, Shrewsbury. Drawn by S.S.F. from a rubbing by R.P.W., 1953.

obverse: countersunk
reverse: five dots

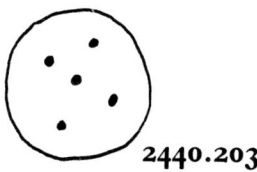

2440.203

For further examples of V see *RIB* 2440.20, 38, 39, 107, 109, 179, 221, 222, 230, 244–246, 260(?), 335 and 347. For another example of five dots see 2440.378.

2440.204. Chichester (*Noviomagus*), West Sussex. Bone roundel (¼), diameter 22.5 mm, thickness 4.5 mm, one of a group of twenty-three found in 1965 in Burial Group 66 in the St Pancras Roman cemetery; for the group see *RIB* 2440.27. Chichester Museum. Drawn by R.P.W., 1965.

JRS lvi (1966), 220 No. 14 g. Wright in A. Down and M. Rule, *Chichester Excavations* i (1971), 83 No. 6 with fig. 5.15.

obverse: slightly countersunk
reverse: V̄Ī

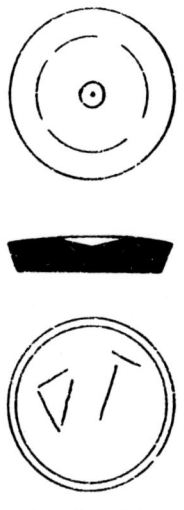

2440.204

2440.205. Colchester (*Camulodunum*), Essex. Bone roundel ($\frac{1}{1}$), diameter 24 mm, thickness 2 mm, found in 1975 in a late or post-Roman context at Balkerne Lane. Colchester Museum. Drawn by P.R. Sealey.

Britannia ix (1978), 478 No. 35.

obverse: five concentric rings
reverse: VI

2440.206. Silchester (*Calleva*), Hampshire. Bone roundel ($\frac{1}{1}$), diameter 19 mm, thickness 2 mm, found in or before 1909. Reading Museum. Drawn by S.S.F. from a rubbing by R.P.W., 1955.

obverse: flat with central hole
reverse: VI and VI (inverted)

For further examples of VI see *RIB* 2440.105, 140, 199, 209, 262(?), 289, 336 and 366; and for six dots *RIB* 2440.170.

2440.207. Chichester (*Noviomagus*), West Sussex. Bone roundel ($\frac{1}{1}$), diameter 25.5 mm, thickness 4.5 mm, one of a group of twenty-three found in 1965 in Burial Group 66 at the St Pancras Roman cemetery; for the group see *RIB* 2440.27. Chichester Museum. Drawn by R.P.W., 1965.

JRS lvi (1966), 220 No. 14 q. Wright in A. Down and M. Rule, *Chichester Excavations* i (1971), 83 No. 2 with fig. 5.15.

obverse: slightly countersunk; two drilled dots near the rim
reverse: X within three drilled dots
edge: VII

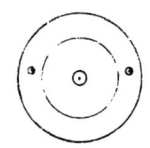
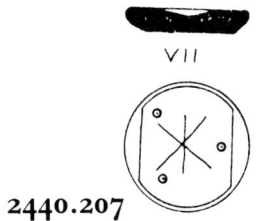

2440.208. Caerwent (*Venta Silurum*), Gwent [Monmouthshire]. Bone roundel ($\frac{1}{1}$), diameter 22 mm, thickness 3 mm, found in 1909 during excavations. Newport Museum. Drawn by S.S.F. from a rubbing by R.P.W., 1947.

obverse: countersunk
reverse: three dots in a grid-pattern of lines
edge: IIIIIII
       'Seven'

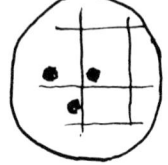

For further examples of VII see *RIB* 2440.26 and 40.

For examples of VIII see *RIB* 2440.222, 243(?) and 381.

2440.209. Ibid. Bone roundel ($\frac{1}{1}$), diameter 19 mm, thickness 3 mm, found in 1899–1912. Newport Museum. Drawn by S.S.F. from a rubbing by R.P.W., 1947.

obverse: countersunk
reverse: scratches
edge: VIIII VI

2440.210. St Albans (*Verulamium*), Hertfordshire. Bone roundel ($\frac{1}{1}$), diameter 24 mm, thickness 3 mm, found in 1958 in Insula XIV. Verulamium Museum. Drawn by M.G. Wilson.

JRS xlix (1959), 137 No. 7 b. S.S. Frere, *Verulamium Excavations* i (1972), 152 No. 213 with fig. 56.213.

obverse: countersunk
reverse: (*left*) VIIII (*centre*) X and M

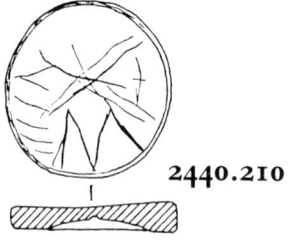

For further examples of VIIII, some retrograde, see *RIB* 2440.222, 297, 336, 347, 364 and 366; and for further examples of IX see *RIB* 2440.140, 264(?) and 329.

2440.211. Marshfield, Avon [Gloucestershire]. Bone roundel (¹⁄₁), diameter 21 mm, thickness 3.5 mm, found in 1982 at Ironmonger's Piece, Marshfield. Bristol Museum. Reproduced from Blockley.

Britannia xiv (1983), 343 No. 14. K. Blockley, *Marshfield, Ironmongers Piece, Excavations 1982–3* (B.A.R. No. 141) (1985), 189 No. 3 with fig. 60.

obverse: slightly countersunk
reverse: blank
edge: IXI, probably to be taken as a numeral on its side between subscript and supra24script lines, i.e. X

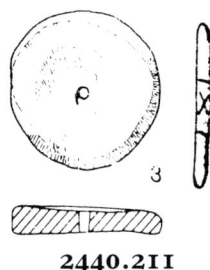

2440.211

2440.212. Aldborough (*Isurium*), North Yorkshire. Bone roundel (¹⁄₁), diameter 22 mm, thickness 1.5 mm. Aldborough Museum. Drawn by S.S.F. from a rubbing by R.P.W., 1952.

obverse: five concentric rings
reverse: X̄

2440.212

2440.213. Bath (*Aquae Sulis*), Avon [Somerset]. Bone roundel (¹⁄₁), diameter 23 mm. Roman Baths Museum, Bath. Drawn by S.S.F. from a rubbing by R.P.W., 1951.

obverse: X
reverse: small hole

2440.213

2440.214. Binchester (*Vinovia*), Durham. Bone roundel (¹⁄₁), diameter 20.5 mm, found in 1878–9. University collection, Durham. Drawn by R.P.W., 1941.

JRS xxxii (1942), 117 No. 11 e. Wright, *PSAN*⁴ x (1942), 17 f.

reverse: X̄

2440.214

2440.215. Caerleon (*Isca*), Gwent [Monmouthshire]. Bone roundel (¹⁄₁), diameter 21 mm, thickness 4 mm, found in 1964–69 at the fortress baths. Caerleon Museum. Not illustrated.

J.D. Zienkiewicz, *The Legionary Baths at Caerleon* ii (1986), 205 No. 25 with fig. 71.

obverse: five concentric rings
reverse: X

2440.216–218. Caerwent (*Venta Silurum*), Gwent [Monmouthshire]. Three bone roundels (¹⁄₁), found in 1899–1912. Newport Museum. Drawn by S.S.F. from rubbings by R.P.W., 1947.

216. diameter 19 mm, thickness 3 mm.

obverse: countersunk
reverse: X

2440.216

217. diameter 12.5 mm, thickness 4.2 mm.

obverse: countersunk
reverse: X

2440.217

218. diameter 19 mm, thickness 3 mm.

obverse: countersunk
reverse: X

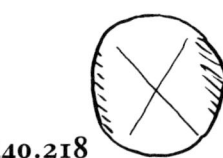

2440.218

2440.219. Canterbury (*Durovernum*), Kent. Bone roundel (¼), diameter 26 mm, thickness 3.5 mm, found in 1978–80 during excavations in the Marlowe Car Park. Canterbury Museum. Drawing: Canterbury Archaeological Trust.

The Archaeology of Canterbury v (1991, forthcoming), No. 1004.

obverse: four concentric rings
reverse: X

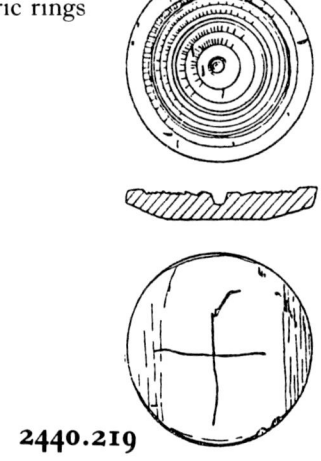

2440.220–223. Chichester (*Noviomagus*), West Sussex. Four bone roundels (¼), part of a group of twenty-three varying in diameter from 16 to 25.5 mm, and in thickness from 2 to 5 mm, found in 1965 in Burial Group 66 in the Roman cemetery at St Pancras. Six are uninscribed; for the remainder see *RIB* 2440.19, 27, 74, 106, 151, 170, 199, 204, 207, 329–331 and 357. Chichester Museum. Drawn by R.P.W., 1965.

JRS lvi (1966), 220 No. 14. Wright in A. Down and M. Rule, *Chichester Excavations* i (1971), 83–8.

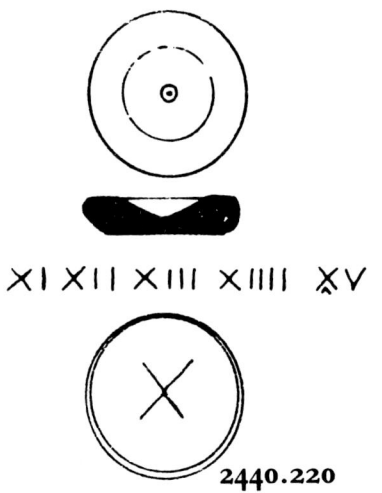

220. diameter 21 mm, thickness 4.5 mm. *JRS* loc. cit., No. 14 j. Wright, 83 No. 23 with fig. 5.5.

obverse: countersunk
reverse: X
edge: XI XII XIII XIIII XV

221. diameter 22.5 mm, thickness 3.75 mm. *JRS*, loc. cit., No. 14 h. Wright, 83 No. 14 with fig. 5.15.

obverse: countersunk
reverse: X̄
edge: II Λ V

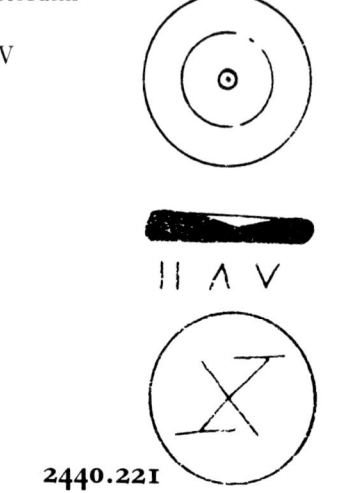

222. diameter 25.5 mm, thickness 4 mm. *JRS*, loc. cit., No. 14 i. Wright, 83 No. 9 with fig. 5.15.

obverse: countersunk
reverse: X with cross-scorings
edge: IV V I VIII (*inverted*) VIIII (*inverted*)

The last numeral could also be read as IIIIΛ.

223. diameter 25.5 mm, thickness 4.5 mm. *JRS*, loc. cit., No. 14 k. Wright, 83 No. 22 with fig. 5.15.

obverse: ⊗
reverse: X with cross-scorings
edge: II·· IIII··I·

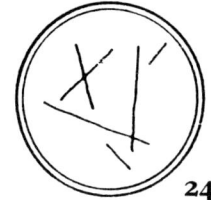

2440.224. Ibid. Bone roundel (¹⁄₁), diameter 22.5 mm, thickness 4.5 mm, one of a group of at least twenty-four (for which see *RIB* 2440.52) found in 1968 in Burial Group 250 in the Roman cemetery at St Pancras. Chichester Museum. Drawn by R.P.W., 1968.

JRS lix (1969), 237 No. 11. Wright in A. Down and M. Rule, *Chichester Excavations* i (1971), 88 No. 250 D with fig. 5.15.

obverse: flat with one circle
reverse: X with scorings (XX is less likely)
edge: IIII

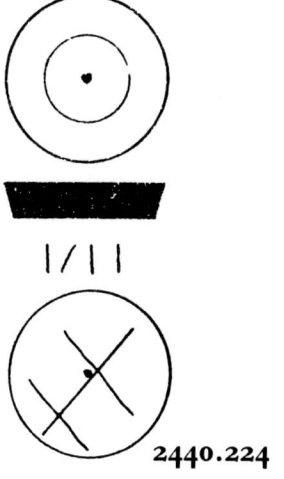

2440.225. Colchester (*Camulodunum*), Essex. Bone roundel (¹⁄₁), diameter 20 mm, thickness 4 mm, found sometime between 1840 and 1888. Colchester Museum (Acton collection). Drawn by S.S.F. from a rubbing by R.P.W., 1943.

JRS xxxiv (1944), 89 No. 9 i.

obverse: countersunk
reverse: X̄

2440.226. Ibid. Bone roundel (¹⁄₁), diameter 17 mm, thickness 4 mm, found in 1973 in a pit with first- and second-century material at The Cups Hotel. Colchester Museum. Drawn by P.R. Sealey.

Britannia ix (1978), 478 No. 37.

obverse: X
reverse: blank

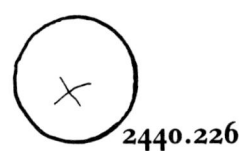

2440.227. Ibid. Bone roundel (¹⁄₁), diameter 19 mm, thickness 1.5 mm, found in 1972 in the second-century rampart at Lion Walk. Colchester Museum. Drawn by P.R. Sealey.

Britannia ix (1978), 478 No. 38.

obverse: four concentric rings
reverse: shallow central hole, X very faintly incised

2440.228. Colchester. Bone roundel (⅟₁), diameter 18 mm, thickness 4 mm, one of a group of twelve ranging in diameter from 16 to 21 mm and in thickness from 2.5 to 5.5 mm, found in 1975 in a pit with third- to fourth-century material at Balkerne Lane. Nine were uninscribed; for the others see *RIB* 2440.33 and 197. Colchester Museum. Drawing: Colchester Archaeological Trust.

Britannia ix (1978), 478 No. 34 c. N. Crummy, *Small Finds* (1983), 91 No. 2244 with fig. 94.

obverse: flat, with four strokes scratched radially from the central lathe-mark
reverse: X with exaggerated serif to the top right-hand terminal

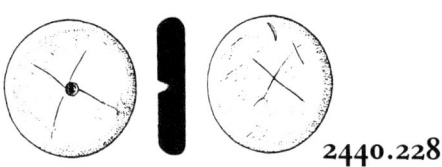

2440.228

2440.229. Ibid. Bone roundel (⅟₁), diameter 21 mm, thickness 1.5 mm, found in 1975 in a pit with third- to fourth-century material at Balkerne Lane (not the same pit as 2440.228). Colchester Museum. Drawn by P.R. Sealey.

Britannia ix (1978), 478 No. 36.

obverse: six concentric rings
reverse: X

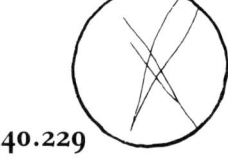

2440.229

2440.230. Ibid. Bone roundel (⅟₁), diameter 23 mm, thickness 3 mm, found in 1936 in the grounds of the Union House, now St Mary's Hospital. Colchester Museum. Drawn by S.S.F. from a rubbing by R.P.W., 1943.

obverse: countersunk
reverse: V heavily inscribed over X

2440.230

2440.231. Corbridge (? *Coria*), Northumberland. Bone roundel (⅟₁), diameter 20 mm, thickness 2.5 mm, found in 1934 south of Site XI. Corbridge Museum. Drawn by R.P.W., 1942.

JRS xxxii (1942), 117 No. 11 b. Wright, *PSAN*⁴ x (1942), 16 (b) No. 4.

obverse: countersunk
reverse: X̄

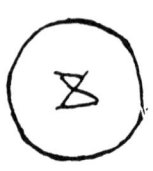

2440.231

2440.232. Ibid. Bone roundel (⅟₁), diameter 23 mm, thickness 2.5 mm, found in 1934 west of Site XI. Corbridge Museum. Drawn by R.P.W., 1942.

JRS xxxii (1942), 117 No. 11 b. Wright, *PSAN*⁴ x (1942), 16 (b) No. 5.

obverse: countersunk, X
reverse: three drilled dots

2440.232

2440.233. Ibid. Bone roundel (⅟₁), diameter 19 mm, thickness 1.5 mm, found in 1941 with a set of nineteen others (from which it differs in style) in an upper level of the Stanegate road. For details of the group see *RIB* 2440.35–36, with 79–80, 120, 145 and 146. Corbridge Museum. Drawn by R.P.W., 1942.

JRS xxxii (1942), 117 No. 11 a. Wright, *PSAN*⁴ x (1942), 16 (a).

obverse: five concentric rings
reverse: X

2440.233

2440.234. Ibid. Bone roundel (¹⁄₁), diameter 19 mm, thickness 3 mm, found in 1934 north of Site XI. Corbridge Museum. Drawn by R.P.W., 1942.

JRS xxxii (1942), 117 No. 11 b. Wright, *PSAN*⁴ (1942), 16 (b) No. 3.

obverse: countersunk
reverse: X

2440.234

2440.235. Ibid. Bone roundel (¹⁄₁), diameter 24 mm. Corbridge Museum. Drawn by S.S.F. from a rubbing by R.P.W., 1941.

obverse: concentric rings, central perforation.
reverse: X

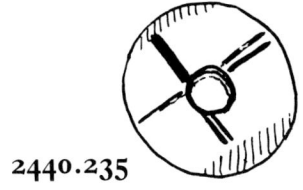
2440.235

2440.236–237. Dorchester (*Durnovaria*), Dorset. Two bone roundels (¹⁄₁), found before 1893 in the south-western sector of the Roman city. Acquired in 1893 by Dorchester Museum as part of the Somerleigh Court collection. Drawn by S.S.F. from rubbings by R.P.W., 1946 and 1951.

236. diameter 12.5 mm, thickness 3 mm.
    obverse: X
    reverse: X
    edge: fifteen vertical cuts (not illustrated)

2440.236

237. diameter 12.5 mm
JRS xlii (1952), 105 No. 12.
    obverse: X
    reverse: X
    edge: +I+II+IIII+IIII

There is a fourth digit in the third group of figures.

2440.237

2440.238–239. Ibid. Two bone roundels (¹⁄₁) found in 1937–8 at Colliton Park. Dorchester Museum. Drawn by S.S.F. from rubbings by R.P.W., 1946 and 1951.

238. diameter 20.5 mm, thickness 3 mm.
    obverse: countersunk
    reverse: X

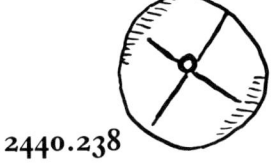
2440.238

239. diameter 20.5 mm, thickness 3 mm.
    obverse: countersunk
    reverse: X

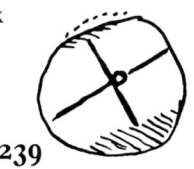
2440.239

2440.240. Leicester (*Ratae*). Bone roundel (¹⁄₁), diameter 17.5 mm, thickness 1.5 mm, found in 1939, unstratified. Leicester Museum. Drawn by S.S.F. from a rubbing by R.P.W., 1951.

obverse: $\overline{\text{X}}$
reverse: blank

2440.240

2440.241. Malton (*Derventio*), North Yorkshire. Bone roundel (¹⁄₁), diameter 22 mm. Malton Museum. Drawn by S.S.F. from a rubbing by R.P.W., 1951.

obverse, countersunk: X̶
reverse: X

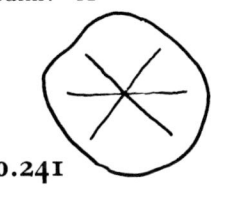 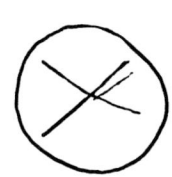
2440.241

2440.242. Ibid. Bone roundel (¹⁄₁), diameter 18 mm, thickness 4 mm, found in 1970 in the *vicus* south of the fort. Malton Museum. Not illustrated.

Britannia ii (1971), 303 No. 88.

obverse: countersunk
reverse: X cut twice with some extra cuts

2440.243–291. Ravenglass (*Glannoventa*), Cumbria [Cumberland]. Forty-nine bone roundels (¹⁄₁), found in 1975–77 as part of a group of 119 bone and seven glass roundels discovered together in a burnt deposit of c. A.D. 190–210 during excavations at the fort. Thirty were uninscribed. Ten were inscribed with letters (*RIB* 2440.42–44, 69, 90–92, 94, 103–104) and three with both letters and numerals (263, 264 and 270): the remaining seventy-nine carry numerals only (*RIB* 2440 152–160, 165–166, 175–182, 201, 243–262, 265–269, 271–291, 337–343 and 355–356). Tullie House Museum, Carlisle. Drawn by T.W. Potter, 1978.

T.W. Potter, *Romans in North-West England* (1979), 75–87.

243. diameter 19 mm, thickness 2.5 mm. Potter, op. cit., 79 No. 1 with fig. 29.

   obverse: four concentric rings
   reverse: X apparently overlying IIIV

2440.243

244. diameter 19 mm, thickness 3 mm. Potter, op. cit., 79 No. 2.

   obverse: five concentric rings
   reverse: X overlying X̶ or XIII with earlier graffiti V and X

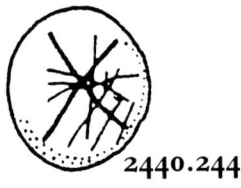

245. diameter 15 mm, thickness 2 mm. Potter, op. cit., 79 No. 3.

   obverse: three concentric rings
   reverse: X overlying V

246. diameter 16 mm, thickness 1.5 mm. Potter, op. cit., 79 No. 4.

   obverse: three concentric rings
   reverse: X overlying V̄

2440.246

247. diameter 16 mm, thickness 2 mm. Potter, op. cit., 79 No. 5.

   obverse: three concentric rings
   reverse: X

2440.247

248. diameter 19 mm, thickness 3 mm. Potter, op. cit., 79 No. 8.

   obverse: three concentric rings
   reverse: X overlying X(?) with other marks

2440.248

249. diameter 18 mm, thickness 3 mm. Potter, op. cit., 81 No. 9.

   obverse: four concentric rings
   reverse: X overlying XI

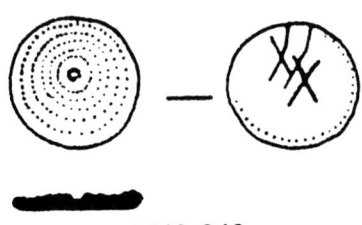

2440.249

250. diameter 20 mm, thickness 2.5 mm. Potter, op. cit., 81 No. 10.

    obverse: three concentric rings
    reverse: X overlying other marks

2440.250

251. diameter 18 mm, thickness 1.5 mm. Potter, op. cit., 81 No. 11.

    obverse: three concentric rings
    reverse: X overlying other marks

2440.251

252. diameter 22 mm, thickness 2.5 mm. Potter, op. cit., 81 No. 13.

    obverse: four concentric rings
    reverse: X overlying II and other marks

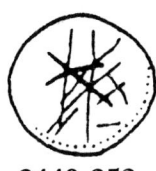

2440.252

253. diameter 15 mm, thickness 1 mm. Potter, op. cit., 81 No. 14.

    obverse: two concentric rings
    reverse: X overlying X

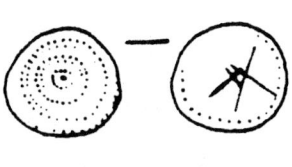

2440.253

254. diameter 14 mm, thickness 2.5 mm. Potter, op. cit., 81 No. 15.

    obverse: three incised concentric circles
    reverse: X

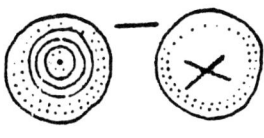

2440.254

255. diameter 20 mm, thickness 3 mm. Potter, op. cit., 81 No. 16.

    obverse: three concentric rings
    reverse: X (twice incised)

2440.255

256. diameter 14 mm, thickness 1.5 mm. Potter, op. cit., 81 No. 17.

    obverse: two concentric rings
    reverse: X

2440.256

257. diameter 16 mm, thickness 2 mm. Potter, op. cit., 81 No. 19.

    obverse: three concentric rings
    reverse: X

2440.257

258. diameter 15 mm, thickness 1.5 mm. Potter, op. cit., 81 No. 20.

    obverse: three incised concentric circles
    reverse: $\overline{\text{X}}$

2440.258

(Ravenglass, continued)

259. diameter 20 mm, thickness 3 mm. Potter, op. cit., 82 No. 24.

obverse: three concentric rings
reverse: X

260. diameter 18 mm, thickness 2 mm. Potter, op. cit., 82 No. 27.

obverse: three concentric rings
reverse: X replacing X which may overlie V

261. diameter 15 mm, thickness 2 mm. Potter, op. cit., 82 No. 29.

obverse: two concentric rings
reverse: X

262. diameter 13 mm, thickness 2 mm. Potter, op. cit., 82 No. 30.

obverse: two concentric rings
reverse: X perhaps overlying VI

263. diameter 18 mm, thickness 1.5 mm. Potter, op. cit., 82 No. 31.

obverse: three concentric rings
reverse: X overlying PE

See *RIB* 2440.94 for another example of PE from this group.

264. diameter 19 mm, thickness 2 mm. Potter, op. cit., 82 No. 32.

obverse: two concentric rings
reverse: X P(?) IX(?)

265. diameter 17 mm, thickness 3 mm. Potter, op. cit., 82 No. 33.

obverse: three concentric rings
reverse: $\overline{X}$

266. diameter 20 mm, thickness 3 mm. Potter, op. cit., 82 No. 35.

obverse: six concentric rings
reverse: $\overline{X}$, X and other marks

267. diameter 18 mm, thickness 2 mm. Potter, op. cit., 82 No. 36.

obverse: three concentric rings
reverse: X

(Ravenglass, continued)

268. diameter 20 mm, thickness 1.5 mm. Potter, op. cit., 82 No. 38.

    obverse: three concentric rings
    reverse: X

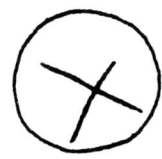

2440.268

269. diameter 18 mm, thickness 1.5 mm. Potter, op. cit., 82 No. 39.

    obverse: three concentric inscribed circles
    reverse: X

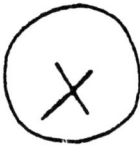

2440.269

270. diameter 18 mm, thickness 2 mm. Potter, op. cit., 82 No. 40.

    obverse: three concentric rings
    reverse: X overlying R

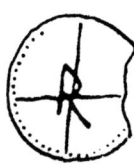

2440.270

271. diameter 18 mm, thickness 3 mm. Potter, op. cit., 82 No. 41.

    obverse: three concentric rings
    reverse: $\overline{X}$ replacing a Y-shaped line, or perhaps $\overline{XI}$

2440.271

272. diameter 20 mm, thickness 3 mm. Potter, op. cit., 83 No. 42.

    obverse: three concentric rings
    reverse: X

2440.272

273. diameter 22 mm, thickness 3 mm. Potter, op. cit., 83 No. 44.

    obverse: three concentric rings
    reverse: $\overline{X}$

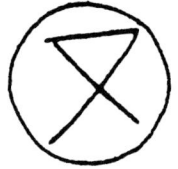

2440.273

274. diameter 15 mm, thickness 1.5 mm. Potter, op. cit., 83 No. 45.

    obverse: two concentric rings
    reverse: X

2440.274

275. diameter 16 mm, thickness 1.5 mm. Potter, op. cit., 83 No. 50.

    obverse: four concentric inscribed circles
    reverse: X

2440.275

(Ravenglass, continued)

276. diameter 20 mm, thickness 1 mm. Potter, op. cit., 83 No. 52.

obverse: five concentric rings
reverse: Perhaps X with other marks

277. diameter 19 mm, thickness 1.5 mm. Potter, op. cit., 83 No. 53.

obverse: four concentric rings
reverse: X

278. diameter 16 mm, thickness 2.5 mm. Potter, op. cit., 83 No. 54.

obverse: three concentric rings
reverse: X overlaid by other marks

279. diameter 15 mm, thickness 1.5 mm. Potter, op. cit., 83 No. 55.

obverse: three concentric rings
reverse: X twice successively and other marks

280. diameter 22 mm, thickness 1.5 mm. Potter, op. cit., 83 No. 56.

obverse: four concentric rings
reverse: X with other marks

281. diameter 15 mm, thickness 1.5 mm. Potter, op. cit., 83 No. 37.

obverse: three concentric rings
reverse: X

282. diameter 16 mm, thickness 1 mm. Potter, op. cit., 85 No. 62.

obverse: three concentric rings
reverse: $\overline{X}$

283. diameter 18 mm, thickness 2 mm. Potter, op. cit., 85 No. 63.

obverse: three concentric rings
reverse: $\underline{\overline{X}}$

284. diameter 15 mm, thickness 1 mm. Potter, op. cit., 85 No. 59.

obverse: three concentric inscribed circles
reverse: X

(Ravenglass, continued)

285. diameter 16 mm, thickness 1.5 mm. Potter, op. cit., 85 No. 65.

obverse: three concentric inscribed circles
reverse: X

286. diameter 14 mm, thickness 2 mm. Potter, op. cit., 85 No. 70.

obverse: two concentric inscribed circles
reverse: perhaps X

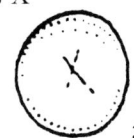

287. diameter 16 mm, thickness 2 mm. Potter, op. cit., 85 No. 71.

obverse: two concentric rings
reverse: X

288. diameter 16 mm, thickness 1.5 mm. Potter, op. cit., 85 No. 79.

obverse: plain
reverse: X̄

289. diameter 12 mm, thickness 2 mm. Potter, op. cit., 85 No. 80.

obverse: plain
reverse: X and VI and another stroke.

290. diameter 18 mm, thickness 2 mm. Potter, op. cit., 86 No. 82.

obverse: plain
reverse: X twice and other lines

291. diameter 16 mm, thickness 1 mm. Potter, op. cit., 87 No. 119.

obverse: three dots
reverse (over other marks): X (*twice*)

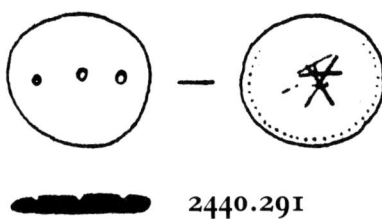

2440.292. Richborough (*Rutupiae*), Kent. Bone roundel (¹⁄₁), diameter 14.3 mm, thickness 2.5 mm. In store at Dover Castle. Drawn by S.S.F. from a rubbing by R.P.W., 1948.

obverse (flat): X
reverse: M

2440.293. St Albans (*Verulamium*), Hertfordshire. Bone roundel (¹⁄₁), diameter 18 mm, thickness 2.5 mm, found before 1942. Verulamium Museum. Drawn by S.S.F. from a rubbing by R.P.W., 1942.

obverse: four concentric rings
reverse: X

2440.294. St Albans. Bone roundel (⅟₁), diameter 17.5 mm, thickness 3 mm, found in 1958 in an early Antonine layer in Insula XIV. Verulamium Museum. Drawn by M.G. Wilson

JRS xlix (1959), 137 No. 7 a. S.S. Frere, *Verulamium Excavations* i (1972), 152 No. 214 with fig. 56.

obverse: five concentric rings
reverse: X

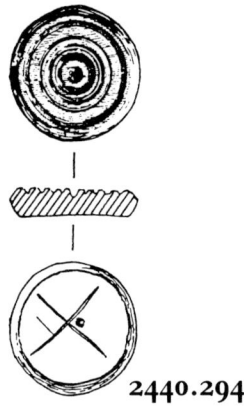

2440.294

2440.295. Ibid. Bone roundel (⅟₁), diameter 23 mm, found in 1958 unstratified in Insula XIV. Verulamium Museum. Drawn by M.G. Wilson.

S.S. Frere, *Verulamium Excavations* i (1972), 152 No. 215 with fig. 56.

reverse: countersunk
reverse: X twice, with intersecting scratched lines, or eight-pointed star.

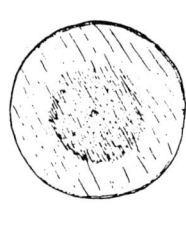

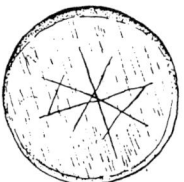

2440.295

2440.296–300. Silchester (*Calleva*), Hampshire. Five bone roundels (⅟₁), found in or before 1909. Reading Museum. Drawn by S.S.F. from rubbings by R.P.W., 1955.

296. diameter 24 mm, thickness 3 mm.
  obverse: countersunk
  reverse: X̄

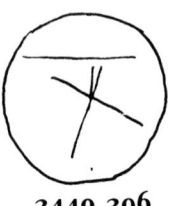

2440.296

297. diameter 22 mm, thickness 3 mm.
  obverse: six concentric rings
  reverse: X
  edge: IIIIV
    Presumably 'nine' retrograde

2440.297

298. diameter 24 mm, thickness 3 mm.
  obverse: countersunk, with central perforation
  reverse: X
  edge: MΛII with I on the opposite edge

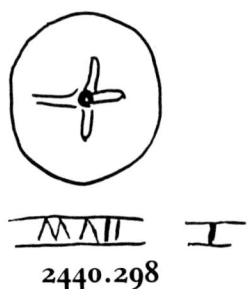

2440.298

299. diameter 19 mm, thickness 3 mm.

    obverse: countersunk
    reverse: X
    edge: I

2440.299

300. diameter 24 mm, thickness 2 mm.

    obverse: seven concentric rings
    reverse: X̄

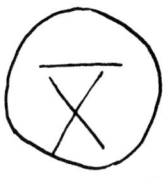

2440.300

2440.301. South Shields (*Arbeia*), Tyne and Wear [Durham]. Bone roundel (⅟₁), diameter 17.5 mm, thickness 4.75 mm. South Shields Museum. Drawn by S.S.F. from a rubbing by R.P.W., 1946.

obverse: countersunk
reverse: X

2440.301

2440.302. Wall (*Letocetum*), Staffordshire. Bone roundel (⅟₁), diameter 16 mm. Wall Museum. Drawn by S.S.F. from a rubbing by R.P.W., 1951.

obverse: central hole, X
reverse: some scratches

2440.302

2440.303–304. Wroxeter (*Viroconium*), Shropshire. Two bone roundels (⅟₁). Rowley's House Museum, Shrewsbury. Drawn by S.S.F. from rubbings by R.P.W., 1953.

303. diameter 17.5 mm.

    obverse: central hole
    reverse: X

2440.303

304. diameter 19 mm.

    obverse: three concentric rings
    reverse: X
    edge: III

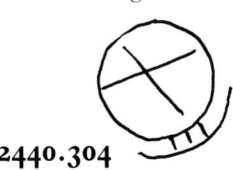

2440.304

2440.305. Ibid. Bone roundel (⅟₁), diameter 17 mm, thickness 3 mm, found in 1967 unstratified at the Baths. Wroxeter Museum. Drawn by S.S.F. from a rubbing by R.P.W., 1967.

JRS lviii (1968), 210 No. 34.

obverse: countersunk
reverse: X̄

2440.305

2440.306–307. (?) York (*Eboracum*). Two bone roundels (⅟₁), Yorkshire Museum, York. Drawn by S.S.F. from rubbings by R.P.W., 1946.

306. diameter 19 mm, thickness 3 mm.

    obverse: countersunk
    reverse: X

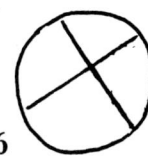

2440.306

307. diameter 24 mm, thickness 3 mm.

    obverse: plain
    reverse: X

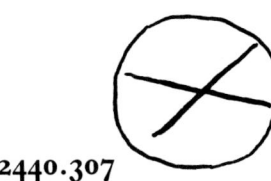

2440.307

2440.308–309. York. Two bone roundels (⅟₁), found in 1972–73 in the Roman sewer in Church Street within the fortress. Yorkshire Museum, York. Reproduced from MacGregor.

A. MacGregor, *Finds from a Roman Sewer System . . . in Church Street* (The Archaeology of York xvii fascicule 1, 1976).

308. diameter 22 mm, thickness 4 mm. MacGregor, op. cit., 22 No. 85 with fig. 3.

    obverse: countersunk, with four radial strokes from the central lathe-mark
    reverse: X

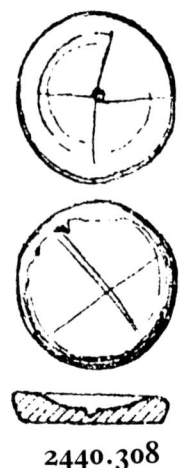

2440.308

309. diameter 23 mm, thickness 4.5 mm. MacGregor, op. cit., 22 No. 79 with fig. 3.

    obverse: countersunk
    reverse: blank
    edge: X

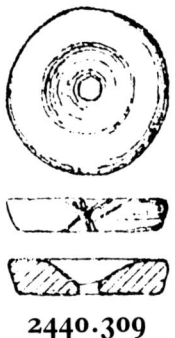

2440.309

2440.310–320. Ibid. Eleven bone roundels (⅟₁), from a group of forty-six found in 1951–59 during excavation of Cremation No. 41 at Trentholme Drive, lying among debris from the pyre, which filled the grave around the cremation vessel. One other bore a scratched mark and the remainder were uninscribed. Yorkshire Museum, York. Reproduced from Wenham.

L.F. Wenham, *The Romano-British Cemetery at Trentholme Drive, York* (1968), 32 and 97 with fig. 40 No. 11.

310. diameter 18.5 mm, thickness 2.5 mm.

    obverse: countersunk: X
    reverse: X

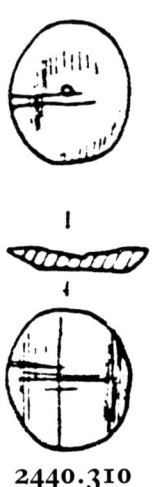

2440.310

311. diameter 21 mm, thickness 3 mm.

    obverse: countersunk
    reverse: X

2440.311

(York, continued)

312. diameter 19 mm, thickness 3 mm.

    obverse: countersunk
    reverse: $\overline{X}$

2440.312

313. diameter 22 mm, thickness 3.5 mm.

    obverse: countersunk
    reverse: X made with repeated strokes

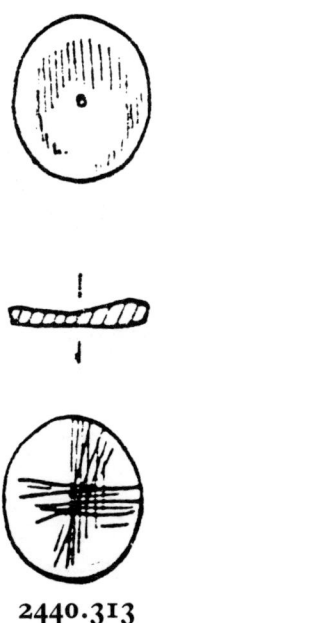

2440.313

314. diameter 22 mm, thickness 2 mm.

    obverse: concave
    reverse: X three times repeated

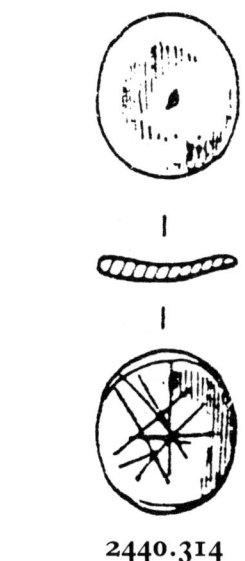

2440.314

315. diameter 25 mm, thickness 4 mm.

    obverse: countersunk
    reverse: X made with repeated strokes

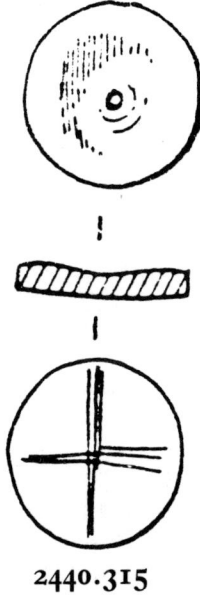

2440.315

(York, continued)

316. partly adhering to a nail: diameter 22 mm, thickness not recorded.

    reverse: X

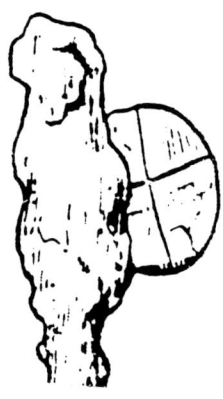

2440.316

317. diameter 21 mm, thickness 5 mm.

    obverse: countersunk
    reverse: X made with repeated strokes

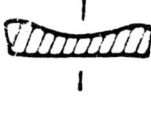

2440.317

318. diameter 22.5 mm, thickness 4 mm.

    obverse: countersunk
    reverse: X

2440.318

319. diameter 20 mm, thickness 2.5 mm.

    obverse: countersunk
    reverse: X made with repeated strokes

2440.319

320. diameter 23 mm, thickness 4 mm.

obverse: countersunk
reverse: X made with repeated strokes

2440.320

2440.321. Caerleon (*Isca*), Gwent [Monmouthshire]. Bone roundel ($\frac{1}{1}$), diameter 19 mm, thickness 4 mm, found in 1979 in the frigidarium drain of the legionary baths. Caerleon Museum. Reproduced from Zienkiewicz.

J.D. Zienkiewicz, *The Legionary Baths at Caerleon* ii (1986), 205 No. 31 with fig. 71.31.

obverse: three incised circles
reverse: ten dots
edge: three single incisions (not illustrated)

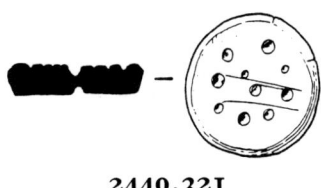

2440.321

For further examples of X see *RIB* 2440.26, 27, 31, 32, 42, 75, 82(?), 90, 91, 103, 104, 107, 134, 143, 150, 155, 161, 180, 198, 199, 201(?), 337, 354 and 372.

2440.322. Chesterholm (*Vindolanda*), Northumberland. Bone roundel ($\frac{1}{1}$), diameter 24 mm, thickness 2 mm, found in excavations directed by R.E. Birley. Vindolanda Museum. Drawing: The Vindolanda Trust.

obverse: X̶
reverse: XI

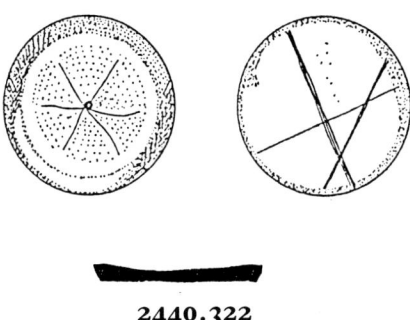

2440.322

2440.323. Ibid. Bone roundel ($\frac{1}{1}$), diameter 16 mm, thickness 2 mm, found in excavations directed by R.E. Birley. Vindolanda Museum. Drawing: The Vindolanda Trust.

obverse: X̄Ī
reverse: blank

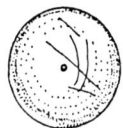

2440.323

2440.324. Ibid. Bone roundel ($\frac{1}{1}$), diameter 17 mm, thickness 3 mm, found in excavations directed by R.E. Birley. Vindolanda Museum. Drawing: The Vindolanda Trust.

obverse, countersunk: XI
reverse: blank.

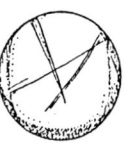

2440.324

2440.325–326. Chichester (*Noviomagus*), West Sussex. Two bone roundels found in 1968 in a group of at least twenty-four (for which see *RIB* 2440.52) in Grave Group 250 at the Roman cemetery at St Pancras. Chichester Museum. No. 325 drawn by R.P.W., 1968.

JRS lix (1969), 237 No. 11. Wright in A. Down and M. Rule, *Chichester Excavations* i (1971), 88.

325. (⅟₁), diameter 25.5 mm, thickness 3 mm. Drawn by R.P.W., 1968. Wright, loc. cit., No. 250 A with fig. 5.15.

obverse: flat
reverse: X̄Ī

326. Not illustrated. Dimensions not recorded. Wright, loc. cit., No. 250 C.

obverse: flat
reverse: X̄Ī

For further examples of XI see *RIB* 2440.76, 197(?), 198, 220, 249 and 354.

2440.327–328. Caerwent (*Venta Silurum*), Gwent [Monmouthshire]. Two bone roundels (⅟₁), found in 1899–1912. Newport Museum. Drawn by S.S.F. from rubbings by R.P.W., 1947.

327. diameter 22 mm, thickness 3 mm.

obverse: countersunk
reverse: X

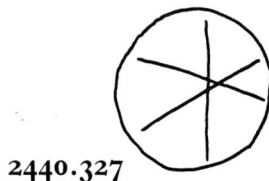

328. diameter 19 mm, thickness 2.5 mm.

obverse: countersunk
reverse: X

See the Introduction to this chapter, p. 106

2440.329–331. Chichester (*Noviomagus*), West Sussex. Three bone roundels (⅟₁), found in 1965 as part of a group of twenty-three in Burial Group 66 in the St Pancras Roman cemetery. For details of the group see *RIB* 2440.27. Chichester Museum. Drawn by R.P.W., 1968.

Wright in A. Down and M. Rule, *Chichester Excavations* i (1971), 83 with fig. 5.15.

329. op. cit., 83 No. 18 (not illustrated).

obverse: blank
reverse: X

330. diameter 22.5 mm, thickness 3.5 mm. op. cit., 83 No. 4.

obverse: countersunk
reverse: X

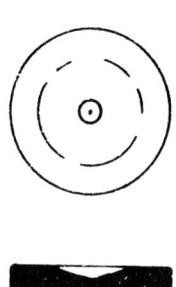
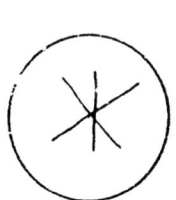

331. diameter 23 mm, thickness 3 mm. op. cit., 83 No. 5.

    obverse: countersunk
    reverse: ӾII

See the Introduction to this chapter, p. 106

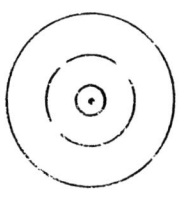

2440.331

2440.332–333. Colchester (*Camulodunum*), Essex. Two bone roundels (⅟₁), found in 1929 in the grounds of the Union House, now St Mary's Hospital. Colchester Museum. Drawn by S.S.F. from rubbings by R.P.W., 1943.

332. diameter 23 mm, thickness 2.5 mm.

    obverse: a small hollow
    reverse: Ӿ

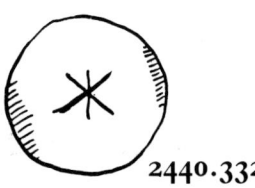

2440.332

333. diameter 22 mm, thickness 3 mm.

    obverse: countersunk
    reverse: Ӿ

See the Introduction to this chapter, p. 106

2440.333

2440.334. Ibid. Bone roundel (⅟₁), diameter 16 mm, thickness 3 mm. No provenance recorded. Colchester Museum. Drawn by S.S.F. from a rubbing by R.P.W., 1943.

    obverse: small central hole and the edge bevelled all round: Ӿ
    reverse: Ӿ

See the Introduction to this chapter, p. 106

2440.334

2440.335. Ewell, Surrey. Bone roundel (⅟₁), diameter 21 mm, thickness 4 mm, one of nine found in 1946 in association with a cremation in the grounds of the lodge of 'The Looe'. For the others see *RIB* 2440.20, 107–110, and 188–190. Bourne Hall Museum, Ewell. Drawn by J. Cotton, 1976.

Britannia viii (1977), 445 No. 104 i with fig. 30.

    obverse: five concentric rings
    reverse: V | Ӿ with other marks

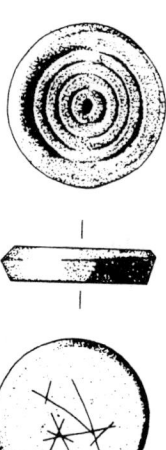

2440.335

2440.336. North Warnborough, Hampshire. Bone roundel (¼), diameter 19 mm, thickness 3 mm, found in 1929–30 during excavations at the villa. At Lodge Farm, North Warnborough. Drawn by S.S.F. from a rubbing by R.P.W., 1953.

Liddell, *P. Hants. F.C.* x (1931), 230 with pl. XIII.5.

obverse: countersunk
reverse: X
edge: VIIII VI VIIII

See the Introduction to this chapter, p. 106

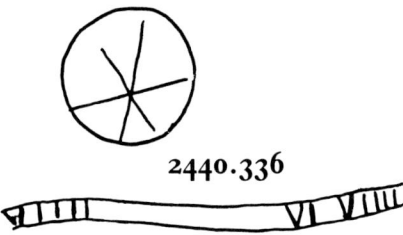

2440.336

2440.337–343. Ravenglass (*Glannoventa*), Cumbria [Cumberland]. Seven bone roundels (¼), found in 1975–77 as part of a group of 119 bone and seven glass roundels discovered together in a burnt deposit of *c*. A.D. 190–210 during excavations at the fort. Thirty are uninscribed. Ten are inscribed with letters (*RIB* 2440.42–44, 69, 90–92, 94, 103–104) and three with both letters and numerals (263, 264 and 270). The remaining seventy-five carry numerals only (*RIB* 2440.152–160, 165–166, 175–182, 201, 243–262, 265–269, 271–291, 337–343 and 355–356). Tullie House Museum. Carlisle. Drawn by T.W. Potter, 1978.

T.W. Potter, *Romans in North-West England* (1979), 75–87.

337. diameter 24 mm, thickness 3 mm. Potter, loc. cit., 82 No. 26.

obverse: five concentric rings
reverse: X overlying other marks

See the Introduction to this chapter, p. 106

2440.337

338. diameter 17 mm, thickness 1 mm. Potter, loc. cit., 82, No. 83.

obverse: three concentric rings
reverse: X and other marks. The cross-bar of the X may be caused by damage.

See the Introduction to this chapter, p. 106

2440.338

339. diameter 20 mm, thickness 2 mm. Potter, loc. cit., 83 No. 57.

obverse: four concentric rings
reverse: X

See the Introduction to this chapter, p. 106

2440.339

340. diameter 19 mm, thickness 2 mm. Potter, loc. cit., 86 No. 85.

obverse: plain
reverse: X

See the Introduction to this chapter, p. 106

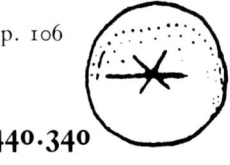

2440.340

341. diameter 20 mm, thickness 2.5 mm. Potter, loc. cit., 86 No. 86.

obverse: plain
reverse: X or possibly X over I

See the Introduction to this chapter, p. 106

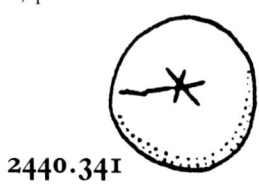

2440.341

342. diameter 17 mm, thickness 2 mm. Potter, loc. cit., 86 No. 89.

obverse: plain
reverse: ✷

See the Introduction to this chapter, p. 106

2440.342

343. diameter 15 mm, thickness 1 mm. Potter, loc. cit., 87 No. 64.

obverse: blank
reverse: ✷

See the Introduction to this chapter, p. 106

2440.343

2440.344–345. Richborough (*Rutupiae*), Kent. Two bone roundels (⅟₁), both 19 mm in diameter and 3 mm thick, found in 1928–31 during excavations at the fort. In store at Dover Castle. Drawn by S.S.F. from rubbings by R.P.W., 1948.

344. obverse: countersunk with two concentric rings
reverse: ✷

2440.344

345. obverse: flat
reverse: ✷

See the Introduction to this chapter, p. 106

2440.345

2440.346. St Albans (*Verulamium*), Hertfordshire. Bone roundel (⅟₁), diameter 25.5 mm, thickness 3 mm, found in 1930–34. Verulamium Museum. Drawn by S.S.F. from a rubbing by R.P.W., 1941.

JRS xxxii (1942), 118 No. 11 g. Wright, *PSAN*⁴ x (1942), 17 (g) No. 14.

obverse: five concentric rings
reverse: ✷

See the Introduction to this chapter, p. 106

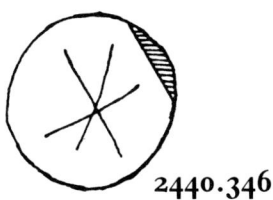
2440.346

2440.347. Silchester (*Calleva*), Hampshire. Bone roundel (⅟₁), diameter 22 mm, thickness 3 mm, found in 1909 during excavations at the forum. Reading Museum. Drawn by S.S.F. from a rubbing by R.P.W., 1955.

obverse: countersunk
reverse: ✷
edge (not illustrated): M III V II VN IIIIV

See the Introduction to this chapter, p. 106

2440.347

2440.348. Ibid. Bone roundel (⅟₁), found in or before 1909. Reading Museum. Drawn by S.S.F. from a rubbing by R.P.W., 1955.

obverse: cross on the rim
reverse: ✷
edge: IIII

See the Introduction to this chapter, p. 106

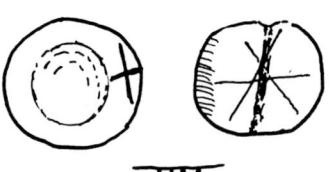
2440.348

2440.349–351. Wroxeter (*Viroconium*), Shropshire. Three bone roundels (⅟₁). Rowley's House Museum, Shrewsbury (No. 350 at Wroxeter Museum). Drawn by S.S.F. from rubbings by R.P.W., 1953.

349. diameter 17.5 mm.

obverse: central hole
reverse: X

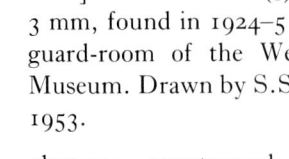
2440.349

350. diameter 22 mm, thickness 3 mm.

obverse: countersunk and perforated
reverse: X

2440.350

351. diameter 19 mm, thickness 3 mm.

obverse: countersunk
reverse: X

See the Introduction to this chapter, p. 106

2440.351

2440.352. York (*Eboracum*). Bone roundel (⅟₁), diameter 24 mm, thickness 2.5 mm. Yorkshire Museum, York. Drawn by S.S.F. from a rubbing by R.P.W., 1946.

obverse: six concentric rings
reverse: X

See the Introduction to this chapter, p. 106

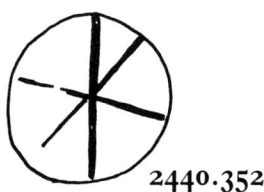
2440.352

For further examples of X see *RIB* 2440.68, 140, 142, 207, 223, 241, 271(?), 322 and 378.

2440.353. Brecon (? *Cicucium*), Powys [Brecknockshire]. Bone roundel (⅟₁), diameter 20.5 mm, thickness 3 mm, found in 1924–5 during excavation of the north guard-room of the West Gate of the fort. Brecon Museum. Drawn by S.S.F. from a rubbing by R.P.W., 1953.

obverse: countersunk
reverse: blank
edge: XII

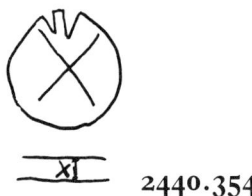
2440.353

2440.354. Colchester (*Camulodunum*), Essex. Bone roundel (⅟₁), diameter 18 mm, thickness 4 mm, found in 1936 in the grounds of the Union House, now St Mary's Hospital. Colchester Museum. Drawn by S.S.F. from a rubbing by R.P.W., 1943.

obverse: countersunk
reverse: X with two notches cut on the edge. Perhaps 'Twelve', R.P.W.
edge: XI

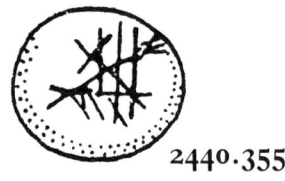
2440.354

2440.355–356. Ravenglass (*Glannoventa*), Cumbria [Cumberland]. Two bone roundels (⅟₁), found in 1975–77 as part of a group of 119 bone and seven glass roundels, in a burnt deposit of c. A.D. 190–210 during excavations at the fort. For other details of the group see *RIB* 2440.337–343. Tullie House Museum, Carlisle. Drawn by T.W. Potter, 1978.

T.W. Potter, *Romans in North-West England* (1979), 75–87.

355. diameter 22 mm, thickness 2.5 mm. Potter, loc. cit., 81 No. 12.

obverse: three concentric rings
reverse: Perhaps XII overlying X̄ with other marks

2440.355

356. diameter 14 mm, thickness 1.5 mm. Potter, loc. cit., 86 No. 81.

obverse: plain
reverse: XII with the II twice incised.

2440.356

2440.357. Chichester (*Noviomagus*), West Sussex. Bone roundel (¹⁄₁), diameter 21 mm, thickness 5 mm, found in 1965 in a group of twenty-three (for which see *RIB* 2440.27) in Burial Group 66 in the Roman cemetery at St Pancras. Chichester Museum. Drawn by R.P.W., 1965.

JRS lvi (1966), 220 No. 14 m. Wright in A. Down and M. Rule, *Chichester Excavations* i (1971), 83 No. 7 with fig. 5.15.

obverse: countersunk
reverse: blank
edge: XII, /XXIIII, XV

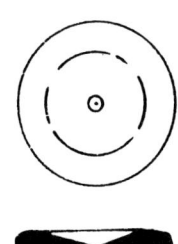

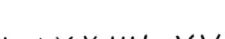

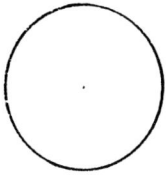
2440.357

For a further example of XII see *RIB* 2440.220; and for twelve dots see *RIB* 2440.33.

For examples of XIII see *RIB* 2440.220 and 244(?)

2440.358. Wroxeter (*Viroconium*), Shropshire. Bone roundel (¹⁄₁), diameter 16 mm, thickness 3 mm, found in 1924–27 during excavations. Rowley's House Museum, Shrewsbury. Drawn by S.S.F. from a rubbing by R.P.W., 1947.

JRS xxxiii (1943), 80 No. 13. Atkinson, *Wroxeter*, 232.

obverse: countersunk, with concentric rings
reverse: XIIIS
xiii s(emis)
'Thirteen and a half'

2440.358

For examples of XIIII see *RIB* 2440.220 and 365(?).

2440.359. Chichester (*Noviomagus*), West Sussex. Bone roundel (¹⁄₁), diameter 21 mm, thickness 4.5 mm, found in 1968 in a group of at least twenty-four (for which see *RIB* 2440.52), in Grave Group 250 at the Roman cemetery at St Pancras. Chichester Museum. Drawn by R.P.W., 1968.

JRS lix (1969), 237 No. 11. Wright in A. Down and M. Rule, *Chichester Excavations* i (1971), 88 No. 250 B with fig. 5.15.

obverse: flat with one ring
reverse (with three earlier shallow cuttings): XV
edge: XII

2440.359

2440.360. Colchester (*Camulodunum*), Essex. Bone roundel (1/1), diameter 20 mm, thickness 4 mm, found sometime between 1840 and 1888. Colchester Museum (Acton collection). Drawn by S.S.F. from a rubbing by R.P.W., 1943.

JRS xxxiv (1944), 89 No. 9 e.

obverse: countersunk
reverse: V̂X

Presumably XV, retrograde

2440.361. Silchester (*Calleva*), Hampshire. Bone roundel (1/1), diameter 19 mm, thickness 4.75 mm, found in or before 1909. Reading Museum. Drawn by S.S.F. from a rubbing by R.P.W., 1955.

obverse: bevelled edge, central hole
reverse: X̂V with added V

For further examples of XV see *RIB* 2440.220 and 357.

For an example of XVII see *RIB* 2440.73.

2440.362. St Albans (*Verulamium*), Hertfordshire. Bone counter (1/1), diameter 19 mm, thickness 3 mm, found in 1933. Verulamium Museum. Drawn by R.P.W., 1942.

JRS xxxii (1942), 118 No. 11 g. Wright, *PSAN*[4] x (1942), 17 (g) No. 13.

obverse: slightly countersunk
reverse: blank
edge: XVIIII Λ

XVIII Λ, incorrectly *JRS*. Λ is more roughly cut and may be unintentional.

For another example of XVIIII see *RIB* 2440.57(?).

2440.363. Aldborough (*Isurium*), North Yorkshire. Bone roundel (1/1), diameter 16 mm, thickness 0.8 mm. Aldborough Museum. Drawn by S.S.F. from a rubbing by R.P.W., 1952.

obverse: small recess
reverse: XX

2440.364. Silchester (*Calleva*), Hampshire. Bone roundel (1/1), diameter 20 mm, found in or before 1909. Reading Museum. Drawn by S.S.F. from a rubbing by R.P.W., 1953.

obverse: one ring and central recess
reverse: XX
edge: VIIII

2440.365. Ibid. Bone roundel (1/1), diameter 19 mm, thickness 3 mm, found in or before 1909. Reading Museum. Drawn by S.S.F. from a rubbing by R.P.W., 1955.

obverse: countersunk, part of the rim missing
reverse: X̂X
edge: [. . .]XIIII XXX

2440.366–368. Wroxeter (*Viroconium*), Shropshire. Three bone roundels (¹⁄₁). Rowley's House Museum, Shrewsbury. Drawn by S.S.F. from rubbings by R.P.W., 1953.

366. diameter 19 mm, thickness 3 mm.

obverse: countersunk
reverse, deeply cut: XX
edge: spaced round the circumference: VI IIIIV NIIΛ XVV

The first two groups may represent 'six' and 'nine'.

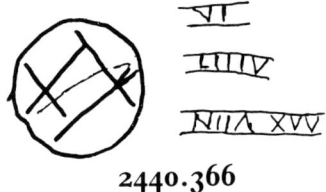

2440.366

367. diameter 17.5 mm.

obvere: central hole
reverse: XX with one cross-cut

2440.367

368. diameter 25.5 mm.

obverse: seven concentric rings
reverse: XX or X cut with double lines

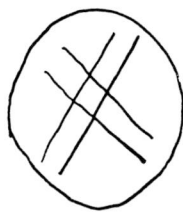

2440.368

For another example of XX see *RIB* 2440.26.

2440.369. London (*Londinium*). Bone roundel (¹⁄₁), diameter 22 mm, thickness 3 mm, found in 1924–34 during excavations on the site of the Bank of England, Princes Street. Bank of England Museum. Drawn by S.S.F. from a rubbing by R.P.W., 1953.

obverse: countersunk
reverse: XXS with an additional line
xx s(emis)
'Twenty and a half'

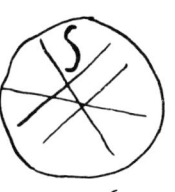

2440.369

For a possible example of XXIIII see *RIB* 2440.365.

2440.370. Aldborough (*Isurium*), North Yorkshire. Bone roundel (¹⁄₁), diameter 19 mm, thickness 0.8 mm. Aldborough Museum. Drawn by S.S.F. from a rubbing by R.P.W., 1952.

obverse: small recess
reverse: XXV

2440.370

2440.371. Ibid. Bone roundel (¹⁄₁), diameter 22 mm, thickness 3 mm. Aldborough Museum. Drawn by S.S.F. from a rubbing by R.P.W., 1952.

obverse: countersunk
reverse, over a horizontal line: XXVI

2440.371

2440.372. Chichester (*Noviomagus*), West Sussex. Bone roundel (1/1), found in 1959–64, unstratified during excavations in the Central Car Park site. Chichester Museum. Reproduced from Down.

A. Down, *Chichester Excavations* ii (1974), 140 No. 8 with fig. 8.14 No. 8.

obverse: countersunk with random scorings
reverse: X and three dots
edge: XXVIIII

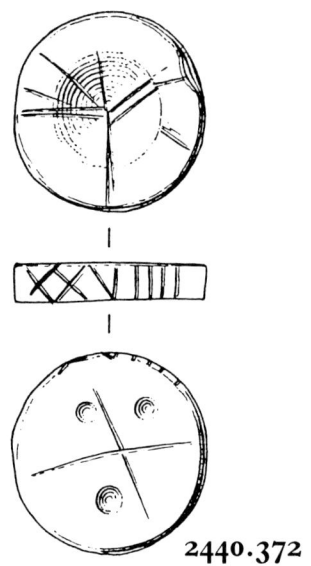

2440.372

2440.373. Caerleon (*Isca*), Gwent [Monmouthshire]. Bone roundel (1/1), diameter 22 mm, thickness 4 mm, found in 1979 in the frigidarium drain of the legionary baths. Caerleon Museum. Reproduced from Zienkiewicz.

J.D. Zienkiewicz, *The Legionary Baths at Caerleon* ii (1986), 205 No. 28 with fig. 71.28.

obverse: five incised circles
reverse: XXX

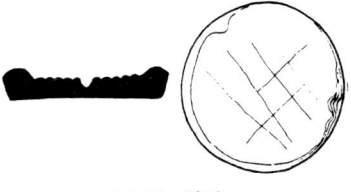

2440.373

2440.374. Richborough (*Rutupiae*), Kent. Bone roundel, diameter 22 mm, thickness 2.5 mm, found in 1929 during excavation of 'Section 53'. In store at Dover Castle. Not illustrated.

obverse: countersunk
reverse: blank
edge: XXX (?)

For another example of XXX, and for a possible example of XXXIIII as well, see *RIB* 2440.365.

2440.375. Colchester (*Camulodunum*), Essex. Bone roundel (1/1), diameter 21 mm, thickness 3 mm, found in 1975 unstratified at Balkerne Lane. Colchester Museum. Reproduced from Crummy.

Britannia ix (1978), 478 No. 39. N. Crummy, *Small Finds* (1983), 91 No. 2238 with fig. 94.

obverse: countersunk
reverse: XLV

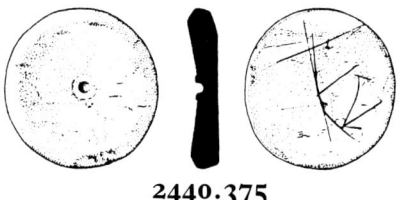

2440.375

2440.376. London (*Londinium*). Bone roundel (1/1), diameter 19 mm, thickness 3 mm, found in 1983 or 1984 during excavations at Billingsgate Lorry Park, London. Museum of London. Drawn by Christine Jones.

Britannia xvi (1985), 329 No. 31.

obverse: flat, blank
reverse: XLIIX
'Forty-eight'

2440.376

For examples of L see *RIB* 2440.97, 197.

2440.377. Ibid. Bone roundel (¹⁄₁), diameter 18 mm, thickness 4 mm. Found in 1974 above the Thames revetment at Billingsgate Buildings, London. Museum of London. Drawn by D. Parfitt.

Britannia ix (1978), 479 No. 50. D. Jones, *Excavations at Billingsgate Buildings . . . 1974* (Lond. Middl. AS. Special Paper No. 4, 1980), 94 No. 488. with fig. 54.

obverse: countersunk
reverse: LΠ
Perhaps 'Fifty-two'

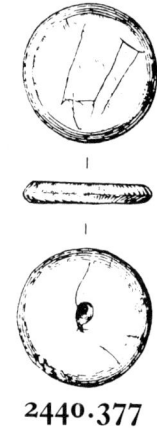

2440.377

2440.378. Bowcombe, Isle of Wight. Bone roundel (¹⁄₁), diameter 22 mm, thickness 2.5 mm, found in 1959 unstratified during excavations at Bowcombe near Carisbrooke. County Archaeological Collection, Newport. Reproduced from Tomalin.

D.J. Tomalin, *Roman Wight* (1987), 52–3 No. D5 with fig. on p. 55.

obverse, slightly countersunk: LX (?)
reverse: X forming six segments on which are five dots.

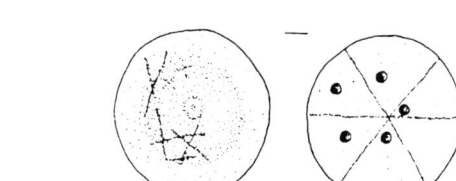

2440.378

For another example of five dots see *RIB* 2440.203.

2440.379. Wroxeter (*Viroconium*), Shropshire. Bone roundel (¹⁄₁), diameter 18 mm. Rowley's House Museum, Shrewsbury. Drawn by S.S.F. from a rubbing by R.P.W., 1953.

obverse: four concentric rings
reverse: XCI

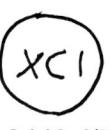

2440.379

2440.380. Caerleon (*Isca*), Gwent [Monmouthshire]. Bone roundel (¹⁄₁), diameter 15 mm, thickness 2.5 mm, found in 1979 in the frigidarium drain of the legionary baths. Caerleon Museum. Reproduced from Zienkiewicz.

J.D. Zienkiewicz, *The Legionary Baths at Caerleon* ii (1986), 205 No. 47 with fig. 72.47.

obverse: countersunk
reverse: four dots

Compare *RIB* 2440.185.

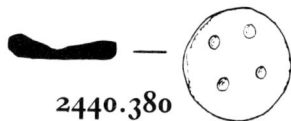

2440.380

2440.381. St Albans (*Verulamium*), Hertfordshire. Bone roundel (¹⁄₁), diameter 21 mm, thickness 4 mm, found in 1957 in an Antonine deposit in Insula XXVII. Verulamium Museum. Drawn by M.G. Wilson.

S.S. Frere, *Verulamium Excavations* iii (1984), 75 No. 292 with fig. 32.292.

obverse: countersunk
reverse: blank
edge: VIII

Compare *RIB* 2440.222 and 243.

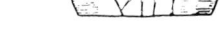

2440.381

RIB 2441. MISCELLANEOUS OBJECTS IN BONE, HORN OR IVORY

This chapter contains four bone handles, probably from knives, five inscribed plaques, one of them with openwork letters, one comb and two scrapers, together with six other miscellaneous inscribed objects, one (No. 19*) being of ivory.

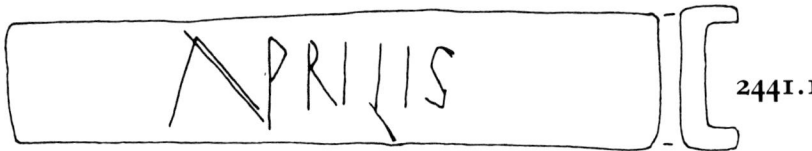

2441.1

2441.1. King's Sedgemoor near Somerton, Somerset. Half a bone handle ($\frac{1}{1}$), 90 by 19 mm, probably of a knife, with incised decoration on one of the partly incomplete sides. Found 'early in the 19th century' in a Roman building. Taunton Museum. Drawn by R.G.C., 1921.

CIL vii 1263. Haverfield, *VCH* Somerset i (1906), 325 with fig. 82. W. Stradling, *Priory of Chilton Polden* (1839), 16; *Arch. J.* ix (1852), 107. *Arch. Inst.* Bristol 1851, lxv with fig. Huebner, *Monatsber. der Kgl. Preuss. Akad. der Wissensch.* (1867), 767 with fig. Gray, *P. Som. AS* xlviii (1902), 85.

incised: APRILIS
'(Property) of Aprilis'

2441.2. York (*Eboracum*). Bone object ($\frac{1}{2}$), length 140 mm, maximum width 14 mm, thickness 6.5 mm, with a sharp point and a drilled hole for suspension, perhaps a stilus with the upper part damaged. The exact provenance is unrecorded, but the object was probably found in the last quarter of the 19th century in one of the Roman cemeteries then being built over. Yorkshire Museum, York. Drawn by S.S.F. after a sketch by R.P.W., 1963, not quite to scale.

JRS lii (1962), 196 No. 31

Four graffiti, perhaps in different hands:
(a) Λ   (c) leaf-stop
(b) VLL   (d) CEX

2441.2

2441.3. South Shields (*Arbeia*), Tyne and Wear [Durham]. Rectangular bone plaque ($\frac{1}{1}$), 28.5 by 20.5 mm, thickness 3 mm, with serrated edges. Found probably about 1878 during excavations at the fort. South Shields Museum. Drawn by R.P.W., 1946.

JRS xxxvii (1947), 181 No. 14. L. Allason-Jones and R. Miket, *Cat.* (1984) 54 No. 2.141 with fig.

scratched on one face: CḄ YSSVS

The second letter is badly finished and might be an attempted R.

2441.3

2441.4. London (*Londinium*). Triangular bone scraper ($\frac{1}{2}$ and $\frac{1}{1}$) made from the scapula of an (?) ox, with the edges and apex corner smoothed and rounded and the working side worn to a blunt edge; a single suspension-hole is pierced near the apex corner. Found in 1974 in rubbish dumped over the wooden river-revetment at Billingsgate Buildings. Museum of London. Reproduced from Jones.

Britannia ix (1978), 479 No. 49. D. Jones, *Excavations at Billingsgate Buildings ... 1974* (Lond. Middl. AS Special Paper No. 4, 1980), 93 No. 490 with fig. 54.

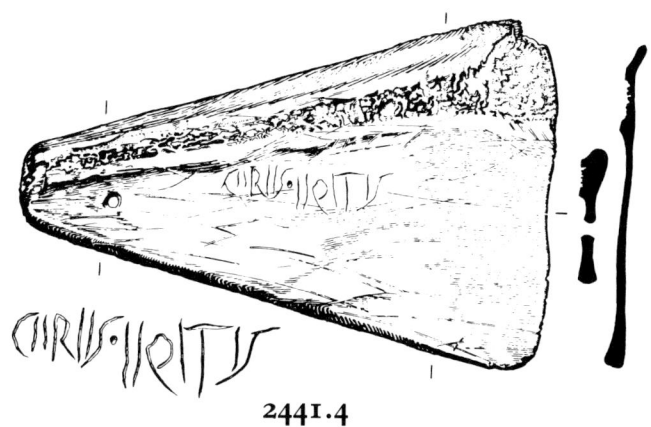

2441.4

incised graffito: CIIRIIS·IIQITIS
Ceres Eq(u)itis
'Ceres, (property) of Eques'

A personal name *Ceres* is not recorded and Ceres as the name of the goddess seems out of place. M.W.C.H., *Britannia*, suggests a possible connection with *cera*, 'wax'.

For the rare cognomen *Eques* see *CIL* ii 5964 and *JRS* xliv (1954), 109 No. 38. where *Eques* was expanded to *Eques(ter)* by R.P.W.

2441.5. Corbridge (? *Coria*), Northumberland. Part of the bone handle perhaps of a knife (⅓), found in 1910 during excavations at Site XVI. Corbridge Museum. Drawn by R.P.W.

EE ix 1343. Haverfield *Arch. Ael*[3] viii (1912), 56 No. 7.

incised: >PVBLISAMA | IOXIITLLIIS
(Centuria) Publi . . .
'Century of Publius . . .'

The first three letters are deeply cut, the rest according to F.H., *Arch. Ael.*, is not certain. *P* is of capital form, but *B* is cursive. *Publius* here is a nomen or cognomen, unless *Publi(cius)* was intended.

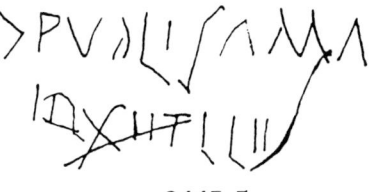

2441.5

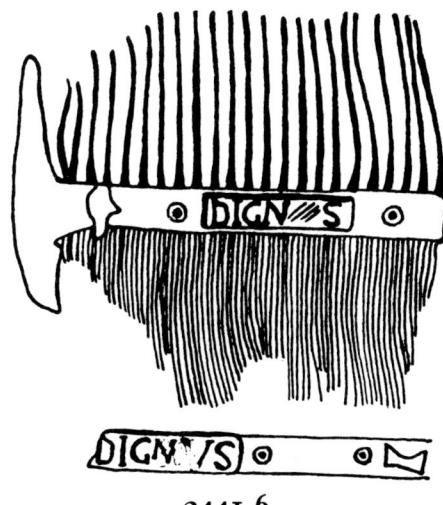

2441.6

2441.6. London (*Londinium*). Bone comb (¹⁄₁) with a row of large and small teeth on either side of a central band, 70 (originally 86) by 53 mm. Found before 1912 in Moorgate Street, when it was acquired by the London Museum. Museum of London. Drawn by R.P.W., 1971.

Britannia ii (1971), 299 No. 61.

obverse, stamped: DIGN[.]S
reverse, stamped: [. . .]DIGNVS
'Dignus (made this)'

2441.7. York (*Eboracum*). Bone plaque (½), 127 by 38 mm, with one suspension-hole, found in 1873 in a sarcophagus in the Roman cemetery at the railway station. Yorkshire Museum, York. Drawn by R.G.C.

EE iii 123. Yorkshire Museum *Cat.* (1875), 94; (1891), 128 d. Huebner, *IBC* (1876), 13*. RCHM, *York* i (1962), 135 No. 149 with pl. 65.149.

incised in good capitals:
DOMINEVICTOR | VINCASFELIX
Domine Victor vincas felix
'Sir Victor, may you be victorious and lucky'

The formula used is associated with gladiators or charioteers.

2441.7

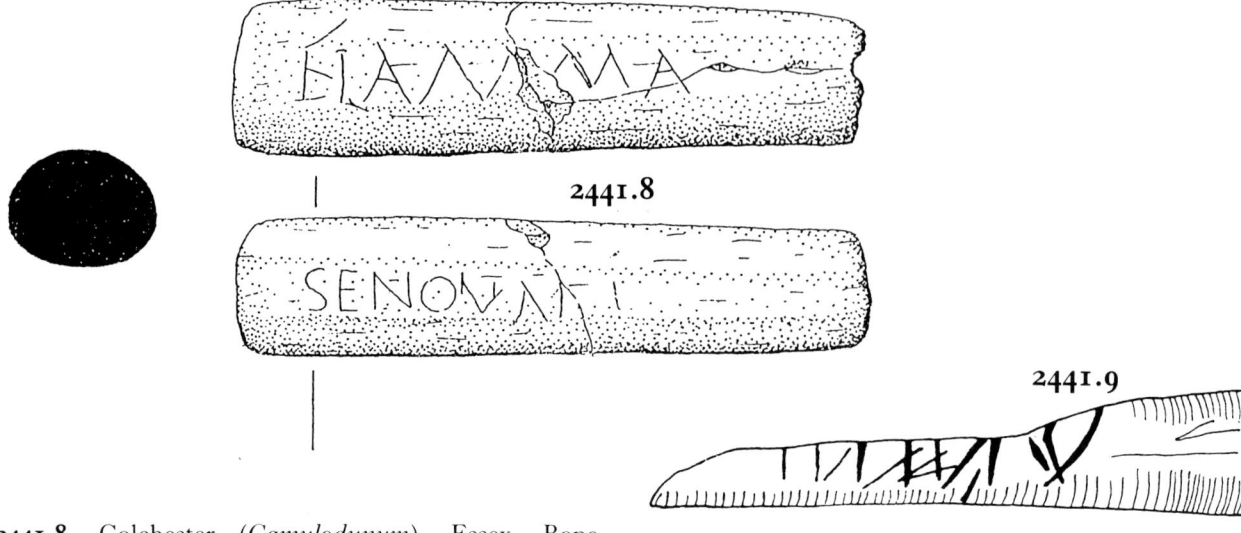

2441.8

2441.9

2441.8. Colchester (*Camulodunum*), Essex. Bone knife-handle (1/1), length 85 mm with oval cross-section, long axis 20 mm, short axis 15 mm, found in 1981 in topsoil during excavations at Culver Street. Colchester Museum. Drawn by Terry Cook.

Britannia xv (1984), 343 No. 26.

cut in neat capitals: FLAMMA|SENOVARI
flamma Senovari
'The flame of Senovarus' or
'Flamma (wife *or* daughter) of
Senovarus'

For *Flamma* as a personal name see Kajanto, *Cognomina* 341. The Celtic name *Senovarus* occurs in an unpublished curse tablet from Uley, cf. *Senovara* (*Britannia* xiii (1982), 398 No. 4 = *Tab. Sulis* No. 9, line 8).

2441.9. East Tilbury, Essex. Bone peg or toggle (1/1), length 82.5 mm with a longitudinal flake broken away, found about 1900 on the foreshore of the river Thames on the site of Roman hut-circles. Gravesend Museum. Drawn by R.P.W., 1960.

JRS li (1961), 195 No. 20

deeply incised: IVLLIAO
Iullia(v)o (est)
'(This belongs) to Iulliavus'

Intervocalic V has been omitted. The name is in the dative of the possessor. R.P.W. (The name *Iulliavus* is unrecorded, and the reading seems uncertain. R.S.O.T.)

2441.10. Newbury, Berkshire. Horn handle with part of an iron blade, length 51 mm, still attached, found in or before 1837 in a cinerary urn inscribed D M | SMI (*EE* iii 57). Now lost. Reprinted from *EE* iii.

EE iii 133; vii 843. *Gent. Mag.* 1837, February, p. 161. Watkin, *Arch. J.* xxxi (1874), 351.

incised on the handle: P·R·M·
P(ubli) R(...) M(...)
'(Property) of Publius R...M...'

2441.11. York (*Eboracum*). Part of a bone plaque (1/1), 136.5 mm by 9.5 mm, thickness 1.5 mm, with open-work letters, perhaps from a casket. Found in 1901 in a sarcophagus containing a woman's skeleton, glass drinking-vessels and some jet jewelry, in Sycamore Terrace, outside the north-west gate of the fortress. Yorkshire Museum, York. Drawn by R.G.C.

EE ix 1345. *Yorks. Phil. Soc. Rep.* (1901), 104 with pl. VII. Home, *York* (1924), 190 with pl. Richmond, *Arch. J.* ciii (1946), 81. RCHM, *York* i (1962), 73 group (v), 135 No. 150 with pl. 65.150. Toynbee in M.W. Barley and R.P.C. Hanson, *Christianity in Britain, 300–700* (1968), 191 with fig.

in openwork letters:
[. . .]S̱[. .]OR͡AVEVI͡VASI͡NDEO
...s[or]or ave vivas in deo
'Hail, sister, may you live in God'

The text is undoubtedly Christian (compare *RIB* 2420.49; 2422.14, 15, 69), but its association with grave-goods leaves the Christianity of the burial in doubt.

2441.11

2441.12. Chesterton (*Durobrivae*), Cambridgeshire [Huntingdonshire]. Five thin pieces (½) of 'white wood', probably really bone (F.H., *VCH*), found in 1754 'beside the high road near Chesterton' in a stone coffin. Now lost. Reproduced from Manning.

CIL vii 1264. Manning, Soc. Ant. (London) *Minutes* vii, 122 (9 May 1754), with fig. Stukeley's *Letters* ii 218. Gough's *Camden* ii (1806), 257 with fig. K. Gibson, *A Comment upon ... Castor* (ed. 2, 1819), 84. Haverfield, *VCH* Northamptonshire i (1902), 170 with fig.

incised: (a) [...] VTERE FELIX [...]
          (b) in Greek, [...]ΑΛΩΙΓΥ[...]
          (c) [...]ΤΛ[...]
          (d) A 'diamond' consisting of a cross within a lozenge.

(a) *utere felix*, 'Good luck to the user'. These two fragments evidently conjoined, but have been drawn in the wrong order.
(b) perhaps [...]αλῳ γυ[...]
(c) may be either Greek (-τλ-) or Latin (-ta-)

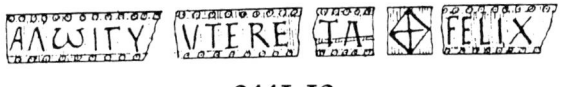

2441.12

2441.13. St. Albans (*Verulamium*), Hertfordshire. Semicircular bone object (¹⁄₁), diameter 38 mm, height 19 mm, thickness 5 mm, bevelled on both sides; the diametrical edge has been cut down to leave a slightly splayed projection 2.5 mm high at the centre, and two recesses have been gouged from it. On the flat face a perforation 3 mm in diameter has been made near the projection. Found in 1964 in an early deposit in Insula XIII, but stolen from the site. Drawn by S.S.F. from a field-drawing by A.D. McWhirr.

JRS lvii (1967), 207 No. 27.

incised: VIIII
          'Nine'

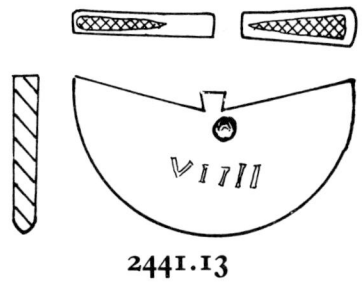

2441.13

2441.14. Castleford (*Lagentium*), West Yorkshire. Part of a sheep's metacarpal (¼), found in 1982 in a Flavian context. It has been scored with a knife in a series of diagonal strokes apparently intended for letters or numerals. West Yorkshire Archaeology Service. Drawn by R.S.O.T.

Britannia xviii (1987), 376 No. 47.

cut with a knife: 3–4 and (more deeply scored) IMXIVI[...]

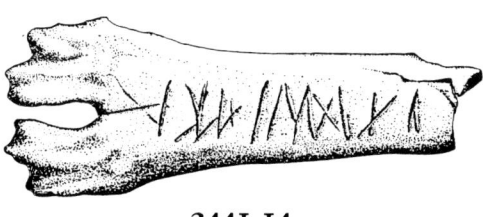

2441.14

2441.15. Ilkley, North Yorkshire. Part of a bone (?) spatula or scraper (¼), surviving length 70 mm, width 25.5 mm, with one side flat, the other slightly convex. Found in 1921 'at a deep level outside the north wall' of the *principia* during excavations at the fort. Ilkley Museum. Reproduced from Woodward.

A.M. Woodward, *The Roman Fort at Ilkley* (1925), =*YAJ* xxviii (1925), 194, 288–9 with fig. 49.

scratched in elongated letters on the flat side of the blade:
[...].HISCONICILLI
'(Property) of ...'

IHIS, or IIIIS (for *ieis*) or LIIIS (for *leis*), R.P.W. The last three letters are small and the two I s may be accidental scratches, Woodward. IKI, R.P.W.

The personal name, a diminutive in -*illus*, is not attested; any restoration is therefore impracticable.

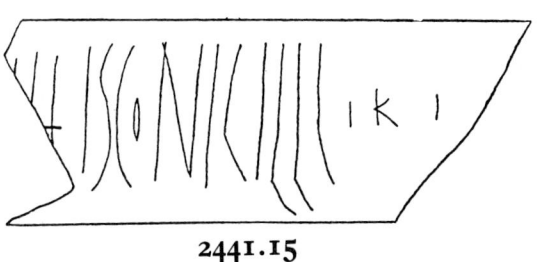

2441.15

2441.16. Rockbourne, Hampshire. Fragment of bone (⅔), 51 by 12.5 mm, found in 1960 in Room X of the Roman Villa. Hampshire Museum Service. Drawn by S.S.F. from a rubbing by R.P.W., 1962.

JRS lii (1962), 196 No. 32.

incised: [. . .] CRA V̩.[. . .]

2441.16

2441.17. St. Albans (*Verulamium*), Hertfordshire. Fragment of bone (⅔), 90 by 28.5 by 9.5 mm, found in 1958 during excavations in Insula XIV. Verulamium Museum. Drawn by S.S.F. from a rubbing by R.P.W., 1959.

JRS l (1960), 195 No. 21.

roughly incised: [. . .]PID̩II

Perhaps the genitive of a personal name, e.g. *Epidius* or *Lepidius*.

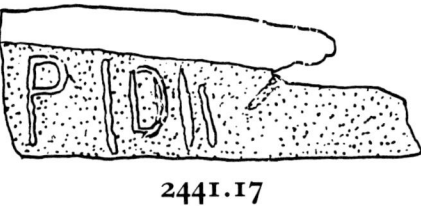

2441.17

2441.18. Richborough (*Rutupiae*), Kent. Part of a bone plaque (¼), 53 by 23 mm, with notched edges and with incised lines enclosing the inscription. Found in 1922–23 during excavations at the fort. In store at Dover Castle. Drawn by R.P.W., 1948.

J.P. Bushe-Fox, *Richborough* i (1926), 45 No. 12 with pl. XIII.12.

2441.18

incised: [. . .]SVIVAS
          [. . .]s vivas
          '. . .s, may you live'

The first letter should be the termination of a personal name, the nominative serving for the vocative.

FALSUM

2441.19.* York (*Eboracum*) (?). Part of an ivory handle (¼), split lengthwise with only the tops of the letters surviving; length 68 mm, surviving width 9 mm, surviving depth 8 mm. The side above the letters is ribbed transversely. Found before 1891, provenance unknown, but probably from York. Yorkshire Museum, York. Drawn by R.S.O.T. from a rubbing by B.R. Hartley.

Yorkshire Museum *Cat.* (1891), 128 *f.* RCHM, *York* i (1962), 134–5, No. 148 with pl. 65.148.

incised within defining lines: H̩N̩ K̩E̩R̩ I̩P[. . .]

IINPES(or Ↄ) ID[. . .], Hartley.
GI(or T)GꓶꓤN̩I(or T)T(or I), R.P.W., 1941 (*RIB* archive), reading the other way up.

Two ivory fan-handles and ivory parasol-ribs have been found in Roman burials at York (Richmond, *Arch. J.* ciii (1946), 79 with figs. 12, 13; *RCHM*, op. cit., 82 with pl. 71), and this object has been included with them. However, its Roman association has only been inferred; the letter-forms though perhaps Roman also resemble 18th/19th-century forms; the first word within its defining lines does not look like Latin, the *K* in particular (if correctly read) making such an interpretation impossible. 'H.N.Ker, Ipswich' looks more probable. R.S.O.T.

2441.19

INDEX OF SITES

Akenham (Suff.), **2423**.23
Alcester (Warwicks.), **2421**.5, 6; **2436**.5
Alchester (Oxon), **2421**.7
Aldborough (Yorks.), **2429**.7, 8; **2440**.64, 81, 212, 363, 370, 371
Ashby de la Launde (Lincs.), **2438**.1
Avebury (Wilts.), **2421**.8

Backworth (Northumb.), **2422**.9
Baldock (Herts.), **2421**.36
Bar Hill (Strathclyde), **2428**.1; **2429**.13
Bath (Avon), **2433**.22*; **2434**.5; **2440**.48, 213
Bedford, **2422**.5
Benwell (Tyne & Wear), **2422**.22
Bermondsey (S. London), **2440**.123–132
Billingford (Norf.), **2422**.30
Binchester (Durham), **2435**.7; **2440**.214
Birchington (Kent), **2422**.7
Bishops Stortford (Essex), **2440**.75
Bowcombe (I.o.W.), **2440**.378
Box (Wilts.), **2436**.11
Bradwell (Essex), **2423**.19
Brafield (Northants.), **2422**.41
Braintree (Essex), **2423**.6
Brampton (Cumbria), **2429**.11
Brancaster (Norf.), **2422**.15; **2432**.5
Brandon (Suff.), **2422**.35
Brecon (Powys), **2440**.18, 113–118, 133, 353
Brentwood (Essex), **2422**.16
Brettenham (Norf.), **2429**.10
Brough on Humber, **2435**.2; **2440**.31
Brough under Stainmore (Cumbria), **2422**.81

Caerhun (Gwynedd), **2435**.9, 13; **2436**.7
Caerleon (Gwent), **2423**.25, 30; **2427**.13, 25; **2433**.7; **2435**.4; **2440**.1, 40, 71–73, 136–7, 168, 215, 321, 373, 380
Caerwent (Gwent), **2440**.41, 46, 49, 50, 82, 89, 150, 208–9, 216–18, 327–8
Caister on Sea (Norf.), **2432**.2
Caistor St Edmund (Norf.), **2422**.4, 32, 53, 65; **2423**.8; **2440**.96, 143
Canterbury (Kent), **2421**.9, 56; **2422**.67; **2423**.33*; **2433**.13, 16, 19; **2440**.219

Carlisle (Cumbria), **2422**.2; **2429**.2
Carrawburgh (Northumb.), **2422**.28
Castell Collen (Powys), **2422**.19
Castleford (Yorks.), **2441**.14
Castlesteads (Cumbria), **2423**.12
Castlethorpe (Bucks.), **2424**.1, 2
Catsgore (Som.), **2421**.10
Catterick (Yorks.), **2428**.17; **2423**.4
Charlton (Som.), **2421**.11
Charterhouse on Mendip (Som.), **2421**.12, 38; **2435**.3
Chester, **2427**.14, 15; **2429**.15; **2433**.11; **2434**.1–4
Chesterholm (Northumb.), **2422**.29, 79; **2423**.4; **2425**.8; **2428**.19; **2431**.2; **2439**.6; **2440**.13, 14, 45, 53, 95, 140, 164, 187, 322–4
Chesters (Northumb.), **2422**.23, 80; **2429**.16, 17; **2435**.5; **2440**.2, 119
Chesterton (Cambs.), **2430**.3; **2431**.1, 4–11; **2441**.12
Chichester (Sussex), **2422**.59, 72; **2433**.10; **2440**.15, 19, 27, 51–2, 67–8, 74, 86, 106, 151, 169–171, 185, 199, 200, 204, 207, 220–24, 325–6, 329–31, 357, 359, 372
Chilgrove (Sussex), **2433**.2
Cirencester (Glos.), **2421**.13, 14, 41; **2422**.26; **2423**.3; **2440**.47
Colchester (Essex), **2421**.2; **2422**.8, 27, 50; **2423**.9, 17, 26; **2427**.27*; **2428**.10; **2432**.8; **2433**.8, 20; **2438**.7*; **2439**.1–5, 8–12, 14, 16–18, 19*–31*; **2440**.3, 32–4, 54, 76, 102, 144, 148, 194–7, 205, 225–30, 332–4, 354, 360, 375; **2441**.8
Corbridge (Northumb.), **2422**.1, 12, 20, 34, 43; **2426**.4; **2428**.11; **2429**.5, 9; **2440**.35–6, 55, 79, 80, 99, 120, 145–6, 231–5; **2441**.5
Covesea (Highland Region), **2433**.17
Croxton Kerrial (Leics.), **2422**.51

Dorchester (Dorset), **2422**.74; **2433**.24*; **2438**.3; **2440**.236–9
Dover (Kent), **2423**.13
Dragonby (Humberside), **2423**.22
Dringhouses (Yorks.), **2423**.35
Durham County, **2421**.57

East Tilbury (Essex), **2441**.9
East Winterslow (Wilts.), **2433**.3
Eastwood (Hants.), **2422**.31
England, **2421**.58

Erickstanebrae (Dumfries & Gal.), **2421**.43
Essex, **2422**.11
Ewell (Surrey), **2440**.20, 107–110, 188–190, 335
Exeter (Devon), **2421**.45; **2427**.28*

Fifehead Neville (Doset), **2422**.44, 45
Folkestone (Kent), **2423**.24

Godmanchester (Cambs.), **2432**.4
Gogmagog Hills (Cambs.), **2423**.18
Great Chesterford (Essex), **2440**.121

Ham Hill (Som.), **2421**.15, 16
Harlow (Essex), **2421**.17
Hawkeden (Suff.), **2425**.9
Hemel Hempstead (Herts.), **2433**.6
High Rochester (Northumb.), **2429**.1
Hod Hill (Dorset), **2440**.98
Holt (Clwyd), **2437**.1
Housesteads (Northumb.), **2440**.4
Hylton (Tyne & Wear), **2435**.14*

Ilkley (Yorks.), **2441**.15

Kempston (Beds.), **2421**.59
Kent, **2422**.33
Keynsham (Avon), **2423**.9, 21
Kilbride (Strathclyde), **2423**.29
Kingsholm (Glos.), **2421**.34; **2423**.21
King's Sedgemoor (Som.), **2441**.1
Kirkby Thore (Cumbria), **2427**.18; **2429**.12
Kirmington (Humberside), **2423**.34*

Lakenheath (Suff.), **2421**.52
Leicester, **2440**.5, 16, 56, 142, 240
Leyland (Lancs.), **2422**.83*
Lincoln, **2422**.36; **2436**.10
Lockleys (Herts.), **2423**.1
London, **2421**.18, **2422**.3, 13, 24, 49, 62, 71, 73, 75, 77; **2423**.2; **2425**.2; **2426**.3; **2427**.2; **2428**.2, 5–9, 12–16, 20; **2432**.1; **2433**.5, 9; **2436**.9; **2438**.4; **2440**.12, 93, 138, 369, 376, 377; **2441**.4, 6
Lydney Park (Glos.), **2436**.1, 3

Maiden Castle (Dorset), **2421**.33
Maidstone (Kent), **2421**.46
Malton (Yorks.), **2423**.27; **2436**.4; **2440**.83, 241, 242
Mancetter (Warwicks.), **2429**.18*
Margate (Kent), **2440**.57, 198

175

INDEX OF SITES

Marshfield (Avon), **2440**.183, 211
Matfen (Northumb.), **2426**.2
Meols (Cheshire), **2437**.4
Mildenhall (Wilts.), **2421**.19
Minster (Kent), **2437**.6*

Neath (W. Glam.), **2438**.2
Nettleton (Wilts.), **2421**.20; **2432**.3; **2435**.10; **2439**.7
Newbury (Berks.), **2441**.10
Newstead (Borders), **2425**.4, 5; **2427**.3–12, 21–24; **2428**.3, 4, 18
Norfolk, **2421**.1
North Warnborough (Hants.), **2440**.336
North Wraxall (Wilts.), **2423**.11

Old Winteringham (Humberside), **2422**.63
Ospringe (Kent), **2440**.6, 122
Owslebury (Hants.), **2422**.55, 56
Oxfordshire, **2423**.20

Piddington (Northants.), **2421**.49
Portchester (Hants.), **2422**.18
Poundbury (Dorset), **2437**.2

Ravenglass (Cumbria), **2440**.42–4, 69, 90–92, 94, 103–4, 152–160, 165–6, 175–82, 201, 243–91, 337–43, 355–6
Ravensden (Beds.), **2421**.47
Reculver (Kent), **2423**.32*
Ribchester (Lancs.), **2423**.7; **2425**.6
Richborough (Kent), **2421**.21, 50; **2422**.70, 84*; **2433**.12; **2435**.8; **2436**.12; **2438**.6*; **2440**. 7, 8, 24, 28, 58–9, 111, 292, 344–5, 374; **2441**.18
Rockbourne (Hants.), **2433**.18; **2441**.16
Rudston (Humberside), **2421**.35

Rugby (Warwicks.), **2422**.57

Saham Toney (Norf.), **2422**.69
St Albans (Herts.), **2421**.51; **2422**.48; **2425**.3; **2440**.9, 39, 65, 77, 134–5, 139, 149, 172, 186, 191–3, 210, 293–5, 346, 362, 381; **2441**.13, 17
Sea Mills (Avon), **2436**.2
Silchester (Hants.), **2421**.39; **2422**.14, 25, 42; **2423**.16, 31; **2427**.1; **2429**.3; **2432**.9; **2440**.22, 25–6, 29, 30, 60, 61, 66, 70, 84–5, 97, 141, 161, 167, 173–4, 184, 202, 206, 296–300, 347–8, 361, 364–5
Slack (Yorks.), **2437**.3
South Ferriby (Humberside), **2421**.22, 40
South Shields (Tyne & Wear), **2422**.68, 78; **2429**.13, 14; **2433**.23*; **2435**.12; **2440**.17, 37, 62, 100, 101, 301; **2441**.3
Southwark (S. London), **2421**.60; **2423**.28
Springhead (Kent), **2433**.15; **2440**.78
Stanwix (Cumbria), **2427**.16, 17, 20
Stonea (Cambs.), **2430**.1
Stonham Aspal (Suff.), **2422**.10
Suffolk, **2422**.17

Tetford (Lincs.), **2422**.39
Thetford (Norf.), **2423**.5, 15
Thistleton (Leics.), **2431**.3
Thruxton (Hants.), **2422**.46
Tilbury, East, see East Tilbury
Traprain Law (Lothian), **2439**.15
Tyne, river, **2426**.1

Uley (Glos.), **2429**.4; **2432**.6, 7, 10
Unknown provenance, **2421**.31, 32, 44, 48; **2422**.38, 58, 64, 76; **2425**.1; **2427**.26*; **2433**.21*; **2434**.6*
Upchurch Marshes (Kent), **2437**.5

Usk (Gwent), **2421**.23, 24; **2433**.14; **2438**.5

Verulamium, see St Albans
Vindolanda, see Chesterholm

Waddon Hill (Dorset), **2433**.1; **2435**.1, 6
Walcot (Avon), **2421**.55
Wall (Staffs.), **2421**.25; **2427**.19; **2436**.13; **2440**.302
Wanborough (Wilts.), **2421**.26; **2422**.61
Warnborough, North, see North Warnborough
Watercrook (Cumbria), **2436**.6
Water Newton, see Chesterton
Welwyn, see Lockleys
Wendens Ambo (Essex), **2422**.52
West Kington, see Nettleton
Whittlesey (Cambs.), **2422**.6
Wickford (Essex), **2421**.53
Willoughby-on-the-Wolds (Notts.), **2422**.40
Winteringham, Old, see Old Winteringham
Winterslow, East, see East Winterslow
Wood Eaton (Oxon.), **2430**.2
Worthing (Norf.), **2425**.7
Wraxall, North, see North Wraxhall
Wroxeter (Shrops.), **2421**.3, 4, 27–9, 37, 42, 54, 60; **2422**.47, **2423**.14; **2435**.11; **2436**.8; **2440**.10, 11, 21, 23, 38, 87–8, 147, 162–3, 203, 303–5, 349–51, 358, 366–8, 379

Yatton (Som.), **2422**.54
York, **2421**.30; **2422**.21, 37, 82*; **2429**.6; **2440**.63, 105, 306–20, 352; **2441**.2, 7, 11, 19*

PLATES

PLATE I

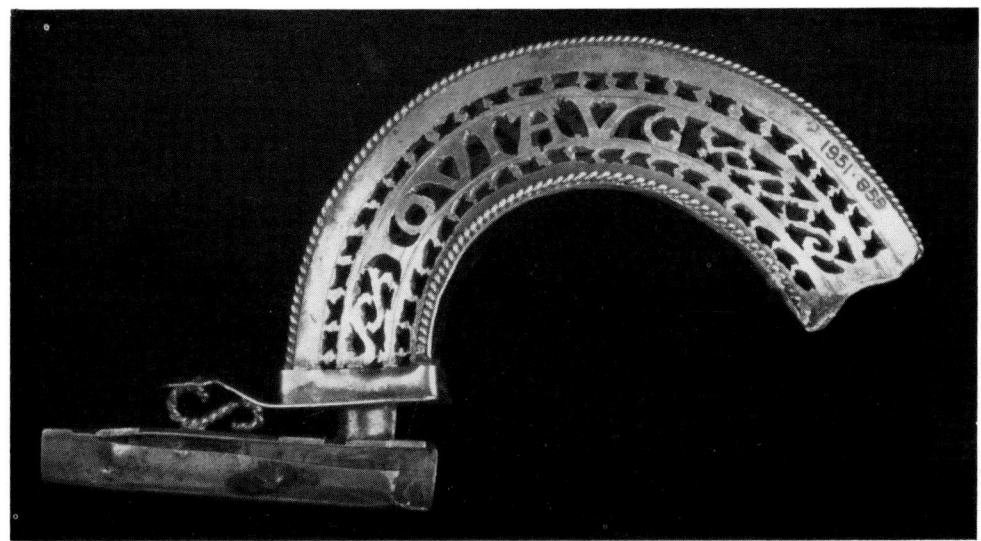

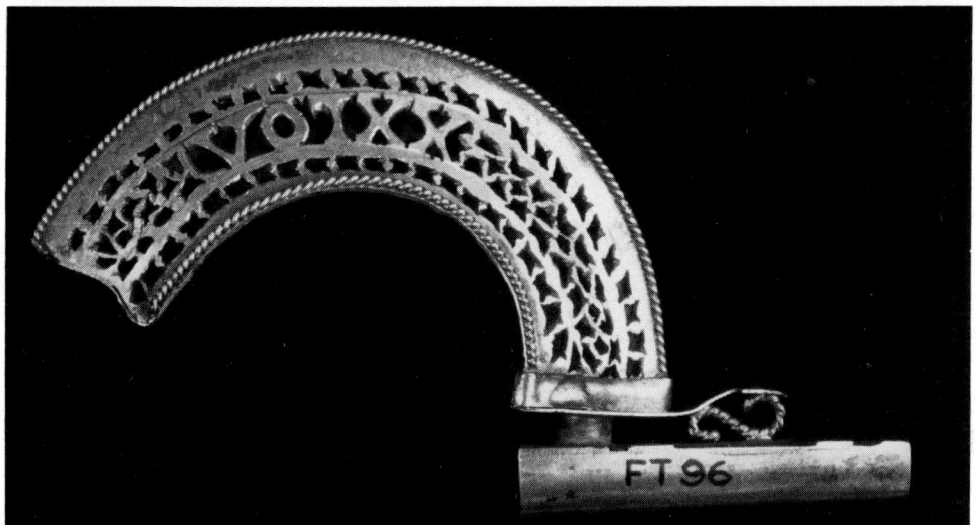

A–B. 2421.43. Gold crossbow brooch from Erickstanebrae, Strathclyde (Scale 1.3:1).
(*Photographs: National Museums of Scotland*)

C. Graffito on the underside of the bow of *RIB* 2421.43.

PLATE II

A. 2421.53. Bronze brooch from Wickford, Essex (¾).
(*Photograph: Southend Museum*)

B. 2421.49. Bronze brooch from Piddington, Northamptonshire (6/1).
(*Photograph: R. Friendship Taylor*)

C. 2421.59. Bronze brooch from Kempston, Bedfordshire (¾).
(*Photograph: Bedford Museum*)

PLATE III

A. 2422.16. Gold ring from Brentwood, Essex (1/1).
(*Photograph: British Museum*)

B. 2422.30. Silver ring from Billingford, Norfolk (2/1).
(*Photograph: Norfolk Archaeological Unit*)

C. 2422.42. Silver disc from Silchester (3/1).
(*Photograph: Reading Museum*)

D. 2422.32. *Impression* from a silver ring from Caistor St Edmund, Norfolk (3/1).
(*Photograph: Norwich Castle Museum*)

E. 2422.38. Silver ring from an unknown provenance (3/1).
(*Photograph: British Museum*)

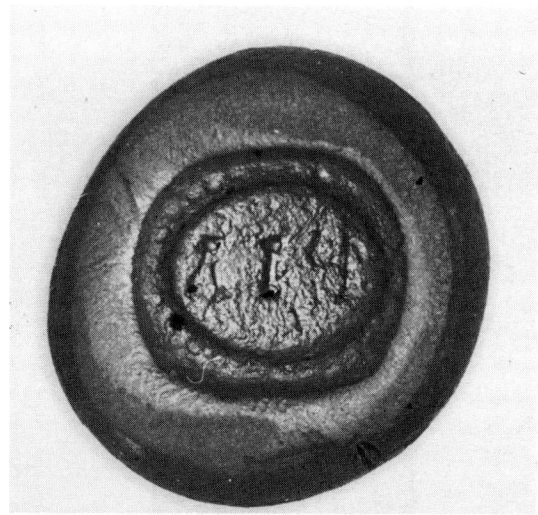

F. 2422.65. *Impression* from a bronze ring from Caistor St Edmund, Norfolk (3/1).
(*Photograph: Norwich Castle Museum*)

G. 2422.75. Iron ring with bronze inlay from London (1/1)
(*Photograph: Museum of London*)

PLATE IV

A–E. 2422.80. Jet ring from (?) Chesters, Northumberland (¾/₁).

(*Photographs: S. Ellaway. Copyright, English Heritage*)

A. 2423.1. Obverse of a haematite amulet from Lockleys, Welwyn, Hertfordshire (3/1).
(*Photographs: Martin Henig*)

B. 2423.1. Reverse of A.

PLATE V

PLATE VI

2423.2. Onyx gem from London ($\frac{10}{1}$).

(*Photograph: Museum of London*)

PLATE VII

A. 2423.6. Cornelian intaglio from Braintree, Essex, showing Asclepius and Hygieia ($\frac{3}{1}$).
(*Photographs: RIB Archive*)

B. *Impression* of A.

C. 2423.8. Jasper intaglio in an iron ring from Caistor St Edmund, Norfolk (c. $\frac{3}{1}$).
(*Photograph: Hallam Ashley, copyright Norwich Castle Museum*)

D. 2423.11. Onyx cameo from North Wraxall, Wiltshire ($\frac{4}{1}$).
(*Photograph: Ashmolean Museum, Oxford*)

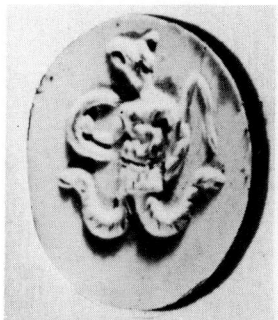

E. 2423.16. Cast of the obverse of a bloodstone amulet from Silchester, Hampshire, showing Abrasax ($\frac{3}{1}$).
(*Photograph: Reading Museum*)

PLATE VIII

A. 2423.17. Obverse of a lapis lazuli amulet from (?) Colchester, Essex, showing Harpocrates (3/1).
(Photographs: Martin Henig)

B. Reverse of A (3/1).

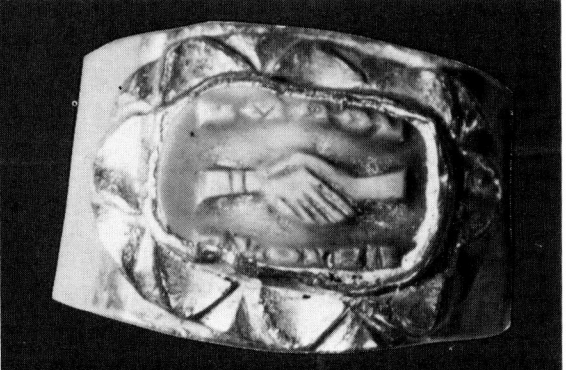

C. 2423.19. Onyx cameo from Bradwell, Essex, set in a gold ring (4/1).
(Photograph: British Museum)

D. 2423.20. Obverse of a nicolo intaglio from Oxfordshire (4/1).
(Photographs: R.L. Wilkins)

E. Reverse of D (4/1).

PLATE IX

A. 2423.21. Cornelian intaglio from Kingsholm, Gloucestershire, showing wheat-stalks and a cow (4/1).
(*Photograph: Martin Henig*)

B. 2423.23. Cornelian intaglio from Akenham, Suffolk, showing Victory (4/1).
(*Photograph: Ipswich Museum*)

C. 2423.25. Cornelian intaglio from Caerleon, Gwent, showing Diana (5/1).
(*Photograph: National Museum, Cardiff*).

D. 2423.30. Intaglio of green prase from Caerleon, Gwent, showing clasped hands, a hippocamp, raven and other symbols (3/1).
(*Photographs: National Museum, Cardiff*)

E. *Impression of D.*

PLATE X

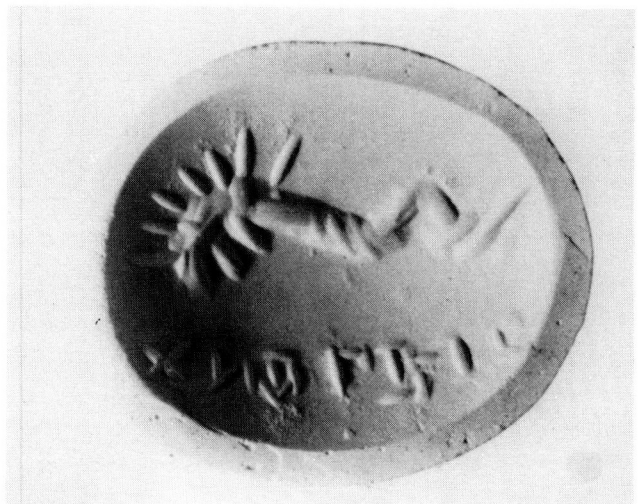

A. 2423.33.* *Impression* of a plasma intaglio from Canterbury Cathedral, showing a lion-headed serpent (4/1).

(*Photograph: R.L. Wilkins*)

B. 2427.26.* Bronze roundel of unknown provenance, showing legionary vexillations and a *venatio* (1/1).

(*Copyright: Cabinet des Medailles*)

PLATE XI

2426.1. Bronze shield-plate from the river Tyne (⁴⁄₇).

(*Photograph: British Museum*)

PLATE XII

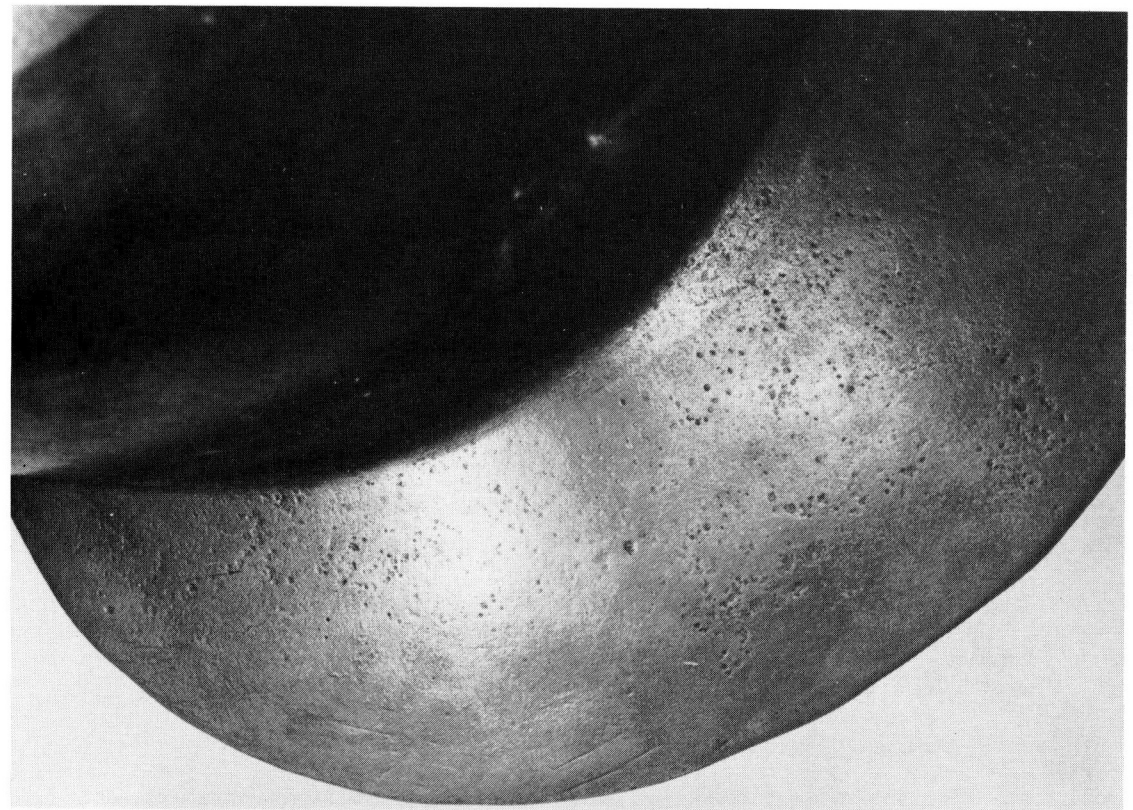

A, B. 2425.2. Neck-guard of a bronze helmet from London with graffiti in punched dots.

(*Photographs: British Museum*)

PLATE XIII

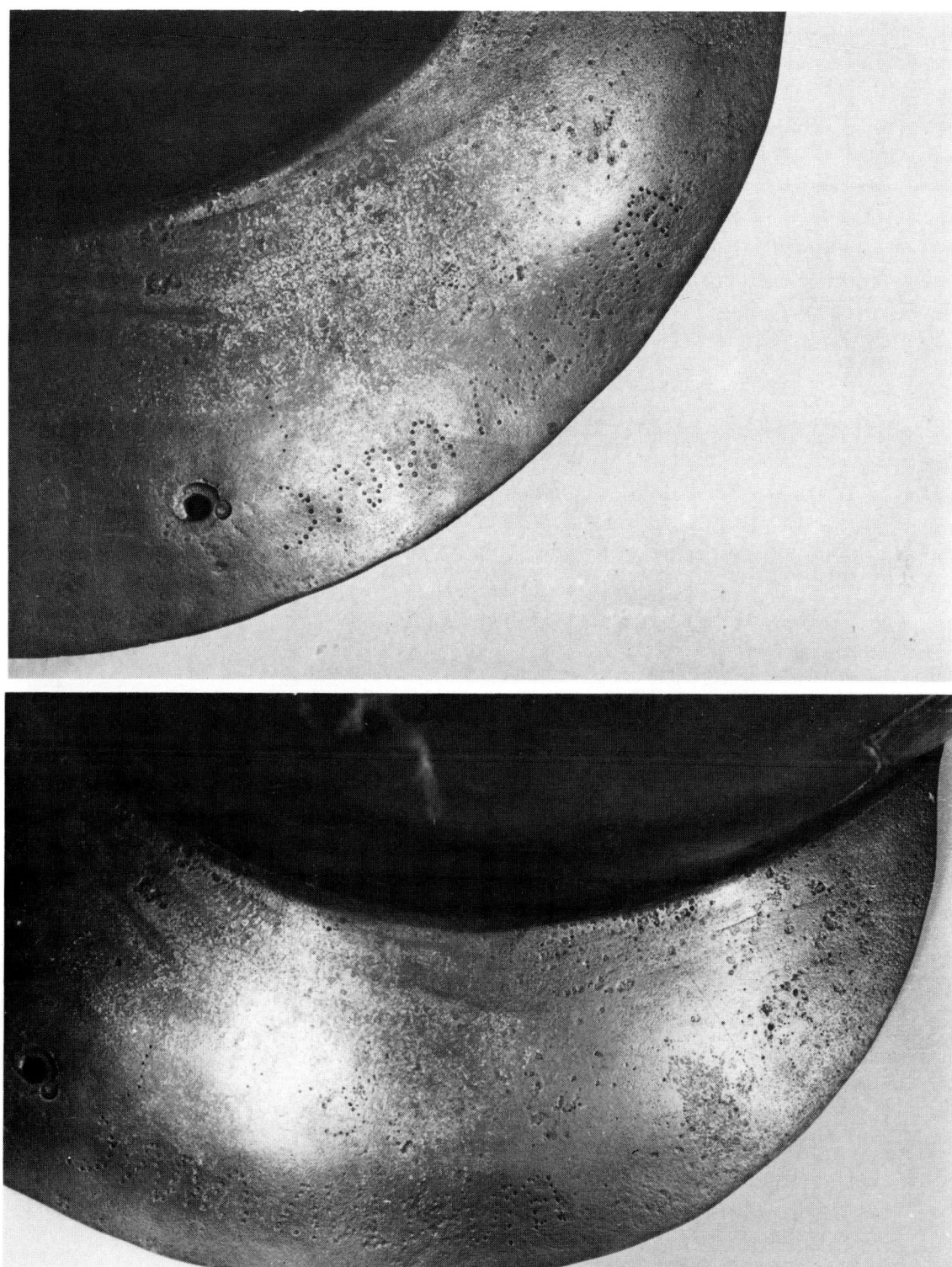

A, B. 2425.2. Neck-guard of a bronze helmet from London with graffiti in punched dots.
(*Photographs: British Museum*)

PLATE XIV

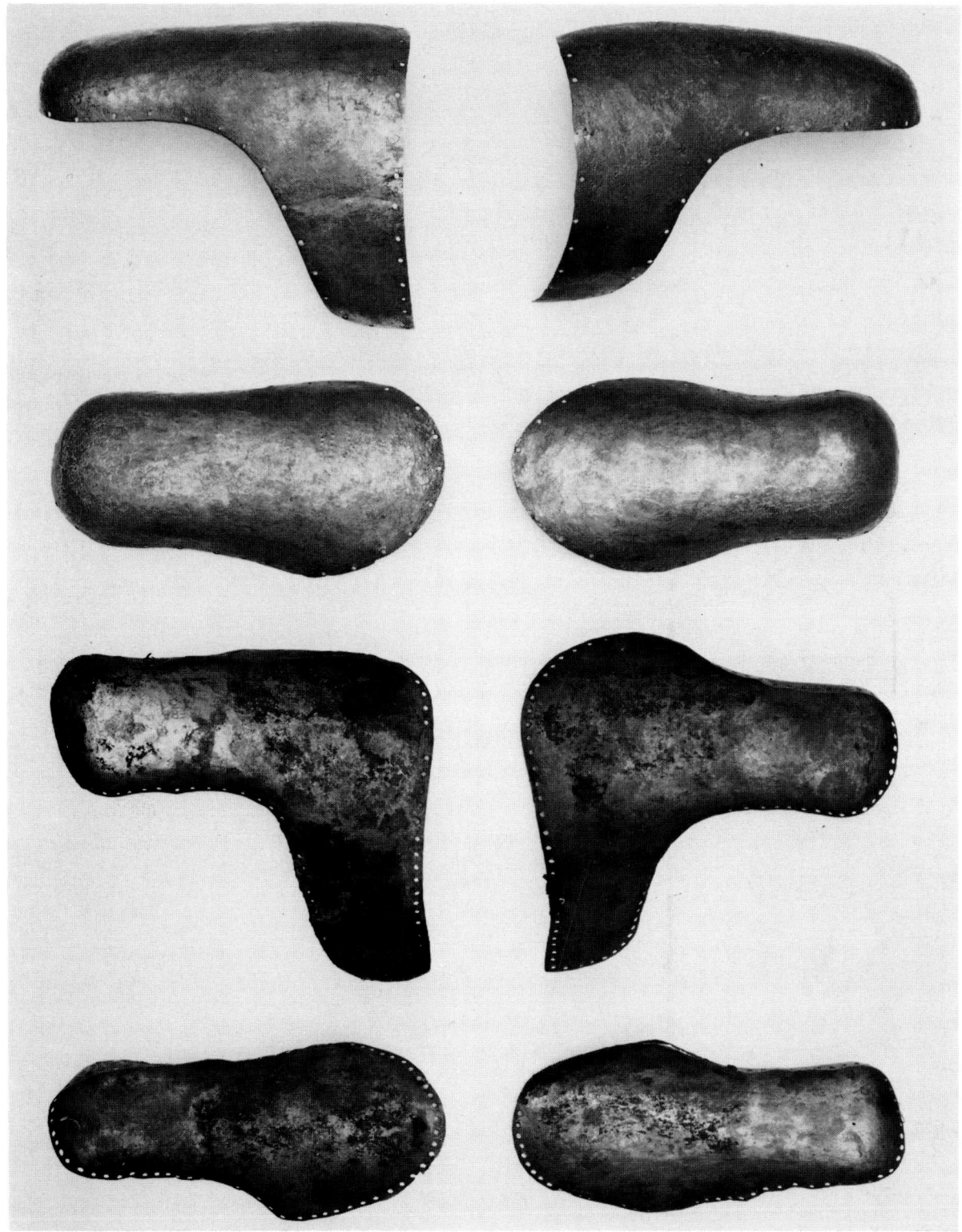

2427.21–24. Four bronze pommel-stiffeners from Newstead ($\frac{1}{3}$).

(*Photograph: National Museums of Scotland*)

PLATE XV

A. 2429.6. Bronze baldric-fitting from York (1/1)
(*Photograph: T. Romans*)

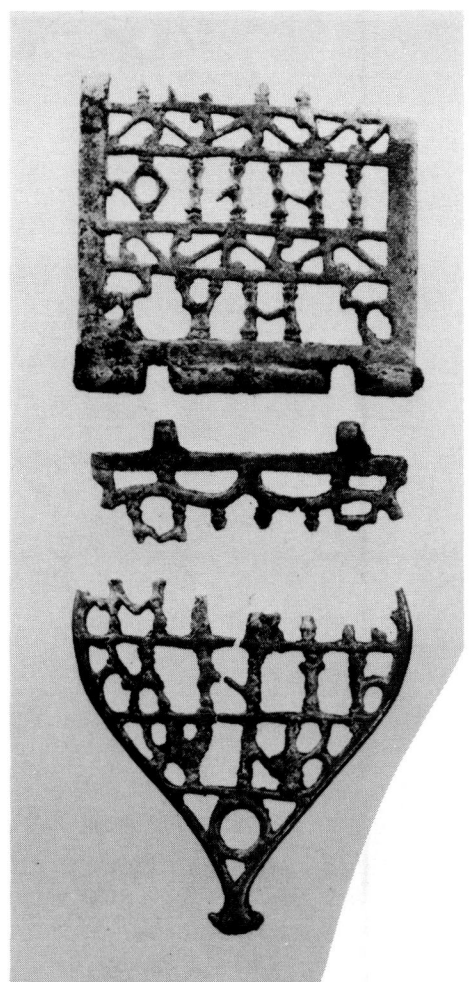

B. 2429.7 (top and bottom) and part of 8 (centre). Bronze baldric-fittings from Aldborough, Yorkshire (4/5).
(*Photograph: Department of the Environment*)

C. 2429.17 and 16. Bronze belt-plates from Chesters, Northumberland (1:2.2).
(*Photograph: R.P. Wright*)

PLATE XVI

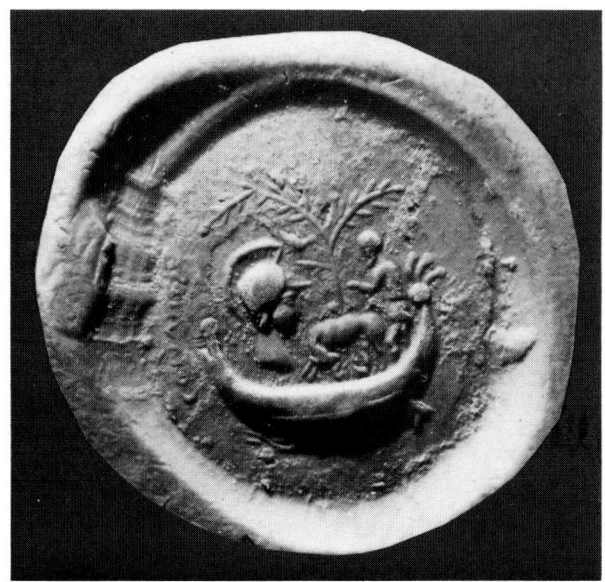

(*Photographs: R.P. Wright*)

A, B. 2427.27.* Impression from the obverse and reverse of jasper pommel from Colchester, Essex ($\frac{2}{1}$).

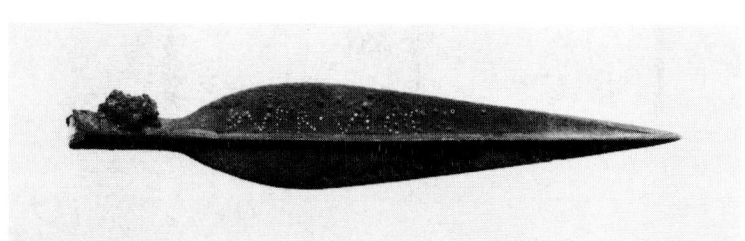

C. 2427.2. Iron spearhead from London with graffito in punched dots ($\frac{1}{3}$).
(*Photograph: Museum of London*)

D. 2440.15. Bone roundel from the Chichester amphitheatre ($\frac{2}{1}$).
(*Photograph: RIB archive*)

E. 2440.51. Bone roundel from the Chichester amphitheatre ($\frac{2}{1}$).
(*Photograph: RIB archive*)

F, G. 2440.68. Obverse and reverse of a bone roundel from the Chichester amphitheatre ($\frac{2}{1}$).
(*Photograph: RIB archive*)